Lecture Notes in Computer Science　14718

Founding Editors

Gerhard Goos
Juris Hartmanis

The series Lecture Notes in Computer Science (LNCS), including its subseries Lecture Notes in Artificial Intelligence (LNAI) and Lecture Notes in Bioinformatics (LNBI), has established itself as a medium for the publication of new developments in computer science and information technology research, teaching, and education.

LNCS enjoys close cooperation with the computer science R & D community, the series counts many renowned academics among its volume editors and paper authors, and collaborates with prestigious societies. Its mission is to serve this international community by providing an invaluable service, mainly focused on the publication of conference and workshop proceedings and postproceedings. LNCS commenced publication in 1973.

Norbert A. Streitz · Shin'ichi Konomi
Editors

Distributed, Ambient and Pervasive Interactions

12th International Conference, DAPI 2024
Held as Part of the 26th HCI International Conference, HCII 2024
Washington, DC, USA, June 29 – July 4, 2024
Proceedings, Part I

 Springer

Editors
Norbert A. Streitz 🆔
Smart Future Initiative
Frankfurt am Main, Germany

Shin'ichi Konomi
Kyushu University
Fukuoka, Japan

ISSN 0302-9743 ISSN 1611-3349 (electronic)
Lecture Notes in Computer Science
ISBN 978-3-031-59987-3 ISBN 978-3-031-59988-0 (eBook)
https://doi.org/10.1007/978-3-031-59988-0

Foreword

This year we celebrate 40 years since the establishment of the HCI International (HCII) Conference, which has been a hub for presenting groundbreaking research and novel ideas and collaboration for people from all over the world.

The HCII conference was founded in 1984 by Prof. Gavriel Salvendy (Purdue University, USA, Tsinghua University, P.R. China, and University of Central Florida, USA) and the first event of the series, "1st USA-Japan Conference on Human-Computer Interaction", was held in Honolulu, Hawaii, USA, 18–20 August. Since then, HCI International is held jointly with several Thematic Areas and Affiliated Conferences, with each one under the auspices of a distinguished international Program Board and under one management and one registration. Twenty-six HCI International Conferences have been organized so far (every two years until 2013, and annually thereafter).

Over the years, this conference has served as a platform for scholars, researchers, industry experts and students to exchange ideas, connect, and address challenges in the ever-evolving HCI field. Throughout these 40 years, the conference has evolved itself, adapting to new technologies and emerging trends, while staying committed to its core mission of advancing knowledge and driving change.

As we celebrate this milestone anniversary, we reflect on the contributions of its founding members and appreciate the commitment of its current and past Affiliated Conference Program Board Chairs and members. We are also thankful to all past conference attendees who have shaped this community into what it is today.

The 26th International Conference on Human-Computer Interaction, HCI International 2024 (HCII 2024), was held as a 'hybrid' event at the Washington Hilton Hotel, Washington, DC, USA, during 29 June – 4 July 2024. It incorporated the 21 thematic areas and affiliated conferences listed below.

A total of 5108 individuals from academia, research institutes, industry, and government agencies from 85 countries submitted contributions, and 1271 papers and 309 posters were included in the volumes of the proceedings that were published just before the start of the conference, these are listed below. The contributions thoroughly cover the entire field of human-computer interaction, addressing major advances in knowledge and effective use of computers in a variety of application areas. These papers provide academics, researchers, engineers, scientists, practitioners and students with state-of-the-art information on the most recent advances in HCI.

The HCI International (HCII) conference also offers the option of presenting 'Late Breaking Work', and this applies both for papers and posters, with corresponding volumes of proceedings that will be published after the conference. Full papers will be included in the 'HCII 2024 - Late Breaking Papers' volumes of the proceedings to be published in the Springer LNCS series, while 'Poster Extended Abstracts' will be included as short research papers in the 'HCII 2024 - Late Breaking Posters' volumes to be published in the Springer CCIS series.

I would like to thank the Program Board Chairs and the members of the Program Boards of all thematic areas and affiliated conferences for their contribution towards the high scientific quality and overall success of the HCI International 2024 conference. Their manifold support in terms of paper reviewing (single-blind review process, with a minimum of two reviews per submission), session organization and their willingness to act as goodwill ambassadors for the conference is most highly appreciated.

This conference would not have been possible without the continuous and unwavering support and advice of Gavriel Salvendy, founder, General Chair Emeritus, and Scientific Advisor. For his outstanding efforts, I would like to express my sincere appreciation to Abbas Moallem, Communications Chair and Editor of HCI International News.

July 2024   Constantine Stephanidis

HCI International 2024 Thematic Areas
and Affiliated Conferences

- HCI: Human-Computer Interaction Thematic Area
- HIMI: Human Interface and the Management of Information Thematic Area
- EPCE: 21st International Conference on Engineering Psychology and Cognitive Ergonomics
- AC: 18th International Conference on Augmented Cognition
- UAHCI: 18th International Conference on Universal Access in Human-Computer Interaction
- CCD: 16th International Conference on Cross-Cultural Design
- SCSM: 16th International Conference on Social Computing and Social Media
- VAMR: 16th International Conference on Virtual, Augmented and Mixed Reality
- DHM: 15th International Conference on Digital Human Modeling & Applications in Health, Safety, Ergonomics & Risk Management
- DUXU: 13th International Conference on Design, User Experience and Usability
- C&C: 12th International Conference on Culture and Computing
- DAPI: 12th International Conference on Distributed, Ambient and Pervasive Interactions
- HCIBGO: 11th International Conference on HCI in Business, Government and Organizations
- LCT: 11th International Conference on Learning and Collaboration Technologies
- ITAP: 10th International Conference on Human Aspects of IT for the Aged Population
- AIS: 6th International Conference on Adaptive Instructional Systems
- HCI-CPT: 6th International Conference on HCI for Cybersecurity, Privacy and Trust
- HCI-Games: 6th International Conference on HCI in Games
- MobiTAS: 6th International Conference on HCI in Mobility, Transport and Automotive Systems
- AI-HCI: 5th International Conference on Artificial Intelligence in HCI
- MOBILE: 5th International Conference on Human-Centered Design, Operation and Evaluation of Mobile Communications

List of Conference Proceedings Volumes Appearing Before the Conference

1. LNCS 14684, Human-Computer Interaction: Part I, edited by Masaaki Kurosu and Ayako Hashizume
2. LNCS 14685, Human-Computer Interaction: Part II, edited by Masaaki Kurosu and Ayako Hashizume
3. LNCS 14686, Human-Computer Interaction: Part III, edited by Masaaki Kurosu and Ayako Hashizume
4. LNCS 14687, Human-Computer Interaction: Part IV, edited by Masaaki Kurosu and Ayako Hashizume
5. LNCS 14688, Human-Computer Interaction: Part V, edited by Masaaki Kurosu and Ayako Hashizume
6. LNCS 14689, Human Interface and the Management of Information: Part I, edited by Hirohiko Mori and Yumi Asahi
7. LNCS 14690, Human Interface and the Management of Information: Part II, edited by Hirohiko Mori and Yumi Asahi
8. LNCS 14691, Human Interface and the Management of Information: Part III, edited by Hirohiko Mori and Yumi Asahi
9. LNAI 14692, Engineering Psychology and Cognitive Ergonomics: Part I, edited by Don Harris and Wen-Chin Li
10. LNAI 14693, Engineering Psychology and Cognitive Ergonomics: Part II, edited by Don Harris and Wen-Chin Li
11. LNAI 14694, Augmented Cognition, Part I, edited by Dylan D. Schmorrow and Cali M. Fidopiastis
12. LNAI 14695, Augmented Cognition, Part II, edited by Dylan D. Schmorrow and Cali M. Fidopiastis
13. LNCS 14696, Universal Access in Human-Computer Interaction: Part I, edited by Margherita Antona and Constantine Stephanidis
14. LNCS 14697, Universal Access in Human-Computer Interaction: Part II, edited by Margherita Antona and Constantine Stephanidis
15. LNCS 14698, Universal Access in Human-Computer Interaction: Part III, edited by Margherita Antona and Constantine Stephanidis
16. LNCS 14699, Cross-Cultural Design: Part I, edited by Pei-Luen Patrick Rau
17. LNCS 14700, Cross-Cultural Design: Part II, edited by Pei-Luen Patrick Rau
18. LNCS 14701, Cross-Cultural Design: Part III, edited by Pei-Luen Patrick Rau
19. LNCS 14702, Cross-Cultural Design: Part IV, edited by Pei-Luen Patrick Rau
20. LNCS 14703, Social Computing and Social Media: Part I, edited by Adela Coman and Simona Vasilache
21. LNCS 14704, Social Computing and Social Media: Part II, edited by Adela Coman and Simona Vasilache
22. LNCS 14705, Social Computing and Social Media: Part III, edited by Adela Coman and Simona Vasilache

https://2024.hci.international/proceedings

Preface

The 12th International Conference on Distributed, Ambient and Pervasive Interactions (DAPI 2024), an affiliated conference of the HCI International Conference, provided a forum for interaction and exchanges among researchers, academics, and practitioners in the field of HCI for DAPI environments.

The DAPI conference addressed approaches and objectives of information, inter-action, and user experience design for DAPI Environments as well as their enabling technologies, methods, and platforms, and relevant application areas. The DAPI 2024 conference covered topics addressing basic research questions and technology issues in the areas of new modalities, immersive environments, smart devices, etc. On the other hand, there was an increase in more applied papers that cover comprehensive platforms and smart ecosystems addressing the challenges of cyber-physical systems, human-machine networks, public spaces, smart cities, and nature preservation. The application areas also include education, learning, culture, art, music, and interactive installations.

Two volumes of the HCII 2024 proceedings are dedicated to this year's edition of the DAPI Conference. The first focuses on topics related to Designing, Developing and Evaluating Intelligent Environments, and Smart Cities, Smart Industries and Smart Tourism. The second focuses on topics related to Intelligent Environments for Health and Wellbeing, Smart Ecosystems for Learning and Culture, and Multimodal Interaction in Intelligent Environments.

The papers in these volumes were accepted for publication after a minimum of two single-blind reviews from the members of the DAPI Program Board or, in some cases, from members of the Program Boards of other affiliated conferences. We would like to thank all of them for their invaluable contribution, support, and efforts.

July 2024

Norbert A. Streitz
Shin'ichi Konomi

12th International Conference on Distributed, Ambient and Pervasive Interactions (DAPI 2024)

Program Board Chairs: **Norbert A. Streitz,** *Smart Future Initiative, Germany,* and **Shin'ichi Konomi,** *Kyushu University, Japan*

- Pedro Antunes, *University of Lisbon, Portugal*
- Kelvin Joseph Bwalya, *Sohar University, Oman*
- Katrien De Moor, *Norwegian University of Science and Technology (NTNU), Norway*
- Morten Fjeld, *Chalmers University of Technology, Sweden*
- Nuno Guimaraes, *Instituto Universitário de Lisboa - ISCTE, Portugal*
- Kyungsik Han, *Hanyang University, Korea*
- Jun Hu, *Eindhoven University of Technology, Netherlands*
- Eiman Kanjo, *Nottingham Trent University, UK*
- Nicos Komninos, *Aristotle University of Thessaloniki, Greece*
- H. Patricia McKenna, *AmbientEase/UrbanitiesLab Initiative, Canada*
- Tatsuo Nakajima, *Waseda University, Japan*
- Guochao Peng, *Sun Yat-Sen University, P.R. China*
- Elaine M. Raybourn, *Sandia National Laboratories, USA*
- Carsten Röcker, *TH OWL, Germany*
- Tomoyo Sasao, *The University of Tokyo, Japan*
- Reiner Wichert, *Darmstadt University of Applied Sciences, Germany*
- Chui Yin Wong, *Intel Corporation, Malaysia*
- Woontack Woo, *KAIST, Korea*
- Mika Yasuoka-Jensen, *Roskilde University, Denmark*
- Takuro Yonezawa, *Nagoya University, Japan*
- Yuchong Zhang, *KTH Stockholm, Sweden*

The full list with the Program Board Chairs and the members of the Program Boards of all thematic areas and affiliated conferences of HCII 2024 is available online at:

http://www.hci.international/board-members-2024.php

HCI International 2025 Conference

The 27th International Conference on Human-Computer Interaction, HCI International 2025, will be held jointly with the affiliated conferences at the Swedish Exhibition & Congress Centre and Gothia Towers Hotel, Gothenburg, Sweden, June 22–27, 2025. It will cover a broad spectrum of themes related to Human-Computer Interaction, including theoretical issues, methods, tools, processes, and case studies in HCI design, as well as novel interaction techniques, interfaces, and applications. The proceedings will be published by Springer. More information will become available on the conference website: https://2025.hci.international/.

General Chair
Prof. Constantine Stephanidis
University of Crete and ICS-FORTH
Heraklion, Crete, Greece
Email: general_chair@2025.hci.international

https://2025.hci.international/

Contents – Part I

Contents – Part II

Smart Ecosystems for Learning and Culture

Designing, Developing and Evaluating Intelligent Environments

Exploring the Motivation of Living Lab Participants for Continuous Co-creation

Mayu Akaki[1]([✉]) [iD], Hiroto Ito[1], Isana Fujii[1], Ao Hirai[1], and Ryutaro Yoshimoto[2,3]

[1] Shunan University, Shunan 745-0000, Yamaguchi, Japan
akaki@shunan-u.ac.jp
[2] Aratana Inc., Shunan 745-0032, Yamaguchi, Japan
[3] Chutoku Holdings, K. K., Shunan 745-0801, Yamaguchi, Japan

Abstract. Living Lab is a co-creation approach receiving attention because of its different advantages compared to the traditional system development process as well as in the HCI field. In this study, we focused on the motivation of the participants to join the team activities in the living labs for continuous co-creation. In particular, we conducted a questionnaire asking about the motivation of the participants of Shunan Living Lab and Yamaguchi Living Lab in Japan. The coding and classification of the free descriptions clarified the seven important motivational factors. Moreover, we indicated the different motivations due to the background of the participants, such as students, working adults in the public, private, and education sectors, which LL they are joining, and the teams they belong to. Furthermore, we conducted a depth interview asking how their motivation and team's motivation changed. Through the interview, the motivation and expectations to enhance their motivation were explicitly different between students and working adults. Finally, we indicated three points as the implications to the living lab organizers, especially in Japan; creating occasions to interact with each other, taking different approaches depending on the background of the participants, and encouraging prototyping in teams.

Keywords: living lab · participatory design · motivation

1 Introduction

Living lab (LL), which is a network or ecosystem for innovation to engage the users from the concept design, is held all over the world, especially in Europe. Accordingly, number of the studies focusing on living labs has increased after 2015 [1, 2]. According to Hossain et al. [1], many living lab studies apply the definition presented by ENoLL (European Network of Living Lab) which networks worldwide LLs; such as 'user-centered open innovation ecosystems based on a systematic user co-creation approach, integrating research and innovation processes in real-life communities and settings' (openlivinglabs.eu/aboutus).

LLs received attention in practice and research because of their different strengths compared to the traditional system development process. Bergvall-Kåreborn et al. [3]

N. A. Streitz and S. Konomi (Eds.): HCII 2024, LNCS 14718, pp. 3–20, 2024.
https://doi.org/10.1007/978-3-031-59988-0_1

described the difference between LL and traditional system design. They indicated that the difference is the clearest in the concept of realism as an LL approach for real-world contexts. Also, in terms of the empowerment of users, the LL sees users as partners, on the other hand, system development sees them as actors. The importance of the relationship with the partners was highlighted to realize the continuity of the lab.

Alavi et al. [2] focused on HCI research taking up LLs. They identified five divergent setups, such as the "Visited Places", "Instrumented Places", "Instrumented People", "Lived-in Places", and "Innovation Spaces" as 'the infrastructure to facilitate data collection and experimental intervention in a LL settings' (p. 7). As the re-emergence of the participatory design movement in HCI is pointed out [2], this study focuses on LLs in innovation spaces, which host co-creation. Likewise, the relevance of the HCI community to shift from passive participants to engaged partners was also pointed out [2].

In order to emphasize the strengths of the LL and to contribute to the work-in-progress HCI research, this study explores the participants' motivation to realize continuous co-creation in LLs. Through the exploration, we indicate how participants are motivated and build trust to become proactive partners.

In particular, we focused on two LLs held in Yamaguchi prefecture, Japan. We coded and classified the free descriptions of the online survey and conducted an depth interview to clarify the motivation of participants in two specific timings; motivation to join the kick-off workshop and to keep joining the team activities. Through the analysis result, seven important factors were extracted. The results implicated the LL organizers especially in Japan in three points to encourage the motivation of the participants.

2 Background

2.1 Research on Motivation of Living Lab Participants

There are limited studies on the motivation of the LL participants although the participants as the users are essential for the LL to be active for the long term [4, 5]. Akasaka et al. [6] indicated 'motivation management' as one of the categories of the key elements to be considered in configuring participation in LLs. They pointed out the importance of enhancing motivation and eliminating obstacles to realize the long period of user involvement in the LL. As another way to realize continuous co-creation, preventing drop-out is considered. Habibipour et al. [7] focused on drop-out behaviors since participation is usually voluntary in the LL approach different from the traditional information systems research. Since there are no drop-outs in the specific LLs dealt with in this study, we focused on the motivations of the participants.

In particular, previous studies focusing on the participants' motivations indicated that intrinsic motivation is more important than extrinsic motivation for participants to remain in the LL community [4, 5]. Also, Logge et al. [5] indicated that there are motivations of the participants to 'become part of communities', which means to be part of the innovation activity and new product development. According to the case study conducted by Logge et al. [5] utilizing the motivation variables consisting of 17 items, the highest number of the participants chose 'collaboration with others' as their motivation. However, when they interviewed the alpha users, 'personal interest' and 'learning' scored higher. It was the characteristics of the alpha users in their study that they belong to IT industries, which they can apply the learnings in the LL community.

- H1: Participants of the LL have intrinsic motivations more than extrinsic motivations.
- H2: Participants of the LL are motivated to be part of the community and collaborate with others.
- H3: Participants of the LL are motivated to learn from the activities when they have fields to apply the learnings.

We also partly followed Logge and Schuurman [4] to take an action research approach to further understand the participants' motivation. The authors of this paper except the first author are the participants of the Shunan LL. The first author is the organizer of the Shunan LL and facilitator of the team-building phase of the Yamaguchi LL.

2.2 Living Labs in Japan

In the context of the dysfunctionality of representative democracy as well as in Japan, Kimura et al. [8] indicated that urban LLs are one of the social design methodologies to transform the social system. The rapidly aging society is another context in that LLs add new values by gathering residents and the stakeholders of urban development to develop new policies needed for the society [9]. There are more than 100LLs in Japan according to the research of JNOLL (https://jnoll.org/living-labs/) in 2023. Although the number of LLs is growing, it is limited (DESIAP research network, 2016) compared to the European countries. There are studies to develop tools that empower the participants in LLs in Japan [9, 10]. Taoka et al. [10] focused on the cultural characteristics of Japan compared to the Scandinavian countries. They especially pointed out three characteristics that affect the co-creation process in Japan; such as power distance, low individualism, and uncertainty avoidance. Kitazume et al. [9] focused on the two points from the 45 characteristics of Japanese proposed by Hirai [11]; such as 'Japanese people speak up while carefully considering the opinions of the members around them' and 'the Japanese value cooperation among participants' (p. 67). The low 'individualism' is related to the two characteristics extracted by Hirai [11]. Referring to those previous studies, we hypothesize the three points below as the motivation factors that affect the participants in Japanese LLs.

- H4: As 'power distance' prevents equal participation in activities, the students and working adults having different roles and statuses in society have different kinds of motivation.
- H5: As the low 'individualism' puts more value on the harmony of a group, the participants are motivated to listen and learn from others rather than express their opinions.
- H6: As the 'uncertainty avoidance' is threatened by ambiguous situations, the participants are demotivated when the information isn't shared enough.

3 Methodology

To clarify the motivation of the LL participants in different settings, we compared two kinds of LLs kicked off in 2023 in Yamaguchi prefecture, Japan.

Shunan Living Lab is held as the research activity in Shunan University to challenge regional social problems through collaborations of students and professionals working for town development from diverse aspects. The kick-off workshop of Shunan LL was held in July 2023 participated by 9 students and 7 professionals. Three teams are organized depending on the themes that the professionals specialize in, such as regional special foods, activation of the onsen site, and zero-waste activities in the region.

Yamaguchi LL was held by the local government as a measure to realize the ideas presented at the Design Thinking College (DTC). The kick-off seminar was held in June to gather the participants interested in LL regardless of their participation in the DTC. Two themes were selected by the participants of the kick-off seminar, which are leisure activities utilizing the local park and fulfilling child-raising through cooking activities. In total 11 participants joined and 6 participants are members of the local government.

We asked the participants to answer the online questionnaire. The questionnaire was composed of two parts. First, we asked about the motivation during the two specific times, such as when the participant joined the kick-off workshop and at the moment, he/she is answering the survey, on a 5-point scale. Secondly, as the written questionnaire, we asked four questions below to clarify the timewise changes and specific factors that influenced the motivation after the kick-off workshop.

1. What was your motivation to join the living lab?
2. What is your motivation to keep joining the activities of the living lab?
3. What are the factors enhancing your motivation?
4. What are the factors that demotivated you?

In total 21 participants (87.5% of the Shunan LL participants and 63.6% of the Yamaguchi LL participants) answered the survey. We analyzed the result by coding and classifying the comments as the steps taken by Habibipour et al. [7]. First, we classified the descriptions of each of the questions and aggregated the numbers for the backgrounds of the participants. We focused on the background whether they are students, or working adults in the public, private, or education sector. Also, we focused on which LL or the team they participate in. The table below shows the background of the participants of each LL.

Furthermore, in order to further clarify the motivations of the individuals, depth interviews were held with seven participants (three participants of Shunan LL and four participants of the Yamaguchi LL). The interviewees were selected to ensure the diversity of the participants' backgrounds. The table below shows the background of the interviewees (Tables 1 and 2).

To further understand the changes in the motivation of the participants, we prepared the questions below to conduct the semi-structured interview. The first question is about the individuals and the second and the third is asking the perceptions of their teams. To encourage the interviewees to feel free to speak directly about their teams, the authors didn't participate in the interviews with the interviewees belonging to the same teams as them.

1. How did your motivation change and why?
2. How did your team's motivation change and why?
3. What is needed to moreover motivate your team?

Table 1. Background of the participants.

Background		Shunan LL	Yamaguchi LL
Total		14	7
Sector	Students	6	1
	Public	0	4
	Private	6	1
	Education	2	1
Team	Zero-waste	6	-
	Onsen-site	4	-
	Food	4	-
	Leisure activity	-	3
	Child-raising	-	4

Table 2. Background of the interviewees.

Interviewee	sector	Living lab	Team
A	Student	Shunan	Food
B	Private	Shunan	Zero-waste
C	Private	Shunan	Onsen-site
D	Public	Yamaguchi	Leisure activity
E	Education	Yamaguchi	Leisure activity
F	Student	Yamaguchi	Child-raising
G	Public	Yamaguchi	Child-raising

4   Survey Result

The figure below presents the motivation of the participants asked by the 5-point scale (1: Low, 2: Not so high, 3: Neutral, 4: Somewhat high, 5: High). In total more than half of the participants answered 4 (somewhat high) or 5 (high) at both timings. The number of participants answering that their motivation is 'high' increased from two to three. However, the number of participants answering 'not so high' increased, from two to five, which means that their motivation decreased through the team activities (Fig. 1).

Figure 2 shows the result comparing the sector of the participants. The result indicated that the motivation of the participants in the public sector grew as the number of the participants answering 'high' increased and 'not so high' decreased. On the other hand, students' motivation decreased as the number of participants answering 'not so high' increased from one to three. There was not a big change in education and the private sector but the motivation slightly decreased as the number of the participants answering 'not so high' increased in both of the sectors.

Fig. 1. Changes in motivation (total).

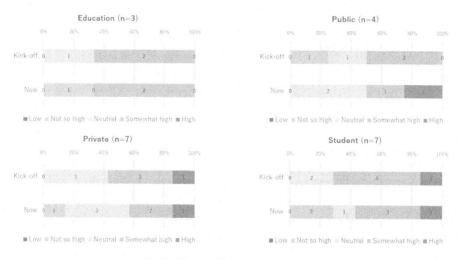

Fig. 2. Changes in motivation (sector).

Figure 3 compares the changes in motivation depending on the LL that the participant joined. The results show that the motivation of the Yamaguchi LL participants increased since all the participants were higher than neutral and the number of the participants answering 'high' increased from one to two participants. Regarding the Shunan LL, the number of participants answering 'not so high' increased from one to five.

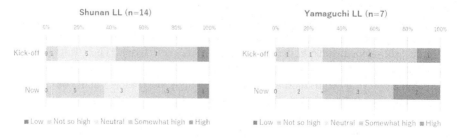

Fig. 3. Changes in motivation (living lab).

Figure 4 shows the changes in motivation depending on the teams that the participants belong to. The participants answering 'not so high' increased in Zero-waste and Onsen-site team. However, the number of participants answering 'slightly high' in the Zero-waste team and 'high' in the Onsen-site team didn't change. In detail, highly motivated members stayed but the 'neutral' members were demotivated. Positive changes were specified in the Child-raising team, in which participants with 'high' motivation increased and 'not so high' disappeared. The food and Leisure activity teams' changes were not remarkable compared to other teams.

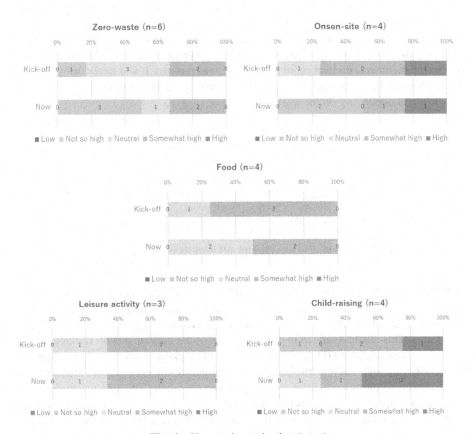

Fig. 4. Changes in motivation (team)

Overall, looking at the motivation of the participants described in numbers, positive changes turned up in participants belonging to the public sector and Yamaguchi LL, especially in the Child-raising team. Negative changes stood out in the student participants joining Shunan LL, especially in the Zero-waste and Onsen-site teams. The reasons for those changes are explored in the next sections.

5 Open Coding Result

5.1 Motivation to Join the Kick-Off Workshop

Since some participants answered more than one factor, 29 comments about the motivation to join the kick-off workshop were extracted. Through the classification of the descriptions, we found out that there are active motivation and passive motivation. Figure 5 shows the ratio of the comments depending on the background of the participants. Regarding the sector of the participants, students and the education sector tend to be passive, in contrast, the public and private sectors are more active. Comparing the two LLs, Yamaguchi LL participants had more active motivation than Shunan LL. This result explains the higher motivation of Yamaguchi LL from the kick-off. Focusing on the teams, the Food team was different from the other two teams in Shunan LL since most of the members' motivation to join the LL was passive. It was noteworthy that all the members of the Leisure activity team were active. We found out that the motivations were different depending on the teams.

Classification	No. of comments	Ratio	Sector				Shunan LL				Yamaguchi LL		
			Stu.	Pub.	Pri,	Edu.	TOTAL	ZW	OS	Food	TOTAL	LA	CR
Active	18	62.1%	44.4%	80.0%	72.7%	33.3%	57.9%	62.5%	83.3%	20.0%	70.0%	100.0%	57.1%
Passive	11	37.9%	55.6%	20.0%	27.3%	66.7%	42.1%	37.5%	16.7%	80.0%	30.0%	0.0%	42.9%

Fig. 5. Motivation to join the kick-off workshop (classification 1)

We created another classification in more precise as Fig. 6. Students and working adults in the private sector tend to expect occasions to interact with people, which supports H2. On the other hand, public sector participants were motivated to realize the team's idea. This result is related to the motivation of the participants of Yamaguchi LL since ideas created at the DTC were presented at the kick-off workshop. Regarding the Shunan LL, although many participants in total expected the occasions to interact with people, the motivations were different depending on the teams. The zero-waste team had the most participants expecting personal growth and the Food team expected occasions to interact. The Onsen-site team's motivations were divided, but it was the only team that had explicit extrinsic motivation. This result supports H1, as others were mostly intrinsic motivations. Regarding Yamaguchi-LL, all of the participants belonging to the Leisure activity team were motivated to realize their ideas. It can be perceived that the members of the Leisure activity team had a close motivation from the beginning. The motivation of the Child-raising team was divided into interaction with other people and interest in the theme.

#	Classification	No. of comments	Ratio	Sector				Shunan LL				Yamaguchi LL		
				Stu.	Pub.	Pri.	Edu.	TOTAL	ZW	OS	Food	TOTAL	LA	CR
1	Occasions to interact with diverse people	8	27.6%	33.3%	0.0%	45.5%	0.0%	31.6%	25.0%	33.3%	40.0%	20.0%	0.0%	28.6%
2	Passive (just because he/she was invited)	4	13.8%	11.1%	20.0%	9.1%	33.3%	15.8%	25.0%	0.0%	20.0%	10.0%	0.0%	14.3%
3	Realize the team's idea	4	13.8%	0.0%	60.0%	0.0%	33.3%	0.0%	0.0%	0.0%	0.0%	40.0%	100.0%	14.3%
4	Personal growth	4	13.8%	11.1%	20.0%	9.1%	0.0%	15.8%	37.5%	0.0%	0.0%	10.0%	0.0%	14.3%
5	Interest in the theme of the team	4	13.8%	22.2%	0.0%	18.2%	0.0%	10.5%	0.0%	16.7%	20.0%	20.0%	0.0%	28.6%
6	Interest in the LL and to enjoy the activities	2	6.9%	11.1%	0.0%	9.1%	0.0%	10.5%	0.0%	16.7%	20.0%	0.0%	0.0%	0.0%
7	Extrinsic motivation related to their job	2	6.9%	0.0%	0.0%	9.1%	33.3%	10.5%	0.0%	33.3%	0.0%	0.0%	0.0%	0.0%
8	Values for the future	1	3.4%	11.1%	0.0%	0.0%	0.0%	5.3%	12.5%	0.0%	0.0%	0.0%	0.0%	0.0%

Fig. 6. Motivation to join the kick-off workshop (classification 2)

5.2 Motivation to Keep Joining the Team Activities

22 comments on the motivation to keep joining the team activities were gathered and classified into nine categories as Fig. 7. 22.7% of participants kept joining the team as they could acquire new perspectives, which supports H3. Regarding the sectors of the participants, the motivations of students and the participants in the education sector were divided. It was the characteristics of the education sector participants to be passive to keep joining the activities. This may be due to their motivation to be extrinsic from the beginning. The public sector participants had two kinds of motivation, such as achievement and excitement. As the characteristic of private sector participants, they are motivated by acquiring new perspectives through the team's activities outside their business, which supports H3. It can be highlighted that more than half of the participants of Yamaguchi LL are excited and enjoying their team activities and are motivated by those emotions. Both teams of the Yamaguchi LL are enjoying their activities. On the other hand, Shunan LL participants are motivated by learning and receiving new perspectives or providing them to other members. It can be assumed that members are divided into receiver and provider in the teams except the Onsen-site team where half of the participants are motivated by acquiring new perspectives. Since there wasn't a category to contribute to others at the beginning, some participants discovered the specific points that they could contribute to what the team was trying to achieve. This may be due to the characteristics of Shunan LL to be participated by professionals in the field and students.

Classification	No. of comments	Ratio	Sector				Shunan LL				Yamaguchi LL		
			Stu.	Pub.	Pri,	Edu.	TOTAL	ZW	OS	Food	TOTAL	LA	CR
1 Acquire new perspectives different from their daily life	5	22.7%	12.5%	0.0%	50.0%	0.0%	26.7%	14.3%	50.0%	25.0%	14.3%	0.0%	25.0%
2 Excitement through the activities	4	18.2%	12.5%	50.0%	0.0%	33.3%	0.0%	0.0%	0.0%	0.0%	57.1%	66.7%	50.0%
3 Achievements through the activities	3	13.6%	12.5%	50.0%	0.0%	0.0%	6.7%	14.3%	0.0%	0.0%	28.6%	33.3%	25.0%
4 Self development and learning	3	13.6%	25.0%	0.0%	16.7%	0.0%	20.0%	28.6%	0.0%	25.0%	0.0%	0.0%	0.0%
5 Contribution to other team members	3	13.6%	12.5%	0.0%	33.3%	0.0%	20.0%	28.6%	0.0%	25.0%	0.0%	0.0%	0.0%
6 No specific motivations	1	4.5%	0.0%	0.0%	0.0%	33.3%	6.7%	14.3%	0.0%	0.0%	0.0%	0.0%	0.0%
7 Interest in the activities	1	4.5%	12.5%	0.0%	0.0%	0.0%	6.7%	0.0%	0.0%	25.0%	0.0%	0.0%	0.0%
8 Sense of duty	1	4.5%	0.0%	0.0%	0.0%	33.3%	6.7%	0.0%	25.0%	0.0%	0.0%	0.0%	0.0%
9 Occasions to participate	1	4.5%	12.5%	0.0%	0.0%	0.0%	6.7%	0.0%	25.0%	0.0%	0.0%	0.0%	0.0%

Fig. 7. Motivation to keep joining the team activities

5.3 Motivational Factors

28 comments were gathered as the motivational factors in Fig. 8. As well as the motivation to join the kick-off workshop, the highest ratio motivator was the interaction with other people, which supports H2. Especially listening to the opinions of people having different backgrounds motivated the participants, which supports H5 expressing the characteristics of Japanese. Easiness, clear vision, and sharing information were the new factors that emerged. Regarding the sectors, students were the only sector that was motivated by ownership, clear vision, and interest in the theme and their highest motivational factor was to realize the idea. Both public and private sector participants were motivated by the interaction with other people. It is noteworthy that it wasn't their motivation to interact with others at the moment of the kick-off workshop for the public sector participants. The passive attitude of the education sector was confirmed in this question as well. The variety of motivational factors was diverse for the Shunan LL participants compared with the Yamaguchi LL because of the diverse answers by the Zero-waste team. The result shows that the participants are motivated by the realization of the idea although many participants were motivated by the self-development and learning to keep joining the activities. It may mean that their motivations to achieve during the activities aren't satisfied enough. The onsen-site team was motivated by the interaction with others. Food team participants' motivational factors were divided but linked to their own interests. Although all the Leisure activity team participants were motivated to realize the idea at the moment of the kick-off workshop, the factors to enhance their motivation were interaction with others and their emotions to enjoy the activities as well as the realization of the idea. The Child-raising team was motivated by enjoying the interactions with others and acquiring new perspectives.

Classification	No. of comments	Ratio	Sector				Shunan LL				Yamaguchi LL		
			Stu.	Pub.	Pri.	Edu.	TOTAL	ZW	OS	Food	TOTAL	LA	CR
1 Interaction with diverse people (especially listening to others idea)	6	21.4%	11.1%	33.3%	30.0%	0.0%	15.8%	14.3%	40.0%	0.0%	33.3%	33.3%	33.3%
2 Interest in the LL and to enjoy the activities	4	14.3%	11.1%	33.3%	10.0%	0.0%	10.5%	0.0%	20.0%	14.3%	22.2%	33.3%	16.7%
3 Realize the team's idea	4	14.3%	22.2%	0.0%	10.0%	33.3%	15.8%	28.6%	20.0%	0.0%	11.1%	33.3%	0.0%
4 Acquire new perspectives	4	14.3%	11.1%	16.7%	20.0%	0.0%	10.5%	0.0%	0.0%	28.6%	22.2%	0.0%	33.3%
5 Easiness to join the activities	3	10.7%	11.1%	16.7%	0.0%	33.3%	10.5%	0.0%	20.0%	14.3%	11.1%	0.0%	16.7%
6 Sense of contribution to the team	2	7.1%	0.0%	0.0%	20.0%	0.0%	10.5%	0.0%	0.0%	28.6%	0.0%	0.0%	0.0%
7 Interest in the theme of the team	1	3.6%	11.1%	0.0%	0.0%	0.0%	5.3%	0.0%	0.0%	14.3%	0.0%	0.0%	0.0%
8 Ownership to the activities	1	3.6%	11.1%	0.0%	0.0%	0.0%	5.3%	14.3%	0.0%	0.0%	0.0%	0.0%	0.0%
9 Clear vision	1	3.6%	11.1%	0.0%	0.0%	0.0%	5.3%	14.3%	0.0%	0.0%	0.0%	0.0%	0.0%
10 Sharing information with others	1	3.6%	0.0%	0.0%	10.0%	0.0%	5.3%	14.3%	0.0%	0.0%	0.0%	0.0%	0.0%
11 No specific motivations	1	0.0%	0.0%	0.0%	.0.0%	33.3%	5.3%	14.3%	0.0%	0.0%	0.0%	0.0%	0.0%

Fig. 8. Motivational factors

5.4 Demotivational Factors

There were 24 comments about the factors that demotivate the participants and the comments were classified into 11 categories as Fig. 9. Most participants (16.7%) answered that there aren't specific factors that demotivate themselves. It is noteworthy that many participants (75.0%) belonging to the Child-raising team didn't come up with demotivational factors. When focusing on the specific demotivational factors, the difference in the ratios was not big among the factors. It means that the demotivational factors are not that much in common. Contribution to the team, shared vision, and information were the factors that motivated the participants when it was positive, but when the situation was negative, they demotivated them. H6 was supported as there were participants demotivated by the lack of shared information.

Regarding the sectors, for students, low contribution to the team and misunderstandings among the team members were the factors that were pointed out the most. Although many participants in the public or private sector didn't have a specific demotivational factor, the specific factors that demotivate them were quite different between the sectors. Regarding the teams, Zero-waste team participants were demotivated by the lack of shared information. Onsen-team participants raised their low degree of contribution and leadership in the team. Food team participants were concerned about the misunderstandings among the team members. Leisure activity team participants were demotivated by the passive participation of themselves and other members.

Classification	No. of comments	Ratio	Sector				Shunan LL				Yamaguchi LL		
			Stu.	Pub.	Pri.	Edu.	TOTAL	ZW	OS	Food	TOTAL	LA	CR
1 No specific demotivational factors	4	16.7%	11.1%	25.0%	28.6%	0.0%	5.9%	0.0%	25.0%	0.0%	42.9%	0.0%	75.0%
2 Low contribution to the team	3	12.5%	22.2%	0.0%	14.3%	0.0%	17.6%	12.5%	25.0%	20.0%	0.0%	0.0%	0.0%
3 Misunderstanding among the team members	3	12.5%	22.2%	25.0%	0.0%	0.0%	11.8%	0.0%	0.0%	40.0%	14.3%	0.0%	25.0%
4 Lacking shared information	3	12.5%	11.1%	0.0%	14.3%	33.3%	17.6%	37.5%	0.0%	0.0%	0.0%	0.0%	0.0%
5 Passive attitude and low participation rate of other members	3	12.5%	11.1%	25.0%	0.0%	0.0%	11.8%	25.0%	0.0%	0.0%	14.3%	33.3%	0.0%
6 Cannot participate to the activities (because of the schedule etc...)	2	8.3%	11.1%	0.0%	0.0%	33.3%	5.9%	12.5%	0.0%	0.0%	14.3%	33.3%	0.0%
7 Not enough leadership role in the team	2	8.3%	0.0%	0.0%	28.6%	0.0%	11.8%	0.0%	25.0%	20.0%	0.0%	0.0%	0.0%
8 Less chances to participate	1	4.2%	0.0%	0.0%	14.3%	0.0%	5.9%	0.0%	0.0%	20.0%	0.0%	0.0%	0.0%
9 Sense of duty	1	4.2%	0.0%	0.0%	0.0%	33.3%	5.9%	0.0%	25.0%	0.0%	0.0%	0.0%	0.0%
10 Delay of the project	1	4.2%	11.1%	0.0%	0.0%	0.0%	5.9%	12.5%	0.0%	0.0%	0.0%	0.0%	0.0%
11 Low feasibility of the idea	1	4.2%	0.0%	25.0%	0.0%	0.0%	0.0%	0.0%	0.0%	0.0%	14.3%	33.3%	0.0%

Fig. 9. Demotivational factors

6   Interview Result

We conducted a semi-structured interview to further explore the motivation of the participants. Figure 10 shows the summarized comments gathered through the interview with participants of Shunan LL, we found out the different attitudes between students and working adults, which supports H4. Students are expected from the working adults to move aggressively and present new ideas. At the same time, working adults consciously avoid speaking out too much and step back to support the students. When the communication between students and working adults is going well, they can learn and be stimulated by each other. All the teams were not sure who should lead the team. Interviewee A answered that the working adult is leading the team, although she thinks that students should. Interviewees B and C implied that the students should lead the team and try not to lead the team too much. Therefore, leadership is lacking and it seems both teams aren't stable enough to maintain the motivation. In order to motivate the team, Interviewees A and B mentioned the frequency of meeting each other. Interviewee A emphasized the importance of meeting in person. This is due to the lack of meetings at this point for the teams. As Interviewee A highlighted, the opportunity should be open (not duty) to maintain the motivation of the students. On the other hand, Interviewee C clearly demanded opportunities to motivate the students. He considers that students find it more difficult to manage their motivation. Through the interview, as there are different attitudes and amounts of experience between students and working adults, we found out that they should be taken care of consciously differently to enhance motivation.

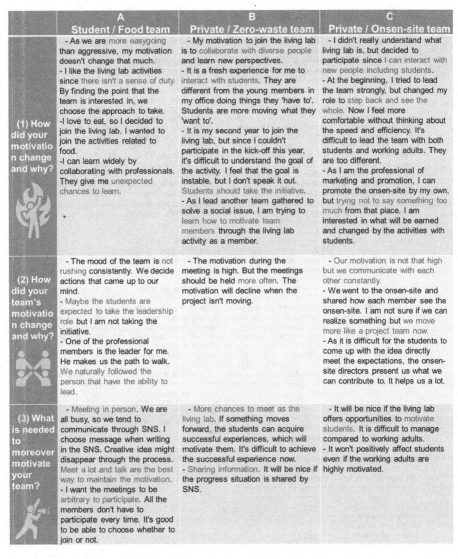

	A Student / Food team	B Private / Zero-waste team	C Private / Onsen-site team
(1) How did your motivation change and why?	- As we are more easygoing than aggressive, my motivation doesn't change that much. - I like the living lab activities since there isn't a sense of duty. By finding the point that the team is interested in, we choose the approach to take. -I love to eat, so I decided to join the living lab. I wanted to join the activities related to food. -I can learn widely by collaborating with professionals. They give me unexpected chances to learn.	- My motivation to join the living lab is to collaborate with diverse people and learn new perspectives. - It is a fresh experience for me to interact with students. They are different from the young members in my office doing things they 'have to'. Students are more moving what they 'want to'. - It is my second year to join the living lab, but since I couldn't participate in the kick-off this year, it's difficult to understand the goal of the activity. I feel that the goal is instable, but I don't speak it out. Students should take the initiative. - As I lead another team gathered to solve a social issue, I am trying to learn how to motivate team members through the living lab activity as a member.	- I didn't really understand what living lab is, but decided to participate since I can interact with new people including students. - At the beginning, I tried to lead the team strongly, but changed my role to step back and see the whole. Now I feel more comfortable without thinking about the speed and efficiency. It's difficult to lead the team with both students and working adults. They are too different. - As I am the professional of marketing and promotion, I can promote the onsen-site by my own, but trying not to say something too much from that place. I am interested in what will be earned and changed by the activities with students.
(2) How did your team's motivation change and why?	- The mood of the team is not rushing consistently. We decide actions that came up to our mind. - Maybe the students are expected to take the leadership role but I am not taking the initiative. - One of the professional members is the leader for me. He makes us the path to walk. We naturally followed the person that have the ability to lead.	- The motivation during the meeting is high. But the meetings should be held more often. The motivation will decline when the project isn't moving.	- Our motivation is not that high but we communicate with each other constantly. - We went to the onsen-site and shared how each member see the onsen-site. I am not sure if we can realize something but we move more like a project team now. - As it is difficult for the students to come up with the idea directly meet the expectations, the onsen-site directors present us what we can contribute to. It helps us a lot.
(3) What is needed to moreover motivate your team?	- Meeting in person. We are all busy, so we tend to communicate through SNS. I choose message when writing in the SNS. Creative idea might disappear through the process. Meet a lot and talk are the best way to maintain the motivation. - I want the meetings to be arbitrary to participate. All the members don't have to participate every time. It's good to be able to choose whether to join or not.	- More chances to meet as the living lab. If something moves forward, the students can acquire successful experiences, which will motivate them. It's difficult to achieve the successful experience now. - Sharing information. It will be nice if the progress situation is shared by SNS.	- It will be nice if the living lab offers opportunities to motivate students. It is difficult to manage compared to working adults. - It won't positively affect students even if the working adults are highly motivated.

Fig. 10. Interview result (Shunan LL)

Figure 11 shows the summarized interview results of four participants of Yamaguchi LL. Regarding the motivation of individuals, the participants of DTC (Interviewee E and G) clearly understood the objectives of LL, but others were not sure. Also, it is one of the characteristics of Yamaguchi LL that some members join the activities as their work. It can be assumed that when the activities are related to their work, extrinsic motivation is enhanced. Interviewees E and F mentioned that their secure feelings enhanced their motivation, which supports H6 that Japanese characteristics tend to avoid uncertainty. Also, Interviewee D and Interviewee E highlighted that they enjoy the activities to apply

	D Public / Leisure activity team	E Education / Leisure activity team	F Student / Child-raising team	G Public / Child-raising team
(1) How did your motivation change and why?	-At the beginning, I wasn't sure my expected role. Since most of the team members were the participants of Design Thinking College (DTC), I felt like I'm in an 'away'. -I even thought myself to be an observer, but as the activities proceed, I gradually found out my role as a team member. -I still haven't clarified whether this activity is private or work. I can enjoy the situation when it is vague. I experienced that joining interesting projects in private leading to a business opportunity. LL is one of the projects that I enjoy to apply the experience to other situations and to meet with interesting people.	-My motivation join the LL was to realize the idea we present at DTC. Since there was a member with very high motivation, I could participate more comfortably. -I was excited the most when we conducted prototyping at the park. My motivation was enhanced. When I see the children enjoying the leisure activities we planned, I became free from anxiety. -Overall, I found out my self motivated when I feel secure and have a bright outlook on our idea. Contrary, feeling anxiety and no light in the tunnel demotivate me. -As I am teaching design thinking to students, LL relates to my job. I can understand students perspective and feeling by being a participant	- At the beginning, I wasn't sure what LL is. However, as the activity proceed my motivation was enhanced by collaboration with working adults and absorbing new ways of thinking. Surprisingly, the team members come up with ideas one after another. Yamaguchi LL was totally different from the activities only with students. Working adults can respect each others' opinion. - I used to be skeptical of the effect of the online meetings, but after the second meeting, I became use to the online communication. - Since I am closest to the target of the team's solution, I am required to present ultimate ideas.	-I was the participant of the DTC. After DTC, I moved to the department that organizes the DTC and Yamaguchi LL. So, it was my work to join the LL in one aspect. Although, it became a good chance for me the output the input acquired at DTC. It is one of my motivation to implement design thinking in the LL activities. -Maybe I hadn't joined LL if there weren't an aspect of work. Many participants of DTC didn't join the LL.
(2) How did your team's motivation change and why?	-I think the team's motivation hasn't change that much. After the prototyping at the park, our idea took shape and the motivation slightly became higher. When the team perceive that the goal is getting closer the motivation is enhanced. -The team members can openly speak up to each other. There is a member leading the team with his strong feelings.	-We maintained high motivation. Two of the members were working on the activities as part of their job. They were especially highly motivated and had a strong ownership.. -I felt the team leader is necessary to participate comfortably. Fortunately, we had a good leader with clear vision.	-The motivation of the team was high and stable. Since the organizer of the LL schedule the next meeting, the meetings were constantly held and were effective to maintain the motivation. Also it was arbitrary to participate. - Cooking as the prototyping in offline settings enhanced our motivation. As the prototype clarified the fuzzy points, we can move forward more concretely.	-When the idea didn't come up the team was in a rut. The team members are nice and cooperative. The bad mood didn't last long. -The chance to meet in person enhanced the understanding of each other. Chatting lack in online meetings to naturally know the personality.
(3) What is needed to moreover motivate your team?	-We took a lot of time to share the goal vision, but taking more time to think about 'how' to realize the idea might be more fun. -We should have meet in person at the park at the earlier timing. The members' frequency to use the park was quite different, so when ideating, the view of the members were quite different as well.	-We should have meet in person at the park at earlier timing and more often. I understood the team members' characteristics naturally by seeing them communicating with their children.	- We should have meet in person at the earlier point and more often.	-Sense of crisis might be lacking in LL. There weren't any chances to present the solution. At the same time, we couldn't receive objective feedbacks to the idea. -Target of the solution was too wide and difficult to ideate. If the target is determined from the beginning, we didn't have to take such a long time to debate about it.

Fig. 11. Interview result (Yamaguchi LL)

the experience to other situations, which supports H3. This comment is close to Interviewee B's motivation to learn effective team building. Regarding the team's motivation, both teams were perceived to maintain high motivation. Interviewee F pointed out that the arbitrary meeting motivated her, which is also mentioned by Interviewee A. Students may be demotivated by duty meetings. All the interviewees were motivated through the prototyping in offline settings. Realizing the idea and knowing other members are the motivation factors satisfied through meeting in person. Therefore, in order to moreover motivate the team, most of the interviewees highlighted that they should have met in person at the earlier point and more often. Interviewees D and G also mentioned that since the time was limited, setting limitations in the process of the activities might motivate the team by avoiding frustrating uncertainty. Additionally, it is noteworthy that Interviewee G pointed out the necessity of the sense of crisis. Chances of the teams to present and receive feedback on their idea might motivate them to finalize their idea effectively.

Through the interview, we found out two specific characteristics of the LL that affect the motivation of the participants. The first is the strong presence of students in the Shunan LL. When the activities are closer to their own business of the working adults, it may be easier to motivate the participants. Secondly, periodical meetings are effective in maintaining the participants' motivation. The meeting setting role of the organizer of Yamaguchi LL affected the team's motivation positively, which is lacking in Shunan LL.

7 Discussions

Through the analysis of the free descriptions and the semi-structured interview result, we extracted the factors related to the motivation of the participants to continuously join the co-creation activities in the two kinds of LL, such as Shunan LL and Yamaguchi LL. Each of the analyses highlighted the difference depending on the background of the participants. As a result, the interview clarified the difference between students and working adults. The different motivations of the participants in the two LLs can be explained by the different classifications they belong to. Referring to the classification of living labs indicated in the previous studies [12–14], Yamaguchi LL is classified as enabler driven approach, bottom-up and exhalation-dominated, since the local government facilitates the community participation by the citizens to fulfill the requirements of the citizens in the region. This is why it is important for the participants to be excited and interested in participating in the community. Referring to the innovation approach point of view indicated by Capdevila [14], Yamaguchi LL took the social innovation approach. The social innovation approach's advantages are the 'citizen-participation and involvement' and the disadvantages are the 'frustration if outcomes are not finally implemented'. The result of this study was in line with the analysis of Capdevila [14] as the Leisure-activity team especially valued to realize their idea. On the other hand, Shunan LL is classified as a provider driven approach, top-down and exhalation-dominated. As it is held in the university, the participants are motivated to acquire new perspectives and learnings. It is noteworthy that some participants are motivated to offer new knowledge to the community not just receive it. At the same time, the participants are demotivated by the weak top-down constructions such as their ambiguous roles of themselves and the goal settings. In Capdevila [14]'s classification, Shunan LL is the 'methods and techniques to channel collective creativity' usually held by non-profit institutions such as universities. However, as the Shunan LL doesn't strongly guide the participants, the participants haven't received the both advantages and disadvantages of this type of activity defined by Capdevila [14].

In the following part of this section, we indicate two points. First, we indicate the important motivational factors extracted through the coding and classification of the free descriptions. The result will contribute to enriching the living lab research in the HCI field requiring the involvement of the participants in the design process as engaged partners. Secondly, we indicate the implications to the practitioners on how to motivate the participants to continuously join the LL. The result contributes to practice for living lab coordinators for the continuity of the lab.

7.1 Important Motivatinal Factors

To indicate the important motivational factors, we focused on the seven common factors extracted beyond the questions. Moreover, the result indicated the importance of encouraging the motivational factors, instead of improving the demotivational factors, since the demotivational factor's individuality was higher and it was more difficult to motivate the participants spontaneously. Figure 12 shows the common motivational factors extracted beyond the questions. The column-colored orange 'interest in the LL and to enjoy the activities' was the most important motivational factor commonly extracted in three questions. The reasons why the participants are interested in the LL differ, but it is important to communicate the advantages of the LL approach and make the participants enjoy those advantages during the activities. Another motivation related to interest was 'the interest in the theme of the team', which was extracted in both the motivation to join the kick-off workshop and motivational factors (colored yellow). Both LLs we dealt with in this study set a specific theme for each team to work on. By letting participants select the theme they are interested in, we can motivate the participants from the beginning of the LL. The motivation to interact with diverse people was pointed out the most in both of the questions, which supports H2. LL can offer the participants to strengthen the weak ties [15] with diverse people to acquire wider information that they can't access generally. However, as it is not extracted as the motivation to keep joining the workshop, only coordinating occasions to interact with others doesn't motivate the participants to keep joining the LL but outcomes are expected. As the outcome of the interactions, 'Acquire new perspectives' was extracted as the common factor for motivation to keep joining the team activities and the motivational factors (colored green). The advantage of the LL to offer chances to acquire learnings that can apply to other scenes (H3) was the unexpected motivation for the participants at the beginning of the LL. Another two factors colored green can be explained by the Japanese characteristics to value harmony of the team (H5). 'Contribution to the team' could be acknowledged after the participants find their roles in the comfortable team with harmony. 'Ownership to the activities' related to the sense of duty can be interpreted as the motivation not to break the harmony of the team for continuous relationships. Finally, the motivation to 'realize the idea' was the factor beyond the generated hypotheses. As we also found out that the prototyping led to excitement through the activities in the interviews, we can motivate the participants by creating chances to prototype their ideas for continuous co-creation. Additionally, the participants avoid uncertainty (H6) and acquire successful experiences. These were the new findings that led to the contribution to the research.

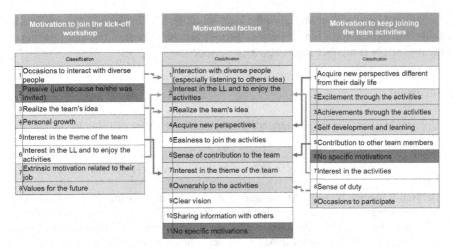

Fig. 12. Important Motivational Factors

7.2   Implications to the Practitioners

Through the findings of this study, we have three points for the implications to the organizers of the LL especially in Japan to motivate the participants. First, it is important to create occasions for participants to interact and collaborate with other participants. It can be periodical meetings, which were effective in Yamaguchi LL. Moreover, it is effective in transforming collaboration occasions into learnings. Secondly, the organizers can detect the different motivations depending on the background of the participants and implement measures to enhance them, especially when there are explicit power distances. For example, when there are both students and working adults in the team, it is expected to manage their motivations differently from the working adults. Finally, the organizers should actively encourage the participants to prototype their ideas, especially by meeting the team members in person. Meeting in person will enhance the understanding of the personality of the team members difficult to find out in online settings. Also, prototyping the concept will lead the LL itself to achieve successful outcomes [16].

As additional implications, shedding light on the motivations of the participants and opening them to others are other measures that can be taken to motivate the participants. In the process of this study taking the action research approach, the participants of the LL researching on the motivation motivated themselves to more actively evolve the activities and communicate with other team members. Especially in the context of Japanese teams emphasizing harmony, it may be difficult to disclose themselves, but taking effective ways will enhance the motivations.

7.3   Limitations and Future Research

Since this study focused on exploring the real voices of the participants in two LLs, the extracted factors are limited depending on the characteristics and the situation of the LLs. In future research, it will be effective to compare the factors extracted in this study to LLs in other countries with different cultural characteristics. Also, as this research was conducted about six months after the kick-off of the LL, further research is possible by following the LL for a longer period. To indicate the impact of the measures taken by the organizers is another future research perspective.

References

1. Hossain, M., Leminen, S., Westerlund, M.: A systematic review of living lab literature. J. Clean. Prod. **213**, 976–988 (2013)
2. Alavi, H.S., Lalanne, D., Rogers, Y.: The five strands of living lab a literature study of the evolution of living lab concepts in HCI. ACM Trans. Comput.-Hum. Interact. **27**(2), 1–26 (2020)
3. Bergvall-Kåreborn, B., Holst, M., Ståhlbröst, A.: Concept design with a living lab approach. In: Proceedings of the 42nd Hawaii International Conference on System Sciences (2009)
4. Logghe, S., Baccarne, B., Schuurman, D.: An exploration of user motivations for participation in Living Labs. In: The XXV ISPIM Conference – Innovation for Sustainable Economy & Society, Dublin, Ireland on 8–11 June 2014 (2014)
5. Logghe, S., Schuurman, D.: Action research as a framework to evaluate the operations of a living lab. Technol. Innov. Manag. Rev. **7**(2), 35–41 (2017)
6. Akasaka, F., Mitake, Y., Watanabe, K., Shimomura, Y.: A framework for 'configuring participation' in living labs. Des. Sci. **8**, e28 (2022)
7. Habibipour, A., Padyab, A., Bergvall-Kåreborn, B., Ståhlbröst, A.: Exploring factors influencing participant drop-out behavior. In: Scandinavian Conference on Information Systems 2017: Nordic Contributions in IS Research, pp. 28–40 (2017)
8. Kimura, A., Haraguchi, H., Yamauchi, Y., Matsuura, K.: Social system design methodology for transitioning to a new social structure – a holistic urban living lab approach to the well-being city. Front. Sociol. **8**, 1201504 (2023)
9. Kitazume, K., Takaku, M., Kubota, K.: Development of a living lab co-creation tool considering Japanese characteristics. In: Proceedings of the Open LivingLab Days Conference 2022 "The city as a Lab, but now for real!", Officine Grandi Riparazioni (Turin) on 21–23 September 2022 (2022)
10. Taoka, Y., Kagohashi, K., Mougenot, C.: Living labs and co-design for social innovation: mapping the European model to Asian societies? In: Cumulus Hong Kong 2016 – Open Design for E-very-thing, Hong Kong on 21–24 November 2016 (2016)
11. Hirai, M.: Stereotypes about the Japanese: differences in evaluations between "The Japanese" and "Myself." Japan. J. Exp. Soc. Psychol. **39**(2), 103–113 (1999). (in Japanese)
12. Leminen, S., Westerlund, M., Nyström, A.-G.: Living labs as open-innovation networks. Technol. Innov. Manag. Rev. 6–11 (2012)
13. Leimen, S.: Coordination and participation in living lab networks. Technol. Innov. Manag. Rev. 5–14 (2013)
14. Capdevila, I.: How can city labs enhance the citizens' motivation in different types of innovation activities? In: International Conference on Social Informatics, Social Informatics, pp. 64–71 (2014)
15. Morgan, J.: Why Every Employee Should Be Building Weak Ties At Work, Forbes, edited on 11 March 2014 (2014). https://www.forbes.com/sites/jacobmorgan/2014/03/11/every-employee-weak-ties-work/?sh=41f970513168. Accessed 02 Feb 2013
16. Shuurman, D.D., Marez, L., Ballon, P.: The impact of living lab methodology on open innovation contributions and outcomes. Technol. Innov. Manag. Rev. **6**(1), 7–16 (2016)

A Study on the Determinants of User Continuance Intention in Social Media Intelligent Recommendation Systems from the Perspective of Information Ecology

Xiao Cheng and Guochao Peng[✉]

School of Information Management, Sun Yat-sen University, Guangzhou, China
penggch@mail.sysu.edu.cn

Abstract. This study employs literature analysis and integrates information ecology theory to categorize the determinants influencing user continuance intention in social media intelligent recommendation systems into four dimensions: individual factors, information factors, environmental factors, and technological factors. Data is collected through a questionnaire survey, and a qualitative comparative analysis method is utilized to validate the paths and combinations leading to user continuance intention in the context of social media intelligent recommendations. The research reveals that user continuance intention in social media intelligent recommendations is the result of the combined influence of individual factors, environmental factors, information factors, and technological factors, with flow experience and social influence playing primary roles in the process.

Keywords: Social media · Intelligent recommendation · Continuous intention to use · Information ecological theory · Qualitative comparative analysis

1 Introduction

The new information era is characterized by semantic networks, artificial intelligence, and personalized customization. Leveraging intelligent recommendation algorithms, social media can grasp and fulfill user information needs based on historical information behaviors of users and similar counterparts, actively providing more accurate information services, thereby alleviating information overload to some extent. Intelligent recommendation, centered around humans and built upon network technology, involves in-depth exploration and analysis of consumer behavior and platform business characteristics. It offers real-time and precise recommendations for products and services in different scenarios.

Mobile social media has become a crucial space for people's life, entertainment, and information acquisition. In order to more precisely deliver information content that aligns with user interests and needs, and to mitigate issues like information overload, intelligent recommendation systems are widely applied. In social media, the "recommendation" channels or related features based on intelligent recommendation systems have had a broad and profound impact on users. These systems personalize information recommendations based on user characteristics and their activities such as browsing, searching, reading, and bookmarking on social media platforms.

Intelligent recommendations help address issues like information overload for users (Zhang et al. 2019). However, they also bring about new challenges, as users transition from actively seeking information to passively receiving it. Social media platforms not only recommend personalized information to users through algorithms, data mining, and analysis but also continuously optimize recommendation algorithms by applying technical means to utilize user data. With the acceleration of people's lifestyle and consumption patterns, personalized intelligent recommendations, based on consumer characteristics, provide personalized products and services, creating more value for platform enterprises. This phenomenon has garnered widespread attention from scholars and entrepreneurs alike.

2 Literature Review

Intelligent recommendation plays a crucial role in facilitating user growth and maintaining user satisfaction for Internet products. However, the effectiveness of intelligent recommendations largely depends on a substantial amount of user data. The more user data a product acquires, the more accurate and efficient the recommendation algorithm analysis becomes (Chang & Yang, 2020). With the advent of the big data era, social media applications have significantly enhanced their ability to utilize and analyze user data to provide targeted services. Through intelligent recommendations, users can effectively and promptly access content of interest, thereby increasing the perceived value of recommended information and further enhancing user satisfaction and continuance intention for the application. However, concerns have been raised regarding the negative impacts of intelligent recommendations, such as user addiction, privacy risks, and information filter bubbles (Lu et al., 2020; Zhang et al., 2019; Chen & Liu, 2020; Meral, 2021). Youn pointed out that the disclosure and loss of control over user data increase perceived risks, leading to concerns about personal monitoring, loss of anonymity, identity theft, and other issues (Youn, 2009). Kim et al. conducted an online survey focusing on respondents with YouTube experience and found that perceived severity had a significant negative impact on the willingness to disclose all types of information. Coping efficacy had a positive impact on the willingness to disclose information other than feedback information, and self-efficacy had a positive impact on the disclosure of feedback information (Kim & Kim, 2018). Mou et al. explored the impact of recommendation algorithms, product reputation, product novelty, privacy concerns, and privacy protection behavior on user satisfaction and the continuance intention to use intelligent recommendation applications (Mou et al., 2021).

The current academic research landscape on intelligent recommendations within the social media environment is relatively limited, and there is a dearth of studies focusing on user information behaviors related to intelligent recommendations in the social media context. Furthermore, existing research has not fully considered the comprehensive impact of multiple dimensions such as platform dynamics, user characteristics, and contextual factors. Studies integrating intelligent recommendations within the context of social media also suffer from insufficient attention.

In an effort to address these gaps, this study, grounded in the Information Ecology theory, aims to employ a qualitative comparative analysis method. It seeks to explore the mechanisms influencing user continuance intention in the context of social media intelligent recommendations, taking into account the interplay of platform dynamics, user behaviors, and situational factors.

3   Theoretical Basis and Analysis Framework

The concept of "information ecology" was introduced by scholar Horton in 1978 within the field of information management. He applied an ecological perspective from the field of ecology to examine the flow of information within organizations. Horton proposed that information, processed data intended to meet users' decision-making needs, does not operate independently but is influenced by the ecological dynamics of the system (Horton, 1978). Information ecology theory is oriented towards user information needs and emphasizes the interactive relationships among information people, information, information environment, and information technology as an active state (Nardi & O'Day, 1999). According to this theory, human behavior is a result of the combined influence of information, environment, and technology (Nardi & O'Day, 1999). In this context, drawing upon the information ecology theory, this paper analyzes the antecedents and configurational pathways influencing user continuance intention in the context of social media intelligent recommendations. It considers factors such as individuals, information, environment, and technology, examining their characteristics and interactions within the social media ecosystem.

The sustained usage intention of social media intelligent recommendations by users is closely associated with factors such as individual attributes, environmental conditions, informational aspects, and technological elements. Grounded in the Information Ecology theory, this paper categorizes the influencing factors of user continuance intention into four dimensions: individual, environmental, informational, and technological. Additionally, based on a comprehensive literature review, the study introduces six variables, namely flow experience, social influence, information overload, recommendation accuracy, feature overload, and algorithm transparency.

1. Flow experience and willingness to use

In 1992, American psychologist Csikszentmihalyi defined the concept of "flow experience" as the subjective perception or psychological state individuals experience when fully engaged in an activity, with undivided attention and unaffected by external factor (Csikszentmihalyi, 2008). This intrinsic motivator has been widely applied in the field of electronic information, and the dimensions of flow experience in the context of mobile information environments differ slightly from the original concept. Immersive experiences are primarily used to measure emotional responses when individuals engage in activities such as online banking, online gaming, social media, online shopping, instant messaging services, and mobile applications. In a computer environment, immersive experiences describe the emotional state people undergo during activities involving interactions with computers, serving as an intrinsic motivator influencing individuals to engage in specific activities (Hoffman & Novak, 2009). Flow experience is considered a factor influencing users' intention for continued usage (Guo et al., 2016). When users experience a sense of pleasure and satisfaction through immersive experiences, it significantly influences their continued usage behavior (Chang & Zhu, 2012). With the rise of big data, Argyris et al. proposed interpreting immersive technology stimuli-cognitive experiences as the maximum satisfaction of perceptual entertainment and usefulness during the mobile digital learning experience in the digital network era (Argyris et al., 2020). Therefore, when users are likely to experience flow and satisfaction while using social media intelligent recommendation apps, their intention to continue using the app for learning and entertainment strengthens. Obtaining a flow experience contributes to sustained usage intention.

2. Social influence and willingness to use

Social influence is a critical factor influencing individuals' willingness to use information technology, defined as the extent to which individuals perceive the influence of their surrounding social groups (Venkatesh et al., 2003). It reflects the degree to which an individual's attitudes and behaviors are influenced by their social circles. In the real world, people exhibit conformity and homophily tendencies, considering the behaviors, viewpoints, or authoritative opinions of family members, friends, colleagues, or societal norms as benchmarks and unconsciously aligning their own behaviors and perspectives with them. In the context of information technology usage, it is generally acknowledged that an individual's technology adoption behavior is influenced by the behaviors of those around them, especially colleagues with similar job roles (Fulk et al., 1995).In this study, social influence refers to the specific individuals or organizations that impact users' adoption of social media intelligent recommendation apps. Zainab et al. posit that social influence has a positive impact on information systems (Zainab et al., 2018). Akram et al., based on the UTAUT model, explored factors influencing employees' behavioral intent to engage in e-learning in the public sector, finding that social influence significantly affects users' behavioral intent for e-learning (Hossain et al., 2019). De Melo Pereira et al. pointed out that social influence has a significantly positive impact on learners' satisfaction and intention to continue using e-learning services (De Melo Pereira et al., 2015).

3. Information Overload and willingness to use

Information overload is a state where an individual's information processing demands exceed their information processing capacity within a specific timeframe, hindering normal processes of information reception, processing, transformation, and decision-making (Galbraith, 1974). Research by Cao et al. found that information overload significantly impacts discontinuous intention, leading to a reduced willingness to continue using social media (Cao & Sun, 2018). Kim et al. suggested that information overload significantly affects social fatigue and diminishes users' intentions to continue using a platform (Kim et al., 2019). Zhang et al. proposed that perceived information overload can stimulate negative emotions among social network users and enhance their discontinuance intention (Zhang et al., 2020).

4. Recommendation accuracy and willingness to use

For users, the advantages of intelligent recommendations lie in their high relevance and precision, delivering accurate information recommendations at appropriate times and locations, thereby saving users time and effort in searching. Precise personalized services and relevant content also enhance users' willingness to consume, exerting a positive impact on their consumption behavior (Tucker, 2014). Lu, through the analysis of four representative service industries (aviation, hospitality, catering, and retail), discovered that consumers' willingness to use service robots increases with the improvement of the robot's intelligence and recommendation accuracy (Lu et al., 2019).

5. Functional overload and willingness to use

Functional overload refers to the perception of functional fatigue caused by system features being too complex for a given task or features exceeding user needs (Maier et al., 2015). System functional overload occurs when the provided information technology features are deemed too complex for the given task, leading to a perception of functional fatigue. In this study, functional overload refers to users perceiving that the features provided by social media intelligent recommendation software exceed their needs. Shokouhyar et al. identified factors leading to user social network fatigue, including information overload, social overload, and system functional overload (Shokouhyar et al., 2018). Fu et al. found that system functional overload leads to user emotional exhaustion, prompting users to discontinue the use of mobile social networks (Fu et al., 2020). Zhang et al. discovered that system functional overload, information overload, and social overload are sources of stress that significantly impact social fatigue, subsequently leading to users' discontinuous usage behavior (Zhang et al., 2016). System functional overload in social media affects users' willingness to use and to some extent induces social media fatigue. When the costs associated with complexity outweigh the benefits of new features, users perceive system functional overload in social media intelligent recommendation software, gradually developing impatience and a negative attitude, eventually leading to discontinuation of use.

6. Algorithmic transparency and willingness to use

Algorithm transparency refers to the disclosure of information about the deployment, operation, and usage of an algorithm's design to users, regulatory authorities, or third parties for oversight. The acquisition and utilization of personal privacy information by social platforms increasingly exhibit automated and covert characteristics. The algorithmic black box significantly blurs the boundaries between public and private spaces, posing a threat to citizens' privacy rights. Moderate transparency in privacy policies can stimulate higher user willingness to use, while too little transparency may trigger perceived threats by users.

4 Research Design

4.1 Research Methods

The Qualitative Comparative Analysis (QCA) method differs from traditional research approaches that focus on the impact of individual factors on outcomes. QCA posits that the occurrence of a particular outcome results from the combined influence of multiple factors, and the impact of a single variable on the outcome is limited (Ragin, 2008). QCA, from a configurational perspective, explores the multiple and simultaneous relationships between variables, providing an effective means to investigate complex causal relationships among factors leading to a particular social phenomenon. Qualitative Comparative Analysis methods include csQCA, mvQCA, and fsQCA. Among them, fsQCA stands out for its consistency assessment, which allows for more precise set-theoretic analysis. In this study, a fuzzy set qualitative comparative analysis method is employed to explore the influencing mechanism of social media intelligent recommendation on users' willingness to continue usage.

4.2 Questionnaire Design and Data Collection

This study investigates the impact of various variables on the continuous usage intention of social media users through questionnaire data collection. In formulating the survey questions, emphasis was placed on adopting questions that have been previously proven to be mature and effective in classical research. The questions were modified slightly based on the context of this study. Each variable was measured using a 7-point Likert scale in the questionnaire.

The questionnaire for this study was distributed through an online survey platform. Before the formal data collection, the researchers conducted a pilot survey with 30 participants to assess the reliability and validity of the collected data. Based on the analysis results, adjustments were made to the questionnaire content before proceeding with the official survey. The study ultimately collected 203 survey responses, and after removing invalid data, there were 168 valid responses. The sample size meets the minimum case requirements for the six conditional variables. Basic information about the sample is presented in Table 1.

Table 1. Demographic characteristics

Category	Sub Category	Frequency	Percent (%)
Gender	Male	82	48.8
	Female	86	51.2
Age(years)	<18	10	6
	18–30	115	68.5
	31–40	25	14.9
	41–50	12	7.1
	>50	6	3.5
Education	Below bachelor degree	16	9.5
	Bachelor's degree	102	60.7
	Master degree or above	50	29.8

4.3 Reliability and Validity Testing

The reliability of a scale is generally measured by the size of the Cronbach's Alpha value. When the Cronbach's Alpha value is greater than 0.7, the scale can be considered to have good reliability. In this paper, SPSS 26 was used to test the reliability and validity of the scale. The Cronbach's Alpha value was used to measure the reliability of the questionnaire, and the KMO value and Bartlett's spherical test significance level were used to measure the validity of the questionnaire. The specific values are shown in Table 2. As can be seen from the values in the table, the minimum value of Cronbach's Alpha is 0.713, indicating that the questionnaire has good reliability. In order to test the construct validity of the scale, this paper conducted exploratory factor analysis on the questionnaire data. The KMO value was 0.765, which was greater than 0.7, and the significance level of Bartlett's spherical test was 0.000, indicating that it was suitable for factor analysis and the questionnaire scale had good construct validity.

Table 2. Reliability and validity indices

Constructs	Cronbach's Alpha	KMO	Bartlett Sphere Test Sig.
Flow Experience	0.812	0.765	0.000
Social Influence	0.881		
Information Overload	0.756		
Recommendation Accuracy	0.811		
Functional Overload	0.809		
Algorithmic Transparency	0.820		
Willingness to Use	0.713		

5 Data Calibration

Qualitative comparative analysis is based on the principle of Boolean algebra, which calibrates a variable against a set to indicate the degree to which the variable belongs to the set (Ragin, 2008), the obtained variable calibration values are the values needed for subsequent data analysis. In terms of calibration methods, there are two main methods: binary calibration and calibration based on Fuzzy sets (Ragin, 2008).The binary calibration method simply divides the relationship between variables and sets into two types: belonging and not belonging, resulting in variable assignments of only 1 and 0. However, the calibration based on fuzzy sets interprets the degree of a variable belonging to a set as a continuous process, so the variable assignment range obtained by the qualitative comparison analysis of fuzzy sets is within the interval [0,1], where 0 means no membership at all and 1 means full membership. In this study, the data were calibrated by calculating the average of the scores of each item under the same variable and then selecting the maximum, minimum and average value of the mean as the "complete membership", "complete non-membership" and "cross point" respectively.

6 Data Analysis

6.1 Univariate Necessary Condition Analysis

Then, the single necessary condition of the outcome variable is further analyzed. In qualitative comparative analysis of fuzzy sets, the adequacy and necessity of the relationship between conditional variables and outcome variables are mainly observed by the size of the consistency index. Consistency refers to the extent to which a given case shares a certain condition that leads to the occurrence of a result (Ragin, 2008), When the consistency index is greater than 0.8, it is considered that the conditional variable is a sufficient condition for the outcome variable; When the consistency index is greater than 0.9, it is considered that the conditional variable is a necessary condition for the outcome variable. Meanwhile, fuzzy set qualitative comparative analysis uses coverage indicators to determine the explanatory power of conditional variables on outcome variables. The larger the coverage, the more effective the conditional variable is in explaining the outcome variable (Ragin, 2008). The results of the univariate necessary condition analysis are shown in Table 3.

Table 3. Single variable necessity test

Constructs	Consistency	Coverage
Flow Experience	0.796345	0.878646
~ Flow Experience	0.557767	0.605384
Social Influence	0.788512	0.844657
~ Social Influence	0.489665	0.547633
Information Overload	0.666450	0.706005
~ Information Overload	0.644908	0.729779
Recommendation Accuracy	0.821367	0.850799
~ Recommendation Accuracy	0.530026	0.614686
Functional Overload	0.651219	0.660852
~ Functional Overload	0.645452	0.766339
Algorithmic Transparency	0.722911	0.831560
~ Algorithmic Transparency	0.555592	0.579748

According to Table 3, when the outcome variable is positive, the consistency values of all conditional variables have not reached 0.8, indicating that a single conditional variable cannot be a sufficient condition for users to continue using social media intelligent recommendation apps.

6.2 Conditional Combination Analysis

Building upon the calibration process based on variable assignment rules, the fsQCA 3.0 software was employed to construct a truth table. This facilitated the combination pathway analysis of the condition variables affecting users' continuous intention to use social media intelligent recommendation. In selecting the pathway solutions, consideration was given to balancing complexity, avoiding overly complicated solutions that might result in uninterpretable combinations, while also avoiding oversimplification that could hinder a comprehensive understanding of the multifaceted causal relationships underlying users' continuous usage behavior. Therefore, this study opted for a middle-of-the-road approach as the pathway combination solution. The results, as shown in Table 4, reveal a total of 3 combination pathways influencing users' continuous intention to use.

Table 4. Analysis of conditional paths

Constructs	Configurational paths		
	1	2	3
Flow Experience	●	●	●
Social Influence	●	●	●
Information Overload	●		●
Recommendation Accuracy	●	●	⊗
Functional Overload	⊗	⊗	●
Algorithmic Transparency		●	⊗
raw coverage	0.386	0.432	0.312
unique coverage	0.028	0.116	0.068
consistency	0.945	0.958	0.957
solution coverage	0.571		
solution consistency	0.951		

Note: ● represents the occurrence of a certain condition, ⊗ represents the absence of a specific condition. Large circles denote core conditions, small circles represent peripheral conditions, and blanks signify conditions that have no impact.

From the results in Table 4, it is evident that the original coverage for all condition combination pathways exceeds the unique coverage, indicating the presence of supporting cases that align with multiple causal pathways, with a relatively even distribution of coverage across the pathways. The consistency for all three combination pathways is above 0.9, signifying that these three configurations are necessary conditions for users' continuous usage of social media intelligent recommendations. The overall consistency is 0.951, and the overall coverage is 0.571, implying that these three pathways can account for 57.1% of the reasons behind users' continuous intention to use social media intelligent recommendations.

Pathway 1: The emergence of users' continuous intention to use social media recommendations is influenced by flow experience, social influence, information overload, recommendation accuracy, and non-functional overload. In this pathway, non-functional overload serves as the core condition, while flow experience, social influence, information overload, and recommendation accuracy act as marginal conditions. Consequently, it is evident that when a social media intelligent recommendation platform induces users to experience flow, demonstrates high precision, avoids functional overload, and is widely adopted by friends, users are likely to maintain a high level of continuous intention to use, even in the presence of information overload.

Pathway 2: The emergence of users' continuous intention to use social media recommendations is influenced by flow experience, social influence, recommendation accuracy, non-functional overload, and algorithm transparency. In this pathway, non-functional overload serves as the core condition, while flow experience, social influence, recommendation accuracy, and algorithm transparency act as marginal conditions. This suggests that when a social media intelligent recommendation platform induces users to experience flow, demonstrates high precision, avoids functional overload, has high algorithm transparency, and is widely adopted by friends, users are likely to maintain a high level of continuous intention to use.

Pathway 3: The emergence of users' continuous intention to use social media recommendations is influenced by flow experience, social influence, information overload, non-recommendation accuracy, functional overload, and non-algorithm transparency. In this pathway, social influence, information overload, and non-recommendation accuracy serve as core conditions, while flow experience, functional overload, and non-algorithm transparency act as marginal conditions. This suggests that when users have a good flow experience and their friends are using the social media intelligent recommendation software, users may still have a high level of continuous intention to use, even if the platform experiences information overload, functional overload, low precision in intelligent recommendations, and algorithmic non-transparency.

By observing the three configuration pathways mentioned above, it is evident that psychological experience and social influence appear in each pathway, indicating that the strength of users' continuous intention to use social media recommendations depends significantly on user experience and the influence of friends. Furthermore, from the observation of these pathways, it is noticeable that recommendation accuracy and functional overload appear in opposite forms, such as "recommendation accuracy * ~ functional overload" or " ~ recommendation accuracy * functional overload." This suggests that when there is functional overload on a social media platform, accurate content recommendations can effectively alleviate the negative experience caused by functional overload.

7   Conclusion and Directions for Future Research

Based on information ecology theory, this paper studies study the impact mechanism of the continuous use intention of social media intelligent recommendation users. A framework of factors affecting the continuous use intention of social media intelligent recommendation users is constructed from four aspects: individual factors, information factors, environmental factors, and technical factors. Relevant data is collected through questionnaire surveys, and fuzzy set qualitative comparative analysis method is applied to verify how the four factors of individual, information, environment and technology interact with each other to affect the continuous use intention of social media intelligent recommendation users.

The research reveals that the sustained intention of users in social media intelligent recommendations is indeed a result of the collective influence and various combinations of individual, informational, environmental, and technological factors. At an explanatory level with a total coverage of 57.1%, there are three configuration paths that contribute to the generation of high sustained usage intentions among users of social media intelligent recommendations. Combining these three paths, it is evident that factors such as flow experience, social influence, information overload, recommendation accuracy, and functional overload play a primary role in the process of fostering high sustained usage intentions among users of social media intelligent recommendations. Notably, both flow experience and social influence are key conditional variables that appear in all three paths, serving as critical factors for the occurrence of high sustained usage intentions. However, they alone cannot induce the high sustained usage intentions; their effectiveness relies on the combination with other influencing factors. The findings of this study offer valuable insights for the operational considerations of social media intelligent recommendation platforms.

This study is subject to certain limitations. The inability to incorporate all influencing factors of user sustained usage intentions into the model, coupled with the subjective nature of data collected through questionnaires, may introduce biases to the research findings. Consequently, future studies should aim to address these limitations by considering the inclusion of additional variables and leveraging objective research data obtained through methods such as web scraping to further enhance the depth of investigation.

References

Argyris, Y.A., Wang, Z., Kim, Y., et al.: The effects of visual congruence on increasing consumers' brand engagement: an empirical investigation of influencer marketing on Instagram using deep-learning algorithms for automatic image classification. Comput. Hum. Behav. **112**, 106443 (2020)

Cao, X., Sun, J.: Exploring the effect of overload on the discontinuous intention of social media users: an S-O-R perspective. Comput. Hum. Behav. **81**(4), 10–18 (2018)

Chang, H., Yang, S.O.: Research on commodity mixed recommendation algorithm. Int. J. Adv. Netw. Monit. Controls **5**(3), 1–8 (2020)

Chang, Y.P., Zhu, D.H.: The role of perceived social capital and flow experience in building users continuance intention to social networking sites in China. Comput. Hum. Behav. **28**(3), 995–1001 (2012)

Chen, S.Y., Liu, T.T.: Research on privacy policy issues and countermeasures of short video applications. Inf. Commun. Technol. Policy **46**(2), 74 (2020)

Csikszentmihalyi, M.: Flow: The Psychology of Optimal Experience. Harper & Row (2008)

De Melo, P.F.A., Ramos, A.S.M., Gouvea, M.A., et al.: Satisfaction and continuous use intention of elearning service in Brazilian public organizations. Comput. Hum. Behav. **46**(5), 139–148 (2015)

Fu, S., Li, H., Liu, Y., et al.: Social media overload, exhaustion, and use discontinuance: examining the effects of information overload, system feature and social overload. Inf. Process. Manag. **57**, 1023076 (2020)

Fulk, J., Schmitz, J., Ryu, D.: Cognitive elements in the social construction of communication technologies. Manag. Commun. Q. **8**(3), 259–288 (1995)

Galbraith, J.R.: Organization design: an information processing view. Interfaces **4**(3), 28–36 (1974)

Guo, J., Liu, Z., Liu, Y.: Key success factors for the launch of government social media platform: identifying the formation mechanism of continuance intention. Comput. Hum. Behav. **55**, 750–763 (2016)

Hoffman, D.L., Novak, T.P.: Flow online: lessons learned and future prospects. J. Interact. Mark. **23**(1), 23–34 (2009)

Horton, F.W.: Information ecology. J. Syst. Manag. **29**(09), 32–36 (1978)

Hossain, A., Quaresma, R., Rahman, H.: Investigating factors influencing the physicians' adoption of electronic health record (EHR) in healthcare system of Bangladesh: an empirical study. Int. J. Inf. Manage. **44**, 76–87 (2019)

Kim, M.S., Kim, S.: Factors influencing willingness to provide personal information for personalized recommendations. Comput. Hum. Behav. **88**, 143–152 (2018)

Kim, S., Park, H., Choi, M.J.: Negative impact of social network services based on stressor-stress-outcome: the role of experience of privacy violations. Future Internet **11**(6), 137 (2019)

Lu, L., Cai, R., Gursoy, D.: Developing and validating a service robot integration willingness scale. Int. J. Hosp. Manag. **80**, 36–51 (2019)

Lu, X., Lu, Z., Liu, C.: Exploring TikTok use and non-use practices and experiences in China. In: Meiselwitz, G. (eds.) HCII 2020. LNCS, vol. 12195, pp. 57–70. Springer, Cham (2020). https://doi.org/10.1007/978-3-030-49576-3_5

Maier, C., Laumer, S., Eckhardt, A., et al.: Giving too much social support: social overload on social networking sites. Eur. J. Inf. Syst. **24**(5), 447–464 (2015)

Meral, K.Z.: Social media short video-sharing TikTok application and ethics: data367privacy and addiction issues. In: Multidisciplinary Approaches to Ethics in the Digital Era, pp. 147–165. IGI Global (2021)

Mou, X.B., Xu, F., Du, J.T.: Examining the factors influencing college students' continuance intention to use short-form video APPII. Aslib J. Inf. Manag. **73**(6), 992–1013 (2021)

Nardi, B.A., O'Day, V.: Information Ecologies: Using Technology with Heart, pp. 36–37, 49–51. MIT Press, Cambridge (1999)

Nardi, B.A., O'Day, V.: Information Ecologies: Using Technology with Heart. MIT Press, Cambridge (1999)

Ragin, C.: Redesigning Social Inquiry: Fuzzy Sets and Beyond. University of Chicago Press, Chicago (2008)

Shokouhyar, S., Siadat, S.H., Razavi, M.K.: How social influence and personality affect users' social network fatigue and discontinuance behavior. Aslib J. Inf. Manag. **70**(4), 344–366 (2018)

Tucker, C.E.: Social networks, personalized advertising, and privacy controls. J. Mark. Res. **51**(5), 546–562 (2014)

Venkatesh, V., Morris, M., Davis, G.B., et al.: User acceptance of information technology: toward a unified view. MIS Q. **27**(3), 425–478 (2003)

Youn, S.: Determinants of online privacy concern and its influence on privacy protection behaviors among young adolescents. J. Consum. Aff. **43**(3), 389–418 (2009)

Zainab, A.M., Kiran, K., Karim, N.H.A., et al.: UTAUT'S performance consistency: empirical evidence from a library management system. Malays. J. Libr. Inf. Sci. **23**(1), 17–32 (2018)

Zhang, S., Zhao, L., Lu, Y., et al.: Do you get tired of socializing? An empirical explanation of discontinuous usage behaviour in social network services. Inf. Manag. **53**(7), 904–914 (2016)

Zhang, S., Yao, L., Sun, A., et al.: Deep learning based recommender system: a survey and new perspectives. ACM Comput. Surv. (CSUR) **52**(1), 1–38 (2019)

Zhang, X., Ma, L., Zhang, G., et al.: An integrated model of the antecedents and consequences of perceived information overload using wechat as an example. Int. J. Mobile Commun. **18**(1), 19–40 (2020)

Zhang, X., Wu, Y., Liu, S.: Exploring short-form video application addiction: socio-technical and attachment perspectives. J. Telemat. Inform. **42**, 101243 (2019)

Exploring Spatial Relation Awareness Through Virtual Indoor Environments

Swe Nwe Nwe Htun[1] , Shusaku Egami[1] , Takanori Ugai[1,2] , Yijun Duan[1] ,
and Ken Fukuda[1(✉)]

[1] National Institute of Advanced Industrial Science and Technology, Tokyo 135-0064, Japan
{swenwe.nwehtun,s-egami,yijun.duan,ken.fukuda}@aist.go.jp,
ugai@fujitsu.com
[2] Fujitsu Limited, Kawasaki, Kanagawa 211-8588, Japan

Abstract. This research addresses the critical challenge of understanding spatial relations in virtual indoor environments. The proposed methodology comprises two core modules: object clustering and spatial relation extraction. Object clustering employs a Bayesian probabilistic model to group closely positioned objects, facilitating a more contextual understanding and simplifying subsequent spatial relation analyses. The spatial relation extraction module integrates depth information with cluster bounding box data, enabling a nuanced assessment of relationships such as above, below, inside, and close between objects. The effectiveness of the proposed approach is evaluated using the VirtualHome2KG dataset, demonstrating its robust performance in capturing spatial relationships. A gold standard is prepared to assess the results of relation extraction, representing a precise set of spatial relationships derived from the 3D object locations in VirtualHome. Experimental phases include clustering stability analysis and 2D spatial relation extraction, providing valuable insights into the temporal dynamics of scenes and the precision of the method. The results underscore the methodology's efficacy, as evidenced by precision, recall, and accuracy metrics, establishing its potential for evolving intelligent monitoring systems in home environments.

Keywords: Spatial Relations · Object Clustering · Bayesian Probabilistic Model · Depth · VirtualHome2KG dataset

1 Introduction

Visualizing and understanding spatial relations in visual data is integral to developing intelligent monitoring systems and robots [1]. The ability to discern the context of human-object interactions is pivotal for distinguishing between normal and abnormal conditions [2], particularly in scenarios involving the safety of older adults. Guaranteeing the safety of older adults at home consists of identifying risks in their daily activities [3, 4]. For example, determining whether a person is resting on the bed (a common scenario) or lying amidst kitchen objects (a potentially hazardous situation) demands a precise definition of spatial relations among objects, such as "person on the bed" or "person on the floor." Achieving these objectives involves recognizing that spatial relations between objects are influenced not only by postural attributes (i.e., pose and shape) but also by object-specific sensory knowledge. For instance, a person lying in the kitchen room with groceries and appliances nearby is a situation that our common understanding can immediately recognize as abnormal.

In addressing this problem, a previous study [2] employed an approach to identify objects closest to a person through bounding box intersections. The centroids of these objects were then connected through the person's centroid, and the degree of orientation from the person to the objects was calculated based on the person's movement. Spatial relations—specifically, "besides," "in front of," and "on"—were determined using this calculated orientation (e.g., the person beside the kitchen table, the person on the floor). However, while effective for a few objects, this method has inherent limitations, as it fails to capture comprehensive relations between objects.

In this study, we explore spatial relations among objects, including humans, focusing on enhancing the safety of older adults in their homes. Our methodology comprises two primary modules: object grouping and spatial relation extraction. As a preprocessing step, we utilize the YOLOv8[1] object detection model [5] on sequential images to identify objects. The object grouping module incorporates a Bayesian probabilistic model. This module, employing Bayesian reasoning to update posterior probabilities, clusters objects based on prior probabilities and the likelihoods. The likelihood calculations assess the probability of objects belonging to the same cluster, taking into account distances and overlapping ratios to update posterior probabilities. Object grouping provides a more comprehensive understanding of the scene by identifying clusters of related objects. For instance, in a kitchen scene, grouping objects like stoves, refrigerators, and utensils close to each other enhances the contextual understanding of the cooking area, facilitating more precise spatial relations analysis. In addition, it facilitates semantically meaningful clusters. For instance, office supplies are usually kept in one group in real-life scenarios. Grouping office-related objects like desks, computers, and chairs creates semantically meaningful clusters, enabling the system to analyze spatial relations relevant to an office environment. Grouping objects also simplifies the complexity of spatial relation analysis. Instead of considering pairwise relationships between all objects that could produce inaccurate relations, the focus is narrowed to relationships within object groups, reducing computational complexity.

The relation extraction in this work offers a comprehensive process for analyzing spatial relationships among objects in scenes. The process begins with extracting depth information from RGB image data, which is achieved by applying the MiDaS v3.1[2] [6, 7] depth estimation model. The acquired depth data is then integrated with cluster bounding box information, providing a nuanced understanding of the spatial layout of objects in the scene. The analysis uses depth-based spatial reasoning to categorize relationships such as "Above," "Below," "Close," and "Inside" between objects in a given scene. This seamless integration of cluster and depth information contributes to a more nuanced and accurate assessment of their spatial interrelations.

---

[1] https://github.com/ultralytics/ultralytics.

[2] https://github.com/isl-org/MiDaS.

In response to the challenges of grasping the spatial connections between objects, this paper proposes an approach for spatial relation awareness using virtual indoor environments. The objectives are twofold: (1) to interpret the environmental context and (2) to evaluate the effectiveness of the VirtualHome2KG dataset[3], which is simulated to mimic real-home settings [4, 8–10].

2   Related Work

The field of high-level computer vision has recently turned its attention to recognizing visual relationships beyond just identifying objects [11, 12]. Sadeghi & Farhadi [13] investigated the identification of visual phrases in images, where a visual phrase might describe a spatial relationship like "the person next to a bicycle." However, their dataset could be more extensive, containing only 17 different visual phrases, with just 9 of them involving spatial relations. It means that each spatial term is only associated with a small number of specific objects. For example, the phrase "next to" is only connected to "person," "car," and "bicycle." As a result, this dataset is not ideal for assessing a comprehensive understanding of "next to" that goes beyond specific types of objects.

While Lu et al. [14] focused on visual relationship detection, precisely predicting subject-predicate-object triplets and object-bounding boxes from images, our work extends beyond by addressing spatial relations in virtual indoor environments. By employing object clustering and spatial relation extraction modules, our methodology offers a nuanced understanding of relationships such as above, inside, and close between objects in simulated indoor scenes. Unlike Lu et al. [14], our approach considers the intricacies of object locations, depth information, and cluster bounding box data.

Ding et al. [15] presented a system for predicting spatial relations in images, incorporating depth guidance and linguistic information to encode common sense knowledge about objects. Unlike prevailing approaches that rely on language or context for relation prediction, Kumar et al. [16] introduced a model that integrates spatial and depth cues with visual features to enhance relation recognition. In contrast to Kumar et al.'s depth-guided relation prediction system, our model emphasizes the significance of depth information in understanding spatial relationships such as "Above," "Below," "Inside," and "Close," especially in scenarios where depth cues play a crucial role in determining the proximity, relative positions, and spatial arrangements of objects within a given scene. Unlike Kumar et al., who focused on integrating spatial and depth cues for relation recognition, we conduct a pairwise analysis within identified object clusters, considering depth scores and vertical positions to precisely evaluate spatial configurations between objects.

3   Proposed Approach

This section delineates our proposed methodology for investigating spatial relations through virtual indoor environments. The framework comprises two primary modules, as depicted in Fig. 1. Detailed technical procedures for each module are elucidated in the subsequent subsections, with Subsects. 3.1 and 3.2 providing an in-depth explanation of their respective components.

---

[3] https://github.com/KnowledgeGraphJapan/KGRC-RDF/blob/kgrc4si/README.md.

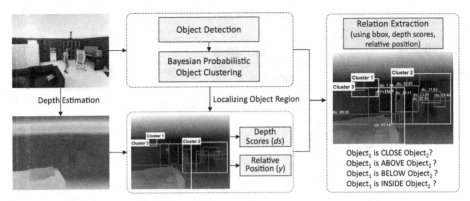

Fig. 1. An overview of proposed approach for exploring spatial relationships among objects.

3.1 Object Clustering

Object grouping or clustering is crucial in scenarios involving multiple objects within a scene. The task is to assign spatially proximate objects to specific clusters, enabling the identification of coherent groups. Our approach employs a probabilistic framework grounded in Bayes' theorem to infer each object's most likely cluster assignments based on observed spatial locations and bounding boxes, as shown in Fig. 2. In this module, we first utilize YOLOv8, a state-of-the-art object detection model developed by Ultralytics [5]. Ultralytics YOLOv8 predicts bounding boxes along with classes for each object in the images. This pre-processing step sets the stage for the subsequent probabilistic clustering module, enhancing the effectiveness of object group assignments.

After that, we denote a set of spatial locations of objects that can be represented as $\{(x_1, y_1), (x_2, y_2), \ldots, (x_n, y_n)\}$ where n is the number of objects. We then compute the pairwise distances between object locations using the Euclidean distance. For a set of spatial locations $\{(x_1, y_1), (x_2, y_2), \ldots, (x_n, y_n)\}$, the pairwise distances matrix can be expressed as in Eq. (1):

$$d_{ij} = \sqrt{\left(x_i - x_j\right)^2 + \left(y_i - y_j\right)^2} \tag{1}$$

The cluster indices for each object is initialized as $[1, 2, \ldots, n]$ and uniform prior probability is assigned as $[1/n]$ to clusters based on the number of bounding boxes. To observe indices of objects that are close to the current object, we calculate a dynamic threshold based on pairwise distances between object locations. In doing so, the median distance ($mDist$) and interquartile range ($iqrDist$) are calculated for a set of distances $\{d_1, d_2, \ldots, d_n\}$, where n is the number of distances. Here, $iqrDist$ is determined by the range between the first quartile (Q_1) and the third quartile (Q_3).

The dynamic threshold (DT) is then determined by adding a scaled value of the interquartile range to the median distance, where the distance multiplier (DM) is the adjustable multiplier as in (2):

$$DT = mDist + DM \times iqrDist \tag{2}$$

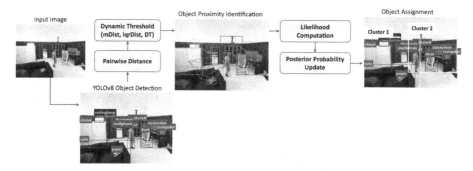

Fig. 2. An overview workflow of the proposed object clustering approach.

After that we identify the indices of objects that are close to the current object i within the specified distance threshold. These objects are assigned to the current cluster by updating their cluster indices. The object's index closest to the current object i is obtained based on pairwise distances, and the bounding box coordinates for the current object i and the nearest object j are retrieved to obtain the likelihood of objects. We computes the likelihood of objects being in the same cluster based on bounding box overlapping ratio. It uses a decreasing exponential method for this calculation as in (3).

$$likelihoodOverlap = exp(-0.1 \times (1 - IoU)) \tag{3}$$

where IoU = Intersection Area / Union Area, $exp(x)$ represents the exponential function and parameter -0.1 in the exponential function controls the rate of decrease. The posterior probability for the closest object j is then updated by (4) and normalizes the posterior probabilities to ensure that they sum to 1 as shown in Eq. (5):

$$posteriorProbabilities_j = posteriorProbabilities_j + likelihoodOverlap \tag{4}$$

$$posteriorProbabilities = \frac{posteriorProbabilities}{\sum posteriorProbabilities_j} \tag{5}$$

Finally, the closest object to the cluster is assigned based on the updated probabilities.

3.2 2D Spatial Relation Extraction

The study introduces a spatial relationship extraction methodology that analyzes relations (Above, Below, Inside, Close) among objects in a given scene. The initial step in this process entails extracting depth images from RGB images, which is achieved by utilizing the pre-trained MiDaS v3.1 model [6, 7] designed for accurate depth estimation. Depth images are helpful for spatial analysis, particularly in understanding relationships such as proximity, relative positions, and spatial arrangements. Thus, we explore the value of depth images in analyzing the spatial interactions between objects. For instance, determining if a person is reaching for an object above or below them or is close to another object enhances the analysis of human-object spatial relationships. Following acquiring depth images through the MiDaS v3.1 pre-trained model, the analysis advances to compute depth scores for individual objects within identified clusters. It involves local-izing bounding boxes onto the depth image for each object, as illustrated in previous Fig. 1. By sampling pixel intensity values within these bounded regions, depth scores are calculated. This process involves mapping the bounding box coordinates onto the depth image's pixel grid. Subsequently, the pixel intensity values within each object's bounded region are extracted to form the depth region. The depth score is then calculated as the mean of these pixel intensities, represented mathematically as:

$$ds_i = \frac{1}{p} \sum_{i=1}^{p} I_i \qquad (6)$$

where p denotes the total number of pixels within the depth region, and I represents the intensity value of the i-th pixel. This process encapsulates the essence of quantifying the depth information associated with a specific object bounding box, contributing to the overall accuracy and granularity of the spatial relationship analysis within the scene.

Object-isAbove/isBelow-Object Relationship. We conduct a pairwise analysis for each pair of objects within the same cluster. This procedure takes into account consider-able factors, including depth scores and vertical positions, to provide a precise analysis of the spatial configuration between two objects. We observe that larger values corre-spond to objects within the specified region closer to the camera when examining the depth scores. In comparison, smaller values indicate that objects in the specified region are generally farther away from the camera. When two objects are far apart in an image, it becomes challenging to accurately determine their relative positions in terms of being above or below one another. Depth perception allows us to perceive the relative dis-tances of objects in a three-dimensional space. When objects are far away, and depth cues are limited, distinguishing whether one object is above or below another becomes less reliable. Additionally, the ability to distinguish the vertical position of objects in an image is closely related to depth perception. Here's a proposed concept as illustrated in Fig. 3. In the figure, if two objects have a significant depth score difference, it suggests that they are likely at different distances from the camera. In this case, comparing their vertical positions in the image may not provide meaningful spatial information, as the depth difference can affect their perceived relationships. If two objects do not have a significant depth score difference, it implies they are relatively close in distance. In this scenario, comparing their vertical positions becomes more meaningful and can provide valuable information about their relative arrangements along the vertical axis.

In our analysis, we comprehensively assess spatial relationships among objects within a cluster by comparing their depth scores and vertical positions. Denoting the depth scores of objects i and j as ds_i and ds_j, respectively, and representing their vertical positions as y_i and y_j, we initiate the evaluation by dynamically calculating a threshold for depth difference. This threshold, determined based on the mean depth scores of all objects in the frame, acts as a critical value. When the absolute difference between ds_i and ds_j is below this threshold, indicating no significant depth difference, the analysis scrutinizes the objects' vertical positions.

This vertical analysis compares the absolute difference between y_i and y_j against a dynamically calculated vertical threshold. This threshold is established by considering

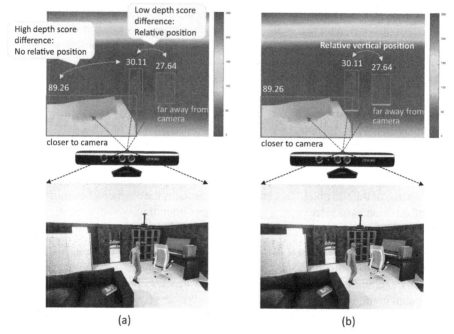

Fig. 3. Analyzing Depth Scores and Relative Position: (a) Explores the impact of depth score differences on relative positions, revealing that high differences suggest no discernible relative position, while low differences indicate the presence of a relative position; (b) Details the subsequent step in cases of low depth score difference, emphasizing the calculation of relative vertical positions.

the average height of objects within the cluster. If the absolute difference falls below this threshold, it implies that both objects share the same level. Further, the spatial relationship between the objects is determined when y_i is less than y_j, suggesting a spatial hierarchy where object i is positioned above object j. When the vertical position of y_i is greater than y_j, it implies a spatial arrangement where object i is positioned below object j. This approach ensures a nuanced interpretation, utilizing depth scores and vertical positions to delineate the spatial connections between objects more precisely.

Object-isInside-Object Relationship. We conduct an analysis of object-inside-object relationships, represented as (Object$_1$, isInside, Object$_2$). To analyze objects' size compatibility, we determine whether one object is completely inside another object. Let (x_1, y_1, w_1, h_1) represent the coordinates, width, and height of Object$_1$ and (x_2, y_2, w_2, h_2) represent the corresponding parameters for Object$_2$. We performs a horizontal check, ensuring that the left edge of Object$_1$ is to the right of or coincides with the left edge of Object$_2$ ($x_1 \geq x_2$), and the right edge of Object$_1$ is to the left of or coincides with the right edge of Object$_2$ ($x_1 + w_1 \leq x_2 + w_2$). Additionally, we conducts a vertical check, ensuring that the top edge of Object$_1$ is below or coincides with the top edge of Object$_2$ ($y_1 \geq y_2$), and the bottom edge of Object$_1$ is above or coincides with the bottom edge of Object$_2$ ($y_1 + h_1 \leq y_2 + h_2$). If all these conditions are satisfied, (Object$_1$, isInside,

Object$_2$) is set to true, indicating that Object$_1$ is entirely contained within Object$_2$. The logical condition for bounding box containment can be expressed as in (7):

$$isInside = \bigcap_{i=1}^{n} (x_i \geq x_j) \bigwedge ((x_i + w_i) \leq (x_j + w_j))$$
$$\bigwedge (y_i \geq y_j) \bigwedge ((y_i + h_i) \leq (y_j + h_j)) \tag{7}$$

where n represents the total number of bounding boxes, ensures that all individual bounding boxes (Object$_1$) satisfy the conditions for containment within Object$_2$.

Object-isClose-Object Relationship. In cases of "Close" spatial relationships, we assume that objects within each cluster have undergone a Bayesian clustering process, confirming their proximity. This assumption is supported by the idea that when two objects show no significant difference in depth scores, it suggests they are relatively close in distance. This aligns with the nature of object clustering, where objects with similar spatial attributes are grouped into clusters for detailed analysis. Recognizing small depth score differences as an indicator of proximity improves the clustering process, forming a basis for more precise spatial relationship analyses.

4 Gold Standard Preparation

To evaluate the results of relation extraction, it is essential to have a gold standard or a correct set of spatial relationships. Accordingly, all object pairs are identified for predicates such as, (Object$_1$, isInside, Object$_2$), (Object$_1$, isClose, Object$_2$), (Object$_1$, isAbove, Object$_2$), etc. Initially, we establish the definitions for five types of spatial relationships, as outlined in Table 1. VirtualHome2KG framework [4, 8–10] generates graph states, focusing on information related to 3D objects within a scene. The dataset contains JSON-formatted data with information about objects, including their identifiers (id), class labels (label), spatial characteristics such as center and size defined by bounding boxes, additional properties, and transformation details like position, rotation, and scale. In the process, we access structures of this data and reconstruct 3D VirtualHome for all scenes to offer a detailed insight into object placements. Our gold standard preparation currently relies on bird's-eye view that encompasses the entire spatial layout of the virtual homes, regardless of specific camera perspectives. The Fig. 4 demonstrates the top view of each scene.

Table 1. Spatial relationships definitions.

Predicate	Definition
Close	Object$_1$ is "Close" to Object$_2$ when Object$_1$ is situated in proximity to Object$_2$, typically implying a short distance or nearness between the two objects
Inside	Object$_1$ is "Inside" Object$_2$ when Object$_1$ is fully contained within the boundaries of Object$_2$
Above (non-touching)	Object$_1$ is "Above" Object$_2$ when Object$_1$ is positioned above relative to Object$_2$
On (touching)	Object$_1$ is "On" another Object$_2$ when object Object$_1$ is positioned directly above or resting on the surface of Object$_2$
Below	Object$_1$ is "Below" Object$_2$ when Object$_1$ is positioned below or in a lower position relative to Object$_2$

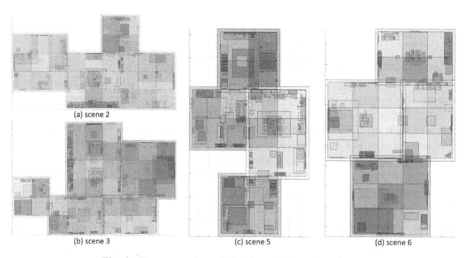

(a) scene 2

(b) scene 3

(c) scene 5

(d) scene 6

Fig. 4. Reconstruction of 3D VirtualHome (Top views).

4.1 Object-isClosed-Object Relationship

We initiate an analysis of spatial relationships, represented as (Object$_1$, isClosed, Object$_2$). Knowing whether an object is close to another is essential for safety assessment and analyses. It helps identify potential risks associated with the interaction between objects and their spatial arrangement. This relationship can be presented by measuring the distance between two objects. We utilize the Euclidean method for calculating the distance between two objects based on their centers in a 3-dimensional space, which can be expressed as follows.

$$d_{3D} = \sqrt{\sum\nolimits_{d=1}^{3} \left(C_{o,d} - C_{ref,d} \right)^2} \tag{8}$$

Here, d_{3D} represents the distance between two objects. $\sum$ indicates a summation over 3 dimensions (x, y, z). $C_{o,d}$ and $C_{ref,d}$ represent the center of object and reference object along d-th dimension, respectively.

4.2 Object-isInside-Object Relationship

This section involves defining the conditions for an object to be inside another through a systematic series of criteria. Initially, we analyze size compatibility, ensuring that each dimension of a smaller object is contained within the boundaries of the larger object. To define the size comparison between 3D objects, let's denote the size of an object as S_o and the size of a reference object as S_{ref}. This size compatibility of 3D objects is expressed in Eq. (9).

$$S = \prod_{d=1}^{3} \left(S_{ref,d} \leq S_{o,d} \right) \tag{9}$$

where S represents the size of object being compared to reference object. d is an index representing the dimension (1, 2, 3) being considered. $S_{ref,d}$ and $S_{o,d}$ are the size of the reference object and the object along the d-th dimension, respectively. The symbol $\prod$ indicates that this condition must hold for all dimensions.

Subsequently, we delve into the object's positional compatibility, confirming whether an object is inside another object as shown in Eq. (10).

$$P = \prod_{d=1}^{3} \left(C_{ref,d} \geq \left(C_{o,d} - \frac{S_{o,d}}{2} \right) \wedge C_{ref,d} \leq \left(C_{o,d} + \frac{S_{o,d}}{2} \right) \right) \tag{10}$$

where P represents the position of object being compared to reference object. $C_{ref,d}$ is the center of reference object and $C_{o,d}$ is the center of object, along d-th dimension.

If both size and positional compatibility conditions are satisfied, we proceed with a more detailed analysis. 3D bounding volumes offer a simplified yet accurate representation of an object's spatial extent. Ensuring that one object's bounding volume fits entirely within another's enables a precise evaluation of the spatial relationship, as expressed in Eq. (11).

$$B = \prod_{d=1}^{3} \left(C_{ref,d} - \frac{S_{ref,d}}{2} \geq C_{o,d} - \frac{S_{o,d}}{2} \right) \wedge \prod_{d=1}^{3} \left(C_{ref,d} + \frac{S_{ref,d}}{2} \leq C_{o,d} + \frac{S_{o,d}}{2} \right) \tag{11}$$

where B represents the condition that the bounding box of object is entirely within the bounding box of reference object in d-th dimension.

Finally, we employ the overlap analysis via volume intersection, providing a quantitative measure of how much the volumes of two 3D objects intersect as in (12).

$$Ovr = \frac{Vol}{min\left(\prod S_o, \prod S_r \right)} \geq thr \tag{12}$$

This equation ensures that the volume of intersection between the two objects is greater than or equal to a specified overlap threshold. We assume that the value of threshold is 0.9. Here, *Ovr* is calculated using the dimensions of the intersection box determined by the minimum and maximum corner points as shown in belows:

$$minCor = max\left(C_o - \frac{S_o}{2}, C_{ref} - \frac{S_{ref}}{2}\right) \tag{13}$$

$$maxCor = min\left(C_o + \frac{S_o}{2}, C_{ref} + \frac{S_{ref}}{2}\right) \tag{14}$$

$$Vol = \prod_{d=1}^{3}(maxCor_d - minCor_d) \tag{15}$$

where *max* and *min* represents the component-wise maximum and minimum, respectively. $\prod$ represents the product of the components. *Vol* represents the process of determining the intersection volume between two bounding boxes. The examples of Object-isInside-Object Relationship are demonstrated in Fig. 5(a).

4.3   Object-isAbove/isOn/isBelow-Object Relationship

This analysis considers three distinct relationships: "Above (not touching), On (touching), and Below." We compute the vertical position of an object relative to a reference object. It assumes that the y-coordinate represents the vertical position as shown in (16).

$$V_{pos} = y_{C_o} - y_{C_{ref}} \tag{16}$$

where V_{pos} represents the vertical position, C_o and C_{ref} are the y-coordinates of the centers of object and reference object, respectively. The horizontal alignment of an object relative to a reference object is then determined by checking if the x and z-coordinates of the object (C_o) fall within the boundaries of the reference object (C_{ref}). The formula is described by Eq. (17):

$$H_{pos} = \left(x_{C_o} \geq x_{C_{ref}} - \frac{x_{S_{ref}}}{2}\right) \wedge \left(x_{C_o} \leq x_{C_{ref}} + \frac{x_{S_{ref}}}{2}\right) \\ \wedge \left(z_{C_o} \geq z_{C_{ref}} - \frac{z_{S_{ref}}}{2}\right) \wedge \left(z_{C_o} \leq z_{C_{ref}} + \frac{z_{S_{ref}}}{2}\right) \tag{17}$$

where H_{pos} is horizontal alignment and symbol $\wedge$ represents the logical AND operation. Then, spatial relationships can be analysed based on 3 criteria as demonstrated in Fig. 5(b). Objects with a vertical position exceeding a defined threshold, lacking horizontal contact, and possessing size compatibility are categorized as "Above." Those with a vertical position within a specified threshold, horizontal touch, and size compatibility are labelled "On." Meanwhile, objects with a vertical position below the reference object (less than zero), size compatibility, and horizontal alignment are classified as "Below."

Therefore, to evaluate the efficacy of spatial relation extraction, we established a gold standard—a precise set of spatial relationships derived from the 3D object locations in VirtualHome. This gold standard serves as a benchmark for assessing the accuracy and performance of our proposed approach.

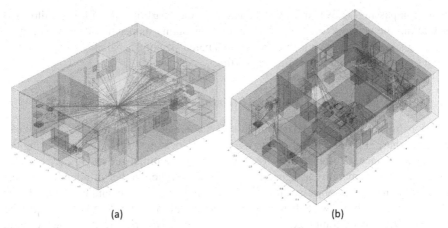

(a)   (b)

Fig. 5. 3D Spatial Relationships Illustration: (a) (Object$_1$, isInside, Object$_2$) - The red line highlights scenarios where Object$_1$ is contained within Object$_2$, exemplified by groceries and kitchen appliances inside the kitchen room; (b) (Object$_1$, isAbove/isOn/isBelow, Object$_2$) - red, yellow, and blue lines respectively denote instances where Object$_1$ is positioned above, on, or below Object$_2$. (Color figure online)

5   Experiments and Discussions

We conducted an empirical investigation to assess the effectiveness of our proposed methodology. This section presents the acquired results and discusses the constraints and avenues for future research. The VirtualHome2KG dataset [4, 8–10] encompasses abnormal activity categories within seven apartments facilitated by a single virtual agent. Our study focuses on 92 activity videos composed of everyday actions such as "walk, sit, grab" and the abnormal action "fall." The experiments comprised multiple scenarios, with Scene 1 (S1) incorporating 59 videos captured from camera views 2–4 and Scene 2 (S2) involving 33 videos from the same camera views. Each video in both scenes represented a composite activity such as, "Fall_while_preparing_meal1_2," "Fall_in_bathroom1_2," "Stand_on_coffee_table1_2," etc.

5.1   Object Detection

We begin by employing YOLOv8, an advanced object detection framework developed by Ultralytics [5]. This framework predicts both bounding boxes and corresponding object classes within images. The groundwork for our study involves gathering 2D bounding boxes from the VirtualHome2KG dataset using provided JSON files and their corresponding images. However, these 2D bounding boxes, initially derived from VirtualHome Unity, are incompatible with the YOLOv8 network due to different image coordinate systems. Consequently, we reform the position of 2D bounding boxes for objects across sequential images to align with the YOLOv8 format. This refined data format serves as the training data for the YOLOv8 network, enabling it to detect custom VirtualHome2KG objects effectively. Notably, this study focuses on a specific category of abnormal human activities, such as Falls in the bathroom, to curate the ground-truth data encompassing 33,591 images. The dataset is then partitioned, with 80% allocated for training the network and 20% reserved for evaluating its performance. We employ a training strategy comprising 25 epochs and a batch size of 32, balancing exposing the model to the dataset and preventing overfitting.

5.2 Object Clustering and Temporal Stability Analysis

The probabilistic object clustering module was conducted following the initial object detection phase. Pairwise distances between object locations were computed using the Euclidean distance. Cluster indices for each object were initialized as $[1, 2,..., n]$, with a uniform prior probability assigned as $[1/n]$ based on the number of bounding boxes. To identify indices of objects, close to the current object, a dynamic threshold was calculated based on pairwise distances. The median distance ($mDist$) and interquartile range ($iqrDist$) were computed for a set of distances $\{d_1, d_2,..., d_n\}$. The dynamic threshold (DT) was then determined by adding a scaled interquartile range value to the median distance. Here, we set 0.1 as a sacred value. Subsequently, objects within the specified distance threshold were identified and assigned to the current cluster by updating their cluster indices. The likelihood of objects being in the same cluster was determined based on the bounding box overlapping ratio (IoU). The posterior probability for the closest object was then updated and normalized to ensure the probabilities.

In this study, we delve into the temporal dynamics of clusters in the video frames. The key objective is to quantify the temporal stability of the object using Jaccard Indices computed with a 5-frame difference. Let C_t and C_{t-5} represent the clusters in consecutive frames t and $t-5$ for a given video. The Jaccard Index (J_t) is computed as the ratio of the intersection to the union of object IDs between C_t and C_{t-5}. Here, the common object IDs represent the set of objects that persist or remain unchanged between consecutive frames as in Fig. 6. This approach allows us to assess how much the clusters in the current frame overlap with those in the previous frame, providing insights into the evolving nature of scenes over time. In the figure, we can observe that objects with dynamic behaviors, such as people walking, items being picked up or put down, or doors opening and closing, can introduce new objects to the scene or alter the relationships between existing objects. Additionally, if an object moves from one location to another, it may create a new cluster or affect the composition of existing clusters.

As shown in Table 2, we culminates in a comprehensive Jaccard Index table, summarizing mean and median values for each scene. Achieving a Jaccard Index of approximately 0.99 indicates high consistency and stability in object clusters between consecutive frames. The following factors contribute to this notable result: (1) The parameters used in the clustering algorithm, such as distance thresholds and cluster updating criteria, seem to be well-tuned to capture the temporal dynamics of object clusters accurately; (2) The nature of the scene and the type of objects involved may influence the stability of clusters, in scenarios where the environment is relatively static, or objects have less movement, higher Jaccard Indices are expected.

Fig. 6. Quantifying Temporal Dynamics: Analysis of object clusters in video frames.

Table 2. Temporal stability of object clusters – Overall Jaccard Index (JI) summary.

Scene	Camera View	Mean JI	Median JI
S1	2	0.9730	0.9763
	3	0.9912	0.9925
	4	0.9883	0.9915
S2	2	0.9796	0.9795
	3	0.9922	0.9939
	4	0.9920	0.9919

5.3   2D Spatial Relation Extraction and Evaluation

We present spatial relationship extraction, focusing on relations like "Above," "Below," "Inside," and "Close" among objects in a given scene. Initial steps involve depth image extraction from RGB images using the MiDaS v3.1 model, optimizing depth estimation accuracy. The subsequent steps involve computing depth scores for individual objects within identified clusters. Depth scores are calculated by localizing bounding boxes onto the depth image and extracting pixel intensity values in these individual bounded regions. We perform pairwise analysis within clusters considering depth scores and vertical positions, determining spatial relations like "Above" and "Below." For "Inside" relationships, the study checks the compatibility of object sizes. Horizontal and vertical checks ensure one object is entirely inside another, considering both objects' coordinates, width, and height. In cases of "Close" spatial relationships, we assume that objects within each cluster have undergone a Bayesian clustering process, confirming their proximity. This assumption is supported by the idea that objects with similar depth scores are relatively close in distance, aligning with the nature of object clustering. This enhances spatial analyses, contributing to experiment effectiveness.

Notably, our gold standard preparation is based on a bird's-eye view encompassing the entire spatial layout of the virtual homes, independent of specific camera perspectives. We performed 2D spatial relation extraction and analysis across 3 camera views, ensuring a comprehensive evaluation. However, due to the 2D nature of our approach, some object pairs extracted from spatial relations may not align with our prepared ground truth, as camera perspectives influence them. Moreover, the 3D virtual homes provides rich spatial relations, even in room structures, such as a kitchen table in the kitchen. Notably, our 2D spatial relation extraction still needs to incorporate object detection and relation extraction for rooms. Consequently, in our evaluation process, we focus on comparing object pairs between actual (gold standard) and predicted relations, acknowledging the inherent limitations of a 2D perspective in capturing the entirety of spatial relationships within 3D virtual homes.

Therefore, we consider 3 key definitions in our evaluation process when comparing object pairs between the actual and predicted relations. In Case 1, we assess definitions where there is an exact match, signifying accurate predictions of both the object pair and the relation, resulting in a true positive outcome. Transitioning to Case 2, we encounter instances where the same object pair is correctly identified, but a different relation is predicted, particularly "Above" or "Below." Depending on the perspective, the evaluation categorizes this case as either a false positive or a false negative. In Case 3, the prediction fails to recognize the object pair entirely, leading to a false negative.

To quantify the performance of our relation analysis, we present the results in Table 3, offering a detailed breakdown of the predicted spatial relationships compared to the actual relationships outlined in the gold standard. Subsequently, we employ evaluation metrics, including precision and recall, to provide a quantitative assessment of the approach's efficacy in capturing correct object pairs and their relations. Figure 7 compares

Table 3. Overall performance evaluation of spatial relationships on each scene.

Scene	Relations	PRC	RCL	ACC
S1	Close	0.9283	0.9615	0.8955
	Above	0.8812	0.9916	0.8739
	Below	0.8791	0.9915	0.8719
	Inside	0.9316	0.9696	0.9046
S2	Close	0.8131	0.9962	0.8106
	Above	0.8173	0.9933	0.8129
	Below	0.8198	0.9933	0.8152
	Inside	0.9055	0.9643	0.8754

the predicted relationships against the spatial relationships delineated by the gold standard. Through this visual analysis, we aim to assess the relation analysis's performance in capturing and predicting spatial relationships between pairs of objects.

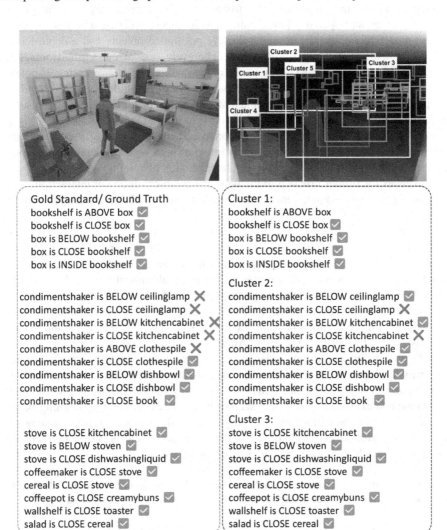

Fig. 7. Comparison of Predicted Spatial Relationships Against Gold Standard: Examples for assessing the performance of relation analysis.

6   Conclusion and Future Work

In conclusion, this research introduces a comprehensive methodology for understanding spatial relations in virtual indoor environments. The proposed approach integrates object clustering and spatial relation extraction modules, utilizing a Bayesian probabilistic model for efficiently grouping closely positioned objects and a depth-based analysis for spatial relationship assessment. The evaluation of the VirtualHome2KG dataset demonstrates the robust performance of the methodology, showcasing its potential for accurately capturing relationships between objects. Additionally, a gold standard is prepared to benchmark the accuracy and performance of the relation extraction results, offering a precise set of spatial relationships derived from 3D object locations in VirtualHome. The results, as measured by precision, recall, and accuracy, affirm the efficacy of the proposed methodology. The seamless integration of object grouping, and depth-based spatial reasoning provides a holistic understanding of complex scenes. This work opens avenues for further research in the field of human-environment interaction, with potential applications in intelligent monitoring systems and robotic assistance for older adults.

In advancing our research, we propose avenues for future work. First, we could expand the preparation of ground truth by incorporating additional perspectives, thereby creating a comprehensive dataset that reflects each camera's views. This expansion is pivotal for a more robust evaluation process, ensuring alignment with real-world scenarios. Additionally, exploring the integration of object detection techniques in both 2D and 3D spaces could hold promise. By incorporating robust object detection models, we anticipate a more accurate identification of object pairs, addressing certain limitations observed in the current evaluation. Another direction could involve enhancing the method's understanding through semantic context awareness. It entails not only considering spatial relations but also incorporating the semantic meaning behind these relations. For instance, recognizing that a kitchen table is typically situated in a kitchen adds a layer of semantic context to the spatial analysis. Furthermore, exploring deep learning-based approaches for relation extraction and recognition could provide a refined framework for improved performance. These proposed directions aim to elevate the spatial relation extraction approach's precision and contextual awareness.

Acknowledgments. This paper is based on results obtained from a project, JPNP20006, commissioned by the New Energy and Industrial Technology Development Organization (NEDO).

Disclosure of Interests.   The authors have no competing interests to declare that are relevant to the content of this article.

References

1. Yang, K., Russakovsky, O., Deng, J.: SpatialSense: an adversarially crowdsourced benchmark for spatial relation recognition. In: 2019 IEEE/CVF International Conference on Computer Vision (ICCV), Seoul, South Korea, pp. 2051–2060 (2019)

2. Htun, S.N.N., Egami, S., Duan, Y., Fukuda, K.: Abnormal activity detection based on place and occasion in virtual home environments. In: Pan, J.S., Pan, Z., Hu, P., Lin, J.C.W. (eds.) Genetic and Evolutionary Computing. ICGEC 2023. Lecture Notes in Electrical Engineering, vol. 1114, pp. 193–205. Springer, Singapore (2024). https://doi.org/10.1007/978-981-99-9412-0_21

3. Htun, S.N.N., Egami, S., Fukuda, K.: A survey and comparison of activities of daily living datasets in real-life and virtual spaces. In: 2023 IEEE/SICE International Symposium on System Integration (SII), Atlanta, 2023, pp. 1–7 (2023)

4. Egami, S., Ugai, T., Oono, M., Kitamura, K., Fukuda, K.: Synthesizing event-centric knowledge graphs of daily activities using virtual space. IEEE Access 11, 23857–23873 (2023). https://doi.org/10.1109/ACCESS.2023.3253807

5. Jocher, G., Chaurasia, A., Qiu, J.: Ultralytics YOLO (Version 8.0.0) [Computer software] (2023). https://github.com/ultralytics/ultralytics

6. Ranftl, R., Lasinger, K., Hafner, D., Schindler, K., Koltun, V.: Towards robust monocular depth estimation: mixing datasets for zero-shot cross-dataset transfer. IEEE Trans. Pattern Anal. Mach. Intell.Intell. 44(3), 1623–1637 (2022). https://doi.org/10.1109/TPAMI.2020.3019967

7. Birkl, R., Wofk, D., Müller, M.: MiDaS v3.1 - A Model Zoo for Robust Monocular Relative Depth Estimation. arXiv, abs/2307.14460 (2023)

8. Egami, S., Nishimura, S., Fukuda, K.: A framework for constructing and augmenting knowledge graphs using virtual space: towards analysis of daily activities. In: Proceedings of the 33rd IEEE International Conference on Tools with Artificial Intelligence, pp. 1226–1230 (2021)

9. Egami, S., Nishimura, S., Fukuda, K.: VirtualHome2KG: constructing and augmenting knowledge graphs of daily activities using virtual space. In: Proceedings of the ISWC 2021 Posters, Demos and Industry Tracks: From Novel Ideas to Industrial Practice, co-located with 20th International Semantic Web Conference. CEUR, vol. 2980 (2021)

10. Ugai, T., Egami, S., Htun, S.N.N., Kozaki, K., Kawamura, T., Fukuda, K.: Synthetic Multimodal Dataset for Empowering Safety and Well-being in Home Environments. arXiv cs.AI 2401.14743 (2023)

11. Krishna, R., Zhu, Y., Groth, O., et al.: Visual genome: connecting language and vision using crowdsourced dense image annotations. Int. J. Comput. Vis.Comput. Vis. 123, 32–73 (2017). https://doi.org/10.1007/s11263-016-0981-7

12. Goyal, A., Yang, K., Yang, D., Deng, J.: Rel3D: A Minimally Contrastive Benchmark for Grounding Spatial Relations in 3D, vol. 33. arXiv, abs/2012.01634 (2020)

13. Sadeghi, M.A., Farhadi, A.: Recognition using visual phrases. In: CVPR 2011, Colorado Springs, CO, USA, 2011, pp. 1745–1752 (2011). https://doi.org/10.1109/CVPR.2011.5995711

14. Lu, C., Krishna, R., Bernstein, M.S., Fei-Fei, L.: Visual Relationship Detection with Language Priors. arXiv, abs/1608.00187 (2016)

15. Ding, X., Li, Y., Pan, Y., Zeng, D., Yao, T.: Exploring depth information for spatial relation recognition. In: 2020 IEEE Conference on Multimedia Information Processing and Retrieval (MIPR), pp. 279–284 (2020)

16. Kumar, A.S., Nair, J.J.: Scene graph generation using depth, spatial, and visual cues in 2D images. IEEE Access 10, 1968–1978 (2022). https://doi.org/10.1109/ACCESS.2021.3139000

User-Centred Repair: From Current Practices to Future Design

Damla Kilic[(⊠)] and Neelima Sailaja

School of Computer Science, University of Nottingham, Nottingham, UK
`damla.kilic3@nottingham.ac.uk`

Abstract. From the kitchen to the bathroom, homes are now equipped with various technological devices like smart vacuums, intelligent mirrors, digital thermostats, wearables, and voice-controlled assistants such as Amazon Alexa. This surge in ubiquitous technologies contributes to the growing concern of electronic waste, or e-waste, globally. Research focuses on developing strategies for e-waste reduction, and is considering a range of approaches on governmental, industrial and societal levels. To gain a comprehensive understanding of smart device repair, our research was structured into several distinct tasks, each supported by semi-structured interviews, each tailored to explore different facets of repair behaviours and decision-making. A total of fifteen one-on-one study sessions were conducted as part of this research. The study's findings will be presented in three primary sections, each shedding light on distinct aspects of repair practices and decision-making. Along with the aforementioned results around current repair practices, repair decision making drivers and future expectations, our paper offers two significant contributions to human-computer interaction (HCI) research and practice. First, we place our findings in a broader context, anchoring them within the existing body of literature on HCI, repair practices, and the IoT. Second, we leverage our findings along with wider literature to conclude our paper with a set of design recommendations that align with current actual user practice around IoT repair; is inclusive of user expectations around every day reparability in future IoT; and enables user decision making around IoT repair thereby making IoT reparability an accessible and equitable process.

Keywords: IoT · consumer · smart products · repair · repair decision · right to repair · design for repair

1 Introduction

The transition towards an interconnected world has led to the widespread integration of Internet of Things (IoT) devices into everyday life, particularly within households. From smart appliances in the kitchen to intelligent gadgets in the bathroom, homes now feature a variety of technological advancements such as smart vacuums, digital thermostats, wearables, and voice-controlled assistants like Amazon Alexa. This proliferation of IoT technologies has heightened concerns regarding electronic waste, or e-waste, on a global scale. Forti et al. project that e-waste could reach approximately 74 million metric tons by 2030 [7].

While efforts to address electronic waste have garnered increasing attention in research circles, the focus has primarily been broad, spanning governmental, industrial, and societal levels. However, within this evolving landscape, the emergence of IoT systems presents distinct challenges to the conventional repair paradigm. Unlike traditional electronic devices, IoT systems integrate hardware, software, and data, creating a complex ecosystem that involves multiple stakeholders including users, designers, manufacturers, and retailers. This intricate network of components presents unique obstacles to the repair process. Notably, despite the growing emphasis on sustainability, the reparability of IoT devices is currently not a primary consideration for designers and manufacturers, as evidenced by existing research [4, 15]. The lack of specific attention to IoT repair highlights the necessity for future studies to explore this area in depth, uncovering the distinctive challenges and dynamics associated with repairing interconnected devices in today's technological landscape.

The aims of this paper are twofold: Firstly, it seeks to explore the evolving landscape of IoT repair by synthesizing insights from diverse academic disciplines, with a particular emphasis on the significant role HCI can play in shaping this emerging field. Secondly, it aims to present the results of a comprehensive user study designed to uncover prevalent repair practices, the key factors influencing repair decisions, and the anticipated future trends in IoT repair. The subsequent sections of this paper are organized to address the aforementioned dual objectives. In Sect. 2, we delve into the research landscape related to the right to repair and the decision-making processes associated with repairing IoT devices. This exploration commences with a thorough examination of multi-disciplinary literature, encompassing various facets of repair. Subsequently, we utilize this examination to underscore a distinct research gap within the current HCI literature concerning the repair of IoT devices. Moving on to Sect. 3, we provide a comprehensive overview of the research design formulated to address this identified research gap, employing a series of empirically supported research activities. Section 4 then presents the empirical findings derived from the study. In Sect. 5, we engage in a thorough discussion of our findings, drawing on existing literature for support, and propose design recommendations to the HCI community in light of our research insights.

2 Literature Review

2.1 Right to Repair

The "right to repair" is the principle asserting that individuals who own a product should have the ability to personally repair it or choose an expert to do so. This concept has been a subject of discourse for several decades, spanning diverse contexts ranging from automobiles to small technical devices. Over the years, discussions surrounding this right have evolved and expanded, encompassing a wide array of consumer products. This ongoing dialogue reflects the growing recognition of consumers' entitlement to access, modify, and repair the products they own, fostering a more sustainable and user-centric approach to technology. As technology continues to advance and permeate various aspects of daily life, the right to repair has become increasingly pertinent, influencing not only consumer rights but also broader considerations related to environmental sustainability, electronic waste management, and the overall longevity of products in the marketplace.

Governments around the world are increasingly recognizing the importance of supporting the right to repair as a fundamental consumer right and a sustainable practice. Many countries are exploring legislative measures to empower consumers in repairing their products. This support often involves advocating for regulations that require manufacturers to provide access to repair manuals, diagnostic tools, and affordable replacement parts. In the year 2021, the UK government enacted regulations known as the Eco-design for Energy Related Products and Energy Information [3], commonly denoted as the Right-to-Repair. This initiative aimed to counteract the issue of electronic product obsolescence. Furthermore, in March 2023, the European Commission introduced a proposal advocating for the repair of goods, amending previous regulations to enhance consumer access to repair services [6]. Both sets of regulations share the overarching goal of fostering a green economy characterized by extended product lifespans, reduced electronic waste, and more sustainable design practices. Nonetheless, the focus of these regulations primarily centres on household appliances such as refrigerators, washing machines, and dishwashers, there is a growing acknowledgment that the existing rules are too narrowly framed, especially due to exclusion of smartphones and computers [11]. Therefore, even these regulations are not that old from now it is obvious that they fall short of addressing the broader environmental and social impacts stemming from the unsustainable production, consumption, and disposal of countless interconnected IoT devices [20]. The role of manufacturers in the context of the right to repair is also significant, influencing both the availability and accessibility of repair solutions for consumers. While some manufacturers have embraced the principles of transparency and consumer empowerment, advocating for the right to repair, others have been criticized for adopting practices that hinder reparability. For example, Fairphone offers consumers the opportunity to reduce e-waste and its negative impacts by purchasing specific repair or upgrade items such as the camera or screen, enabling extended phone use within the product's five to seven-year lifecycle, contributing to environmental sustainability goals [16]. However, Apple has actively opposed measures aimed at increasing the reparability of iPhones. This includes lobbying against right-to-repair legislation in various states, refusing to sell iPhone replacement parts directly to consumers, legal actions against independent repair professionals like in Norway, collaborating with Amazon to remove iPhone and MacBook refurbishes from its marketplace, and enforcing agreements with electronics recyclers that mandate the destruction of iPhones and MacBooks rather than allowing them to be refurbished [10].

2.2 The Decision to Repair

While the concept of the Right to Repair is often discussed by various entities, including governments, disciplines, and industries, the decision to repair ultimately rests with everyday users. These users face numerous technological, financial, and social barriers that significantly influence their decision-making process when confronted with the choice to repair or replace a malfunctioning product. Existing literature extensively explores this multifaceted decision-making process, leading to the identification of various barriers and motivations [11, 17, 18].

Research in this area has proposed categorizations that consider stakeholders' perspectives, the intricate relationship between product and consumer attributes, and the dynamic interplay between external influences and individual preferences [13, 17, 19]. Despite valuable insights from these perspectives, comprehensively understanding user behaviour in the context of repair decisions remains an evolving area with limited empirical research. Studies, including those conducted by [8, 11, 17, 18], have used consumer surveys to untangle the web of factors influencing individuals in their repair decisions, shedding light on the nuanced decision-making processes.

Roskladka et al.'s [17] recent study identifies seven significant barriers shaping a user's willingness to repair, including a lack of trust in repair services, fear of potential further failures, emotional detachment from the product, desire for novel features or products, lack of clarity regarding the repair process, unawareness of the impact of repair, and a societal lack of engagement with repair practices. Lefebvre [11] introduces a comprehensive analysis of determinants for repair decisions, emphasizing factors such as perceived reparability, available support, past experiences, attitudes, knowledge, and individual skills. However, the lack of clarity regarding distinctions between traditional and connected technology devices raises considerations about repairing various household appliances.

Russell et al. [18] extend the exploration into temporal aspects of repair, highlighting that scalability is contingent not only on technical challenges but also on temporal factors like the timing of decisions, needs, or activities. Social challenges, such as willingness to pay, physical access, awareness, and motivation, are pivotal contributors to overall repair initiative scalability. In addition to factors identified in the aforementioned studies, gender and age have been recognized as influential in repair decisions. Perez-Belis et al.'s [14] survey in Spain suggests that variables like gender and age significantly impact the repair response of small household electrical and electronic equipment (EEE). For instance, older females demonstrate a higher inclination toward repairing appliances, and gender differences are identified in the repair of mobile phones, specifically regarding concerns about data privacy related to women's phone numbers in different countries [1, 9]. These cultural nuances add complexity to understanding repair behaviours in diverse societal contexts.

2.3 HCI and IoT Repair

In recent years, Sustainable Human-Computer Interaction (SHCI) has emerged as a critical aspect of HCI, aiming to address environmental concerns and minimize the ecological footprint of technology. Mankoff et al. [12] outlined two fundamental perspectives within SHCI: sustainability through design and sustainability in design. The former emphasizes integrating sustainability principles directly into the design process, including material selection, energy efficiency, and product lifecycle management. Conversely, sustainability in design focuses on utilizing interactive systems to promote sustainable behaviours among users, such as energy conservation and responsible consumption. Despite the growing recognition of sustainability in HCI, research in this area has revealed a lack of comprehensive evaluations concerning the sustainable attributes of technology interventions. DiSalvo et al. [5] stressed the need for more systematic assessments to understand better the environmental and social impacts of HCI technologies and guide design decisions toward sustainability. Additionally, Remy et al. [16] identified five essential elements crucial for evaluating SHCI interventions, offering valuable insights into refining evaluation methods in this field. However, the absence of standardized sustainable design guidelines presents a significant challenge, particularly for complex technologies like IoT devices. As these devices become increasingly interconnected, managing their data, hardware, and software becomes more intricate [2]. Addressing this challenge requires collaborative efforts to develop adaptable guidelines that consider the unique characteristics and requirements of IoT technologies, ensuring alignment with sustainability goals and reducing environmental impact. This is a challenge that the HCI community, with its multidisciplinary, user-centred methodologies, and applied nature, is uniquely positioned to address.

In summary, the discussion surrounding the repair challenges of IoT devices reveals several notable facets. Firstly, from the government's perspective, there is recognition of the intricate nature of IoT repair, prompting attempts to address this complexity. However, current governmental endeavours to establish comprehensive frameworks for addressing the challenges associated with repairing IoT devices are still in the nascent stages. While there is acknowledgment of the need for regulation, specific and nuanced regulations facilitating effective repair practices for IoT devices are yet to be fully realized. Secondly, the role of manufacturers in supporting the right to repair IoT devices remains a topic of concern. Despite the growing emphasis on the right to repair various consumer products, including electronic devices, manufacturers have not fully embraced or implemented measures to facilitate reparability in the IoT ecosystem. The gap between recognizing the importance of repair and translating that recognition into tangible support for consumers, particularly in the context of IoT devices, underscores a notable industry challenge. Moreover, the existing body of research on factors influencing user repair decisions lacks contextualization and specificity when it comes to IoT devices. Many studies have explored various determinants of repair decisions for electronic products, but none have distinctly focused on the repair dynamics specific to the complex landscape of interconnected IoT devices [11, 17]. This literature gap highlights the need for targeted research efforts specifically addressing the unique challenges associated with repairing IoT devices, contributing to a more comprehensive understanding of the factors influencing repair decisions in this rapidly evolving technological domain.

3   Methodology

3.1   Design of the Fixing the Future Study

This research aims to address the identified gap by employing a multifaceted methodology. It involves a combination of interviews, online questionnaires, and scenario-based design to comprehensively understand participants' current repair practices and their considerations regarding IoT repair.

Semi-structured interviews are utilized to delve into various aspects of IoT use and repair. These discussions are guided by the researcher's prompts while remaining flexible to accommodate diverse responses from participants, reflecting their unique approaches to IoT usage and repair. Additionally, online questionnaires are employed to provide additional detail and depth to research-supported concepts, such as factors influencing repair decisions. Participants engage in activities within these questionnaires, such as listing and ranking exercises, to further explore and elaborate on these concepts.

To facilitate this comprehensive understanding, the study is structured into distinct tasks, each aimed at exploring different facets of repair behaviours and decision-making processes as identified in existing literature. This section provides a detailed overview of the study design and the transitions between these tasks.

Task1. The first part of the study was focused on to understand current practices of participants around repair. Therefore, participants were engaged in a comprehensive exploration of their repair experiences and practices regarding smart devices. The inquiry encompassed a range of questions aimed at delving into their repair behaviours and decision-making processes. Initially, participants were asked whether they had encountered the need to repair their smart devices. If affirmative, they were prompted to provide a succinct overview of their actions, including details about who facilitated the repair, the incurred cost, and the rationale behind opting for repair. Additionally, participants were inquired about the duration of the overall repair process and the financial investment involved. Further, those who hadn't encountered the need for smart device repair were encouraged to share their general approach to fixing household items that had experienced malfunction. This line of questioning aimed to gather insights into their broader repair practices and expenditure in situations outside the realm of smart devices.

Task2. Following an analysis of existing literature and participating in personal discussions, we established a compilation of ten factors: cost of repair services and device parts, warranty condition and original cost of the device, availability for repair, accessibility of repair services, technical difficulty, age of devices, time required for repair and physical attributes of the devices that influence their repair decision making. Throughout the study sessions, we provided participants with Microsoft Form links and requested them to prioritize these factors based on their significance while making repair decisions. In this particular section of the study, our primary objective was to delve deeper into the concerns and apprehensions of our participants when it came to the process of repairing their devices. By focusing on this aspect, we aimed to gain a comprehensive understanding of the various factors that influenced their decision-making in this context. Through this exploration, we sought to uncover nuanced insights that could shed light on the underlying motivations and considerations that guided their choices regarding device repair.

Task3. Within this specific segment of the study, we introduced five distinct scenarios, each centred on a different category of smart devices: Smart Watch, Smart Speaker, Smart Thermostat, Smart Toy, and Smart Washing Machine. These scenarios encompassed a range of situations, including considerations such as device pricing when received as a gift or purchased second-hand, alongside limited details regarding the nature of the device fault. The smart washing machine scenario is shown below as an example.

"You purchased a top-of-the-line smart washing machine for your home (1250 GBP), but you decided not to buy the warranty offered by the manufacturer because of its high cost. You thought that since the washing machine was expensive and of high quality, it would be unlikely to have any issues. For the first few months, the washing machine worked perfectly, while doing laundry, you noticed that the machine was making strange noises and wasn't draining the water properly."

Participants were tasked with reading each scenario and making decisions about five distinct factors associated with repairing the defective items. Specifically, they were required to indicate: (1, 2) The amount they were willing to allocate for repair services and the cost of the device part. (3) The age until which they were willing to continue repairing the devices. (4) The level of technical difficulty they were comfortable with in repairing the devices. (5) The duration they were prepared to wait for the repair of these items. By presenting participants with these diverse scenarios, we aimed to simulate current and future real-world scenarios around repair and gather insights into their decision-making processes, towards different devices and different factors.

Task4. In an initial endeavour to gain insights into the forthcoming landscape of repair practices, we presented participants with a set of 10 distinct hardware and 10 software issues encompassing various smart devices (Please see the Table 1). Participants were tasked with making informed decisions about their preferences or anticipated choices for repair approaches in the future. The range of repair options spanned a spectrum, including Individual Repair, Individual Repair supported by online resources, Repair Cafes, Independent Repair Shops, Manufacturers (such as Amazon or Apple), Professional Repair Services (like iCracked or uBreakiFix), and Warranty Services offered by third parties outside the original manufacturers. This phase of the study was structured using the Miro platform. The researcher utilized Microsoft Teams to share her screen, adhering to the participants' guidance for each unique scenario presented.

Table 1. Hardware and Software Repair Scenarios

S1: Your wearable health tracker starts generating unexpected or incorrect data about your physical activities. What will you do?
S2: Your smart shoes may not be able to sync with the companion app, preventing the user from accessing up-to-date fitness data. What will you do?
S3: Your wearable health tracker may become damaged, and it results in cracked screens. What will you do?
S4: Your brand-new smart shoes have the battery problem, and this results in reduced functionality. What will you do?
S5: If your smart washing machine run endlessly or repeatedly start and stop without completing a cycle. What will you do?
S6: If you have programmed your robot vacuum cleaner to clean every Saturday morning around 10 am, but the device starts cleaning at 3 am while you are sleeping. What will you do?
S7: When a smart washing machine experiences mechanical issues such as a broken belt, pump, or motor. What will you do?
S8: If your robot vacuum cleaner is having trouble navigating around obstacles and getting stuck in tight spaces or corners during your cleaning routine. What will you do?
S9: When your CCTV is having trouble connecting to your Wi-Fi network or other devices in your home. What will you do?
S10: If the thermostat is giving inaccurate temperature readings and lead to waste of energy. What will you do?
S11: When you realized that your smart thermostat is hacked, and your login credentials, financial information, or other sensitive data are under risk. What will you do?
S12: Your smart CCTV may be affected by harsh weather conditions, such as rain and not working properly. What will you do?
S13: When you realized that your children's smart doll is collecting and transmitting sensitive user data (such as their reading habits) without proper security measures in place. What will you do?
S14: If you discover that, despite having enabled parental controls on your children's educational tablets, they are still able to access web pages that are not part of the approved content. What will you do?
S15: If the sensors on your children's smart dolls are not working correctly, and the doll is unable to respond to requests to perform physical actions. What will you do?
S16: When you realized that your children's educational tablet have a cracked or unresponsive screen sometimes in a day. What will you do?
S17: When you ask anything to Alexa, it provide inaccurate or irrelevant responses. For example, when you ask a recipe of carrot cake, it tells you about the weather in the UK. What will you do?
S18: The Chabot that you use daily is leaking user data to unauthorized third parties. What will you do?
S19: You realized that your Alexa cannot accurately recognize voice commands. It may be because of microphone of your Alexa is not functioning properly. What will you do?
S20: Your smart speaker may not respond to button presses to turn it on/off. What will you do?

3.2 Participant Recruitment

Recruitment of participants was carried out through a combination of a mailing list and social connections. As an incentive for their involvement, participants received a modest payment of £15 amazon voucher each. Eligibility criteria included being at least 18 years of age and owning a minimum of one smart device.

A total of 15 participants took part in the study, representing a variety of occupations and household statuses. The participants encompassed a diverse group, including students and researchers spanning a wide array of disciplines ranging from computer science to food sustainability. Out of the 15 participants, 7 were married, while 6 identified as single. The number of household members for the participants varied, ranging from 1 to 5 individuals. Regarding house status, the participants were categorized into three groups: homeowners, renters, and those living in student accommodations. Also, approximately 9 participants reported an income of less than 35,000 GBP.

3.3 Data Collection and Analysis

The research was conducted using Microsoft Teams as the platform for fieldwork. Ahead of each study session, a welcoming email along with a reminder was sent to a member of each household participating in the study. This email contained the Microsoft Teams meeting link and provided clear, detailed instructions on how participants could easily join the meetings. Also, Microsoft Forms and Miro were actively utilized throughout the sessions to enhance participant engagement in various parts of the study. Ethical approval for this research was obtained from the Ethical Committee of the Computer Science Department at the University of Nottingham. Participants engaged in the study by utilizing their personal networked devices, typically within the comfort of their own homes. The study sessions occurred from February to July 2023, with each session lasting approximately 50 to 70 min. The data gathered during the study comprised audio recordings of conversations between participants and researchers conducted through Microsoft Teams. Subsequent to transcribing the recordings, the researcher removed the names and any direct identifying details of the participants from the interview notes and transcripts.

4 Findings

The study's findings painted a vivid picture of the technological landscape inhabited by our participants. All 15 individuals showcased an impressive array of smart devices, including but not limited to energy-monitoring smart plugs, smart heating controls, robot vacuum cleaners, security cameras, Wi-Fi-enabled air purifiers, well-being health trackers, smart TVs, and voice assistants like Alexa and Google Home, not to mention the ubiquity of smartphones, tablets, and laptops tailored for varied tasks and research. Beyond merely owning these devices, the participants deeply integrated them into the very fabric of their daily routines. Voice assistants like Alexa were no longer fancy gadgets but had become virtual household members, assisting with weather updates and setting alarms. Smart heating controls weren't just about warmth but symbolized energy efficiency and remote convenience. Devices like Google Home took on the mantle of a digital caretaker, fine-tuning home ambiances with tasks such as lighting adjustments and musical accompaniments. As the discussion shifted to the control mechanisms of these smart devices, a common theme emerged: participants often intertwined the use of physical controls with mobile apps to orchestrate their technological symphony. Voice control, facilitated effortlessly by Alexa and Google Home, was underscored by many as the epitome of convenience in this smart era.

4.1 Current Practices Around Repair

Exploring the repair practices of our participants unveiled a fascinating tapestry of experiences, spanning a spectrum of devices from modern smart products like smart washing machines, smart TVs, Fitbits, robot vacuum cleaners, smartphones, laptops, headphones to older, traditional technologies fridges, freezers, and televisions.

Common smartphone issues included broken screens, as faced by P1 and P14, and charging port malfunctions, a challenge for both P2 and P6, with the latter highlighting complications due to the device being a less-known brand in the UK. Smart appliance troubles were highlighted by P2 and P8, who both dealt with smart washing machine hardware and software breakdowns. Meanwhile, robot vacuum cleaners, as noted by P15 and P14, presented challenges too. While P15's issues were more hardware-centric, P14 grappled with software-related mapping issues, necessitating a remapping of his house layout.

On the traditional front, P5 pinpointed a washing machine electronic board malfunction, P6 discussed issues with a fridge and manual washing machine, and P15 creatively addressed a latch problem on a non-smart vacuum cleaner.

4.2 Decision Making Around Repair

One of our study's primary objectives was to delve into participants' decision-making processes concerning faulty items – whether they chose to repair or disregard them. By exploring participants' experiences with malfunctioning devices, we aimed to uncover their troubleshooting strategies. Typically, participants would first assess the gravity of the malfunction and its effect on their daily operations.

Here, there were instances where participants chose to live with minor glitches in their devices. P4 overlooked smart vacuum cleaner inaccuracies, P9 accepted a persistent digital camera issue, and P11 endured laptop problems before ultimately replacing it. Minor glitches often saw participants adopting a DIY approach, turning to a slew of online resources like forums, user manuals, helplines, Google, YouTube, and technical blogs to guide their repair efforts.

Yet, when issues became more intricate or surpassed their skill set, participants adopted a more collaborative strategy, reaching out to tech-savvy friends for advice. This network often provided varied solutions and insights. In unresolved cases, formal repair avenues became the focus – this could be third-party services, manufacturers, or local experts. Some participants even mentioned community-known individuals adept at troubleshooting, affectionately referred to as "that man" or "our repair guy."

P3's experience perfectly encapsulates this methodical approach. When things go wrong with her smart devices, P3 follow a step-by-step plan. First, P3 figures out how bad the problem is and how much it messes up my daily use. If it's a small issue, she tries to solve it herself. P3 search online to learn what's causing the trouble and if she can fix it by reading and understanding. But if the problem is bigger and makes a big mess of my gadgets, she switches to asking for help. She talks to people she knows who might know more about these things than him. It's like asking a friend who's good with tech stuff. This way, she gets different ideas and solutions. So, when something goes wrong, she starts by checking it out himself. If it's too much, she asks people who know more. It's like a team effort to get things working again. And if things are still a mess after that, she looks for more technical help. She might check out company websites or technical blogs, but that's not his first go-to. She tries to keep it simple and stick to Google and YouTube mostly. So, she guesses you could call it a "try it yourself, ask friends, then get technical" process. It's like when you're trying to build a puzzle – you start on your own, ask a friend for help if you're stuck, and then maybe ask an expert if you still can't figure it out.

4.3 Responsibility of Repair Decision

Social repair dynamics presented themselves across a range of approaches that spread between individual autonomy, collaborative efforts and shared responsibility. P1 assumes repair responsibility within their household due to their family's composition and their comprehensive understanding of gadget insurance terms, which empowers them to effectively manage repairs. Their role as the repair person is influenced by both family dynamics and their specialized knowledge of insurance provisions.

P9 and P14 illustrated how a mix of autonomy and teamwork guided their repair decisions alongside their partners. P9' mentioned that *"It's shared responsibility and I'm quite autonomous in that sense."* Here, a balance was struck between individual autonomy and shared decision-making. P14 echoed a similar sentiment, highlighting a collaborative attempt at repair while ultimately embracing individual responsibility.

P6's household revealed a shared responsibility for repairs, often undertaken by the participant's father or their own expertise as a physics teacher. Also, P4 and P7 exemplified the influence of interest and expertise, stepping forward as primary repair figures due to their familiarity with repair tasks and household systems. Additionally, P5 and P6 contributed to our understanding of shared responsibilities within households. P5 disclosed, *"My brother is very good with laptops... between the two of us we try to resolve what we need to resolve."* This collaborative dynamic illustrated the collective effort to address repair issues, leveraging the strengths of different family members.

However, others, like P2, divided responsibilities practically, with certain family members handling hands-on tasks while others tackled tech-related issues. P2 stated that *"If something broke, it would be either me or my dad that would fix it. If it's something more practical, like water or something that needs a power drill, it's usually my dad and although I have those skills as well, whereas if it's something technological like a computer or TV, if they wanted it, fixing it would come to me"*. This approach underscored the interplay between technical proficiency and hands-on skills, with specific individuals stepping up based on practical considerations.

4.4   Key Drivers of Decision Making Around Repair

The most common factors influencing decision making around repair are the cost of repair (P5, P7, P10, P11), age of devices (P2, P11, P14) and time taken to repair (P2, P5, P9). P2's perspective, as articulated in the following quote, underscores that alongside the *cost of repair,* the *age of the device and time taken to repair*, other factors such as the *personal value a device holds* in one's life plays a pivotal role in shaping the repair or replacement decision:

P2: Let's say, my TV is worth, I don't know, £300, and it would cost £150 to repair it. My TV is now 12 years old and has been with me across three cities and 12 houses. At this point, I would probably just replace it. However, if it were my computer, the value of my computer is far more than what it actually costs. It's probably only worth £700 these days because the parts are so old. But because I use it every day and it has all of my stuff on it, I would happily pay £400 or £450 before I even thought about replacing the whole thing.

Formative Phase of the Decision.   Participants listed different factors that they consider before (and those that thereby influence) their actual repair decision making: *Their mental and physical capacity to sit down and work out how to repair the devices* (P2), *who you trust to repair* (P3), *whether the device is first or second-hand* (P4)*, warranty status of the devices* (P5,) *accessibility of the device's spare parts in different countries* (P6, P11, P15) and *how confident the users feel to fix the problem themselves* (P9). Moreover, the intended user of a device emerged as a significant determinant influencing the decision to pursue repair. P7 illustrated this with an example: when dealing with devices intended for the entire household, such as central heating control systems, the inclination to invest time in perusing online documentation, reading forums, or watching instructional videos on platforms like YouTube diminishes.

Process of the Decision.   In terms of prioritizing the ten distinct factors influencing the decision to repair or not among the participants, at the forefront of their considerations was the *cost of repair services*, a pivotal determinant in their choices. Directly followed by *the cost of device parts*, carrying significant weight in the decision-making process. The *warranty condition of the device* held its place as a key aspect, influencing choices considerably. The *original cost of the device* emerged as an influential factor. If the original cost of the device is lower, P9 believes that it is often more practical to consider replacement over repair. They emphasize that affordability plays a significant role in their decision-making process. For items that are relatively inexpensive to replace, P9 tends to view repairs as less cost-effective and time efficient. However, they also acknowledge that for high-value items such as a car, where repair costs may be substantial but still less than the expense of buying a new vehicle, the repair option becomes more appealing. *Availability for repair* followed closely in importance, with participants giving it serious consideration. The *accessibility of repair services* also played a notable role. The perceived *technical difficulty* of the repair task influenced decisions, with participants tending to favour tasks they felt competent to handle. The *age of devices* had low impact on participants' decision making. When discussing the importance of a device's age in the context of repairs, one participant, P8, emphasized that age alone is not a decisive factor. They pointed out that the significance of the device's age hinges on other variables. Whether a device is expensive and relatively new or an expensive one that has aged, P8 stated that they would assign it the same level of importance when considering repairs. The *time required for repairs* ranked lower in the hierarchy of importance. Finally, *the physical attributes of the devices*, such as size and weight, were the least significant factors when it came to repair decisions. P11 expressed the perspective that when a device requires repair, its size becomes inconsequential.

As delineated in the methodology section, beyond exploring the factors influencing repair decisions, one of the other aims of our study is to delve into participants' repair choices across various devices (Please see Fig. 1 below). Thus, the figure provided herein displays five distinct devices alongside participants' rankings regarding five different repair-influencing factors. The color-coding adjacent to the table denotes rankings, with pink indicating the highest ranking and purple indicating the lowest.

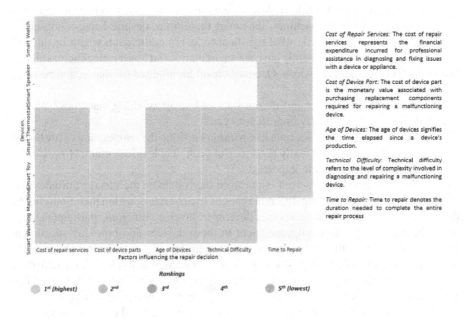

Fig. 1. Devices and factors influencing the repair decision

Participants expressed varying preferences depending on the type of device in question. They mentioned considering different factors at the same time and trying to come up with a final thought is challenging. One of the participants stated that she is trying to find a good balance between all the factors. The price of the device, the people involved, the purpose of the device, whether it was firsthand or second hand, and whether you had the warranty were all considered among a lot of different factors (P3).

Upon closer examination of the findings presented in the table above, it becomes apparent that, for instance, concerning washing machines, the majority of participants expressed a willingness to invest more in both repair services and the necessary parts for repairs. Additionally, participants anticipated that washing machines, given their crucial role in household functioning, might have a higher age and technical complexity compared to other devices. However, given the essential role of washing machines in maintaining household operations, participants were reluctant to endure prolonged repair durations, emphasizing the need for timely resolution to ensure the continuity of household services. As one of the participants put it with respect to washing machine (P2), for example:

P2: I think I would be willing to pay more to get the washing machine repaired and obtain the reports. And again, with the assumption that I would want it to last at least five years for the washing machine. So, if I could repair it and it could last that long, I'd happily spend the money. Whereas if it was just going to be a temporary fix, I wouldn't. Um, but I would want it back immediately. You know, I'd really struggle to send it off, as it would suck to live without a washing machine since there are 6 adults there, a baby, and a dog, and it would be awful. So, I'd want it back immediately. And if it couldn't be fixed really quickly, then I would replace it because it's a necessity to have it for me.

In contrast to washing machines, the smart thermostat, despite being a household device, does not hold the same level of significance for our participants when considering repair. Our participants consistently gave the smart thermostat lower ratings across all five factors influencing repair decisions. One participant highlighted the distinction between these two devices:

Researcher: What about smart thermostats and smart washing machines? We use them daily, but are they equally important to you?

P15: Yeah, I wouldn't say so. I can live without knowing the temperature of my home. I can measure it manually if I really need to. But yeah, it is less important. However, for the washing machine, it's quite important.

This differentiation in perceived importance sheds light on the varying attitudes participants hold towards repairing different types of smart devices within their households. Moreover, when contemplating various devices in diverse situations, participants also raised the subject of emotional attachment to these devices and how this attachment influences the factors they take into account when deciding whether to repair them. This discussion highlights the profound personal connection individuals have with their devices and how this emotional bond plays a pivotal role in shaping their repair-related considerations and choices, illustrates P13 with respect to smart children toy:

P13: The children's toy holds an emotional connection. I just think about it this way: my child may be very attached to that specific toy, and you know how children can be – they often need that exact same toy. So, yeah, I'm willing to pay whatever it takes, I'm willing to wait, and I'll do whatever I can to ensure it gets fixed and returned to the child.

4.5 Current and Future of Repair and Expectations

In fact, 14 out of the 20 scenarios revealed that most participants shared similar preferences when it came to their favoured repair approach (please see Fig. 2 for more information). This consistency in preferences suggests that certain factors or considerations strongly influence participants' decision-making processes. Therefore, in the remaining part of this section, we will delve deeper into the practical and everyday reasoning of our participants that emerged as they discussed their preferences.

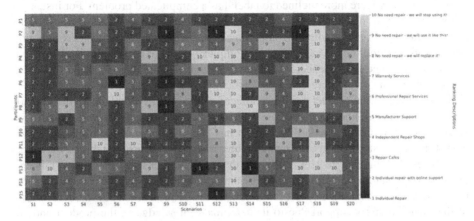

Fig. 2. Spectrum of the Repair

Self-repair.

In 8 of the 20 scenarios presented (as evidenced in Fig. 2), participants leaned towards self-repair with online support, such as YouTube videos or websites like iFixit. While varied reasons drove this choice, some common factors emerged. For example, *past experience* with a similar issue often gave participants the confidence to handle the repair themselves. For example, P9 had prior experience of fixing a cracked screen on her wearable health tracker with the aid of online tutorials. Participants also leaned towards individual repair with *online support* due to the prevalence of shared experiences on common issues. They believe that the ubiquity of a problem often leads to a wealth of insights and solutions available on various online platforms. The shared collective wisdom, often detailed on websites, forums, and social media, instils confidence in individuals facing similar issues, encouraging a DIY approach to repairs.

Participants who preferred online support for self-repair also often chose websites, forums, and general web searches over brand-specific applications. They expressed concerns that individual apps for different devices and brands could lead to clutter and inefficiency. As P5 elaborates, *"When I face a technical issue, I first look for solutions on user forums or online communities,"* a sentiment rooted in the practicality and accessibility of real-world advice and solutions. This gravitation towards peer insights underscores a communal level trust, where real-life experiences are deemed more valuable than official manufacturer guidance, as P8 echoes, *"Manufacturer manuals are often too technical... I prefer watching YouTube videos where someone walks me through the troubleshooting process."*

Seeking Support for More 'Complex' Repairs. Our study participants frequently associated the complexity of a problem with their level of prior experience in troubleshooting and repair. In essence, if they lacked prior experience in addressing a particular issue, they were more inclined to label it as a complicated problem. For instance, if a smart washing machine exhibited behaviour such as running endlessly or repeatedly starting and stopping without completing a washing cycle, participants commonly regarded these symptoms as indicative of a complex issue (P3) and emphasized the need for expert guidance (P1). Hence, it is noteworthy that the majority of our participants, specifically 9 out of 15, expressed a preference for reaching out to the manufacturer's support as their initial contact point when faced with software problems in their smart washing machines. Other examples are, encountering a battery issue with brand-new smart shoes or realizing a smart thermostat has been compromised, putting sensitive data at risk. In these situations, the manufacturer is seen as the most reliable resource for assistance. The tendency to seek help from the manufacturer highlights the significant level of trust users have in the companies that create these products, particularly for resolving software and security issues. P5 echoed this sentiment, emphasizing the value of the manufacturer's support due to their intimate knowledge of the product and an inherent obligation to assist their customers, underscoring their accountability for the products they produce.

Social anxiety emerges as another factor affecting the decision to repair as it is influenced by the communication preferences of participants when seeking repair support. The aversion to direct phone conversations is identified here, with participants like P11 articulating, *"I don't want to talk to someone on the phone, but I would be happy to chat to customer support."* This inclination towards text-based interactions underscores the nuanced role of social dynamics in shaping engagement with support services.

Not Choosing to Repair. Certainly, repair does not always represent the chosen course of action for our participants. At times, participants deemed certain device malfunctions too critical to even attempt a repair. Instead, they chose to discontinue its use entirely.

Participants were happy to have reduced functionality and use the smart devices without smart future of it. Instead of having smart watch, P2 is happy kept using it as a watch, if the wearable health tracker starts generating unexpected or incorrect data about their physical activities. P13 provides another reason for participant to prefer not choosing to repair:

P13: If health tracking is very important to me, I would say there is no need to repair it. I'll just replace it because when it comes to health, accuracy is crucial. You need something that provides correct information, especially since health data is very sensitive. So, I prefer to have a brand new one that's working perfectly rather than a repaired one that might still provide inaccurate information.

Furthermore, participants exhibited similar attitudes towards issues such as reduced battery life in smart shoes (P3) or synchronization problems with companion apps (P12, P13). Additionally, instances were noted where participants discovered privacy concerns with certain smart devices, such as a child's smart doll transmitting sensitive user data insecurely (P2, P3, P4, P6, P7, P8, P10, P11, P12, P13, P14), or a chatbot inadvertently exposing user data to unauthorized entities (P2, P3, P4, P5, P6, P7, P8, P10, P11, P12, P13, P14).

Lastly, sometimes the decision to repair or not is dependent upon the context, culture and resources available. Some participants expressed that in urban environments, accessing repair services was straightforward, as opposed to rural settings, where repair resources, services and alternatives might be scarce. P10 shared their perspective, contrasting their current urban living situation with an upcoming move to rural Malaysia, where repair resources might be less accessible.

5 Discussion

As stated in the literature review section, our findings also emphasized that the repair decision-making process is complex, influenced by various factors that emerged in distinct contexts within the study. Factors influencing repair decisions varied among participants and malfunctioning devices, but the most common included cost of repair, age of devices, and time of repair. Similar to general technological devices, our study indicates that users evaluating IoT devices take into account factors such as their ability to perform repairs, trust in repair sources, device condition (first or second-hand), warranty status, parts accessibility, confidence in personal repair skills, and the intended user of the device.

Building upon the research by Roskladka et al. [17], we extended our inquiry to explore participants' repair attitudes towards a diverse array of smart devices, including Smart Watches, Smart Speakers, Smart Thermostats, Smart Toys, and Smart Washing Machines. Contrary to the notion that repair attitudes may be specific to certain device types, our findings indicate a nuanced adaptation of decision-making strategies based on the device's nature and specific usage scenarios. For instance, participants demonstrated a greater willingness to allocate resources towards repairing essential household devices like washing machines, driven by the imperative of household continuity. However, this commitment to repair was tempered by a reluctance to endure prolonged repair durations, highlighting the delicate balance between practical necessity and inconvenience. Furthermore, our investigation revealed the significant influence of emotional attachment to devices on repair decisions, particularly evident in scenarios where participants considered the sentimental value associated with certain smart devices. As exemplified by P13's experience with a smart children's toy, emotional connections to such devices can often outweigh purely pragmatic considerations, complicating the decision-making process. This underscores the multifaceted nature of repair attitudes and the need for a holistic understanding of users' emotional and practical motivations in navigating repair decisions across various smart device categories.

In conjunction with the literature highlighting age [14] and gender [1, 9] as influential factors in repair decisions, our study extends these considerations to repair responsibilities within households. Additionally, we unveil a range of household-specific factors that impact repair decisions among participants. One such factor is the expertise level of household members in handling different types of repair tasks. While some individuals may excel in hands-on tasks, others may be more adept at tackling technical issues related to devices. This division of labour based on skillset contributes to the allocation of repair responsibilities within households.

Furthermore, social dynamics within the household, such as parental responsibilities and financial situations, play a crucial role in shaping repair decisions. For instance, individuals may prioritize repairs differently based on familial obligations or budget constraints. Additionally, repair decisions often involve collaborative efforts among household members, with discussions and negotiations taking place to determine the most feasible course of action. These social dynamics add layers of complexity to the repair decision-making process within households, reflecting the intricate interplay of personal, familial, and financial considerations.

Also, the role of manufacturers concerning the right to repair holds significant importance [10, 16]. While some companies actively contribute to sustainability efforts by offering repair options and reducing electronic waste, others oppose right-to-repair legislation and restrict repair opportunities for users. However, there remains a gap in research regarding the specific areas where users require manufacturer assistance and their underlying concerns in this regard. In our study, we delved into this aspect and uncovered valuable insights. Participants in our research demonstrated a clear correlation between the perceived complexity of a repair issue and their level of prior experience in troubleshooting and repair. When faced with unfamiliar or intricate problems, participants tended to view them as more challenging and sought expert guidance. Notably, for issues such as software problems or security breaches, participants expressed a preference for reaching out to the manufacturer for support. This preference underscores the substantial trust users place in manufacturers to effectively address product issues. Participants emphasized the value of manufacturer support, citing the company's intimate knowledge of the product and their perceived responsibility to assist customers. These findings shed light on the critical role of manufacturers in providing technical support and assistance to users facing complex repair challenges. Moreover, they underscore the accountability of manufacturers in ensuring the functionality and longevity of the products they produce. Moving forward, further research in this area can help elucidate users' specific needs and concerns regarding manufacturer assistance, contributing to more informed policy discussions and industry practices related to the right to repair.

5.1 Design Recommendations

Based on the above empirical study and its resulting findings and discussion, we propose a focused set of recommendations to the HCI community, who is positioned uniquely in terms of it multidisciplinary which brings together computing, design, education and policy. These recommendations are set forth to be taken up by researchers, designers and developers aiming to embed reparability as an inherent property into future IoT making, management and maintenance. These recommendations, derived from actual user wants and needs unveiled in the study, when applied, become a practical and tangible set of guidelines that would help support the users' with their everyday repair decisions and processes.

Making the process of troubleshooting easy, quick and accessible: Helping the user quickly understand what is wrong with their device, the alternatives available for fixing it and the expense (time, money and effort) the process entails become an important necessity that is currently underserved. This needs to be responded to so that the users are informed enough to make decisions around the next steps of who to contact, what spare parts or tools to access, the most efficient and effective pathway to getting their device repaired etc. HCI research, through its user centred approach and design led methodologies becomes the premier pathway to solutions in this scope which calls for responses that distil large knowledgebase around repair to the focused and user-friendly interventions that this gap seeks.

Effective use of multi-media: To allow for effective dissemination of repair related information, a call to move away from just text based instructional guides is highlighted. Here, we see a need for a mix of media, from audio-based call support or conversational agents to instructional videos to detailed specification documents, each designed to suit a different kind of user and their unique contexts and needs around repair. To understand user contexts around their optimal media type and the very design and dissemination of the instructional asset through this media requires meticulous user centred research, yet another challenge the HCI community should undertake.

Regulated online communities: Where official support is not often prevalent, users turn to post-official communities, Facebook groups and other social media forums that support the repair of their devices. But being unregulated, the trust in these measures would be less than if such communities for repair support are maintained in conjunction with manufacturer stake. This would help with access to official documentation, more accurate recommendations and mitigation of risks from unofficial repairs which could prove harmful if done by inexperienced users. Bringing together the interests of multiple stakeholders, prioritising the user requirements and developing novel strategies for computer supported co-operative work that enable this emergent landscape of technology circularity through repair are challenges that need a holistic, yet multi-disciplinary and applied intervention, all of which speak to the HCI ethos.

Access to manufacturer: Currently, repair as an alternative to replace stays very weak due to the lack of support from manufacturer side. To move away from this status-quo to one that actively enables repair requires multiple avenues of connection between the manufacturer and user. This could be through direct customer support, manufacturer regulated communities and forums, manufacturer whetted instructional resources or even manufacturer enabled processes for quickly assessing a fault, acquiring legal and appropriate spare parts etc. HCI, being the host to several research domains identified here (online communities, computer supported co-operative work, interaction design and user-centred research) would be the perfect point of amalgamation of these priorities to support the realisation of a technology future where repair is live through an active system of communication and collaboration between the key stakeholders of a circular (technology) economy.

Equal responsibility through empowerment: Our findings show a spectrum of responsibility levels around repair decision making and actions. These variations are often socially derived and a reflection of lack of resources and support that cater to a more diverse set of all backgrounds and contexts. Within families and co-located situations, we see a dependence on certain individuals who are assumed to have more knowledge and experience. On a wider scale, we see reports of a complete lack of access to repair resources depending upon the geographic location. This social divide that exists on a global scale seeks to be alleviated, for which future design needs to look into alternatives of empowerment through open access to repair information, more accessible knowledge assets, modularity in device design, transparency of software architectures and more inclusive efforts towards maintenance and repair initiatives. Understanding equitability challenges at several levels of the social system (from the home to a global scale) is a herculean challenge that requires a combined effort from social science, psychology, computing and design together to explore the landscape, explicate the nuances at each level and expound responses that speak to the myriad different contexts across layers. Here, again HCI being a hub for these very domains, along with its methods that render it capable to work at the different social strata, with different sets of stakeholders and their corresponding situations make HCI a key player in the near future of reparability research for technology and beyond.

6 Conclusion

In conclusion, our study sheds light on the intricate factors influencing repair decisions for IoT devices, particularly within households. We've highlighted the importance of economic, emotional, and practical considerations in repair choices, emphasizing the role of factors such as device age, household repair expertise, social dynamics, and manufacturer support. Proposing design recommendations for the HCI community, we advocate for embedding reparability into future IoT devices and promoting user-centred approaches to troubleshooting. Regulated online communities and improved access to manufacturer support are also essential. Addressing social inequalities in repair access is crucial, requiring collaborative efforts across disciplines. Our findings contribute to informed policy discussions and industry practices, aiming to foster sustainable and user-centric repair solutions in the evolving landscape of IoT technology.

Acknowledgments. This work is supported by the Engineering and Physical Sciences Research Council funded project **Fixing the Future: The Right to Repair and Equal-IoT [EP/W024780/1].**

References

1. Ahmed, S.I., Guha, S., Rifat, Md.R., Shezan, F.H., Dell, N.: Privacy in repair. In: Proceedings of the Eighth International Conference on Information and Communication Technologies and Development (2016)
2. Boniface, C., Urquhart, L., Terras, M.: Towards a right to repair for the internet of things: a review of legal and policy aspects. Comput. Law Secur. Rev. **52**, 105934 (2024)
3. Conway, L.: Research briefing right to repair regulations. Research briefings (2021). https://researchbriefings.files.parliament.uk/documents/CBP-9302/CBP-9302.pdf
4. Cooper, T., Salvia, G.: Fix it: barriers to repair and opportunities for change (2018)
5. DiSalvo, C., Sengers, P., Brynjarsdóttir, H.: Mapping the landscape of sustainable HCI. In: Proceedings of the SIGCHI Conference on Human Factors in Computing Systems (2010)
6. EU. Report on the proposal for a directive of the European Parliament and of the council on common rules promoting the repair of goods and amending regulation (EU) 2017/2394, Directives (EU) 2019/771 and (EU) 2020/1828: A9-0316/2023: European Parliament. REPORT on the proposal for a directive of the European Parliament and of the Council on common rules promoting the repair of goods and amending Regulation (EU) 2017/2394, Directives (EU) 2019/771 and (EU) 2020/1828 | A9-0316/2023 | European Parliament, 2023. https://www.europarl.europa.eu/doceo/document/A-9-2023-0316_EN.html

7. Forti, V., Balde, C.P., Kuehr, R., Bel, G.: The Global E-waste Monitor 2020: Quantities, flows and the circular economy potential (2020)
8. Hansson, L.Å., Cerratto Pargman, T., Pargman, D.S.: A decade of sustainable HCI. In: Proceedings of the 2021 CHI Conference on Human Factors in Computing Systems (2021)
9. Haque, S.M., Haque, M.R., Nandy, S., et al.: Privacy vulnerabilities in public digital sevice centers in Dhaka, Bangladesh. In: Proceedings of the 2020 International Conference on Information and Communication Technologies and Development (2020)
10. Koebler, J.: Tim Cook to investors: people bought fewer new iphones because they repaired their old ones. VICE (2019). https://www.vice.com/en/article/zmd9a5/tim-cook-to-investors-people-bought-fewer-new-iphones-becausethey-repaired-their-old-ones
11. Lefebvre, M.: To repair or not to repair: an investigation of the factors influencing prosumer repair propensity (2019)
12. Mankoff, J.C., Blevis, E., Borning, A., et al.: Environmental sustainability and interaction. In: CHI 2007 Extended Abstracts on Human Factors in Computing Systems (2007)
13. van Nes, N., Cramer, J.: Influencing product lifetime through product design. Bus. Strateg. Environ. **14**(5), 286–299 (2005)
14. Pérez-Belis, V., Braulio-Gonzalo, M., Juan, P., Bovea, M.D.: Consumer attitude towards the repair and the second-hand purchase of small household electrical and electronic equipment. A Spanish case study. J. Clean. Prod. **158**, 261–275 (2017)
15. Perzanowski, A.: The right to repair (2021)
16. Remy, C., Bates, O., Dix, A., et al.: Evaluation beyond usability. In: Proceedings of the 2018 CHI Conference on Human Factors in Computing Systems (2018)
17. Roskladka, N., Jaegler, A., Miragliotta, G.: From, "right to repair" to "willingness to repair": exploring consumer's perspective to product lifecycle extension. J. Clean. Prod. **432**, 139705 (2023)
18. Russell, J.D., Svensson-Hoglund, S., Richter, J.L., Dalhammar, C., Milios, L.: A matter of timing: System requirements for repair and their temporal dimensions. J. Ind. Ecol. **27**(3), 845–855 (2022)
19. Sonego, M., Echeveste, M.E., Debarba, H.G.: Repair of electronic products: consumer practices and institutional initiatives. Sustain. Prod. Consumption **30**, 556–565 (2022)
20. Stead, M., Coulton, P., Pilling, F., Gradinar, A., Pilling, M., Forrester, I.: More-than-human-data interaction. In: Proceedings of the 25th International Academic Mindtrek Conference (2022)
21. Svensson, S., Richter, J.L., Maitre-Ekern, E., Pihlajarinne, T., Maigret, A., Dalhammar, C.: The emerging 'right to repair' legislation in the EU and the U ... - lu (2018). https://lucris.lub.lu.se/ws/portalfiles/portal/63585584/Svensson_et_al._Going_Green_CARE_INNOVATION_2018_PREP RINT.pdf
22. Svensson-Hoglund, S., Richter, J.L., Maitre-Ekern, E., Russell, J.D., Pihlajarinne, T., Dalhammar, C.: Barriers, enablers and market governance: a review of the policy landscape for repair of consumer electronics in the EU and the U.S. J. Clean. Prod. **288**, 125488 (2021)

Exploring Opportunities from the More-than-Human Perspective for Investigating Wicked Problem in Our Entangled World

Risa Kimura[✉] and Tatsuo Nakajima

Department of Computer Science and Engineering, Waseda University, Tokyo, Japan
{risa.kimura,tatsuo}@dcl.cs.waseda.ac.jp

Abstract. This paper emphasizes the significance of embracing the more-than-human perspective, which goes beyond conventional human-centered design approaches and offers a foundation for innovative design methodologies. We will delve into the fundamental concepts underpinning the more-than-human perspective, elucidating its core principles. Following this, we will present recommendations on integrating this perspective into distinct design methodologies, fostering a comprehensive and inclusive approach to design. Furthermore, the paper will illuminate the practical implications of adopting the more-than-human perspective through three detailed case studies. These case studies will serve as practical illustrations of how this perspective can influence the design process, unlock novel design possibilities, and contribute to the development of innovative solutions. By delving into these real-world scenarios, we aim to showcase the tangible benefits and transformative potential of the more-than-human perspective in the realm of design.

Keyword: Entanglement · More-than-Human · Posthuman · Hybrid · Affordance · Ontological Turn · Practice Theory · Generative AI

1 Hybrid and Entangled World

In recent years, the design field has witnessed a growing interest in shifting away from the traditional human-centric approach, ushering in a more inclusive design paradigm referred to as More-Than-Human Design (MTHD) [9, 14, 30, 35] for investigating a variety of wicked problems in our entangled world. The term" entangled world" refers to the interconnectedness and interdependence of various elements and phenomena in the contemporary global context. It suggests that different aspects of our world—such as technology, economies, cultures, societies, and the environment—are deeply intertwined and influence each other in complex ways. This interconnectedness can be observed on various levels, including social, economic, political, and environmental dimensions. Design researchers and practitioners are actively exploring collaborative design methods and strategies that encompass not only humans but also objects, animals, and robots as integral constituents of the design process. MTHD research finds strong resonance with postpluralist ideologies, including actor-network theory, philosophy of science, and the critical intersection with posthuman concepts [14]. In the domain of human technology hybrid design, researchers are proactively forging their distinct approaches and methodologies, finely tailored to the realm of design. This paradigm shift reflects an evolving landscape in design thinking, where the boundaries of design expand to accommodate a richer and more diverse set of actors in the design process.

The burgeoning MTHD approach in the design domain exhibits two notable trends. One of these trends is rooted in the growing environmental crisis, which has led scientists to reevaluate the concept of human dominance over other species [8, 12, 32]. Design methodologies focused on sustainability are moving away from presumptions of one species' superiority over another, and instead, they are exploring alternatives that promote the overall well-being of the ecosystem. Some proponents suggest that MTHD theory could serve as a valuable framework for reevaluating global human-nonhuman interactions during the "Anthropocene" epoch, transcending the reliance on human-centric criteria [5].

Another significant trend is related to the evolving concept of what defines a product. A crucial driver behind this profound shift in the product's definition is the move from static physical objects, as commonly seen in traditional "industrial products" to dynamic and adaptable entities [14, 38]. This transformation has been significantly accelerated by the widespread integration of connectivity, machine learning, and artificial intelligence into our daily lives. The emergence of new sensing technologies and advanced data processing capabilities has enabled products to undergo substantial evolution, moving beyond their previous roles as passive objects to become active agents that influence relationships and interactions with individuals [35]. This change in concept and ontology prompts a reevaluation of the boundaries between humans and technology.

For instance, domains like virtual reality, social robotics, digital assistants, and neuroimplants challenge the conventional boundary between humans and machines, raising questions about the essence of humanity versus technology. Furthermore, this transition emphasizes the relational nature of design, positioning intelligence not as an inherent trait of machines or humans, but as an emergent property arising from their interactions [36, 40]. Designers must now shift their focus away from the traditional singular user or product to encompass multifaceted considerations involving various products, services, stakeholders, and their intricate interplay. This shift presents a challenge to the established paradigm of human-centered design [9, 14, 16, 32]. Together, these elements suggest the potential for a paradigm shift in Human-Computer Interaction (HCI), marking the advent of the third wave of HCI [4]. However, it's important to note that the HCI and design discourse on MTHD is still in its early stages [14].

This paper focuses on the "more-than-human" perspective, departing from conventional human-centered design paradigms to encompass nonhuman elements. Its purpose is to introduce the foundational concepts that underpin this perspective and explore the potential for innovative design methodologies it offers. Additionally, it delves into how the more-than-human perspective can impact design through the lens of three case studies. It's clear that this emerging perspective, in contrast to the traditional human-centered design approach, provides a spectrum of viewpoints and the potential to unlock new possibilities.

2 Research Background

2.1 Agential Realism and Entanglement

Agential realism is a theoretical approach rooted in the entanglement theory of physics, conceptualizing the close interconnection of matter and meaning, as well as human beings and the environment. Proposed by physicist and philosopher Karen Barad and extensively detailed in her primary work, "Meeting the Universe Halfway: Quantum Physics and the Entanglement of Matter and Meaning" [3], the theory employs the notion of agential cuts to underscore the process of segregating material agency and situating it within specific relationships and states.

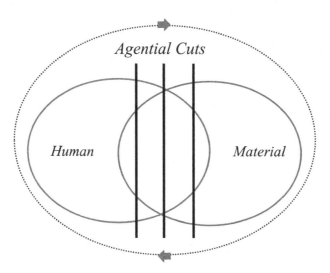

Fig. 1. Agential Realism and Agential Cuts

Agential realism introduces the concept of "intra-action" to emphasize that entities (both human and nonhuman) do not preexist their interactions but rather emerge through those interactions. This challenges traditional notions of interaction and causality. Intra-action underscores the entanglement of different elements and the continuous process of becoming through their relations. Also, agential realism stresses the agency of both human and nonhuman actors. It recognizes that material entities, such as technologies and objects, play an active role in shaping social practices. The material world is not passive but actively participates in the constitution of reality.

As illustrated in Fig. 1, agential cuts reject the dichotomy between material and meaning, defining agency interactions with precision. This process is arbitrary, allowing researchers and observers to opt for different cuts. The flexibility and richness of agential realism emerge from these various cuts, generating diverse understandings and interpretations. In this theory, the separation facilitated by agential cuts signifies an inseparable interrelationship between the observer and the observed. Implicit in the observer's analysis of the object is the notion that the observer is intricately intertwined with the object. This introduces a novel theoretical approach to the intricate interactions of matter and humanity, meaning and the environment, fostering a comprehensive understanding of the entangled phenomenon.

2.2 Actor Network Theory

Latour criticizes the concept of "social explanations" rooted in the binary division of society and the individual, which is prevalent in traditional sociology and, in his view, overly simplistic and homogenous [31]. He labels this as the "sociology of society." In contrast, Latour advocates for a "sociology of relations," a perspective that emphasizes the intricate and unpredictable interactions among actors in everyday practices, where individual "actor" entities play essential roles in reshaping various aspects of the world [31]. In this framework, "society" is no longer the central focus of analysis; instead, attention shifts to the connections between actors and the dynamic processes through which these connections undergo transformation.

From this perspective, Actor-Network Theory (ANT) provides a unique analytical approach compared to traditional HCI methodologies. ANT places its emphasis on the interrelated and inseparable nature of various actors, including humans, objects, social factors, and technology. Services, in essence, emerge as hybrid networks composed of these human, object, social, and technological elements, requiring their consideration as a unified entity. Changes in one actor are understood to have an impact on the entire network. Therefore, when exploring the meaning of services concerning the affordances provided by these hybrid networks, it's inadequate to focus solely on human actors. It is essential to reevaluate the dynamic behaviors of stakeholders from a perspective that encompasses both humans and their associated actors. This opens up new interpretations that diverge from traditional research and provide insights into novel understandings that take into account the influence of nonhuman actors.

ANT conceives social phenomena as intricate networks involving a diverse array of actors. It adopts a relational perspective in which every actor, be it human, natural object, artifact, or any other element, is intricately interconnected, forming an inseparable network [7]. The actor-network is a concept that not only encompasses human connections but also signifies a condition in which various actors, including humans, objects, society, technology, and nature, are interlinked and function as indivisible entities. Each actor is accorded equal status as a constituent of this network. Latour further characterizes ANT as a "sociology of translation," asserting that there are no notions of society, social domains, or social bonds. The essence of ANT lies in tracing the translation activities undertaken by the actors that constitute the network.

Despite their distinct theoretical origins, both agential realism and ANT share a common emphasis on relationships and interactions for attacking a variety of wicked problems in our entangled world. They diverge from reductionist perspectives and recognize the intricate connections within systems. While agential realism underscores entangle-ment and the inseparability of the observer and the observed, ANT focuses on networks of relations among various actors. The interplay of these perspectives enriches our com-prehension of complex phenomena. Therefore, agential realism and ANT contribute to a nuanced understanding of complex systems, each providing unique insights into the relational nature of phenomena while stemming from different academic disciplines.

2.3 Posthuman and Speculative Realism

Contemporary developments in posthumanism focus on the interaction between humans and technology, exploring key themes that leverage cutting-edge technologies such as vir-tual reality (VR) and augmented reality (AR). These technologies aim to enhance human capabilities and perceptions, create new realities, and transcend physical constraints [5, 13, 18, 19].

The ontological shift represents a significant advancement in posthumanism, moving beyond the limits of anthropocentrism to emphasize the status and agency of nonhuman entities [21]. This includes exploring the complex relationships with nonhuman ele-ments, like animals, technology, and the environment, and examining their impact on the shaping of society. Ethical perspectives are also under scrutiny, encompassing rela-tionships with animals, the use of artificial intelligence (AI) and autonomous technology, and environmental consequences—all while taking into account the needs and interests of nonhuman entities.

Furthermore, contemporary posthumanism focuses on the human body and physical-ity, as well as the integration of humans and technology facilitated by advances in biotech-nology, wearable devices, and human-machine interfaces. Environmental posthumanism emphasizes the interconnectedness of humans and the environment, breaking down the traditional human-nature binary. In this context, research explores the ecological impact of human activities and their interplay with the environment.

Lastly, posthumanism explores scenarios in which the boundary between human and nonhuman existence becomes blurred, along with considerations about future existence and intelligence. These discussions are of paramount importance in the context of ethical implications and challenges associated with technological interactions. Recent trends in posthumanism bring forth new perspectives on human-technology interactions, and we are deeply concerned about their far-reaching implications.

Speculative Realism encompasses a collection of philosophical movements within contemporary philosophy that challenge conventional philosophical paradigms [20]. A fundamental characteristic of this philosophical wave is its critical departure from estab-lished anthropocentrism and subjectivism. Speculative realist philosophers emphasize the existence not only of human beings but also of matter, nature, and the universe. They argue that these entities possess autonomy and significance.

The connection between speculative ontology and posthumanism can be elucidated through the following pivotal points. Firstly, in their exploration of concepts, both engage in imaginative and creative conceptual investigations, encouraging us to contemplate novel facets of reality. Speculative ontology delves deeply into the nature of reality, whereas posthumanism encourages us to envision future possibilities among diverse entities, transcending our current understanding.

Secondly, in their efforts to dismantle anthropocentrism, both challenge conventional anthropocentric viewpoints. Instead, they offer more inclusive perspectives that recognize the subjectivity and significance of nonhuman entities. Additionally, within their ethical considerations, both frameworks incorporate ethical concerns. Speculative ontology scrutinizes the ethical ramifications of hypothetical scenarios, while posthumanism centers on ethical issues like human augmentation and environmental impact.

Finally, in relation to speculative posthuman futures, speculative ontology and posthumanism share a mutual interest in the future. Speculative ontology explores possibilities that extend beyond the traditional human condition, whereas posthumanism contemplates a future shaped by technological, ecological, and social transformations. In summary, speculative ontology and posthumanism enhance our understanding of reality and existence, prompting us to reconsider our relationship with the world and the uncharted possibilities that lie ahead.

2.4 Anthropology and Ontological Turn

The ontological turn in anthropology signifies a significant paradigm shift that unfolded in the early 21st century, representing an effort to question conventional methodologies and reevaluate the nature of human existence and social realities [15, 21]. Unlike earlier approaches that focused on external observations and analyses of culture and society, the ontological turn adopts a distinct viewpoint, centered on the multifaceted and intricate ways in which individuals perceive and engage with their own world [10, 24, 30].

The ontological turn in anthropology exhibits several distinctive features:

1. Recognition of Diverse Ontologies: This shift acknowledges that various cultures and social groups hold distinct ontological perspectives. It challenges the assumption of a single, universal reality and underscores the coexistence of multiple ontological viewpoints. Anthropologists embracing the ontological turn value and respect these differing beliefs, striving to comprehend the various realities they entail.
2. Relational Nature of Existence: This paradigm shift examines the interrelationships between humans and nonhuman entities. It challenges anthropocentric Cartesian dualism, emphasizing the interconnectedness and interdependence of all beings.
3. Reevaluation of Subjectivity: The ontological turn reevaluates conventional notions of subjectivity and personality. It questions the assumption that only humans possess subjectivity and influence over social and natural phenomena. Instead, it offers a fresh perspective on the constituent elements that constitute personhood.

Indeed, the ontological shift in anthropology signifies a fundamental change in perspective. It highlights the significance of comprehending and honoring diverse ontological convictions and the intricate interplay between humans and their surroundings. Through an inclusive and participatory approach, anthropologists aim to cultivate a deeper appreciation of the intricacies inherent in human existence and social reality. This paradigm shift not only enriches the field of anthropology but also makes meaningful contributions to wider discussions on cultural diversity, indigenous rights, environmental conservation, and various other pertinent topics.

2.5 Affordance and Thoughtless Act

Suri's concepts of the "Thoughtless Act" and "affordance" hold significance in comprehending human interactions with their environment within the realm of design [45]. "Thoughtless Act", as articulated by Suri, pertains to those minor actions that individuals perform in their everyday lives without conscious deliberation. These actions typically arise from what are known as "affordances" embedded in familiar situations and environments. The notion of "affordance" was originally introduced by Gibson [17] and refers to the inherent potential behaviors and interaction opportunities that an object or environment offers based on its physical attributes and human capabilities. For instance, a chair affords sitting, a doorknob affords turning, and a touchscreen affords tapping. These concepts shed light on how individuals instinctively and intuitively respond to their surroundings, guided by their perception of these affordances. From a design perspective, comprehending these subconscious human behaviors can lead to the creation of more effective designs. By taking into account the affordances presented by design elements, designers are better equipped to deliver intuitive and user-friendly experiences.

Individuals frequently perceive affordances, a phenomenon driven by their adaptive capacity shaped by previous experiences and the contextual factors in their surroundings. This perceptual process often results in actions performed instinctively, with individuals responding in accordance with their perceived affordances. Consequently, unconscious actions influenced by affordances play a pivotal role in how we navigate objects and spaces, fostering innovative approaches and novel uses. When affordances are transparent and intuitive, individuals are more inclined to experiment with diverse methods and explore innovative ideas. The comprehension of unconscious behavior and affordances carries immense significance in user-centered design. Designers endeavor to ensure that design elements align with people's inherent inclinations, facilitating users to engage in an intuitive experience with minimal cognitive load. In essence, the concepts of "unthinking action" and "affordance" constitute fundamental aspects in comprehending people's subconscious behaviors and interactions with their environment within the realm of design, ultimately contributing to the attainment of more effective design solutions.

2.6 Safety-I and Safety-II

In a context distinct from anthropology, a parallel trend is emerging, centering around discussions related to the ontological shift. Safety-II, an approach to safety endorsed by prominent international human factors authorities like Hollnagel, places its focus on adaptive flexibility to ensure and enhance safety, in contrast to the traditional Safety-I approach that primarily seeks to eliminate human error [22]. Human error, viewed as a root cause of accidents, is defined as "human actions leading to unintended consequences," and the conventional approach has revolved around the minimization of human error to ensure safety. This involves preventing "deviations from predefined and correct procedures" while emphasizing the enhancement of human reliability. Crucially, the safety of a technical system hinges on its proper functioning. Systems that operate flawlessly contribute to safety, while those that malfunction are prone to accidents. This concept extends its applicability to both physical systems and business processes. In the pursuit of safety, enhancing human reliability becomes imperative, with the ultimate goal of reducing the incidence of human error to nearly zero.

Safety-I primarily approaches safety from a technical standpoint, operating under the premise that accidents can be averted by correct system operation. Nevertheless, Safety-I, on its own, may not offer a comprehensive solution for accident prevention within complex social and natural settings. In contrast, Safety-II places a strong emphasis on adapting to varying situations and circumstances, aiming to secure safety by enhancing human reliability. Referred to as resilience, this approach underscores the enhancement of coordination competencies. Safety-II represents a reevaluation of the conventional safety paradigm, aligning it with the requirements of contemporary society. The term "resilience" finds applications across diverse fields, encompassing biology, ecology, and psychology, and underscores the capacity for adaptability and robustness. In the context of Safety-II, the goal is to optimize the resilience of the system, requiring a focus on management responsibilities as a pivotal component of the approach.

3 More-than-Human Perspectives and Postpluralism

3.1 Superhuman

The connection between the concept of "superhumans" and technology is multifaceted. Generally, "superhumans" surpass the conventional duality of nature and society, possessing extraordinary capabilities that exceed those of typical individuals. Technology serves as a facilitator or amplifier for these superhuman capacities.

1. Human Augmentation: Technology provides the tools to enhance physical capabilities. Artificial limbs, exoskeletons, brain-computer interfaces, and similar devices have the potential to significantly improve the abilities of individuals with physical disabilities, elevating them to superhuman levels.
2. Artificial Intelligence and Cognitive Enhancement: Cutting-edge artificial intelligence can perform complex tasks at high speeds and sometimes exhibit cognitive abilities that exceed those of humans. Machine learning and natural language processing have the potential to enhance human cognition and improve decision-making processes.
3. Biohacking and Transhumanism: Through genetic engineering and nanotechnology, biohacking aims to enhance both the body and the mind, potentially paving the way for the development of superhuman attributes.
4. Cybernetics and Cyborgs: The convergence of humans and machines through cybernetics has the potential to create cyborgs and amplify human capabilities. For example, brain-computer interfaces can enhance cognition and memory.
5. Blurred Boundaries: The interaction between technology and superhuman enhancements blurs the lines between humans and machines, prompting profound philosophical inquiries. This intersection gives rise to profound questions about the essence of humanity and individual identity.

Technology plays a pivotal role in shaping and redefining the concept of "superhuman." However, it is of paramount importance to adopt a balanced approach that considers ethical considerations and social repercussions.

3.2 Hybrids and Boundary Objects

The connection between ANT and hybrids plays a fundamental role in understanding the complexities of the social domain. ANT challenges traditional social theories by presenting a network-centric perspective in which various actors, including both human and nonhuman elements, influence each other. Hybridity, a conceptual framework, explains how diverse actors come together within the network to create new entities or assemblages. According to the ANT paradigm, actors encompass not only humans but also any conceivable entities, such as animals, technology, institutions, ideas, and natural forces. These actors interconnect to form networks that are in a constant state of change. ANT assigns equal importance to all actors and views agency as dispersed and dependent on relationships.

Hybrids are essentially products or combinations that emerge as a result of diverse actors influencing each other, creating new connections and interdependencies. They serve as evidence of the fresh meanings and capabilities that result from these intricate interactions among actors. Hybrids can take on either stable or transient forms, depending on how these interconnected actors come together. The primary purpose of hybrids is to provide a framework for understanding how different actors connect, interact, and shape the social landscape. This concept of hybrids is invaluable for understanding the complexities of organizational restructuring, transformation, and societal evolution. In essence, actor-network theory introduces a novel approach that enables a comprehensive understanding of the vast diversity and complexity inherent in the real world.

Boundary objects are a pivotal concept in sociology and in the realm of scientific and technological research, where they serve various roles across different communities. These objects represent flexible units of information and data, open to different interpretations within diverse communities. However, beneath this diversity, they encapsulate a core identity or content that remains consistent. The concept of boundary objects was first introduced in 1989 by Star and her colleagues [43]. These objects play a vital role in fostering adaptability and resilience among various stakeholders working collaboratively. While they assume varied meanings across disparate social contexts, they share a common underlying structure. As such, they function as a medium for facilitating information recognition and translation between distinct communities.

The concept of boundary objects is widely accepted and applicable across a range of fields, including computer science, informatics, and management. Their adaptability allows them to meet the diverse requirements of different organizations and communities, serving as a medium for effective collaboration on shared tasks. Boundary objects play a significant role by having the ability to reconcile localized understandings among various actors and coordinate them, even in the absence of complete consensus. Furthermore, the concept of boundary objects has expanded and has been applied to facilitate cooperation between disparate communities and domains. They influence the meaning-making process, especially in interdisciplinary and cross-cultural communication, harnessing the potential of digital technologies to enable users to customize boundary objects to their specific needs.

3.3 Co-performance and Practice Theory

Co-performance aims to provide researchers and practitioners of HCI with a new perspective on the role of artificial agency in everyday life [29]. Co-performance is developed based on the practice theory [37, 41] and make the design focus from the issue of agency distribution during design to the issue of embodied learning of both human and artificial performers in everyday practice. The perspective recognizes the dynamic differences between human and artificial capabilities and emphasizes the fundamentally inverse relationship between professional design and use.

Agency in the practice theory refers to the ability or capacity to act that is demonstrated through the performance of a practice. According to Schatzki, agency is classified into two types: causal and performance [41]. Causal agency relates to making something happen or helping it happen, while performance agency is the performance of an action in a particular situation, while at the same time continuing the practice of which it is a part. The performance of a practice tied to an entity as a social practice is a socially shared idea of appropriate practice and persists across time and space. Social practice consists of the sum of its performances, each performance representing a reinterpretation of appropriate behavior in a situation. Performance is an important factor in shaping and changing social practice.

Social practices are ideas of appropriate forms of shared and materially embedded action. These are not abstract entities, but concrete knowledge and know-how as "body/mind" [37]. The concept of co-performance applies this to both humans and artifacts, emphasizing that changes in social practice involve concrete learning. In line with repeated performances and altered bodies/minds, ideas of appropriate practices are embodied and changed in the bodies/minds of both humans and artifacts. In other words, what is considered appropriate is adaptive in context and changes over time, but from a design perspective, the collaboration will focus on the changing division of roles and responsibilities between human and artifact body/mind and envision appropriate interactions between them. The co-performance integrates all the elements mentioned by Reckwitz [37] in the situation and integrate them into the embodiment of the practice in a way that makes sense and also summarized by Shove et al. as meanings, materials, and competences [42]. In this way, the social practice is jointly formed by the human and the artifact.

This approach is consistent with the idea of interaction and reciprocity between nonhuman actions and human objectives in HCI, but focuses on the level of social practice rather than interaction, and on the passage of time rather than just specific actions, which offers a new perspective on recursive relationships from a design perspective. Co-performance requires that design must follow at the time of use, and at the time of design involves the embodiment of ideas about specific appropriate performances, and in interaction with the human performer, the artificial performer's embodied tendencies may lead to "appropriate" performances and inhibit others. Important in this interaction are the differences between human and artificial body/mind and how these can be capitalized both during design and during use.

3.4 Invisible Things and Affordance

Smart cities are initiatives aimed at addressing a variety of local challenges through the deployment of cutting-edge technologies to improve urban and regional functions and services [1, 48]. This effort promises increased comfort and added value. By systematically monitoring various aspects within a city and leveraging computer software, processes can be automated, and resources can be used more efficiently. Smart cities have now become a focal point not only for the research community but also for businesses and policymakers alike. However, the distinction between smart cities and digital transformation (DX) has become increasingly blurred, complicating understanding for those involved in these domains. To address these complex issues, adopting an affordance perspective offers a valuable approach. This perspective is well-suited for designing and analyzing multifaceted platforms like smart cities. Smart cities use technology to visualize aspects of urban life that remain imperceptible to the naked eye, enabling them to adapt services in real-time to current conditions. Moreover, these visual representations of various urban phenomena empower citizens to lead comfortable lives while remaining aware of potential urban challenges. However, as exemplified in works like "Hyper-Reality," we must exercise caution, as an excessive provision of affordances can inadvertently transform society into a dystopian reality [34]. It's worth noting that visualizing the imperceptible may lead to particular interpretations influenced by the designer's intentions [46]. Thus, careful attention is imperative when designing visually presented affordances.

As mentioned earlier, the concept of affordance pertains to the potential actions and utility offered by a specific environment or object, often shaped by concealed attributes and elements. This concept is a focal point in the realms of cognitive science and epistemology, closely entwined with imperceptible elements. It encompasses the range of actions and uses implied by an object's or environment's characteristics, including not only those attributes readily discernible by sight but also the hidden elements that influence these affordances. For instance, consider a doorknob as part of an object, facilitating the affordance of turning. In this instance, the action of turning, though invisible in itself, holds paramount significance. Affordances associated with an environment or object may extend to include attributes or information not visible to the eye. For example, stairs provide affordances for ascending and descending, yet they are influenced by factors that evade visual detection, such as step height and the presence of handrails. These concealed attributes assist individuals in their actions and decision-making when using stairs. In the realm of technology and systems, invisible elements can similarly contribute to the formation of affordances. Take, for example, a smartphone's touchscreen, which can detect finger movements and touch pressure, offering corresponding operations and functions. The affordances provided by these touchscreens depend on unseen sensor technology and software features.

In essence, the concepts of affordances and invisible elements share a symbiotic relationship. When we seek to comprehend the spectrum of actions and utilities offered by an object or environment, it is imperative that we consider the presence of these imperceptible elements. Affordances, coupled with the influence of concealed attributes and elements, underpin human actions and decisions, enabling individuals to effectively engage with objects and surroundings. These perspectives hold particular significance in the context of comprehending postpluralism, where the intricate interplay between nature and society unfolds in multifaceted ways.

3.5 Postphenomenology and Multistability

Postphenomenology is a philosophical framework firmly grounded in the tradition of phenomenology [23, 39]. It seeks to uphold the core tenets of phenomenology while engaging in an extensive examination of the profound impact of technology on human experience and perception. Here is a brief overview of some of the central principles of postphenomenology:

1. Technological Mediation: Postphenomenology places significant emphasis on the role of technology as a vital medium through which we interact with the external world and with each other. It delves into the diverse forms of technology, encompassing smartphones, medical devices, and more, to investigate how they influence our perception, cognition, and physical bodies.
2. Embodiment and Perception: Postphenomenologists delve into the intricate relationship between technology and our bodies, as well as how it molds our perceptions. This inquiry extends to examining how technology enhances our sensory experiences, such as through the use of hearing aids and virtual reality goggles.
3. Human-Technology Relationship: Postphenomenology scrutinizes the intricate relationship between humans and technology, underscoring that technology is not merely a tool but an active entity that shapes our experiences and perspectives.

In addition, the concept of "multistability" holds significance in postphenomenology. It pertains to the idea that technology can provide multiple distinct yet stable interpretations or perceptions of the same phenomenon. This concept gains particular relevance in the realm of postphenomenology, which posits that technology introduces a multitude of perspectives into our perceptions. Postphenomenology provides a philosophical framework for comprehending this diversity and intricacy inherent to technology.

Postphenomenology departs from the standpoint that technology actively shapes our worldview and perceptual faculties, and it is far from being a neutral tool. In this context, the diversity introduced by technology implies the potential for a range of stable interpretations and experiences regarding a particular situation or phenomenon. These multiple interpretations can arise from the presence or use of specific technologies, as well as physical alterations. Examples of postphenomenological multiplicity include digital photography and AR. In the realm of digital photography, for instance, the same photograph can assume distinct interpretations and meanings through editing and the application of filters. Consequently, technology introduces a sense of multiplicity into the perception of a photograph. Conversely, AR overlays digital information onto the physical environment, creating a scenario where different layers of reality coexist. With AR, we simultaneously perceive both reality and digital information, thereby infusing multiplicity into our perception. In this philosophical context, postphenomenology's notion of multiplicity challenges the idea of a single, objective reality and suggests that our experiences are significantly shaped by the technology we engage with. Furthermore, it's essential to recognize that different technologies yield varying interpretations and experiences of the same phenomenon. Postphenomenologists use the concept of multistability to examine how technology mediates our experiences and how divergent technologies give rise to diverse interpretations of reality.

4 Case Studies

4.1 Overview

By integrating the more-than-human perspective, this study delves into three case studies within the philosophical framework of three distinct concepts: postpluralistic ontology, affordance, and, notably, a hybrid perspective.

Postpluralistic ontology represents a philosophical perspective that extends beyond the conventional singular and monistic interpretation of reality. Within this framework, it acknowledges the existence of diverse forms of reality and modes of existence. Postpluralist ontology rejects the notion of a solitary, unified reality, recognizing instead a multitude of distinct levels or modes of existence. These encompass physical, spiritual, social, cultural, and various other dimensions. This ontology underscores the coexistence and interplay among these diverse ontologies, unveiling the intricate nature of reality. It challenges the concept of a solitary, objective reality, opting instead for the recognition of multiple, interwoven realities.

The concept of affordances, as introduced in Sect. 2, is predominantly utilized within cognitive science and ecopsychology to elucidate the possibilities for action and interaction presented by environments and objects to individuals. It posits that environments and objects possess distinct properties and characteristics, shaping how individuals can utilize and engage with them. Affordances are intricately linked to an individual's capabilities, intentions, and perceptions. Recognizing these affordances aids individuals in understanding and discerning their surroundings, enabling them to take action and navigate within them effectively. The significance of postpluralistic ontology and affordance lies in their collective contribution to comprehending the dynamic and multifaceted nature of reality, perception, and interaction. Particularly within the context of postpluralistic ontology, the concept of affordance extends beyond physical attributes, encompassing various ontologies and forms of existence. Affordance is not confined to the physical realm but extends to encompass spiritual, social, and cultural dimensions. Consequently, individuals perceive affordances through their interactions with these diverse ontologies and forms of existence. In a world where multiple ontological layers and realities coexist, it becomes evident that a single object or phenomenon can present several different affordances. Individuals or groups, influenced by distinct ontological perspectives, may discern diverse affordances for the same object or situation. This underscores the intricate interplay between postpluralistic ontology and the concept of affordances.

The coexistence of multiple ontologies and affordances underscores the intricate nature of human-environment interactions. Postpluralistic ontology challenges the notion of a singular, objective reality, while the concept of affordance acknowledges the pivotal role of perception and action in shaping our experiences within these multifarious realities. Both postpluralistic ontology and the concept of affordance share a common emphasis on the diversity of existence and the various ways individuals perceive and engage with their surroundings. By comprehending and applying the concept of affordance within the framework of postpluralistic ontology, we gain insights into how diverse ontological perspectives shape the perception of affordance within a complex and interdependent world. This approach allows us to explore the profound influence of different ontological viewpoints on our interactions with the environment, enriching our understanding of the multifaceted nature of reality.

4.2   Collective Sharing Human Eyes and Ears

The initial case study revolves around a digital platform designed to aggregate a diverse array of perspectives and viewpoints contributed by individuals worldwide. These individual viewpoints, or listening points, are then digitized, as illustrated in Fig. 2, and replicated within a virtual environment for further data processing. The ultimate objective is to reassemble these gathered perspectives and listening points into innovative hybrid entities, which are subsequently presented in the physical world. The overarching goal of this endeavor is to prompt users to recognize the richness of global diversity and broaden their horizons.

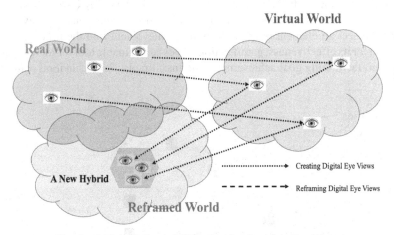

Fig. 2. A Hybrid Created by Reframing People's Eye Views

The existing design of CollectiveEyes [26] and CollectiveEars [27] has not placed significant emphasis on hybrid viewpoints. Nevertheless, there is an opportunity to broaden the range of applications that digital platforms can offer by taking into account the context of the contributors of these viewpoints and listening points. In a more advanced iteration introduced in [28], known as Posthuman CollectiveEyes, the platform leverages the contextual information of the individuals from whom these viewpoints and listening points are collected. This opens up new potential use cases, essentially suggesting the expansion of possibilities by treating viewpoints and listening points as hybrid entities and constructing networks centered around them.

These examples revolve around the affordances associated with two distinct hybrids. The first hybrid concerns the affordances of viewpoints and listening points contributed by individuals. In the initial iterations of CollectiveEyes and CollectiveEars, the networks supporting these hybrids were simplified, primarily relying on context-independent viewpoints and listening points. However, subsequent enhancements delve deeper into the network of viewpoints and listening points, considering the affordances of this hybrid in various contexts. The second hybrid focuses on the affordances generated by the amalgamation of collected viewpoints and listening points. The affordances of this hybrid enable the synthesis of multiple viewpoints, facilitating the construction of meaning for the user. For instance, by presenting the user with perspectives from diverse angles of their current location, this amalgamated hybrid of multiple viewpoints can offer a multifaceted understanding of that particular place.

4.3   Gamification Design from a Hybrids' Perspective

Gamification is a strategy used to enhance user motivation and engagement by incorporating elements and principles commonly found in games into non-game environments [11]. Its application spans diverse domains, including education, business, healthcare, and marketing, among others. The primary goal of gamification is to encourage task completion and promote behavioral changes. This is achieved by introducing various components such as points, badges, rankings, competitions, missions, and rewards, all designed to inject an element of enjoyment and achievement into the user experience. Recognized for its effectiveness, gamification serves as a valuable tool for increasing user engagement, facilitating goal achievement, and instilling lasting behavioral patterns.

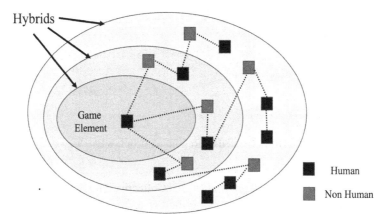

Fig. 3. Hybrids in a Gamified Service

Traditional gamification approaches have primarily focused on using game elements to enhance user motivation. In contrast, this second case study explores the affordances provided by hybrids, which consist of a combination of game elements, human elements, and nonhuman elements, while also considering the intricate interplay between these components. As depicted in Fig. 3, the innermost hybrid consists solely of game elements. The subsequent layers of hybrids include both human and nonhuman elements, directly interacting with game elements, and they create affordances through their inter-connected relationships. The outermost hybrid encompasses not only the human and nonhuman elements directly involved but also those indirectly connected to the process. Through an analysis of these distinct hybrids, we aim to understand the diverse impacts of various hybrid layers on user motivation. Specifically, as the network of relevant human and nonhuman elements within a service becomes more intricate, multiple hybrids that incorporate the same game elements can emerge. In such cases, friction between these hybrids can lead to complex shifts in user motivation. By shifting the focus toward hybrids, this case study provides fresh insights into the design of complex gamification services that cannot be adequately addressed through traditional human-centered design methodologies.

4.4   Paragraphica: An AI-Enhanced Context-to-Image Camera

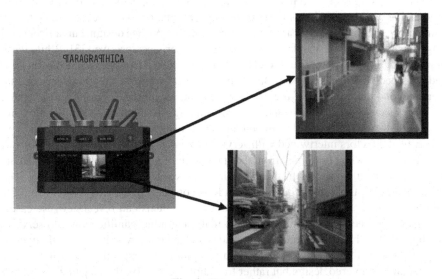

Fig. 4. Paragraphica

The third and final case study is Paragraphica, developed by Karmann[1]. Paragraphica is a context-to-image camera that employs location and artificial intelligence technology to generate visual representations of specific places and moments. These cameras exist in both physical prototype and virtual forms, which can be experimented with. Figure 4 showcases a screenshot of the virtual camera in action. The viewfinder provides real-time descriptions of the current location, and by pressing a trigger, the camera produces a scintigraphic depiction of that description. The camera features three physical dials that govern data and AI parameters, influencing the appearance of the image, much like conventional cameras. It operates by utilizing an open API to gather data from location-related information, incorporating details such as the address, weather, time of day,

---

[1] https://bjoernkarmann.dk/project/paragraphica.

and nearby surroundings. Paragraphica amalgamates all these data points to generate prompts that elaborate on the current location and moment. Using text-to-image AI, the camera transforms these prompts into "photos". The resulting "photo" is more than just a snapshot; it serves as a visual data point and a reflection of the specific location and, to some extent, how the AI model perceives the location.

In this case study, the hybrid consists of a reality generated by a generative AI. The resulting virtual reality successfully creates a compelling experience by maintaining a unique connection with the real world. The question of whether the world is made up of distinct entities or interconnected relationships has been a topic of philosophical and scientific debate for centuries. Paragraphica suggests that both perspectives hold merit and can offer valuable insights into the nature of reality.

4.5 Discussion

Design methodologies rooted in the more-than-human perspective empower us to transcend and expand our horizons beyond the conventional dualism that separates nature from society and aligns with postpluralism. In traditional service design, human-centered design has long been the standard, prioritizing the user's perspective [33]. While these conventional design approaches excel at improving user-friendliness and meeting the needs of specific users, they may fall short when it comes to creating services that extend beyond the confines of the user's viewpoint. Moreover, focusing solely on the user's perspective proves inadequate for considering the numerous complexities and contexts that extend beyond the immediate scope of the user, such as economic and environmental factors intertwined with service provision.

Affordances, when examined from the standpoint of postpluralism, provide insights into the complexities arising from interactions between individuals and society. The first case study in this section demonstrates how considering hybrids formed from the multifaceted viewpoints and listening points of individuals can reveal new use cases. Conversely, the second case study suggests that integrating gamification into services and aligning it with the affordances of hybrids can lead to more suitable and thoughtful designs. As a result, MTHD, grounded in a postpluralist perspective, does not aim to replace human-centered design but rather to complement it. It offers a path to explore a broader range of possibilities and address a wider spectrum of challenges.

The next crucial aspect to consider is the inherent nature of meaning as conveyed by affordances. In the field of computer science, various approaches attempt to articulate the meaning of a program, employing methods such as operational, axiomatic, and representational semantics [47]. These methodologies aim to provide an explicit definition of a program's meaning through mathematical or similar frameworks. In this context, it's essential to view the meaning of affordances as a structural entity. When multiple affordances share a common underlying structure, the possibility arises to abstractly encapsulate these affordances and assign them a universal significance. For example, [28] outlines the affordances of a digital platform as abstract entities provided by the platform. Similarly, [25] elucidates the essence of affordances by naming those offered by digital artifacts as "virtual forms" and imbuing them with a structured framework of value and rhetoric. Hence, in future endeavors, it becomes pivotal to deliberate on the appropriate structure for the discourse surrounding affordances in this specific case study.

An essential dilemma arising in these considerations concerns how to address the scale of the hybrid. As Strathern astutely notes, real-world hybrids encompass networks of infinite dimensions. However, contemplating an infinite network is inherently impractical [44]. Therefore, it becomes imperative to deliberate on the network's boundaries and establish a specific cutoff point. In contrast to conventional human-centered design methodologies, which often employ exceedingly brief network cutoffs for the sake of simplicity in analysis, neglecting the existence of hybrids, this paper argues that we should extend our considerations to include longer-than-usual network cutoffs. This extended perspective is vital, especially in scenarios involving interactions among diverse human and nonhuman elements. Debates about the appropriate length of network cutoffs are currently ongoing, and we plan to explore suitable methods for defining these cutoffs in future studies, informed by various case studies involving networks of varying lengths.

5 Conclusion

The more-than-human perspective represents a departure from traditional human-centered design, with the potential to inject diversity and innovation into the design process. In the future, we anticipate the integration of this perspective into both research and practical applications to advance sustainable design and foster novel innovations. A crucial aspect of future research involves making comparisons. Typically, quantitative comparisons use statistical methods. However, when the objective of the comparison is not to determine superiority but to gain fresh insights and perspectives, traditional vertical comparisons based on scientific methods may not be suitable. Instead, it is essential to approach comparisons by starting with the unique elements being compared. To facilitate these comparisons, one typically identifies common structures or abstract elements and then proceeds to examine the distinctions within those structures. For instance, in [25], the authors explore how values and rhetoric can be applied to the world based on a structured framework known as the Dimension World Model. Nevertheless, when it proves challenging to assume the existence of a common structure, devising meaningful comparisons and extracting insights from differences becomes a complex task. In such scenarios, the more-than-human perspective can introduce novel avenues for comparative analysis.

While traditional technologies like digital transformation (DX) and gamification undoubtedly offer benefits in terms of efficiency and automation, there is an inherent risk associated with overreliance on these tools. Organizations that become overly dependent on such technologies may find themselves becoming rigid and ill-equipped to adapt to the ever-changing landscape [6]. Although algorithms can deliver consistent outcomes and streamline processes, they also have their limitations, including the potential for erroneous decisions stemming from data inaccuracies [2]. Hence, organizations must strike a delicate balance between leveraging algorithms and embracing technology while preserving flexibility. The danger of over-reliance on algorithms is that it can stifle adaptability, jeopardizing an organization's competitive edge and market relevance. In a rapidly evolving business environment, adaptability and flexibility are of paramount importance, as a failure to exhibit these qualities increases the likelihood of an organization falling behind. Therefore, achieving harmony between algorithms and the organization is imperative. Algorithms can undoubtedly enhance efficiency and automation, but concurrently, organizations must safeguard creativity, maintain sound decision-making processes, and uphold flexibility. This task poses a significant challenge, necessitating organizations to adopt a strategic approach to technology adoption. They should leverage the more-than-human perspective to unlock maximum value through human-machine collaboration.

References

1. Allam, Z., Newman, P.: Redefining the smart city: culture, metabolism and governance, smart. Cities **1**(1), 4–25 (2018). https://doi.org/10.3390/smartcities1010002
2. Baer, T.: Understand, Manage, and Prevent Algorithmic Bias: A Guide for Business Users and Data Scientists. Apress (2019)
3. Barad, K.: Meeting the Universe Halfway: Quantum Physics and the Entanglement of Matter and Meaning. Duke University Press (2007)
4. Bødker, S.: Third-wave HCI, 10 years later—participation and sharing 2015. Bowke, G.C., Star, S.L.: Sorting Things Out: Classification and Its Consequences. The MIT Press (2000)
5. Braidotti, R.: Posthuman Knowledge. Polity Press (2021)
6. Bruni, A., Tirabeni, L.: Disentangling digital technologies and power relations in work and organization. TECHOSIENZZA Italian J. Sci. Technol. Stud. **12**(2), 69–78 (2022)
7. Callon, M., Law, J.: After the individual in society: lessons on collectivity from science, technology and society. Can. J. Sociol. **22**(2), 165–182 (1997)
8. Cielemęcka, O., Daigle, C.: Posthuman sustainability: an ethos for our anthropocenic future. Theory Cult. Soc. **36**(7–8), 67–87 (2019)
9. Coulton, P., Lindley, J.G.: More-than human centred design: considering other things. Des. J. **22**(4), 63–81 (2019)
10. Descola, P.: Beyond Nature and Culture. University of Chicago Press (2013)
11. Deterding, S., Dixon, S., Khaled, R., Nacke, L.: From game design elements to gamefulness: defining "gamification". In: Proceedings of the 15th International Academic MindTrek Conference: Envisioning Future Media Environments (MindTrek 2011), pp. 9–15. Association for Computing Machinery, New York (2011). https://doi.org/10.1145/2181037.2181040
12. Elhacham, E., Ben-Uri, L., Grozovski, J., Bar-On, Y.M., Milo, R.: Global human-made mass exceeds all living biomass. Nature **588**(7838), 442–444 (2020)
13. Ferrando, F.: Philosophical Posthumanism. Bloomsbury Academic (2019)
14. Frauenberger, C.: Entanglement HCI the next wave? ACM Trans. Comput.-Hum. Interact. **27**(1), 1–27 (2019)
15. Gad, C.: A postplural attitude reflections on subjectivity and ontology. Nat. Cult. **2**, 50–79 (2013)
16. Giaccardi, E., Redström, J.: Technology and more-than-human design. Des. Issues **36**(4), 33–44 (2020)
17. Gibson, J.: Senses Considered As Perceptual Systems. Praeger Pub Text (1983)
18. Haraway, D.: Simians, Cyborgs, and Women: The Reinvention of Nature. Routledge (1991)
19. Haraway, D.: Staying with the Trouble: Making Kin in the Chthulucene. Duke University Press (2016)
20. Harman, G.: Speculative Realism: An Introduction, Polity (2018)

21. Holbraad, M., Pedersen, M.A.: The Ontological Turn: An Anthropological Exposition. Cambridge University Press (2017)
22. Hollnagel, E.: Safety-I and Safety-II: The Past and Future of Safety Management. CRC Press (2014)
23. Ihde, D.: Experimental Phenomenology, Second Edition: Multistabilities. State University of New York (2012)
24. Ingold, T.: Anthropology and/as Education. Routledge (2017)
25. Kimura, R., Nakajima, T.: Digitally enhancing society through structuralism: virtualizing collective human eyesight and hearing capabilities as a case study. In: Streitz, N., Konomi, S. (eds.) Distributed, Ambient and Pervasive Interactions. HCII 2020. LNCS, vol. 12203, pp. 400–414. Springer, Cham (2020). https://doi.org/10.1007/978-3-030-50344-4_29
26. Kimura, R., Nakajima, T.: Collectively sharing people's visual and auditory capabilities: exploring opportunities and pitfalls. SN Comput. Sci. **1**, 298 (2020). https://doi.org/10.1007/s42979-020-00313-w
27. Kimura, R., Nakajima, T.: A digital platform for sharing collective human hearing. J. Data Intell. **3**(2), 232–251 (2022)
28. Kimura, R., Nakajima, T.: A design approach for building a digital platform to augment human abilities based on a more-than-human perspective. Multimedia Tools Appl. **82**(26), 39961–40008 (2023)
29. Kuijer, L., Giaccardi, E.: Co-performance: conceptualizing the role of artificial agency in the design of everyday life. In: Proceedings of the 2018 CHI Conference on Human Factors in Computing Systems, CHI 2018, vol. 125, pp. 1–125. ACM, New York (2018)
30. Kuper, A.: Anthropology and Anthropologists: The Modern British School. Routledge (2005)
31. Latour, B.: Reassembling the Social: An Introduction to Actor-Network-Theory. Oxford University Press (2005)
32. Lewis, S.L., Maslin, M.A.: Defining the anthropocene. Nature **519**(7542), 171–180 (2015)
33. Maeda, K.: Hyper-Reality (2016). http://km.cx/projects/hyper-reality. Accessed 10 Aug 2021
34. Norman, D.: The Design of Everyday Things: Revised and Expanded Edition. Basic Books (2013)
35. Nazl, C., Smit, I., Giaccardi, E., Kröse, B.: Products as agents: metaphors for designing the products of the IoT age. In: Proceedings of the 2017 CHI Conference on Human Factors in Computing Systems, CHI 2017, pp. 448–459. Association for Computing Machinery, New York (2017)
36. Pendleton-Jullian, A.M., Brown, J.S.: Design unbound: Designing for emergence in a white water world, vol. 1. MIT Press (2018)
37. Reckwitz, A.: Toward a theory of social practices: a development in culturalist theorizing. Eur. J. Soc. Theory **5**(2), 243–263 (2002)
38. Redström, J., Wiltse, H.: Changing Things: The Future of Objects in a Digital World. Bloomsbury Visual Arts (2018)
39. Rosenberger, R., Verbeek, P.-P.: Postphenomenological Investigations: Essays on Human–Technology Relations. Lexington Books (2015)
40. Rozendaal, M.C., Boon, B., Kaptelinin, V.: Objects with intent: designing everyday things as collaborative partners. ACM Trans. Comput. Hum. Interact. (TOCHI) **26**(4), 1–33 (2019)
41. Schatzki, T.: The site of the social: a philosophical account of the constitution of social life and change. Penn State Press, University Park, PA (2002)
42. Shove, E., Pantzar, M., Watson, M.: The Dynamics of Social Practice: Everyday Life and How it Changes. Sage, London (2012)
43. Star, S.L., Grieseme, J.R.: Institutional ecology, 'translations' and boundary objects: amateurs and professionals in berkeley's museum of vertebrate zoology, 1907–39. Soc. Stud. Sci. **19**(3), 387–420 (1989). https://doi.org/10.1177/030631289019003001

44. Strathern, M.: Cutting the network. J. Roy. Anthropol. Inst. **2**(3), 517–535 (1996)
45. Suri, J.F.: Thoughtless Acts?: Observations on Intuitive Design. Chronicle Books (2005)
46. Thaler, R.H., Sunstein, C.R.: Nudge: The Final Edition. Penguin Books (2021)
47. Winskel, G.: The Formal Semantics of Programming Languages. MIT Press (1993)
48. NEOM: an accelerator of human progress (2021). https://www.neom.com. Accessed 10 Aug 2021

An Exploratory Study of Artificial Intelligence Technology in Game Design for a New Interpretation of Historical Events

Yanlin Liu[1]([✉]), Tingwei Zhao[2], Yue Peng[1], and Kaihua Liu[3]

[1] University of Jinan, No. 336, West Road of Nan Xinzhuang, Jinan, Shandong, China
`liuyanlin269@163.com`
[2] CDI College, 3D Modeling and Animation Design, Mississauga, Canada
[3] Marymount Academy International, 5100 Côte Saint Luc Road,
Montreal, QC H3W 2G9, Canada

Abstract. In the digital era, the field of education is undergoing a technology-driven revolution. Traditional methods to history learning - which rely on texts, images, and teacher explanations - have been useful in delivering knowledge, but have faced limitations in stimulating student interest and engagement. To address these limitations, an entirely new mode of learning was explored: using artificial intelligence (AI), virtual reality (VR) and augmented reality (AR) technologies to create a dynamic historical simulation game with the aim of providing an immersive historical experience.

Keywords: Artificial Intelligence · Gaming · History · Education

1 Introduction

With the development of technology, VR and AR technology have become powerful tools for creating immersive experience, which can bring users into a completely different world or enhance their perception of the reality. These technological advances have provided unprecedented opportunities for education, especially in the field of history education. Through VR and AR, learners can directly participate in historical events, so as to understand the complexity and dynamics of history in a new way. In addition, the development of brain-computer interface provides new possibilities for user interaction, allowing users to interact directly with digital content through thinking, further enhancing the sense of immersion and participation. The addition of AI technology provides the ability of dynamic content generation for historical games, so that each player's choice can affect the development of the game plot and the process of history. This method not only increases the playability of the game, but also provides players with a deeply customized learning environment, in which their decisions can bring actual consequences and historical changes. This design allows learners to enjoy the game while also thinking deeply about the significance of history and the importance of personal decision-making (Fig. 1).

© The Author(s), under exclusive license to Springer Nature Switzerland AG 2024
N. A. Streitz and S. Konomi (Eds.): HCII 2024, LNCS 14718, pp. 93–109, 2024.
https://doi.org/10.1007/978-3-031-59988-0_6

Fig. 1. Immersive Experience

However, creating a game that allows players to freely explore and alter the course of history also raises significant moral and ethical questions. By setting legal and moral standards within the game, players must make their own new interpretation of historical events on the premise of following legal and moral rules. This design not only maintains a high degree of freedom in the game but also reflects the principles of morality and law from real life within the game world, so as to promote the players' thinking of morality in the real world and the compliance with the law and the realization of social responsibility.

Due to its combination of education and entertainment, such games have the potential to attract a wide range of players, especially in historical education. Young players can learn about history in a novel and interactive way through this platform, while adult players can use it to review and deepen their understanding of history. By providing historical events from different perspectives and allowing players to set historical process according to their own preferences, this platform has become a new tool for learning history.

Using AI, VR and AR technologies to create dynamic history simulation games has great potential. It not only opens up new prospects for the application of technology in the fields of education and entertainment, but also provides a new and interactive mode of learning for historical education. Through such games, players can acquire new knowledge as well as develop critical thinking and moral judgment skills, which will be the new direction of history education in the future (Fig. 2).

Fig. 2. Historical Scenes Reproduced in Games

2 The Feasibility of Technological Implementation

The maturity of virtual reality (VR) and augmented reality (AR) technologies, along with the brain-computer interface technology, has created an unprecedented immersive experience. These technological innovations provide new dimensions for historical education and entertainment, making it possible to reproduce historical scenes, characters, and events in a more intuitive and interactive way.

Virtual reality (VR) enables users to fully immerse themselves in a computer-generated environment through comprehensive visual and auditory simulation. This technology can transport users to historical moments, such as the construction site of the pyramids in ancient Egypt or the battlefields of Europe during World War II. Users can experience historical events from a first-person perspective, providing a deeper understanding and experience than traditional learning methods. In recent years, the popularity and performance of VR headwear devices, along with advancements in content production tools, have made it increasingly feasible to create immersive experiences for history learning.

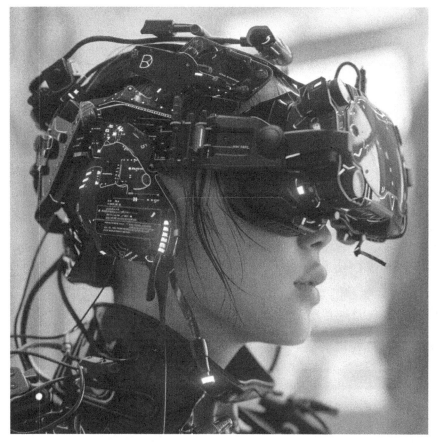

Fig. 3. Intervention of Brain-Computer Interface Technology

Augmented reality (AR) technology overlays computer-generated images onto the real world, enhancing users' perception. Compared to VR, AR provides a more flexible learning method, enabling users to interact with historical content in their own environment. For instance, AR technology enables students to witness the expansion of the Roman Empire on their desks or view 3D reconstructions of ancient works of art in museums on their mobile phones. This application of technology enhances history education by making it more engaging and personalized, and by stimulating learners' curiosity and desire for exploration.

The development of brain-computer interface (BCI) technology provides a new way for user interaction. BCI enables users to control games or simulated environments by directly interpreting their brainwave signals, without relying on traditional input devices such as keyboards and mice. Although this technology is still in a relatively early stage, it has great potential. In the future, it may allow users to explore and interact with the historical simulation environment through thinking, providing a more direct and natural immersive experience.

Combined with these technologies, developers can now create complex historical simulation games, which not only reproduce historical scenes but also allow players to participate in them from a first-person or third-person perspective, and even affect the historical process. The development of such games requires in-depth study of historical events to ensure the accuracy of the content and educational value, as well as mastering the latest technical trends, so as to give full play to the potential of VR/AR and BCI (Fig. 3).

3 The Application of AI in Game Design

The application of AI technology in historical simulation games can offer learners a new educational platform and promote the development of educational technology. This can open up new possibilities for future history education. With the continuous progress of technology and the continuous evolution of educational needs, these advanced tools will play an increasingly important role in shaping how we learn and experience history.

The application of artificial intelligence (AI) technology in the field of game design has opened up new possibilities, especially in creating dynamic historical simulation games. The core value of AI lies in its ability to comprehend, predict, and respond to player behavior, so as to provide a personalized and dynamic game experience. This ability not only enhances the playability of the game, but also provides a powerful tool for education. It allows for a more interactive and experiential method to learning history, rather than passive reception (Fig. 4).

The application of dynamic content generation in AI game design, especially in the field of historical simulation games, has opened up a new way of teaching and entertainment. This technology enables the game environment to evolve in real-time based on every choice and action of the player, creating unique historical paths. This not only enhances the playability and attraction of the game but also significantly increases its educational value.

3.1 Real-Time Plot Adjustments and Personalized Experiences

In traditional game design, story lines and character responses are often static and preset, and players' choices are largely limited, resulting in consistency and predictability of experience. The AI driven dynamic content generation technology breaks this limitation. When players make choices in the game, AI can not only recognize these choices, but

Fig. 4. Intervention of AI Technology

also adjust the game environment and plot in real- time to reflect the consequences of these choices. This means that even under the same historical background, each player's game experience will be unique, and their decisions will directly affect the direction of history, so as to obtain a more personalized and immersive experience.

3.2 Stimulating Learners' Curiosity and the Desire for Discovery

An important educational value of dynamic content generation is that it can stimulate learners' curiosity and exploration. By personally participating in the simulation of historical events and witnessing how their choices affect the historical process, learners can understand history from multiple perspectives and dimensions and experience the non-linearity and complexity of history. This kind of active participation and experience transforms learners from mere spectators of history into active participants who can experience and influence historical events. This learning method helps to cultivate learners' ability to think historically, enabling them to better comprehend the reasons and results of historical events, as well as the diverse consequences of different historical choices.

3.3   Enhancing the Interactivity and Engagement of Education

Traditional history education often relies on textbooks and teacher instruction, which may lack interactivity and participation. The application of dynamic content generation technology has greatly improved the interest and participation of learning by providing a new interactive learning method. Learners are no longer passive receivers of knowledge, but can actively explore history through their own choices. This sense of participation and achievement can significantly improve the learning effect.

Fig. 5. Representation of Engagement in Game Scenarios

The application of AI in dynamic content generation in game design, especially in historical simulation games, not only improves the playability and attraction of the game, but also brings innovation to history education, making learning history an interactive, immersive and personalized experience. In the future, with the continuous progress of AI technology and the continuous innovation of educational philosophy, this type of games will play an increasingly important role in promoting learners' deep understanding and active participation in history learning (Fig. 5).

3.4 Player Behavior Response

AI can also be used to analyze players' behaviors, so as to provide a more personalized game experience. By collecting and analyzing players' choices, strategies and preferences in the game, AI can adjust game difficulty, tips and help information, and even the behavior of characters in the game to better adapt to the needs and levels of different players. The use of this technology not only makes the game accessible to beginners but also provides challenges and novelty for experienced players.

3.5 Enhancing Playability and Educational Value

The application of the aforementioned technologies not only enhances the playability of the game but also significantly improves its educational value. In an AI-driven dynamic history simulation game, each player experiences a unique learning journey. This personalized learning experience can more effectively attract learners' attention and improve learning efficiency. At the same time, it also provides a powerful tool for educators to teach history in a new and interactive way, so that learners can acquire knowledge through practice and experience.

The application of AI technology in game design opens up new possibilities, especially in creating educational historical simulation games. By generating dynamic content and responding to player behavior, AI makes games not only more engaging but also more educationally valuable, offering a new, interactive method for historical education. With further technological advancements, we can anticipate seeing more innovative applications that utilize AI to create educational and entertainment experiences in the future (Fig. 6).

Fig. 6. Interactive Learning Methods

4   Discussion on Moral and Ethical Issues

When designing a game that enables players to freely explore and alter the course of history, moral and ethical issues become particularly important. This type of game not only challenges players' understanding of history but also raises questions about the reflection of moral and ethical standards in the real world. How to embed these standards in the game without excessively restricting the freedom of players has become a key issue in game design.

4.1   Legal Norms and Moral Standards

Game designers need to deeply study the historical background, understand the legal and moral concepts in different periods, and ensure the historical accuracy and cultural sensitivity of the game content. Based on these studies, designers can set a set of internal legal and moral standards for the game world that align with the historical background and resonate with modern players. These standards will become the basis for judging players' decisions and behaviors, and guide them to make more deliberate choices in the game.

4.2 Preserving Player Freedom

Although legal and moral standards are set within the game, it is important to maintain players' freedom, allowing them to explore different choices and possibilities in the game. This design philosophy encourages players to explore their moral boundaries and experience the different outcomes that different decisions bring, rather than simply following a pre-set correct path. To accomplish this, the game can provide numerous scenarios and decision points, each with multiple options and outcomes, so that every decision of the player becomes a unique experience.

To promote players' moral thinking, games should have consequences on their decisions and behaviors through built-in mechanisms. The consequence mechanism plays a crucial role in game design, particularly in historical simulation games for educational purposes. This mechanism enables the game world to respond to players' behavior and provides a framework for their decisions to have real and meaningful consequences. Through the carefully designed consequence mechanism, the game can effectively promote the moral thinking of players, enhance the educational value of the game, and maintain its entertainment.

4.3 Moral and Legal Consequence Mechanisms

To achieve moral and legal consequences in the game, it is crucial to establish clear and consistent standards that are closely related to the game's historical background. When players make decisions, the game analyses whether these decisions meet the established standards through AI, and produces corresponding consequences. For example, if the player chooses to achieve his goal through deception or betrayal, other characters in the game will change their attitude towards the player according to this behavior, which may lead to the player being ostracized or losing important allies. This consequence is not only reflected in the interaction of game characters, but also may affect the development of the game plot and the resources that players can access.

4.4 Social Ostracism and Loss of Trust

Social ostracism and loss of trust are two key consequences in the game. When players take immoral measures, they may find that their status in the game society is affected, making it difficult to cooperate with other characters or gain their help. This not only increases the challenge of the game, but also simulates the possible social consequences of immoral behavior in the real world (Fig. 7).

Fig. 7. Embodiment of rules

4.5 Legal Accountability

In some game scenes, players' behavior may violate the laws in the game world, leading to them facing trial or other legal consequences. This design allows players to experience the moral and legal constraints of their actions, and urges them to consider the consequences when making decisions.

4.6 Educational Value and Innovative Thinking

Through the consequences mechanism, the game becomes a platform for the interpenetration of entertainment and education, allowing players to experience history while reflecting on their actions and their consequences. This interactive learning method helps players develop a complex worldview, emphasizing the importance of individual choices and the impact these choices can have on the individual and society, leading to a deeper understanding of moral and legal issues in the real world.

The consequence mechanism is a core element in the design of historical simulation games, enhancing the realism and immersion of the game while also increasing its educational value. By simulating moral and legal consequences in the game, developers can encourage players to engage in deep moral thinking, while providing an enjoyable and challenging gaming experience. The realization of this game design philosophy requires game developers to have profound historical knowledge, cultural sensitivity, and innovative thinking about game mechanics and storytelling (Fig. 8).

Fig. 8. Educational Methods Linking Games and Real-World Significance

5   Market Potential and Target Audience

In the current digital age, games as a medium have transcended mere entertainment functions to become powerful tools for education and learning. A game that combines education and entertainment and focuses on history learning is expected to break the boundaries of traditional education and attract a wide range of player groups, including young and adult players. Such a game not only has the potential to be an innovative tool for history education, but may also reshape the way people learn history.

With the rapid development of global technology, especially innovation in mobile devices and home entertainment systems, the demand for interactive and immersive experiences from modern consumers is growing at an unprecedented rate. This change not only affects the development direction of the entertainment industry, but also brings new opportunities to the education sector. In this context, the educational game market, especially in the field of games focused on historical learning, has shown enormous untapped potential. Although this field is still in its early stages, its growth prospects and potential impact cannot be ignored.

History education games, especially those that combine profound educational content with engaging entertainment experiences, have the potential to fill the market gap. This type of game provides dynamic content and participatory learning experiences, enabling players to deepen their understanding of historical knowledge while enjoying the game. This can not only attract players who are interested in history, but also stimulate the curiosity of learners who may not be interested in traditional learning methods.

Fig. 9. History Teaching Models

In addition, with the increasing demand for diverse learning resources in the public education system and households, as well as the pursuit of improving learning efficiency and participation, this type of games are expected to become valuable resources in educational institutions and households. Schools and educators can use this type of game as a supplement to classroom teaching, utilizing its interactivity and immersive experience to enhance students' interest and understanding of the subject of history. For families, this type of game provides an educational and entertaining activity that can be participated in at home, enabling children to learn through play while promoting interaction and communication among family members.

Market research shows that despite fierce competition in the educational game market, high-quality educational games focused on specific subject areas still have significant market potential. Consumers, especially young parents and educators, are increasingly inclined to choose educational products that provide both knowledge-based content and high engagement. Therefore, developing a high-quality game that combines history education and entertainment is expected to attract widespread attention and interest, meeting the modern society's demand for diversified and innovative educational resources.

In conclusion, history education games have enormous potential in the market, especially those that can effectively combine advanced technologies such as AI, VR, and AR to provide interactive and immersive learning experiences. Through continuous pursuit of innovation and quality, this type of game is expected to become an important tool for changing the way history education is conducted, promoting active participation and in-depth understanding of history by learners, and bringing considerable market opportunities for game developers (Fig. 9).

Identifying and understanding the target audience is crucial for the success of any game project, especially when developing a historical simulation game aimed at both education and entertainment. With a primary target audience of young and adult players, this game aims to stimulate interest and engagement in history through innovative methods.

5.1 Young Players: School Students

Young players, especially school students, represent a key target audience for this game. Players in this age group usually feel dissatisfied with traditional educational methods, believing that it lacks interactivity and attractiveness. However, they are also the group most enthusiastic about exploring new technologies and games, which provides a unique opportunity for history education games.

Combining history education with game learning can significantly enhance the interest of young players in history. Students can participate in historical events in a more interactive and immersive way through games, gaining a deeper understanding of the complexity and impact of history. For example, players can take on the role of historical figures in a game, make key decisions, and personally experience the impact of these decisions on the historical process. This proactive learning approach is more effective in stimulating students' curiosity and exploration than passively receiving information taught in the classroom.

5.2 Adult Players

Adult players constitute another important target audience. Many adults have a sustained interest in history, but due to the busyness of work and life, they may not have enough time and resources to delve deeper into history. For this audience, a history game that combines educational content and entertainment experience provides an ideal learning path.

This game can provide adults with an accessible channel to historical knowledge, allowing them to supplement or expand their understanding of history in their leisure time. Additionally, the game can serve as a social tool, enabling adult players to play with family or friends, explore history together, and foster communication and understanding. This shared learning experience not only increases the entertainment value of the game, but also helps adult players establish a deeper historical knowledge system and understanding.

Through careful design, historical simulation games that combine educational content and entertainment experiences have the potential to attract a wide range of players from school students to adults. This game not only provides players with a novel way to learn history, but also opens up a way to promote cross generational communication and knowledge sharing. With the continuous advancement of technology and the continuous innovation of game design concepts, historical simulation games are expected to become an important field of education and entertainment in the future.

6 The High Integration of Education and Technology

A history simulation game that combines education and entertainment, providing a new way to learn and experience history, is expected to become an innovative tool for history education and attract a wide range of players. The game has the potential to stimulate the learning interest of young players and satisfy the curiosity of adult players for historical knowledge. With the continuous development of technology and the expansion of market demand, the market potential of historical themed games is enormous, foreshadowing a bright future in the field of educational games (Fig. 10).

This in-depth exploration of the integrated application of artificial intelligence (AI), virtual reality (VR), and augmented reality (AR) technologies in the design of historical simulation games reveals how these cutting-edge technologies will revolutionize the future of education and entertainment. By creating a platform that allows players to experience history firsthand in unprecedented ways, it not only opens up new avenues for learning history, but also brings innovative inspiration to the field of game design.

6.1 The Future of Technology Integration

This study shows that the integration of AI, VR, and AR provides powerful tools for creating dynamic, interactive, and immersive learning environments. With the continuous development and improvement of these technologies, historical simulation games will be able to provide richer and more realistic experiences in the future, enabling players to have a deeper understanding of the complexity and diversity of history. In addition, with the lowering of technological barriers and increasing user acceptance, these games are expected to become mainstream educational tools, providing customized learning experiences for learners of all ages and backgrounds.

Fig. 10. The Integration of Education and Technology

6.2 The Forefront of Educational Innovation

By combining gamified learning with history education, this study demonstrates how to use technological innovation to stimulate learners' interest and engagement. The innovation of this educational method can improve learners' absorption and understanding of historical knowledge, as well as cultivate their critical thinking, problem-solving ability, and moral and ethical concepts. Therefore, historical simulation games have the potential to become an important component of the future education field, supplementing and innovating traditional educational methods.

6.3 Challenges and Opportunities

Although AI, VR, and AR technologies offer great potential for historical simulation game design, there are still technical and design challenges that need to be addressed.

These challenges include improving technology accessibility, reducing costs, ensuring content accuracy and appropriateness, and designing gameplay that is both educational and enjoyable. Future research needs to delve deeper into these fields to ensure that these technologies can maximize their potential in both education and entertainment.

7 Conclusion: Looking into the Future

With the continued development of technology and increasing collaboration among academia, industry, and education, it is expected that historical simulation games and their applications in education and entertainment will continue to evolve. This will provide new learning and entertainment opportunities for players and learners, as well as drive innovation in the fields of educational technology and game design. Further exploration and analysis have led to the conclusion that historical simulation games, created by combining AI, VR, and AR technologies, represent an important direction in the development of educational technology. These games provide players with a new learning and entertainment platform, while also opening up new paths for technological applications in education and entertainment. This heralds a more interactive, immersive, and personalized learning future.

References

1. Hao, L.: Indoor Scene Reconstruction Technology Based on Depth Information. Yanshan University, Qinhuangdao (2022)
2. Xuan, L.: Talking about the Technology and Application of Motion Capture (2019). http://blog.sina.com.cn/s/blog_6be92b950101bqtt.html
3. Jie, J.: Human Body Gesture Recognition and Robot Control Based on Kinect. Shenzhen University, Shenzhen (2020)
4. Chuan, Z.: Analysis of the application and development status of virtual reality technology, vol. 7, pp. 75–76. Industry and Technology Forum (2021)
5. Research on the Application of Artificial Intelligence Based on Machine Learning in Video Games. https://zhuanlan.zhihu.com/p/532933578
6. Reenactment and Reconstruction: A Typological Analysis of Digital Games Based on Cultural Heritage. https://www.zhangqiaokeyan.com/academic-journal-cn_science-education-museums_thesis/0201290473380.html
7. Research on the Impact of Functional Games on User Emotion Arousal and Cognitive Performance in the Context of Historical and Cultural Knowledge Dissemination. https://www.zhangqiaokeyan.com/academic-degree-domestic_mphd_thesis/020316021755.htm
8. Reshaping Learning Methods: The Core Educational Value of Games and Their Application Prospects. https://zhuimeng.qq.com/web201912/report-details.html?newsid=10074436

Purpose Model Simulation - Purpose Formation of Multi-stakeholder by Dialog with LLM-Based AI

Takashi Matsumoto[1]([⊠]), Yurie Kibi[2], and Tetsuro Kondo[3]

[1] Digital MATSUMOTO Lab, 1-17-24 Ooka, Minami, Yokohama, Kanagawa 232-0061, Japan
digital-matsumoto-lab@googlegroups.com
[2] NIKKEN SEKKEI LTD, 2-18-3 Iidabashi, Chiyoda-Ku, Tokyo 102-8117, Japan
[3] Zukai Institute, Inc., 1-5-10 Sekiguchi, Bunkyo-Ku, Tokyo 112-0014, Japan

Abstract. The increasing complexity of social and industrial structures emphasizes the importance of collaborative projects with diverse stakeholders in areas
such as urban development and digital service development. Implementing AI-
based digital services requires considering the impact on a wide range of stakeholders, including developers, users, AI data providers, and workers affected by
the rise of AI. While incorporating diverse perspectives can enhance service value,
aligning the goals and participation of all stakeholders presents challenges, including conflicts of interests and expectations. The "Purpose Model" framework was
developed to visualize the roles and objectives of various stakeholders, fostering mutual understanding and aligning common goals and direction. However,
identifying all stakeholders and ensuring their fair participation is difficult, with
some struggling to clearly express participation and objectives. The rapid expansion of Large Language Model (LLM)-based conversational AI services, such as
ChatGPT, offers the potential to simulate perspectives of less active stakeholders by mimicking specific human personas. Although this approach can provide
valuable insights, the information generated by AI may not always be accurate or
unbiased. This paper presents a comparative study using LLM-based AI to simulate the review process of the Purpose Model in multi-stakeholder co-creation
projects, testing the feasibility of comprehensive stakeholder identification and
role analysis. The study acknowledges the need for a combination of human and
AI-driven reviews to ensure inclusivity and comprehensiveness in stakeholder
engagement in co-creation projects.

Keywords: Purpose Model · LLM · Generative AI · Multi-Stakeholder

1 Introduction

In the contemporary era, characterized by the continuous evolution and increasing complexity of societal and industrial structures, the importance of co-creative projects conducted by multiple stakeholders across diverse sectors, including urban development and
digital transformation, has become more pronounced [1–3]. The involvement of diverse

stakeholders presents the potential for comprehensive and innovative innovation. However, the alignment of the varied expectations and objectives of all stakeholders to form a unified direction is challenging. Because each stakeholder brings their own unique values and purposes to a project, achieving mutual understanding is difficult, which complicates the progress and consensus-building within co-creative projects. To address these challenges, the "Purpose Model" framework was developed by our research team, kibi and kondo, and has been examined in various co-creative projects [4]. This framework aims to visualize the purposes and roles of participants in multi-stakeholder co-creative projects, promoting mutual understanding and consensus on a co-purpose throughout the project lifecycle.

In a society where lifestyles and work styles are becoming increasingly diverse, ensuring comprehensive and equitable participation of all stakeholders in a project is significantly challenging. Barriers to participation and expression may exist for some stakeholders. Some may join projects with unclear purposes, which become apparent as the project progresses, making early-stage consensus difficult. Moreover, as projects extend over time, changing circumstances for stakeholders may lead to shifts in their engagement purposes. Frequent agile adjustments to project plans require dynamic revisions of stakeholders' roles and purposes. Even when using the Purpose Model, it is absolutely difficult to appropriately reflect the voices of all stakeholders in such environments. This research investigates the effectiveness and limitations of the Purpose Model in multi-stakeholder projects, aiming for more comprehensive consensus-building and clarification of purposes.

The advancement of Large Language Model (LLM) has enabled dialogue at levels closely resembling human interaction [5], including the capacity to mimic specific individuals' speech patterns and ideas [6, 7]. For instance, in experiments conducted by our team, when ChatGPT was asked about workplace challenges in Tokyo as a person living in a wheelchair, it provided specific responses regarding accessibility issues, transportation limitations, workplace adaptations, misconceptions and biases towards disabled people, and safety in emergencies. These findings suggest that using LLM-based generative AI to simulate dialogues based on specified personas can offer insights into diverse perspectives and opinions, potentially unexplored through human deliberation alone. Such AI-facilitated simulations could serve as a crucial tool for decision-making and planning in projects, leading to more comprehensive and effective outcomes.

This research team developed prompt templates to replicate the process of examining the Purpose Model and conducted simulations with LLM-based generative AI on a project where human deliberation of the Purpose Model had taken place. By facilitating dialogue between project stakeholders and comparing the human deliberation results with the AI simulation outcomes, this study explores how AI can complement human deliberation by highlighting additional points for consideration.

2 Related Works

The Large Language Model (LLM) equipped with the self-attention mechanism of the Transformer architecture [8] have demonstrated superior performance over traditional natural language processing models across various benchmark tests, thanks to training on extensive text data resulting in an enormous number of parameters [5]. Furthermore, even when the information generated by AI is accurate, it may not always align with human preferences. This alignment issue has been addressed by optimizing LLM to human preferences through supervised fine-tuning using Reinforcement Learning from Human Feedback (RLHF), thus enabling the generation of information suitable for human interaction [9]. Instruct GPT, the base model for OpenAI's ChatGPT, has adopted RLHF to facilitate dialogues that are more acceptable to humans [9].

A notable recent advancement is in-context learning, which, rather than updating model parameters, understands tasks from the context included in LLM inputs and generates appropriate outputs [10]. Various methods for providing context have been identified, such as Few-Shot Prompting, which involves including examples of queries and responses in the LLM prompts to induce similar outputs [11]; Chain of Thought (CoT), which adds instructions like "Let's think step by step." to consider problems incrementally [12]; and ReACT, which iterates through three steps of Thought/Action/Observation to produce highly accurate answers [13]. Additionally, Role-Play Prompting, where responses are generated by embodying specified characters or individuals in the prompts [7], Metacognitive Prompts that mimic human cognitive processes [14], and emotion prompts that use emotional expressions to enhance the quality of responses [15] have also been explored. These techniques for inputting prompts to LLM, known as "prompt engineering", allow for the enforcement of specific in-context learning styles in response to any inquiry by using them as prompt templates [16], demonstrating the versatility and effectiveness of tailored interaction with LLM.

3 Approach

The examination process of the Purpose Model through prompts consists of two phases: the "Purpose Exploration Phase," where the common objective of the project is sought, and the "Purpose Analysis Phase," where the individual objectives and roles of each stakeholder are scrutinized. This study has developed prompt templates using LLM-based conversational generative AI to replicate the "Purpose Analysis Phase" of the Purpose Model.

3.1 Purpose Model

The Purpose Model serves as a blueprint for co-creative projects centered around a purpose, facilitating activities among diverse stakeholders. It is a framework designed for deliberation in a multi-stakeholder setting [4]. The Purpose Model facilitates the exploration of a co-purpose among all stakeholders (Purpose Exploration Phase) and the analysis of individual purposes that stakeholders genuinely hold regarding the co-purpose (Purpose Analysis Phase), all while visualizing these components in a single diagram. This approach enables mutual recognition of the purposes and challenges faced by stakeholders other than oneself, advancing co-creative projects without bias towards the interests of any specific stakeholder group. In the Purpose Model, the co-purpose of the co-creative project is placed at the center in a white circle, with stakeholders involved in the project positioned around it. Active stakeholders are placed below the center, while other stakeholders are positioned above it. Stakeholders are categorized by their attributes on the model, with businesses in green, government agencies in yellow, citizens in red, and universities, research institutions, and professionals in purple. The roles of stakeholders are noted inside, along with their individual purposes concerning the co-purpose of the project (see Fig. 1). Visualizing the Purpose Model throughout the life cycle of the co-creative project promotes mutual understanding among stakeholders.

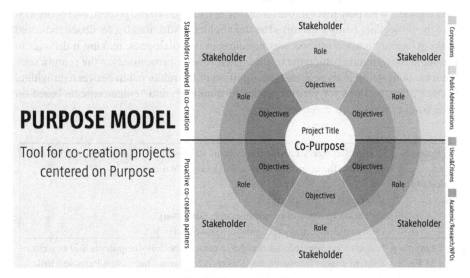

Fig. 1. Purpose Model

3.2 Prompt Templates for Simulating the Purpose Model by LLM-Based Generative AI

In pursuit of replicating the examination process of the Purpose Model through LLM-based conversational generative AI, this research team, comprising experts with extensive experience in facilitating co-creative projects involving multiple stakeholders, developed prompt templates. These templates aim to simulate the "Purpose Analysis Phase" of the Purpose Model and compare the simulation results with those obtained from human-led examinations. In the "Purpose Exploration Phase," the co-purpose of the co-creative project is examined extensively, equivalent to brainstorming, making it challenging to evaluate against human examination results. Therefore, this research focuses on the "Purpose Analysis Phase," simulating the examination of individual purposes and roles of stakeholders after establishing the co-purpose of project.

Initially, a simple prompt template was written to replicate the examination process in the Purpose Analysis Phase (see Fig. 2). This template sets up the "co-purpose, situation (place and circumstances), and stakeholders recognized in the initial phase" of the co-creative project and instructs a comprehensive recognition of key stakeholders towards achieving the co-purpose (a). Subsequently, for each recognized stakeholder, the template instructs the examination and tabulation of "individual purpose, role, and agency (whether the stakeholder is actively involved in promoting the project)" (b). Multiple dialogue experiments were conducted with OpenAI's web-based ChatGPT (selecting GPT-4 as the model) from December 1 to December 15, 2023. However, discussions based on the experimental results revealed challenges such as the general nature of recognized stakeholders and purposes, difficulty in discerning harmonizing or conflicting relationships between stakeholders' purposes as recognized within co-creative projects, a lack of reflective examination on conventional activities and wisdoms, non-recognition of stakeholders who play pivotal roles from the early stages of the project, and beneficiaries of the project not being recognized as stakeholders. Additionally, feedback indicated that the AI's examination process was not clear in two dialogues, making it difficult to understand the rationale behind the results. Therefore, improvements to the prompt template were considered in three areas: "recognition of the relationship between individual purposes", "instructions for various modes of thinking", and "enhancements based on advice from experts in co-creative projects."

a. Recognition of Stakeholders	Comprehensively examine important stakeholders to be recognized towards achieving the co-purpose in the following situation:
	-Co-purpose: {co_purpose}
	-Situation (place and circumstances): {situation}
	-Stakeholders already recognized: {stakeholders}
b. Examination of Each Stakeholder's Purpose	For each recognized stakeholder, examine the following items and organize them in a table format under "Stakeholder Name / Individual Purpose / Role / Agency":
	-Individual Purpose related to the co-purpose: within 20 characters
	-Role: within 15 characters
	-Agency (whether the stakeholder is actively involved in promoting the project towards the co-purpose): Yes or No

Fig. 2. Simple Prompt Template Based on the Purpose Model *Parts included in { } such as {co_purpose} are to be set individually for each project.

Recognition of the Relationships Between Individual Purposes. Feedback from facilitators in co-creative projects involving multiple stakeholders suggests that as the diversity of stakeholders increases, the likelihood of strong harmony or conflict arising between specific stakeholders' purposes within the project also increases. Facilitators are considering these relationships to foster mutual understanding and consensus-building among stakeholders. Additionally, individual purposes held by stakeholders towards the co-purpose of the project can include newly desired purposes (acquired purposes) and purposes they wish not to lose despite changes brought about by the project (protected purposes). Harmony can emerge between different acquired purposes, and conflicts can arise when the realization of an acquired purpose jeopardizes a protected purpose. These relationships of harmony and conflict inherently occur not between stakeholders, but between the individual purposes they hold, leading to situations where some individual purposes can establish the relationship in harmony, while others may lead to conflict.

For example, in a co-creative project aimed at creating a continuous event hall that attracts people from outside a region, residents might hold the acquired purpose of wanting the town to flourish and develop, while also holding the protected purpose of maintaining the traditional comfort of living. Similarly, local businesses may expect to increase their sales by attracting new customers, the tourism sector may expect to expand their tour offerings, and event planners and artists may expect to get new fans. The economic revitalization of the town through the co-creative project can harmonize with the residents' acquired purpose of development, but constant gathering of outsiders in the town center might conflict with the residents' protected purpose of preserving living comfort. Facilitators of the co-creative projects should consider these harmonies and conflicts in setting appropriate targets for attracting visitors to the area.

Conversational generative AI has the feature of reflecting the context of past dialogues within a single chat instance through in-context learning for generating subsequent responses [10]. To reflect the examination of the harmony and conflict between stakeholders' purposes within the context learning of generative AI, the dialogue that was established in two instances with a simple prompt template was changed to nine instances (see Fig. 3). Initially, the recognition of stakeholders (a1) was conducted, followed by instructions to examine the acquired and protected purposes of each stakeholder (b1), and then to consider the harmony (c1) and conflict (d1) between purposes. Unlike the simple prompt template where examination of each stakeholder's purpose (b) was conducted simultaneously, the examination contents (a1/b1/c1/d1) are set to allow human observers to view narrative information while overviewing it, dividing the prompts for examination (a1/b1/c1/d1) and for information organization (a2/b2/c2/d2).

Instructions for Various Modes of Thinking. Feedback from the examination with the simple prompt template indicated a lack of reflective consideration on conventional activities and dogmas. Therefore, various modes of thinking, such as divergent thinking and paradoxical thinking, were experimented with, and those confirmed effective were explicitly included in the prompt template. Experiments were conducted to see if new information would be recognized by explicitly instructing various modes of thinking for each prompt template concerning the recognition of stakeholders (a1), the examination of acquired and protected purposes (b1), and the examination of harmony (c1) and conflict (d1) between purposes. The prompt templates began with the addition of a sentence, "Now, please examine the following content using XX thinking" (see Fig. 4 (Prompt Template for Verifying Modes of Thinking)), where "XX thinking" was replaced with each mode of thinking being tested, comparing it with prompt templates without set thinking methods. This examination required fixing the context information for each prompt and was conducted using the API version of GPT-4 ("gpt-4-32k-0613" with default parameters) to include the context in "past dialogues" comparing prompt templates with and without set modes of thinking (see Fig. 4 (Prompt Template for Verifying Modes of Thinking)). As a result, among the 14 types of modes of thinking trialed by the research team in five trials, there were modes that recognized new information more than four times compared to prompts without set modes of thinking, confirming their effectiveness (see Fig. 5).

Furthermore, as a prompt engineering technique, there is a technique called Chain of Thought (CoT) that displays the examination process for a query in steps [12]. For each prompt template where effective modes of thinking were confirmed, prompts were improved to consider using CoT for each category of modes of thinking (see Fig. 4 (Multiple Modes of thinking with CoT)). Each step in CoT prompts was written to expand upon the examination of the previous step. When running the improved prompt template including CoT, generative AI outputs the examination process using each mode of thinking, enabling humans to observe the examination process (see Fig. 6).

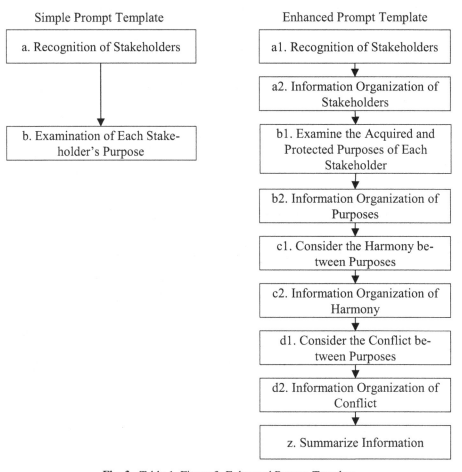

Fig. 3. Table 1. Figure 3. Enhanced Prompt Template

Enhancements Based on Advice from Experts in Co-creative Projects. In the context of co-creative project facilitation using the Purpose Model, experts with extensive experience were present to conduct walk-through tests of dialogue experiments with ChatGPT, utilizing both a simple prompt template and a prompt template that had undergone two improvements: "Recognition of the relationships between individual purposes" and

"Instructions for various modes of thinking". The tests revealed two prevalent issues in both execution outcomes: stakeholders responsible for driving the project from its initial stages were not recognized, and beneficiaries of the project were not identified as stakeholders. Consequently, modifications of prompt template were made to the recognition of stakeholders (a).

To address the issue of stakeholders responsible for driving the project from its initial stages were not recognized, a distinction was made between "leadership stakeholders" and "already recognized stakeholders." For the issue of beneficiaries of the project were not identified as stakeholders, an instruction to "Please add beneficiaries as stakeholders" was incorporated into the prompt template. (see Fig. 7 ("a1. Recognition of Stakeholders" prompt template)).

Simulation of the Purpose Model Using Generative AI. Through the implementation of three improvements to a simple prompt template - "Recognition of the Relationships between Individual Purposes", "Instructions for Various Modes of Thinking", and "Enhancements Based on Advice from Experts in Co-Creative Projects." and the addition of a concluding prompt (z)[1] for organizing conclusions towards the creation of the Purpose Model, the prompt template was finalized (see: Fig. 7). The prompt template is designed to include four variables tailored to the project's specifics: "co-purpose {co_purpose}", "situation {situation}", "leadership stakeholders {leaders}", and "already recognized stakeholders {stakeholders}", with the capability to list multiple entities for {leaders} and {stakeholders}. Utilizing these prompt templates allows for the simulation of the "Purpose Analysis Phase" in the examination process of the Purpose Model through instructions provided to web-based conversational generative AI[2].

4 Use Case

4.1 Targeted Co-creative Project

This study examines a co-creative project known as Arch to Hoop, active in Okinawa Prefecture, Japan, as an example of a project where the Purpose Model analysis had previously been conducted by humans [17]. Arch to Hoop was initiated in April 2023, spurred by the hosting of the Basketball World Cup in Okinawa. The project was led by the sports equipment manufacturer Molten, in collaboration with FIBA (the International Basketball Federation) and the Local Organizing Committee (LOC), involving NPOs, companies, and children within Okinawa Prefecture. Focusing on the social issue of "experience disparity among children" in Okinawa, Arch to Hoop set forth the project purpose of "creating opportunities for goals and dreams for children in Okinawa through basketball," offering them various vocational experiences related to basketball, including

---

[1] Following the input format of Purpose Model Studio, character limits are set for each item. https://purposemodel.zukai.co/

[2] The current investigation is being conducted with ChatGPT (GPT-4), utilizing contextual learning only, making similar assessments technically feasible in other conversational AI models.

Simple Prompt Template	Comprehensively examine important stakeholders to be recognized towards achieving the co-purpose in the following situation: -Co-purpose: {co_purpose} -Situation (place and circumstances): {situation} -Stakeholders already recognized: {stakeholders}
Prompt Template for Verifying Modes of Thinking	Now, please examine the following content using XX thinking Comprehensively examine important stakeholders to be recognized towards achieving the co-purpose in the following situation: -Co-purpose: {co_purpose} -Situation (place and circumstances): {situation} -Stakeholders already recognized: {stakeholders} {past dialogues}
Multiple Modes of Thinking with CoT	We want to comprehensively recognize the important stakeholders for achieving the co-purpose in the following situation. Please identify specific stakeholders through the following examination process. Situation: - Co-purpose: {co_purpose} - Situation: {situation} - Already Recognized Stakeholders: {stakeholders} Examination Process: Step 1. Use divergent and lateral thinking to broadly recognize stakeholders. Step 2. Use analogical thinking to add stakeholders by referencing similar activities. Step 3. Use strategic thinking to add stakeholders relevant to policies, economic activities, and social issues. Step 4. Use paradoxical thinking to add stakeholders from perspectives that differ from conventional wisdom. Step 5. Ensure all recognized stakeholders are organized without any omission or duplication.

Fig. 4. Prompt Example for "a. Recognition of Stakeholders" Using Modes of Thinking *Parts enclosed in { } such as {co_purpose} are set individually for each project.

event setup and operation of experiential events. Continuing beyond the conclusion of the Basketball World Cup, it persistently offers vocational experience opportunities related to the B.LEAGUE basketball games and events, with the participation of several NPOs supporting children, various sponsoring companies, the Okinawa Prefecture Board of Education, local governments, and citizens in the co-creative project.

Arch to Hoop conducts ongoing examinations using the Purpose Model in response to changes in the project's environment and context, with this instance focusing on the project's activities as of July 2022. The Purpose Model examined at that time recognized the Okinawa Youth Independence Support Center Churayui, the project's main body

Mode of Thinking	a1. Stakeholder	b1. Purpose	c1. Harmony	d1. Conflict
Divergent Thinking	Y			
Lateral Thinking	Y			
Creative Thinking				
Analytical Thinking			Y	Y
Contextual Thinking			Y	Y
Analogical Thinking	Y		Y	
Critical Thinking		Y		
Reflective Thinking				Y
Paradoxical Thinking	Y	Y		
Structural Thinking			Y	Y
Systems Thinking			Y	Y
Structural Thinking	Y	Y		
Intuitive Thinking				
Emotional Thinking		Y	Y	Y

Fig. 5. Results of Testing Different Modes of Thinking (Out of five trials conducted by the research team, modes of thinking that recognized new information at least four times compared to when no specific mode of thinking was set are marked with "Y")

Arch to Hoop, Molten, and the company Ridilover aiming to solve social issues as proactive co-creation partners. Stakeholders involved in the co-creation included children participating in the project from Okinawa Prefecture, child support organizations in Okinawa, basketball affiliates, sponsoring companies, and Okinawa Prefecture itself. The project's activities are funded by sponsorships from companies and grants from Okinawa Prefecture (see Fig. 8).

4.2 Experimental Environment

In this study, simulations of the Purpose Model were conducted using the ChatGPT service provided by OpenAI as of January 28, 2024 (model version: GPT-4 model) [18], using the finalized prompt template. Observations were made on a series of responses generated by AI, which were then compared with the human-conducted Purpose Model. The parameters in the prompt template were set based on the information from the Purpose Model of the Arch to Hoop project, as examined in July 2022 (see Fig. 9).

5 Evaluation

The results of the Purpose Model simulations conducted using the prompt template (see Fig. 7) targeting the Arch to Hoop project as of July 2022 were examined through a walkthrough of the outputs generated by generative AI and a comparison with the human-conducted Purpose Model. The simulation, involving the research team and stakeholders from the Arch to Hoop project, was completed in approximately two hours.

Query (Prompt Template)	We want to comprehensively recognize the important stakeholders for achieving the co-purpose in the following situation. Please identify specific stakeholders through the following examination process.
	- Co-purpose: {co_purpose} - Situation: {situation} - Leadership Stakeholders: {leaders} - Already Recognized Stakeholders: {stakeholders}
	Examination Process: Step 1. Use divergent and lateral thinking to broadly recognize stakeholders. Step 2. Use analogical thinking to add stakeholders by referencing similar activities. Step 3. Use strategic thinking to add stakeholders relevant to policies, economic activities, and social issues. Step 4. Use paradoxical thinking to add stakeholders from perspectives that differ from conventional wisdom. Step 5. Please add beneficiaries as stakeholders.
Response from AI	Recognizing stakeholders in this project is crucial. Let's consider each step. Step 1: Divergent and Lateral Thinking - Local educational institutions: Schools and universities serve as places to introduce basketball to children and youth and provide training. - Local community groups: Involvement of local sports clubs, youth organizations, and non-profits can extend the impact to a broader community. - Media and advertising companies: Important for increasing awareness and interest in the project. - Basketball coaches and players: They can serve as role models for children and provide skill coaching. Step 2: Analogical Thinking - Other sports organizations: Refer to youth development programs conducted by soccer or baseball organizations. - International sports events: Analyze the impact on children from major sports events like the Olympics or World Cup. Step 3: Strategic Thinking - Government agencies: Ministries like the Ministry of Education, Culture, Sports, Science and Technology and the Sports Agency play key roles. - Tourism industry: Basketball events can promote tourism and contribute to the local economy. - Social welfare organizations: Organizations supporting children in disadvantaged positions are also crucial. Step 4: Paradoxical Thinking - Competitors in basketball: Companies and organizations normally in competition can collaborate towards a co-purpose. - Groups with critical views: Organizations pointing out issues in sports or education can provide valuable perspectives for project improvement.
	Step 5: Beneficiaries - Children in Okinawa: The main beneficiaries of this project. - Okinawa community: The project could strengthen community bonds and benefit the region as a whole. By considering these steps, a wider and more multifaceted perspective of stakeholder recognition can be achieved, laying the foundation for an effective project implementation.

Fig. 6. Example of Responses When Implementing "Multiple Modes of Thinking with CoT" (Prompt Template for a1)

a1. Recognition of Stakeholders	We want to comprehensively recognize the important stakeholders for achieving the co-purpose in the following situation. Please identify specific stakeholders through the following examination process. - Co-purpose: {co_purpose} - Situation: {situation} - Leadership Stakeholders: {leaders} - Already Recognized Stakeholders: {stakeholders} Examination Process: Step 1. Use divergent and lateral thinking to broadly recognize stakeholders. Step 2. Use analogical thinking to add stakeholders by referencing similar activities. Step 3. Use strategic thinking to add stakeholders relevant to policies, economic activities, and social issues. Step 4. Use paradoxical thinking to add stakeholders from perspectives that differ from conventional wisdom. Step 5. Please add beneficiaries as stakeholders.
a2. Information Organization of Stakeholders	Step6. Ensure all recognized stakeholders are organized without any omission or duplication.
b1. Examine the Acquired and Protected Purposes of Each Stakeholder	Please concisely examine the "acquired purposes" and "protected purposes" related to the co-purpose that each recognized stakeholder. *Include "{leaders}, {stakeholders}, {stakeholders recognized in Step6}" in the stakeholders to be considered. Examination Process: Step7. Use critical thinking to examine the "background issues" of the co-purpose within the situation. Step8. Use critical thinking to evaluate the "fundamental challenges" for each stakeholder. Step9. Use strategic and paradoxical thinking to explore "strategic objectives" and "objectives divergent from conventional wisdom" for all stakeholders. Step10. Use emotional thinking to assess the "motivations" of all stakeholders towards their purposes and challenges.
b2. Information Organization of Purposes	Step11. Please concisely organize "acquired purposes", "protected purposes", "challenges", and "motivations" for each recognized stakeholder. *Include "{leaders}, {stakeholders}, {stakeholders recognized in Step6}."
c1. Consider the Harmony between Purposes	These identified purposes can form the relationships of "Harmony" and "Conflict." Following the examination process in Step11, purposes that form harmonizing relationships are to be examined and displayed in combinations of "stakeholder and purpose."

Fig. 7. Finalized Prompt Template*Parts included in { } such as {co-purpose} are to be manually set for each project.

	Examination Process: Step 12. Use analytical, contextual, and analogical thinking to analyze synergies and similarities among purposes, considering the background to identify harmonizing relationships. Step 13. Use structural and systems thinking to clearly examine combinations of stakeholders and purposes that exhibit harmony. Step 14. Use emotional thinking to assess the "motivations" of stakeholders for purposes in harmonious relationships.
c2. Information Organization of Harmony	Step 15. Based on these examinations, please concisely summarize combinations of purposes in harmony, detailing the "content of harmony," "purpose," "stakeholder," and "motivation."
d1. Consider the Conflict between Purposes	Following the examination process in Step 11, purposes that form conflicting relationships are to be examined and displayed in combinations of "stakeholder and purpose". Examination Process: Step 16. Use analytical, contextual, and reflective thinking to analyze contradictions and conflicts among purposes, identifying those in conflictual relationships. Step 17. Use structural and systems thinking to clearly examine combinations of stakeholders and purposes in conflict. Step 18. Use emotional thinking to assess the "motivations" of stakeholders for purposes in conflicting relationships.
d2. Information Organization of Conflict	Step 19. Based on these examinations, please concisely summarize combinations of purposes in conflict, detailing the "content of conflict," "purpose," "stakeholder," and "motivation."
z. Summarize Information	Based on all examinations, please organize information in a table format for each stakeholder, listing "Stakeholder Name/Detail/Role in Project/Acquired Purposes/Protected Purposes/Agency/Challenges/ Motivations". *Include "{leaders}, {stakeholders}, {stakeholders recognized in Step6}." *"Agency" should be determined as Yes or No, indicating whether the stakeholder actively promotes the project towards the co-purpose.

Fig. 7. (*continued*)

5.1 Walkthrough of Outputs Generated by Generative AI

The walkthrough was conducted using ChatGPT provided as a web service by OpenAI as of January 28, 2024, with participants reviewing the results generated in response to instructions given through the prompt template (see Fig. 7) on a case-by-case basis.

Recognition of Stakeholders (a1/a2). Inquiry was made to ChatGPT, setting the project information (see Fig. 9) in the parameters of scripts for a1 and a2 of the prompt template (see Fig. 7), and the recognized stakeholders and their examination process

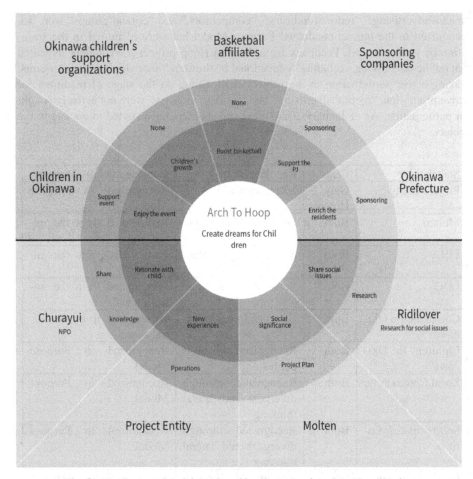

Fig. 8. The Purpose Model Analyzed by Humans of Arch to Hoop Project

- Co-purpose: To create opportunities for goals and dreams for children in Okinawa through basketball
- Situation: Okinawa Prefecture
- Leadership stakeholder: Molten

Fig. 9. Parameters in the prompt template (Arch to Hoop)

were reviewed. It was observed that all stakeholders identified in the human-conducted Purpose Model were recognized except for the "project entity" (see Fig. 10). Since "Molten" was set as the leadership stakeholder in the prompt template, it is likely that the "project entity" was not distinguished as a separate stakeholder, with Molten's employees centrally involved in the actual "project entity." "Educational institutions," "media/advertising," "tourism industry," "competitors," and "critical groups" were not recognized in the human-conducted Purpose Model but were identified in the simulation by generative AI. Feedback from Arch to Hoop project stakeholders indicated that public institutions, including "educational institutions," face significant constraints, making active participation in the project challenging. At the stage of readiness for active promotion, "media/advertising" and "tourism industry" were not actively sought for participation. As of January 2024, these stakeholders have started to engage in the project.

Stakeholder	Class	Recognition by AI	Consideration by Humans
Project Entity	Only Human	Not recognized	Recognized in Purpose Model
Molten	Both	Set as an initial value	Participated from the initial stage
FIBA	Both	Set as an initial value	Participated from the initial stage
LOC	Both	Set as an initial value	Participated from the initial stage
Companies in Okinawa	Both	Set as an initial value	Participated from the initial stage
Children in Okinawa	Both	Recognized as beneficiaries	Recognized in Purpose Model
Local Community	Both	Recognized through divergent and lateral thinking	Recognized in Purpose Model
Sports-related Entities	Both	Recognized through divergent and lateral thinking	Recognized in Purpose Model
Government/Public Institutions	Both	Recognized through strategic thinking	Recognized as Okinawa Prefecture
Social Welfare Organizations	Both	Recognized through strategic thinking	Recognized in Purpose Model
Groups Raising Social Issues	Both	Recognized through paradoxical thinking	Recognized in Purpose Model
Educational Institutions	Only AI	Recognized through divergent and lateral thinking	Not solicited for participation
Media/Advertising	Only AI	Recognized through divergent and lateral thinking	Not solicited for participation
Tourism Industry	Only AI	Recognized through strategic thinking	Not solicited for participation
Competitors	Only AI	Recognized through paradoxical thinking	Not recognized
Critical Groups	Only AI	Recognized through paradoxical thinking	Not recognized

Fig. 10. Simulation-Driven Stakeholder Identification Results

Examine the Purposes (b1/b2). Inquiries were made to ChatGPT using the b1 and

Stakeholder	Purpose recognized by Human	Acquired Purposes	Protected Purposes
Project Entity	Experiences through basketball	None	None
Molten	Redefining the social significance of Sports	Strengthening brand position	Product quality and reliability
FIBA	Elevating Japanese Basketball from Okinawa	Basketball promotion	Fairness in sports
LOC	Elevating Japanese Basketball from Okinawa	Successful event	Safety
Companies in Okinawa	Supporting the Project	Contribution to the community and business growth	Corporate image and regional economic contribution
Children in Okinawa	Enjoying the Event	Pursuit of dreams	Safe environment
Local Community	Connecting Children's Growth through the Project	Community bonds	Local culture
Sports-related Entities	Elevating Japanese Basketball from Okinawa	Sports promotion	Sportsmanship
Government/Public Institutions	Enriching the Lives of the Prefecture's Residents	Regional development	Public benefit
Social Welfare Organizations	Activities Attuned to Children's Needs	Support for the socially vulnerable	Principles of social welfare
Groups Raising Social Issues	Making Social Issues a Concern for Everyone	Interest in social problems	Social change
Educational Institutions	None	Expansion of educational opportunities	Equity in education
Media/Advertising	None	Expansion of outreach	Fairness in media
Tourism Industry	None	Revitalization of the local economy	Economic sustainability
Competitors	None	Acquisition of market share	Uniqueness
Critical Groups	None	Highlighting issues	Social improvement

Fig. 11. Simulation-Driven Stakeholder Identification Results

b2 scripts of the prompt template (see Fig. 7), setting the stakeholders identified by AI (see Fig. 10). Upon reviewing the acquired and protected purposes for each stakeholder, it was found that only the purposes of "Molten" differed between human-conducted and AI simulation (see Fig. 11). Human examination had considered purposes aligned with the project's aim, such as "Redefining the social significance of sports," while AI examination recognized commercial purposes for "Molten," including "brand position strengthening" and "product quality and reliability." For stakeholders other than "Molten," there were no discrepancies between human and AI examinations.

Harmony (c1/c2) and Conflict (d1/d2) between Purposes. Upon reviewing the outputs generated by AI through scripts c1, c2, d1, and d2 of the prompt template (see Fig. 7), it was observed that harmony between purposes was consistent with recognition and showed no discrepancies. No actual conflict between purposes occurred (see Fig. 12).

Purposes in Harmony	Purposes in Conflict
1. Contribution to the regional economy and society (Companies in Okinawa, Government/Public Institutions, Tourism Industry) 2. Education and growth of children (Educational Institutions, Children in Okinawa, Local Community) 3. Promotion of sports and enhancement of competition (Sports-related Entities, Molten, FIBA)	1. Economic benefits (Companies in Okinawa Prefecture) vs. Support for the socially vulnerable (Social Welfare Organizations) 2. Commercial success of sports goods (Molten) vs. Fairness in sports (FIBA) 3. Revitalization of the local economy (Economic Entities) vs. Environmental protection (Groups Raising Social Issues)

Fig. 12. Results of Purpose Identification by Simulation

5.2 Comparison of Purpose Models

Comparing the human-conducted Purpose Model (see Fig. 8) with the Purpose Model based on the AI simulation (see Fig. 13), it was noted that the "Groups Raising Social Issues", which are typically recognized as proactive co-creative partners, were identified as stakeholders involved in co-creation in the AI simulation results. Conversely, the basketball affiliates (FIBA, LOC, Sports-related Entities), traditionally recognized as stakeholders involved in co-creation, were identified as proactive co-creative partners.

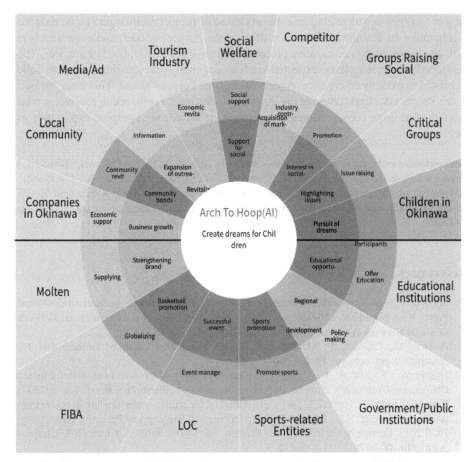

Fig. 13. Purpose Model based on the AI simulation of Arch to Hoop Project

6   Conclusion

The examination using the prompt template for conversational generative AI to analyze the Purpose Model has demonstrated that stakeholders and purposes can be recognized with a certain level of comprehensiveness. It was also confirmed that stakeholders not involved at the time were broadly recognized. However, Molten's purpose, a key player in the project, was recognized not as the original "desire to redefine the social significance of sports" but rather as purposes related to commercial activities, specifically "strengthening of brand position" and "product quality and reliability." Discrepancies were also noted in the identification of primary stakeholders, indicating the difficulty in completing the Purpose Model solely through AI examination. Thus, it is advisable to use generative AI with Human-in-the-loop, where human intervention is required to supplement additional information based on the AI's outputs. According to stakeholders involved in the Arch to Hoop project examined in this study, approximately 50% of their labor time is spent on project facilitation, suggesting that the workload of project facilitation can be reduced if generative AI is utilized to create a draft of the Purpose Model, and even members with less experience in co-creative projects can perform a certain level of analysis. The developed prompt template is expected to advance mutual understanding among multiple stakeholders in many co-creative projects through the Purpose Model. This study focused on the Purpose Analysis phase of the Purpose Model, but it is planned to conduct similar examinations using conversational generative AI in the phase of purpose exploration as well.

Acknowledgement. We would like to thank Shunpei Katsuta from Molten Corporation for advice and discussion on the use case. Additionally, we would like to thank Yuki Yamamoto, Mikio Shoji, Makoto Fukushima, Ayuto Makiguchi, Ryo Harashima, Naomi Sato, Tokio Kibata, and Yiyang Hao from the Deloitte AI Institute of Deloitte Tohmatsu Group for their advice on experiments for LLM.

References

1. Schiffer, E.: Net-map toolbox influences mapping of social network. In: International Food Policy Research Institute Presented at the Sunbelt Conference of the International Network of Social Network Analysis, Corfu, Greece, 01–06 May 2007 (2007)
2. Persson, U., Olander, S.: Methods to estimate stakeholder views of sustainability for construction projects, pp. 19–22 (2004)
3. Hashimoto, T., Mukai, T., Suita, R.: Community Ship Shimokita Line Street Project: Challenging Community. Supporting Railway Company. Gakugei Publishing, Tokyo (2022)
4. Kibi, Y., Kondo, T.: Purpose Model - visual method for mutual understanding in co-creation projects. In: Streitz, N.A., Konomi, S. (eds.) Distributed, Ambient and Pervasive Interactions. HCII 2023. Lecture Notes in Computer Science, vol. 14036. Springer, Cham (2023). https://doi.org/10.1007/978-3-031-34668-2_5
5. OpenAI.: GPT-4 Technical Report. In: Computation and Language (2023). https://doi.org/10.48550/arXiv.2303.08774
6. Serapio-Garcia, G., et al.: Personality traits in large language models. In: Computation and Language of Computer Science (2023). https://doi.org/10.48550/arXiv.2307.00184
7. Kong, A., et al.: Better zero-shot reasoning with role-play prompting. In: Computation and Language of Computer Science (2023). https://doi.org/10.48550/arXiv.2308.07702
8. Vaswani, A., et al.: Attention is all you need. In: Advances in Neural Information Processing Systems, pp. 6000–6010 (2017)
9. Ouyang, L., et al.: Training language models to follow instructions with human feedback. In: Computation and Language of Computer Science (2022). https://doi.org/10.48550/arXiv.2203.02155
10. Dong, Q., et al.: A survey on in-context learning. In: Computation and Language of Computer Science (2023). https://doi.org/10.48550/arXiv.2301.00234
11. Brown, T.B., et al.: Language models are few-shot learners. In: Computation and Language of Computer Science (2020). https://doi.org/10.48550/arXiv.2005.14165
12. Wei, J., et al.: Chain-of-thought prompting elicits reasoning in large language models. In: Computation and Language of Computer Science (2022). https://doi.org/10.48550/arXiv.2201.11903
13. Yao, S., et al.: ReAct: synergizing reasoning and acting in language models. In: Computation and Language of Computer Science (2023). https://doi.org/10.48550/arXiv.2210.03629

14. Wang, Y., Zhao, Y.: Metacognitive prompting improves understanding in large language models. In: Computation and Language of Computer Science (2023). https://doi.org/10.48550/arXiv.2308.05342
15. Li, C., et al.: Large language models understand and can be enhanced by emotional stimuli. In: Computation and Language of Computer Science (2023). https://doi.org/10.48550/arXiv.2307.11760
16. Prompt Engineering Guide Homepage. https://www.promptingguide.ai/techniques. Accessed 30 Jan 2024
17. Arch To Hoop Homepage. https://arch-to-hoop-okinawa.com/. Accessed 30 Jan 2024
18. Open AI ChatGPT Homepage. https://openai.com/chatgpt. Accessed 30 Jan 2024

Utilizing Data Spectrum to Promote Data Interoperability Across Industries and Countries

Ruizhi Wang[1], Yahan Chen[2], Xuzheng Zhang[1], Xucheng Zhang[1], Xiying Chen[1], Dayou Wu[3], and Guochao Peng[1(✉)]

[1] School of Information Management, Sun Yat-Sen University, Guangzhou 510006, Guangdong, China
`penggch@mail.sysu.edu.cn`
[2] Diginova Management Consulting (Guangzhou) Co., Ltd., Guangzhou 510006, Guangdong, China
[3] International Institute for Advanced Data Management Study, Hongkong, China

Abstract. Interoperability of industrial data is crucial for promoting digital transformation of industries and grasping the trend of integrated development of industries. This study starts with data standards and characterizes the level of data standardization through quantitative statistical results of industry standard construction at nodes in the industry's ecological chain. The difficulty of data interoperability between industries is characterized by quantitative statistical results of differences in overall standard construction. The corresponding relationships between international industry and standards' scores as well as nation, industry and international standards' scores are both examined, and two major tools, data spectrum and data light wave, are pioneered, which build a visual measurement system for the interoperability level of industrial data. By using data spectrum and data light wave, the scope of data interoperability research can be further expanded, then a cost evaluation system for data interoperability can be explored; Guide the direction of data standard construction and optimize the industrial data governance architecture; Identify obstacles to data flow in the industrial ecosystem and guide the path of digital development in the industry.

Keywords: Data interoperability · Data standards · Data spectrum · Data light wave

1 Introduction

1.1 Research Background

With the growth of data volume and the revolution of digital technology, the speed of data circulation continues to improve, the scenarios of digital intelligence empowerment continue to extend, and the digital economy formats continue to develop. In order to continuously cultivate the development momentum of the digital economy, countries around the world attach great importance to the construction of data element systems and data infrastructure systems, and have introduced a series of data policies. For example, the European Union introduced the Digital Trade Strategy earlier in 2017, committed to eliminating barriers to data localization and ensuring the free flow of cross-border data. With the proposal of the strategy of innovation-driven development, the digital integration of industries has also become the main lever for China to vigorously promote the construction of a modern industrial system. The Central Committee of the Communist Party of China and the State Council issued the "Overall Layout Plan for Digital China Construction" in February 2023, which clearly proposed strategies such as consolidating the foundation of data resource circulation, comprehensively empowering the digital development of industries, and strengthening the deep integration ability of industry, academia, and research, which also places the digital development of industries in an important position. In this context, the Ministry of Finance officially issued the Provisional Regulations on Accounting Treatment of Enterprise Data Resources in August, which provides strong support for activating the enthusiasm of data market entities, enhancing the willingness of all parties to circulate data, and standardizing the data transaction governance system.

Although international organizations and relevant departments of various countries have planned the development direction of industrial digitization, data assetization, and data element circulation at the level of strategic guarantee and institutional design, how to construct an evaluation system for industrial data interoperability at the international level from a theoretical perspective, and how to open up data circulation channels between industries from a practical perspective are still fundamental issues in the development of the digital economy. Therefore, this study aims to focus on the construction of international industrial data standards, creatively proposing the concepts of data light wave and data spectrum, to construct a measurement system for the difficulty of data interoperability between industries. The research has the following significance:

Firstly, quantitative analysis of the construction of industrial data standards help to standardize the construction of data governance systems. By examining the distribution of data standards corresponding to international industry categories and the participation of countries in international data standards' construction, we can further guide the direction of industrial and national standards' construction, thereby optimizing the data governance structure of industries and countries;

Secondly, quantitative examination of the degree of standardization of industrial data is helpful for the sustainable development of industries and enterprises. Through graph representation, the differences in data standardization among various trades on the international level of the industrial ecological chain can be intuitively identified, and opportunities and challenges in data circulation and business cooperation between industries can be identified, thereby further guiding the focus of digital transformation of industries in various countries and the direction of innovative development of international enterprises;

Thirdly, the innovative introduction of the concepts of data light wave and data spectrum is an extension of research ideas in the field of data interoperability. Through algorithm design and graph drawing, it can provide innovative practices for measuring and representing data interoperability between industries at the international level, thereby further expanding the research scope of data interoperability.

1.2   Overview of Current Research

Data interoperability is the ability of systems to use data resources across boundaries without or with minimal information loss [1]. Currently, existing research on this topic has mainly focused on the following two aspects:

(1) Research on data interoperability methods. Most existing research focuses on solving the problem of data heterogeneity from a semantic perspective through the construction of technology and conceptual models. Fareh et al. [2] used ontology alignment technology to construct a unified data model that integrates the resource transformation of the model layer, metadata layer, and knowledge layer; Shi et al. [3] constructed a BIM, GIS, IoT integrated heterogeneous model based on ontology technology, including data instantiation, ontology construction and mapping, query application, and other levels. These studies mainly focused on the field of information organization, utilizing tools such as metadata, meta models, and ontology to explore the syntax and semantic specification methods of entities such as concept description, semantic association, and knowledge extraction, in order to support the consistency of data structures and conceptual patterns in interoperability.
(2) Research on data interoperability applications. Existing research was mainly conducted in the context of industries such as transportation, healthcare and manufacturing, and was designed by scholars based on specific situations in different disciplinary fields. However, its themes also have semantic interoperability characteristics that focus on conceptual models. At the same time, the industries covered by the research have a narrow span and do not have universality. From the perspective of urban transportation big data, Liu et al. [4] constructed a semantic fusion framework based on deep learning's input side, output side, and bidirectional stages; Prabath et al. [5] created a conceptual framework for PGHD/EHR interoperability through the main patient index and the DH Convener platform; Moeid et al. [6] constructed a data exchange model for urban disaster management between use cases from the perspective of conceptual consistency recognition by reusing model view definitions.

In summary, existing research mainly considers the interoperability problem of heterogeneous data, and proposes solutions to achieve data model consistency from both structural and semantic levels. However, these approaches cannot fully understand and eliminate the data heterogeneity problem caused by business changes in the industrial interconnection environment. What's more, relative research on industries only considers the data circulation system within each industry, without extending to data interoperability between industries. On the one hand, with the deepening practice of the international economic community, the scale of cross-border digital trade has steadily increased, and the large amount of cross-border flow data has posed new challenges to the complexity of data interoperability between industries; On the other hand, with the acceleration of global industrial integration, the complexity of industries, organizations, and information systems makes it difficult for multiple parties to reach consensus on a certain model [7]. Therefore, research on data interoperability between industries is relatively blank but more necessary, and traditional research methods are not applicable to the existing system and development path of industrial interconnection. Furthermore, due to the diversity of business interaction modes, more data assets detached from information systems are shared and applied on a larger scale [8]. When supply and demand entities make decisions on data interoperability across systems, organizations, industries, and even borders, they inevitably need to consider their difficulty and cost. Therefore, exploring the construction of a measurement and representation system for the level of data interoperability between industries is necessary, it is also of great significance for promoting the digital transformation of industries and the standardized development of international digital trade.

1.3   Research Questions and Aims

To solve the problem of cross-industrial and cross-national data interoperability in the industrial interconnection environment, this study firstly focuses on the core issue that affects the possibility and necessity of data interoperability between industries at the international level: how to measure and represent the difficulty and cost of data exchange and sharing among industries. Under this problem orientation, the author firstly carried out conceptual construction and theoretical analysis, proposing the concept of data spectrum and data light wave, as well as the theoretical basis for international data standards to measure industrial data interoperability; Subsequently, data collection and algorithm design were carried out, and the current international standard data of the selected industry was crawled from the ISO's official website, then the extracted data standards were scored and statistically analyzed; Finally, data analysis and graph drawing were conducted to obtain corresponding data for industry data standards' scores at the international level, national data standards' scores, and industry data standards' scores within typical countries. Based on this, data spectrum and data light wave were plotted to respectively demonstrate the difficulty of data interoperability between industries from the international perspective, as well as the participation of countries in international data standards' construction and the specific performance of industry data interoperability levels within typical countries.

In summary, this study conducted a comprehensive investigation of the construction of international industrial data standards and completed the exploration process of the basic issues of data interoperability between industries from theoretical analysis, and conceptual construction to empirical analysis. The aim is to answer the following questions: What is the level of data interoperability between industries worldwide, and how much participation does each country have in the construction of international data standards? What is the specific performance of industry data interoperability among typical countries at the national level? How to promote targeted industrial data governance and data interoperability in the industrial interconnection environment at the historical node where data elements are ushering in areas of great development?

2   Conceptual Definition and Theoretical Analysis

2.1   Data Standards

There is no unified consensus in the academic community on the definition of data standards. The Chinese Academy of Information and Communications defines it as a normative constraint to ensure consistency and accuracy in the internal and external use and exchange of data [9]. In terms of category classification, some scholars have divided the data standards of the biological industry into three categories: vocabulary and authoritative standards, semantic standards, and data exchange standards [10], while others have divided the data standards of the geographic industry into categories such as data interface, classification, coding, and model [11]. Their research is mostly conducted from the perspective of analyzing the construction of existing data standards in a single industry. This study refers to multiple data standard definitions and combines the characteristics of the standards to define data standards as a set of relevant standards that regulate data encoding forms, data exchange forms, communication protocols, storage forms, collection forms, etc. through the development of a system composed of management systems, control processes, and technical tools.

Since data standards directly guide the production and application of data service products and are the foundation of data standardization in the business field [12], many scholars have studied the construction of data governance systems in the field from this perspective. For example, Song et al. [13] have developed a blockchain-based data collaborative governance method from the perspective of improving the efficiency of standard terminology application in traditional data standard construction methods and promoting data standard sharing applications. There are also international data standards aimed at supporting data integration and interoperability, providing data standardization solutions for metadata registration [14]. Therefore, as a direct specification of various types of circulating data in the industry, data standards are not only a key path for data governance within the industry, but also a basic tool for promoting the process of data interoperability between industries. They are suitable as a fundamental basis for examining the difficulty of data interoperability in the context of industrial interconnection.

2.2 Data Spectrum

The data spectrum is an innovative concept proposed in the context of this study, which is a dynamic hierarchical map that presents the levels of different entities in the system in circles. This study applies it to both the industrial and national levels. The industrial spectrum is a dynamic hierarchical chart that presents the difficulty of data interoperability between different industries at the international level. It can be used to measure the difficulty of converting data from different industries into accounting data, as well as the difficulty of data interoperability between any two industries. The national spectrum is a dynamic hierarchical chart that shows the degree of participation of different countries in international standard construction, which can be used to identify the status and contribution of each country in the international standard construction system. The data spectrum example is shown below Fig. 1.

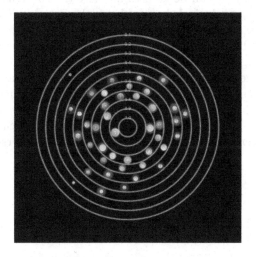

Fig. 1. Sample pf Data Spectrum

Specifically, the data spectrum is composed of multiple concentric circles, and the circles formed between them are called circles. The points distributed in the concentric circles represent industries or countries, and the size of the points within the circles is positively correlated with the data standards' score of that industry or country. In the industrial spectrum, the points representing each industry data are arranged in ascending order of their difficulty in converting to accounting data, distributed from the inner circle to the outer circle; The closer the point is to the center, the easier its data is to convert, while the farther it is from the center, the more difficult it is to convert accounting data. Besides, the interoperability of data between two industries located in the same circle is easy to achieve, while the interoperability of data between two industries crossing one circle requires a certain cost. The higher the cost of crossing more circles, the greater the difficulty of interoperability. In the national spectrum, the closer the point is to the center, the higher the enthusiasm and contribution rate of the country in the international standard construction industry within the circle, while the farther it is from the center, the lower its participation in the international standard construction. Besides, Countries in the same circle have similar positions and investments in the international standard construction. Conversely, if countries cross multiple circles, it indicates a significant gap in their positions and investments in the international standard construction.

2.3   Data Light Wave

The data light wave is also an innovative concept proposed in the context of this study. It is a two-dimensional coordinate graph presented in the form of a transverse wave that represents the standard scores of industry data in different ecological chain nodes. It can be used to measure the construction level of data standards at different ecological chain nodes in the industry. The example figure is shown below.

Specifically, the horizontal axis of the graph represents the nodes (trades) in the industrial ecological chain, arranged according to their order, importance, and relevance in the industrial supply chain. The vertical axis represents the existing standards' score on the corresponding node. By using data light wave to horizontally compare the development of trade standards within the industry, it is possible to strengthen the standardization work of weak trades in data standard development and identify key trades for data conversion Fig. 2.

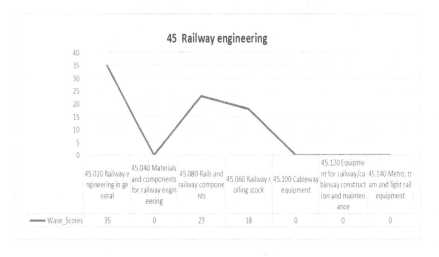

Fig. 2. Sample of Data Light Wave

3   Research Design

3.1   Data Sources and Sample Selection

Firstly, to ensure the authority and accuracy of the data, this study selected ISO, the most universally applicable international standard setting organization, as the data source. The research team crawled the industry category and specific information of international standards included in each industry from its official website according to the International Standard Classification (ICS), as well as the corresponding information of participating standards and participating member countries of each Standardization Technical Committee (TC), as the initial data for the study.

Next, in terms of sample selection, in order to reflect the ranking results of the industrial ecological chain, this study follows the International Standard Classification (ICS), treating the first level classification in the above industry classifications as the industrial chain and the second level classification as the industrial nodes, that is, the trades. The selected trades that have been arranged in order or importance of the supply chain among industries are the more reasonable ones, which ultimately including 127 countries, 25 international industries, and 255 subordinate trades. This is the sample for subsequent research.

3.2   Data Analysis and Algorithm Design

Based on the theoretical analysis in the previous text, in order to characterize the difficulty of data interoperability between industries, this study is based on international industry standard data extracted from the official website. Firstly, Excel software is used to screen and count the data standards in the industry standards, while the other standards are referred to as general standards; Then, based on the TC numbers in the specific items of each international standard obtained, analyse the distribution of observed countries in the Technical Committee for Standardization (TC). Then, based on the algorithm, the variables of "light wave score" and "light spectrum score" are quantified to represent the standard scores of various industries at the international level, the participation of each country in the construction of international standards, and the standard scores of various industries within typical countries. To measure the difficulty of converting industry data into data from other industries, mathematical statistics are conducted to comprehensively consider the content of data standards and general standards in international standards to evaluate the standardization level of data organization, coding, and storage in this industry.

Light Wave Score. The product of data standards' amount and data standards' weight values in each trade, as well as the product of general standards' amount and general standards' weight values, are added together to obtain the light wave score of the trade, which is used to measure the difficulty of data conversion in that trade. Specifically, since data standards directly regulate all data collected and generated in trade business activities, while general standards play an indirect role in standardizing business processes and organizations, we assign a weight of 10 to data standards and 1 to general standards for processing.

$$C_i = A_i * 10 + B_i * 1 \tag{1}$$

A_i: data standards' amount;B_i: general standards' amount;C_i: trade i's light wave score.

Light Spectrum Score. Divide international standards into two categories: data standards and general standards, assign different weights to the two types of standards, and calculate the standard score based on industry or country analysis in the form of amount product weight value, named as data spectrum score. Then the scores are processed by algorithms and converted into spectral score processing values located in the 0–1 range. When drawing a data spectrum graph, divide it into ten circles with an interval value of 0.1. Industry or national representative points are processed according to their spectrum scores and distributed in the corresponding circles.

In the industry spectrum, the standard scores V_j^i of different trades in a certain industry are calculated, where variable j represents the industry, for example, the j value of the Information technology industry is 35. The variable i represents different trades, that is, the industry's nodes. For example, the General IT trade ranks first in the Information technology industry in supply chain order, so its i value is 1. By summing up the standard scores V_j^i of various trades in the industry, the total score (spectrum score)V_j of the industry is obtained. For data spectrum containing different industries, all spectrum scores of the included industries are first statistically analyzed and sorted. Then, the standardized results of natural logarithmic values L_j are taken. Finally, through mathematical statistics, the results are evenly distributed between 0 and 1. Therefore, the standardized values of natural logarithms are divided into circles with intervals of 0.1, Divide into ten circles, with each circle equidistant, and take the natural logarithmic standardized value as the point diameterD_j.

$$V_j = \sum_j^{i=1} V_j^i \tag{2}$$

$$D_j = L_j = lnV_j / lnV_{max} \tag{3}$$

D_j: industry j' s point diameter;L_j:standardized values of natural logarithms for industry j' s spectrum score ;V_j: industry j' s spectrum score.

In the national spectrum, the industry spectrum scores of the corresponding industries within the country V_j are summed up to obtain the total standard scores (spectrum scores) C_k of all industries in the country. The standardized natural logarithmic values S_k are taken. Finally, through mathematical statistics, the results are uniformly distributed between 0 and 1. Therefore, the natural logarithmic standardized values are divided into ten circles with intervals of 0.1, and the circles are equidistant, Take the normalized value of the natural logarithm as the diameter of the point D_k.

$$C_k = \sum_{j=1}^n V_j \tag{4}$$

$$D_k = S_K = lnC_K/lnC_{max} \tag{5}$$

D_k: nation k' s point diameter;C_k: nation k' s spectrum score;S_k:standardized values of natural logarithms for nation k' s spectrum score; V_j: industry j' s light wave score in nation k.

4   Research Results

4.1   Industrial Data Spectrum and Data Light Wave

After following the above steps and algorithm, the international standard samples' processing work for the industry was carried out. Based on the spectrum scores of each industry, this study drew the international industry data spectrum as follows: In terms of individual performance in industries, according to research results, the Information technology industry, Manufacturing engineering industry, Services, Company organization, management and quality, Administration, Transport, and Sociology industries have the highest data spectrum scores at the international level, with significant good performance scores of 24990, 9781, and 4844, reflecting that the above industries have a good foundation in data interoperability, then distributed to the first layer, second layer and third layer of the spectrum. This is closely related to the reality that under the background of the Fourth Industrial Revolution, the information industry has become a new engine driving the development of the world economy [15], and emerging technologies

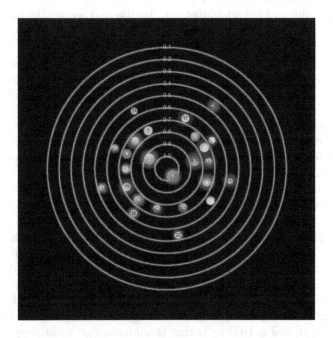

Fig. 3. International Industry Data Spectrum

such as artificial intelligence, automation, blockchain, etc. are rapidly developing, which have integrated information technology and mechanical manufacturing as the core and external drive [16]. It is also determined by the inherent characteristics of the above-mentioned industries, where business activities rely heavily on production factors such as data and information, and produce more data services and products. On the contrary, the Glass and ceramic industry, Paper technology industry, Electrical engineering industry, Wood technology industry, and Railway engineering industry have the lowest data spectrum scores at the international level, with a sluggish performance ranging from the lowest score to 76, showing a significant gap of magnitude compared to other industries, reflecting the shortcomings of these industries in terms of data interoperability. It is undeniable that its performance is constrained by the production materials and methods of traditional industries. However, with the advocacy of global consensus such as green development and circular economy, world organizations and governments should give full attention to the transformation and development of the above-mentioned industries [17], and promote their information transformation and digital empowerment mechanisms through data standardization and regulatory system construction as soon as possible Fig. 3.

In terms of the distribution of industrial circles, industries such as Construction materials and building, Aircraft and space vehicle engineering, Metallurgy, Rubber and plastic, Petroleum and related technologies, Chemical technology, and Agriculture are concentrated and distributed in the spectral circles with individual performance above average, while industries such as Telecommunications. Audio and video engineering, Mechanical systems and components for general use, Paint and colour industries, Textile and leather technology, Mining and minerals, and Food technology are concentrated and distributed in the spectral circles with individual performance below average. Due to being in the same or adjacent circles, the difficulty and cost of data interoperability between the aforementioned industries are relatively low. It can be observed that the light dots in the spectrum with close circle positions represent industries that have interdependent and cooperative relationships in the overall industrial chain, from downstream industries such as mining, petroleum, and agriculture that provide raw materials, to rubber and plastic industries, mechanical equipment and parts industries that process raw materials, finally to upstream industries that design and provide consumer-oriented product services, because of the continuous development of production factors and business cycles [18], these industries face smaller obstacles to business connectivity and are more data interoperable Fig. 4.

In terms of the performance of trade nodes within the industry, on the one hand, the trend of the curve in the data light wave graph represents the corresponding trend of the standard scores of each node in the industrial ecosystem, which can reflect the differences in data interoperability performance among various trades within the industry, identify and develop advantageous trades in the industrial system, and promote the establishment and improvement of relevant standards for vulnerable trades. Taking the information technology industry in

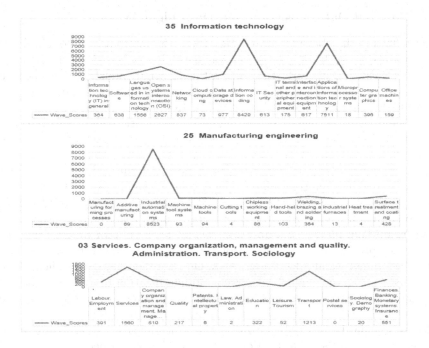

Fig. 4. Sample of International Industries' Data Light Waves

the above figure as an example, its Open system interconnection, Information coding, and Applications of information technology trades are the most dynamic in terms of data interoperability, and should be regarded as key trades to expand their advantages in data elements; On the contrary, the Microprocessor system, Cloud computing, and Office machinery trades have performed poorly in data interoperability, and should be supported as resources for the post distribution trades and encouraged to standardize data construction. On the other hand, enterprises can identify the development slump in their industry data spectrum, identify potential areas for development, and comprehensively carry out research and development innovation, patent asset precipitation, etc., thereby enhancing their market competitiveness and shaping more specialized, innovative, and small giant enterprises. Taking the Manufacturing engineering industry in the above figure as an example, enterprises can determine the development potential of trades such as Manufacturing forming processes, Cutting tools, Heat treatment, and Industrial furnaces as innovation directions, and seize their own development opportunities through technological research and development, patent development, data asset construction, and other practices, jointly seeking a new chapter in industrial development, and truly realizing the pattern of data elements empowering the real economy.

4.2   National Data Spectrum and Data Light Wave

After following the above steps and algorithm, the international standard samples' processing work for the nation was carried out. Based on the spectrum scores of each nation, this study drew the national industry data spectrum as follows: In terms of individual performance of countries, China, Germany, the United Kingdom, Japan, Russia, South Korea, the United States, France, Switzerland, and Sweden have the highest participation and contribution in international standard construction, with spectrum scores exceeding 50000 and small differences. It is not difficult to see that the countries that occupy a major position in the construction of the international standardization system are composed of developed countries and leading developing countries. On the one hand, these countries actively develop the digital economy domestically and improve the global digital trade governance structure through free trade agreements and other means [19], playing an important role in the world economic order. These advantages provide strong support for their influence and discourse power in the international standardization process. On the other hand, from the development history of major industrial powers, standardization has played a positive role in their industrialization process and economic efficiency improvements [20]. Against the backdrop of the inseparable binding relationship between core technologies, standards, and patents [21], actively participating in the construction of the international standardization system has become a necessary means for them to promote the development of core technologies, grasp patent competitive

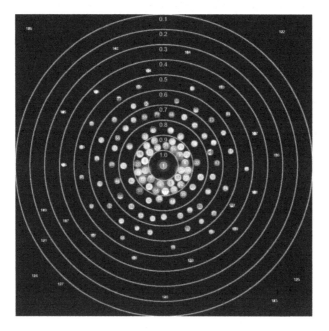

Fig. 5. National Data Spectrum

advantages, and support sustainable economic development. On the contrary, countries such as Fiji, Nepal, and the Bahamas, which have smaller areas, a single industrial structure, lower per capita GDP and human development index, have become the group of countries with the lowest participation and contribution in international standard construction. Among them, African countries such as Afghanistan, Sudan, Gabon, and Benin even showed a dismal performance of 0 in spectrum scores, and are on the edge of the global standardization process Fig. 5.

In terms of the circle distribution of nations, western developed countries such as Spain, Finland, Hungary, Canada, as well as developing countries such as India, Israel, and Kazakhstan, are all in the first circle with the highest participation and contribution in international standard construction mentioned above, while countries such as Poland, Malaysia, Thailand, and New Zealand are in the second circle. These countries with the Philippines, Egypt, Mexico and other countries in the third circle have shown so-so performance slightly above average in international standard construction. However, countries such as Pakistan, Vietnam, and Jordan in the fourth circle, as well as countries such as Iraq, Qatar, and Tunisia in the fifth circle, only perform in the lower middle of international standard construction Fig. 6.

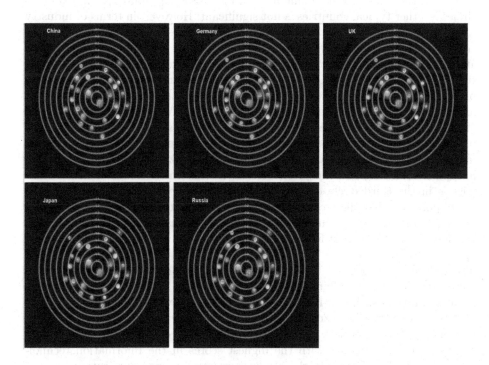

Fig. 6. Industrial Data Spectrum in Typical Nation

In order to conduct a more in-depth and specific analysis of the data interoperability level of industries within each country, this study selected China, Germany, the United Kingdom, Japan, and Russia, which performed the best, as typical country samples from a total of 127 countries, and continued to draw their data spectrum and light waves for analysis.

Focusing on the industrial data spectrum of typical countries, similar to the overall distribution of industries at the international level, the Information technology industry, Manufacturing engineering industry, and Services. Company organization, management and quality. Administration. Transport. Sociology industries in the five typical countries still occupy the center of the data spectrum, with a high level of data standardization and data interoperability, However, the Glass and ceramic industry, Electrical engineering industry, Wood technology industry, and Railway engineering industry are still far from the edge of data spectrum, and the level of data standardization is relatively low, making it difficult to carry out data interoperability. However, in terms of the distribution of industries in different circles, except for Germany, which has a special situation where traditional industries such as leather and mining enter the third circle more than other countries, unlike the situation where the amount of the third circle's industries is significantly more than the fourth circle's in the international data spectrum, the difference in the number of industries distributed within the two circles in other typical countries is not significant; However, in terms of industry categories, each country still exhibits the characteristic of easy data interoperability among upstream industries such as Mining and minerals, Petroleum, and Agriculture that extract raw materials, corresponding midstream industries such as Metallurgy, Chemical technology, Rubber and plastic industries that process raw materials, as well as downstream industries such as Construction materials and building, Food, Telecommunications. Audio and video engineering that directly produces consumer-oriented products. At the same time, basic pillar industries related to Construction, Steel, Chemical industry, Equipment manufacturing, etc. have high levels of data standardization and interoperability in typical countries, and except for Russia, the healthcare industry in all countries is in the third circle close to the spectrum's center, fully demonstrating the importance that these countries attach to livelihood industries that directly affect people's livelihood interests, those are also fundamental industries that provide important support for social welfare and social security in national development. Especially, except for China, Agriculture in other countries is located in the third layer closer to the spectrum's center, reflecting the lagging level of digital development in China's agriculture and rural areas, which may lead to negative impacts such as widening the urban-rural development gap [22] Fig. 7.

Focusing on the industrial data light waves of typical countries, the information application services and information coding sectors are the development focus in all five countries with the highest scores in the Information technology industry, demonstrating the characteristics of a huge application layer in the Information technology industry and the widespread application of information products and services in practical fields. Although the development trend

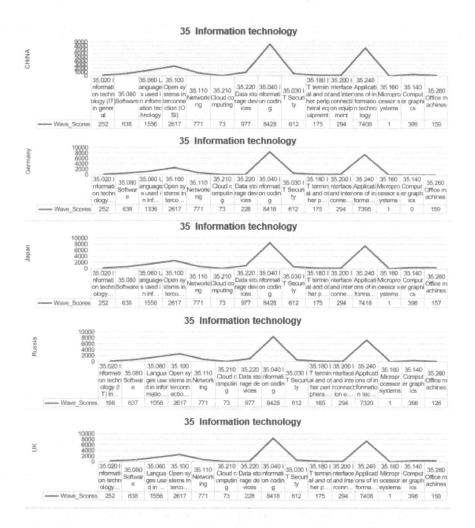

Fig. 7. Information technology's Industrial Data Light Wave in Typical Nation

of Information technology industry nodes within the five countries is basically the same, Germany has the worst development in the Computer Graphics trade compared to other countries; In the Data storage devices trade, Germany and the UK have the worst development compared to each other. On the one hand, these two trades may become constraints on the international development of the corresponding country's Information technology industry, but on the other hand, Germany and the UK can provide research and development support and patent accumulation to these trades, forming new potential trades in the overall industry. In terms of Packaging and distribution of goods industry, the industrial data scores of the four countries are significantly higher than those of Russia. Specifically, Russia lags behind the other four countries in Bottles and Pots

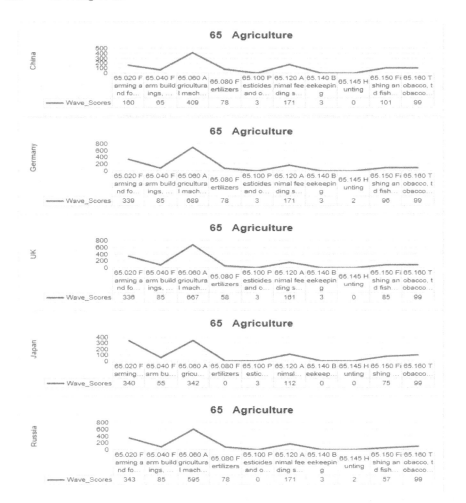

Fig. 8. Agriculture's Industrial Data Light Wave in Typical Nation

transportation, as well as Jars transportation trades. The reason for this may be due to Russia's insufficient emphasis on the development of light industry manufacturing in its past economic history, and may lead Russia to be in a relatively weak position in terms of goods assembly in import and export trade Fig. 8.

In addition, the overall scores of China and Japan's Agriculture industry are significantly lower than those of other three countries. Through datalight wave, China and Japan have lower scores in Agricultural machines, implements, and equipment compared to other three countries. Considering that China is still in a critical period of agricultural modernization and there are significant differences in agricultural development between different regions, although relevant agricultural machinery purchase subsidy policies have accumulated implementation experience in various regions, they will still be constrained by current subjective and objective conditions; The difference in Japan, on the other hand, is that its Farming and forestry trade's score is not lower than those of other countries. The main reason for this is that Japan has accumulated rich experience in forest management, state-owned forest management, comprehensive ecological benefits of forests, forestry industry, forestry basic guarantee, and forestry innovation [23]. In addition, the government's emphasis on forestry has put Japan's forestry industry at a relatively developed level.

5   Conclusion and Future Research

This study explores the measurement system and representation method of data interoperability between industries through the theoretical construction and algorithm design of data spectrum and data light waves. Through mathematical statistics on the scores of various industry standards at the international level, the participation of various countries in international standard construction, and the scores of various industry standards within typical countries, the following conclusions are finally drawn:

(1) The industrial data spectrum of the international community and typical countries have similarities. The Information technology industry, Manufacturing engineering industry, sociology, and Services. Company organization, management and quality. Administration. Transport. Sociology industries with significantly better data interoperability, and are distributed in the first, second, and third circles of the spectrum. On the contrary, the Glass and ceramic industry, Electrical engineering industry, Wood technology industry, and Railway engineering industry are peripheral industries located on the outer layer of the data spectrum, with their poor data interoperability, which indicates that the cost and difficulty of their data interoperability with other industries are high, so it is necessary to accelerate the establishment and improvement of relevant standard systems. At the same time, the cluster distribution of industries in the data spectrum layer exhibits an ecological system of industrial chain clusters [24]. The basic feature of the data spectrum is that the upstream, midstream, and downstream industries with resource integration and configuration optimization linkage are distributed in the same or similar circles, making it easier to carry out data interoperability.

(2) The industrial data spectrum of various countries around the world has their own characteristics based on their industrial structure and economic system models. However, basic industries such as construction, food, and communication, which are directly related to people's livelihood interests, are all distributed close to the center of data spectrum, making it relatively easy to carry out data interoperability with other industries. At the same time, the level of participation and contribution of countries around the world in international standard construction varies greatly, with China, Germany, the United Kingdom, Japan, Russia, South Korea, the United States, France,

Switzerland, and Sweden being the countries with the highest level of participation and contribution in international standard construction.

(3) The trade nodes within the industry at the international and national levels are represented by data waves, with the highest point being trades with better data standard construction, better data standardization level and interoperability potential, which are the core development trades for industrial digital transformation; Its low point is the trade with poor data standard construction, which is the keynote of industrial data standard system's construction and the potential development trade for enterprise's technology research and development, patent precipitation, and innovation investment.

In summary, this study innovatively proposes a measurement system and representation method for identifying and locating the level of industrial data interoperability: data spectrum and data light wave, responding to the basic question of how to measure the difficulty and cost of data interoperability between industries, filling the gap in related research fields, but there are still certain limitations. Firstly, this study only uses data standards as quantitative research objects, so the data sources are not diverse and comprehensive enough; Secondly, this study only attempted to characterize the difficulty of industry data interoperability through the circle distance of data spectrum, but without conducting further research on quantifying the difficulty of interoperability, so the research content is not in-depth enough. In future research, it may be considered to introduce measurement objects such as patents to expand data sources and conduct algorithm construction research on quantifying the level of data interoperability between industries.

References

1. Masud, M., Hossain, M.S.: ALAMRI A: data interoperability and multimedia content management in e-health systems. IEEE Trans. Inf Technol. Biomed. **16**(6), 1015–1023 (2012)
2. Fareh, M., Boussaid, O.: CHALAL R: reconciliation model of heterogeneous information in decisional information systems. Int. J. Metadata Semant. Ontol. **10**(1), 37–54 (2015)
3. Shi, J., Pan, Z., Jiang, L., et al.: An ontology-based methodology to establish city information model of digital twin city by merging BIM. GIS and IoT. Adv. Eng. Inform. **57**, 102114 (2023)
4. Liu, J., Li, T., Xie, P., et al.: Urban big data fusion based on deep learning: An overview. Information Fusion **53**, 123–133 (2020)
5. Prabath, J., Mahdi, S., Josef, N., et al.: Patient-generated health data interoperability through master patient index: the DH-convener approach. Stud. Health Technol. Inform. **305**, 20–23 (2023)
6. Moeid, S., YongCheol, L.: Urban-level data interoperability for management of building and civil infrastructure systems during the disaster phases using model view definitions. J. Comput. Civil Eng. **37**(1), 04022045 (2023)
7. Boeckhout, M., Zielhuis, G.A., Bredenoord, A.L.: The FAIR guiding principles for data stewardship: fair enough? Europ. J. Humangenetics **26**(7), 931–936 (2018)

8. Vilminko-Heikkinen, R., Pekkola, S.: Changes in roles, responsibilities and ownership in organizing master data management. Int. J. Inform. Manage. **47**, 76–87 (2018)

9. Institute of Cloud Computing and Big Data, Chinese Academy of Information and Communications Technology.: White Paper on Data Standard Management Practice. 1st edn. China Academy of Information and Communications Technology, Beijing (2019)

10. Meng, C.: Biological information standards. Bull. Am. Soc. Inf. Sci. Technol. **30**(2), 15–17 (2004)

11. Lun, W.U., Yi-Qin, X.U., Xiao-Ming, W., et al.: Study on Data Standards of the Digital Community. Geography and Geo-Information Science (2005)

12. Zhan, J., Guo, C., Lei, T., et al.: Comparative study on data standards of autonomous driving map. J. Image Graph. **26**(1), 36–48 (2021)

13. Song, J., Dai, B., Jiang, L., et al.: Data governance collaborative method based on blockchain. J. Comput. Appl. **38**(9), 2500 (2018)

14. INTERNATIONAL ORGANIZATION FOR STANDARDIZATION. ISO\IEC-11179-3:2023: Information technology: Metadata registries (MDR) . part3: metamodel for registry common facilities (2023)

15. Wang, L., Chen, Y., Ramsey, T.S., et al.: Will researching digital technology really empower green development? Technol. Soc. **66**(10), 101638 (2021)

16. Bai C , Dallasega P , Orzes G ,et al.: Industry 4.0 technologies assessment: A sustainability perspective. International Journal of Production Economics **229**, 107776 (2020)

17. Olsen, T.L., Tomlin, B.: Industry 4.0: opportunities and challenges for operations management. Manufact. Serv. Oper. Manage. **22**(1), 113–122 (2020)

18. De Angelis, R., Howard, M., Miemczyk, J.: Supply chain management and the circular economy: towards the circular supply chain. Prod. Plann. Contr. **29**(6), 425–437 (2017)

19. Baier, S.L., Bergstrand, J.H., Feng, M.: Economic integration agreements and the margins of international trade. J. Int. Econ. **93**(2), 339–350 (2014)

20. Standards&economic growth-ISO members' research on the impact of standards on their national economies,https://www.iso.org/files/live/sites/isoorg/files/store/en/PUB100456.pdf. Accessed 15 Jan 2024

21. Wang, P.: A brief history of Standards and Standardization organizations: A Chinese perspective. East West Center Working Papers Economics (2011)

22. Baure, J.M.: The internet and income inequality: socio-economic challenges in a hyperconnected society. Telecommun. Policy **42**(4), 333–343 (2018)

23. Ministry of Agriculture,Forestry and Fisheries, Japan: Annual Report on Forest and Forestry in Japan: Fiscal Year 2018 (2019)

24. Hannah, D.P., Eisenhardt, K.M.: How firms navigate cooperation and competition in nascent ecosystems. Strateg. Manag. J. **39**(12), 3163–3192 (2018)

Iterative Design Process of Smart Door Lock Interaction System in Homestay Scenario

Diyan Xian[1(✉)] and Ningchang Zhou[2]

[1] Wuyi University, Jiangmen 529020, Guangdong, China
`xiandy2@wyu.edu.cn`
[2] South China Agriculture University, Guangzhou 510505, Guangdong, China
`znc1116@scau.edu.cn`

Abstract. This study investigated the users of smart door locks and home systems in the scene of homestay space, and promotes the optimization of smart home systems. It was found that in preliminary investigation the convenience and security of smart door locks and smart products required a suitable framework to regulate user behavior and meet the interactive needs of users. User journey maps were used to record the user's experience, and comprehensively perceive the user's behavior, touch points, emotions, opportunities, etc. and were of great help to the scene of homestay and the design of its management system. In this study, the personas of homestay were established while creating the user journey map. By studying the different stages (stages and different nodes), activities, touchpoints, design opportunities, etc., these findings were applied to the iterative design process of smart home system or product interface. This paper developed a prototype of a smart home system-a framework of smart home manage APP, which was suitable for user interactions in homestays.

Keywords: Smart Door Lock · Smart Home System · User Journey Map · Interface Design

1 Introduction

1.1 The Interaction of Smart Door Look in Homestay

The scenarios that smart door locks were used including semi-open and interactive spaces such as office space, warehouse, laboratory, and homestay. There are various kinds of users, and their access level to the lock are different. Probably, the most complicated scenarios that smart lock used is homestays or short rental apartments, where the users are short-term visitors from different countries or regions.

Homestay, also known as Minshuku or B&B, is a kind of accommodation in the category of vocational short rental. Through the shot rental platform or vocational rental system, such as Air B&B, homestay owner would have the opportunity to contact with variable visitors from all over the world. One of the features that homestays differ from traditional hotel accommodations is that there may not be a front desk. The guest (visitors) and hosts (owner or landlord) get in touch online, instead of face-to-face interaction. Usually, guests contact hosts by email or through the short rent platform (such as Air B&B) when booking a homestay. Owners may run many homestays scattered in different areas, and may need to manage homestays and arrange visitors remotely. Smart door locks can support remote operation, and are more efficient when guests stay in homestays, compared to ordinary physical keys. Furthermore, the integration of smart lock with vacation rental management system is supported to increase the interaction of users [1].

Based on the Internet of Things(IoT) system, smart door locks can be operated in different interactive modes, and are widely used in short rent homestay [2].Currently, the interactions utilized in smart locks includes but not limited to, knowledge-based (eg, pin/passwords), post based (eg, smartphones, smart cards), or physical biometric based (eg, fingerprint, face) methods [3].User is important factor to be considered when designing interactions with smart locks [4], and the user mental model is an important aspect that needs to be understood in designing the smart lock user interface in the Internet of Things [5]. New features and devices can be added to such a system through integration with the central controller.

The host of the homestay is the administrator of the smart lock, and can send pass-words to guests and other users (such as cleaning staff, maintenance staff, housekeepers, etc.) to realize remote management of the B&B. Not the landlord can set the valid dura-tion of the password, that is, the length of time the tenant stays in the B&B (for example, 3 days, one week, etc.). The "Owner" password/key can be used to lock and unlock the smart lock at any time. The administrator can grant or revoke keys of any access level and apply any other administrative feature of the lock. "Resident" keys allow a user to access the home in a certain period, while temporary visitors can only access to short-term keys [6].

1.2 Integration of Smart Home Products

There are a wide range of smart home products, and the smart home products widely used in homestays usually include humidifiers, air purifiers, other smart products, as well as the control systems. Base on IoT, Energy Efficient Embedded System was developed for indoor intelligent lighting, air quality monitoring, and ventilation [7].The interaction of smart home products is not limited to one product, the whole system and the scenarios applied should also be taken into account [8]. Some smart home products are utilized to save energy, while others are used to improve the quality of life or facilitate the care of the elderly.

Most of the researches on smart home product and Internet of Things system focused on household daily scenarios, but there is little in-depth research about the smart home products and system in the scenarios of homestay. Therefore, this paper gave out a hypothesis: on the infrastructure of Internet of Things, smart door locks and other smart home products can also be integrated into a system, and developed as an interact system interface for a homestay host and guest.

2 Related Works

2.1 Interaction of Smart Home Products

Research on interaction and user experience of smart home products have developed various interactions, including voice control, gesture control, touch control, etc., and even multimode mixed interaction. Research has been conducted on how to control smart home devices by employing four different interaction techniques for elderly people [9]. Multimodal User Interfaces also been developed for Hybrid Collaboration from the User-Centered perspective [10]. Effective user interface, effective general control panels, variable accessibility, and secure privacy are essential for Smart Home Product system [11].

The Internet of Things provides the possibility for intelligent door lock and even remote management of the whole home system. Generally speaking, the working mechanism of smart home products needs to be connected with the Internet of Things, and stable Internet of Things and sufficient power supply are the foundation. Every home appliance is a unit in the Internet of Things. Remote intelligent control and interaction can be easily realized through the system interface through a linked network [12]. Mao et al. reviewed smart home products and presented cross-device interaction from the perspective of user experience. How to deal with scattered smart devices and how to coordinate diversified user needs in the complex smart home system is a challenge [13].

However, there are some complex issues related to smart home products, such as privacy problems, interaction conflicting. Edu et al., studied Smart Home Personal Assistants on Security and Privacy issues [14]. These issues have to be considered when dealing with smart home products infrastructure design [15].

2.2 The Application of Persona and Journey Map

Persona can be used as goal-oriented design techniques to support all stages of design and iteratively optimize design process [16]. Boyle et al. investigated the creation of different persona and the difficulties encountered in revising persona [4]. The user journey map is another critical tool for recording and investigating the user behavior as well as insights to innovative designs. The different adaptation stages of smart home product users, from low expansion, trust building, behavior change to minimum use were all recorded in the user journey map [17]. Physical journey map has been leveraged for visualizing the experience of users, with the form of a physical and interactive installation, and this process arose the empathy of the stakeholders and help improving the design iterative [18].

In an ordinary home, smart home products users are relatively fixed. Therefore, smart home products can be maintained and used appropriately. However, compared to the scenarios in homestays or short-rental apartments, the users of smart home systems are diversified and complex, so the requirements for smart home management systems are higher, while it is easier to find new needs and pain points. Iterative design of interactive smart home products systems APP may also require the tool of user journey map. The user journal map records the story of the users' experiences, from initial contact, through the process of engagement and into a long-term usage, providing essential information of interactions in the whole process.

3 Methods

3.1 Surveys

Quality survey methods, including questionnaire and interviews, were employed in this study. Night interviews were held with three different types of users who involved with homestay. A pilot interview was produced to investigate the users' attitude towards interaction method for unlocking the doors of Homestays (see Fig. 1). Open questions were asked in the interviews, collecting the users' opinions and understanding their behavior. From the results, we can identify problems and sort out the improvements for the existing products. In these semi-structured interviews, a degree of consistency can keep between different interviews. The users can express ideas, opinions and explanations to specified why and how actions were performed. In this way, the insight into user's motion and need can help define future direction during the design process.

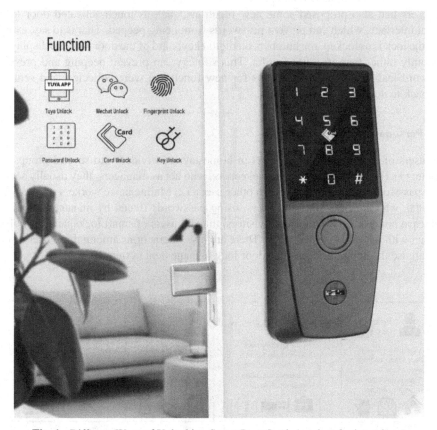

Fig. 1. Different Ways of Unlocking Smart Door Lock (product for interviews)

The existing product provides six different ways for unlocking the doors in the scene of homestay. However, at present, the existing APP interface is only used for issuing password locks and setting the effective duration of passwords, and does not provide other functions for interaction. In the Interviews, users also express their need and suggestions for new functions.

In addition to the existing unlocking methods, homestay users expressed their needs for fingerprint unlocking, face ID or other biometric identified methods to unlock the door. However, users' fingerprints should be collected and entered in the lock in advance, which is not practical for guest who come to the homestay for the first time. The guests can only enter fingerprint or face ID data after their arrival. For cleaning staff or maintenance workers who often visit the homestay for cleaning and maintenance, they are free to use all kind of interactive methods for unlocking. Because their fingerprints are collected in advance.

On the other hand, if these interactive unlocking methods are applied in homestays, all guests will need to enter their biological data and store them in the APP. This will involve privacy and data security issues. To meet this demand of users, it is essential to ensure that data is not leaked and personal privacy and security are protected.

Users had also proposed some new functions, such as touch-activated door lock digital interface, which can prevent passwords from being peeped. That is to say, every time the lock is unlocked, the numbers on digital keyboard of the door lock are displayed randomly rather than in a fixed order. This strategy can prevent peeping and prevent password leakage. These suggestions for new functional were collected, and sent as feedback to door lock manufacturers.

3.2 Personas and Interactions

The users of digital smart door locks in homestay are divided into several groups of people: (1) The hosts(owner) or housekeepers, who act as managers, they usually set or issue passwords, or authorize them to other users. (2) Maintenance workers or cleaning personal, who are both staff and users, using passwords issued by managers to enter and leave homestays. (3) Guests or visitors, the end users of smart locks, and they also interact with door locks extensively. There are also interactions among these users, and they all use the app interface of the door lock management system (Fig. 2).

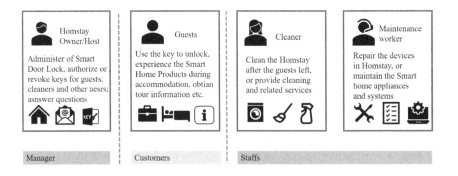

Fig. 2. Personas in Homestay

As the administrator, the access level of the host/ owner is higher than the guest and cleaning and maintenance personnel. Generally, the guest can apply for higher access level from the administrator, and the users can interact with each other through the APP. Base on the outcome from the interview, sometimes, guest would like to contact the cleaners or maintainers for services. Before the iterative design, the guest had to ask owner or host to arrange cleaning or repairment. The interactions between different types of users can be promoted by adding a new function to the lock management system APP, such as "message" function. The guests and staff (cleaner and maintainer) can have direct communication through the management system interface. Guest will be able to contact cleaner or maintenance worker any time they needed during accommodation. For example, the maintenance worker can ask guest the specific items that need to be repaired, and guest can provide details (Fig. 3).

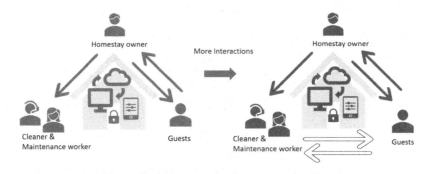

Fig. 3. The Interactions Between Personas

3.3 User Journey Map

This study created a User Journey Map with focus on the users' experience in homestay smart door lock and management system. The time line of this Journey Map is: (1) before check in (inquiry and order), (2) check in, (3) during accommodation, (4) check out. Each of the user actions, user psychology and feeling changes in each subdivision stage were all recorded.

This process was repeated six times with different users, including six parts: (1) the user/person, (2) the phase/timeline of the experience, (3) the users' actions, (4) the users' thoughts and emotional experience, (5) the touch points, and problems, (6) the design opportunities or ideas for improvement with APP or interactions between users.

Base on previous interview, the Stage1 User Journey Map was created, recording the subjective feelings of users about smart door locks and smart home systems, so as to seek opportunities for improvement. Stage2 User Journey Map was the insight into smart home products and systems, also defining touch points and problems in depth. In this stage, integration of all smart home products and finding for further design opportunities, which keep the user focusing on the development processes.

Stage 1 Journey Map
(See Fig. 4).

Stage 1 Journey map

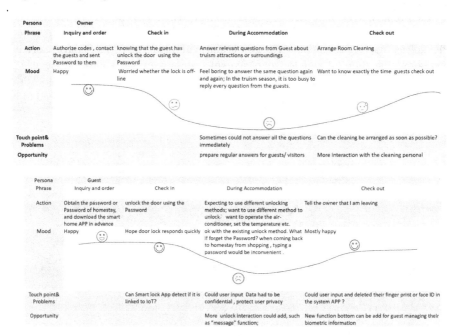

Fig. 4. Stage1 User Journey Map of Owner and Guests

Stage 2 Journey Map
(See Fig. 5).

The Touch Point/Problems

1. The door lock must connect to the Internet of Things before it works. The host hoped that the guests can check in without any problems and unlock smoothly.
2. Homestay users wanted to unlock the door in different unlocking methods and experience different interactions (such as face ID unlocking), but they worried about personal information leakage or insecurity.
3. Hosts and housekeepers might be bored or tired of answering questions from different guests. In the peak season of tourism, especially for people who manage a series of homestay at the same time, it is difficult for them to deal with the problems immediately.
4. Guests would like to get more access to smart home products, and can remotely control them. However, some guests were unfamiliar with smart home appliances.
5. The owner hoped that the guests could turn off the lights and air conditioners before leaving, in order to save power. They also wanted to know when exactly the guests

Stage 2 Journey map.

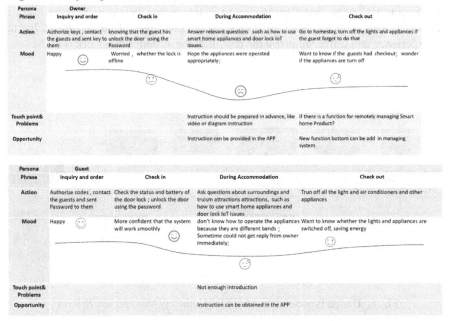

Fig. 5. Stage2 User Journey Map of Owner and Guests

will check out. They can arrange cleaning and change bedlinen before the next guests or visitor arrive.

The Solutions

1. In case of network disconnect or failure, the guest can help to recover and ensure that the door lock is online. The system can add a detection function for the network.
2. New function developed for guests, they can enter fingerprints and other information by themselves during their stay, and delete relevant biometric information by themselves before checking out.
3. An automatic reply robot can be employed in the dialogue with guests, which can help respond to the questions in time and host can set the authority for the use of any facilities and equipment in the house.
4. If the Instructions or videos of the homestay can be obtained from the management system at any time, the homestay users can use and maintain the smart appliances in the homestay appropriately.
5. Corresponding functions can be added to the system APP to help the host or guest to check if smart home products are running normally.

3.4 The Iterative Design Process

The first step of the design process was to study the interaction between users and smart locks, to sort out the problems, promote the functional improvement of products and enhance the experience of users.

The second step of the design process was to find touch points through interviews and user journey maps, and then increase the interaction between different users to improve the user interface. Also, by upgrading the privileges of guests, enhancing the user experience and further improve the design of the system framework (Fig. 6).

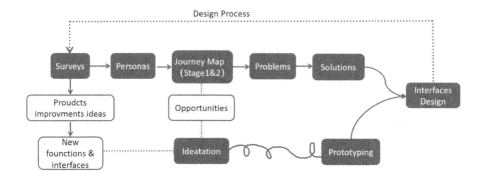

Fig. 6. Design Process of Interfaces for Homestay Management System

Ideation and Prototyping. Ideas were generated and communicated from users' interview, problems and users' needs in homestay scenario. Based on the existing door lock management system, different smart home devices are integrated in an IoT system APP, which is used for unified general management. For example, guests want to know the instructions for smart home products, just like getting the Wi-Fi password of a homestay. During the accommodation in homestay, guests also wanted to take the control of smart home products. As different smart products were different brands and with different functions. Even if the same product, different users might have different usage preferences or different cognitive levels. If the App provides instructions and tutorials for guests, they might probably have better experience in homestay.

Visualize the Function-APP Interfaces Design

According to the data from previous research and user map, both guests and owners were worried about whether the door locks were stably linked to the Internet of Things, because this directly affected the unlocking speed. Similarly, the power of door lock was also a key factor. If the power was low, it may not be possible to open the door with password, so a mechanical key was required in case. Therefore, the top of the APP interface is the control system, showing whether the door lock status (online or off line) and the power consumption. Other function buttons were designed in different interfaces according to different persona (Fig. 7).

In the first stage, the user interface was designed according to the touch point and opportunities in the user journey map:

(a) App Interface for Host/Owner   (b) App Interface for Guests   (c) App Interface for Cleaner/worker

Fig. 7. Interface for different users

1. App Interface for Host/Owner

   As administrator, host or homestay owner have to operate the function buttons "Authorize Password "and "Delete Password" in the interface, and also need to manage users through the function button of "Manage Users", set the valid time for the passwords. Also, they can check the open record of the door through "unlocking records". The "Message" function is designed as a convenient function for directly communication between hosts and guests. The "Setting" button is a function button that can access other functions or settings.

2. App Interface for Guests

   Some guests would like to experience other interactive unlocking methods besides password unlocking. However, since most of the guests have never been to the homestay, they did not have the opportunity to enter their personal biological information into the door lock system before. The "input biometric" allows guests to experience other unlocking methods after opening the door with password for the first time. For example, if residents enter fingerprints after check in, they can use corresponding function (like finger print unlock) to unlock. "Delete password and information" helps guests delete passwords or other personal information (biological information) when they are ready to check out. "Instruction for Smart Home" can provide instructions or tutorial videos of all smart home products in the homestay to help guests have a better experience. The "Message" function is a more direct platform for guests to ask questions, and book cleaning or maintenance during their stay.

3. App Interface for Cleaner/Worker

   The interface of cleaning workers or maintenance workers can be similar to that for guests. The staff can choose different unlocking methods to unlock. The "work log" function can help them recording the clean or maintenance work contents, abnormal situations, or items left by guests, etc. (Fig. 8).

   According to the opportunities provided by the second stage user's journey map, all smart home products in the homestay can be integrated, and the status and power of each

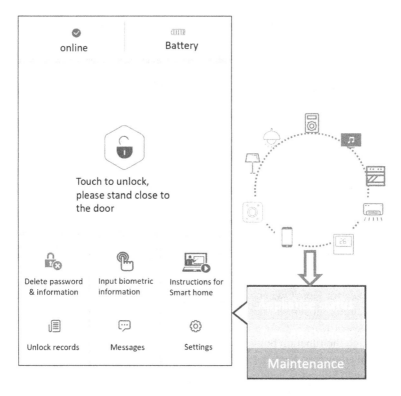

Fig. 8. The interface design for next step

device are viewed from the system APP. For example, the "Appliance Status" button is convenient for users to check whether all smart home products are linked to the Internet of Things. It is also hoped that the function of "turning off electrical appliances" can be designed in the interface for host and guest. So that they can turn off the lights and electrical appliances just by one click when the guest checking out. The "maintenance" button can facilitate checking and repairing electrical appliances or equipment, so as to better maintain the equipment in the Homestay.

4   Results and Discussion

Among the various interactive ways of unlocking, using digital password was a relatively convenient and safe interactive mode. Fingerprint unlocking or face ID unlocking might bring about certain potential privacy issues. The solution was to authorize guests the operate privilege in the system. Guests were able to enter and delete the relevant biometric data by themselves, and use fingerprint unlocking or face ID Unlocking during the stay. Before checking out, guests deleted relevant personal information or data by themselves. In this work, relevant interactions were study in the smart home system and the interface were finally designed. Suggestions on upgrading door locks were sent to smart lock manufacturers, which would be helpful for further research and development.

This work studied the interaction between users and smart locks, and the interaction between users captured and identified users' intentions in variable stages in homestay. By gathering a couples of ideas, the phototype interfaces were developed with the help of user journey map. Consequently, the touch points were applied to further improve the design of the system framework. After the integration of intelligent systems, users checked whether each smart home product was running normally and which need repair through the system interface. If necessary, the maintenance personnel can be notified in time for maintenance, so that the homestay guests got a good experience with the system. The interface designs of the system were then generated.

In the further, more functions can be designed, such as "Welcome Mode", "Outing Mode", "Sleeping Mode", personalizing light mode or product experience mode for users. The limitation of this study is that a more in-depth study could had been conducted on the interaction of smart home products, and promote the upgrading of products or systems. Overall, this paper elaborated steps on the iterative design process of smart home product management system interface, through the application of the user journey map.

Acknowledgement. This paper was funded by 2021 Education Constructive Reform Project of Wuyi University (Project No. KC2021013) and 2023 Jiangmen Social Science Planning Project (Project No. 106, Research on Service Design Strategies for Homestays in Overseas Chinese Hometowns).

Disclosure of Interests. It is now necessary to declare any competing interests or to specifically state that the authors have no competing interests.

References

1. Law, C.Y., Goh, K.O., Ng, W.S., Loh, C.Y., Sek, Y.W.: The integration of smart lock in vacation rental management system. In: 2020 IEEE 20th International Conference on Communication Technology (ICCT). pp. 846–850. IEEE, Nanning (2020)
2. Toapanta, J., Miranda, M., Andaluz, V.H., Palacios-Navarro, G., Varela-Aldás, J.: Control of a security door through the internet of things. In: Stephanidis, C., Antona, M., Ntoa, S. (eds.) HCI International 2022 Posters, pp. 391–397. Springer, Cham (2022). https://doi.org/10.1007/978-3-031-06388-6_52
3. Gupta, S., Buriro, A., Crispo, B.: SmartHandle: a novel behavioral biometric-based authentication scheme for smart lock systems. In: Proceedings of the 2019 3rd International Conference on Biometric Engineering and Applications, pp. 15–22. ACM, Stockholm (2019)
4. Boyle, R., Pledger, R., Brown, H.-F., Vanderbilt, R.: A case study in organizational adoption of user personas: assessing perceptions, awareness, and hesitation to adopt. In: Marcus, A., Rosenzweig, E., Soares, M.M. (eds.) Design, User Experience, and Usability, pp. 51–65. Springer, Cham (2023). https://doi.org/10.1007/978-3-031-35699-5_5
5. Yarosh, S., Zave, P.: Locked or not?: mental models of IoT feature interaction. In: Proceedings of the 2017 CHI Conference on Human Factors in Computing Systems, pp. 2993–2997. ACM, Denver (2017)
6. Ho, G., Leung, D., Mishra, P., Hosseini, A., Song, D., Wagner, D.: Smart locks: lessons for securing commodity internet of things devices. In: Proceedings of the 11th ACM on Asia Conference on Computer and Communications Security, pp. 461–472. ACM, Xi'an (2016)

7. Mahbub, M., Hossain, M.M., Gazi, M.: IoT-Cognizant cloud-assisted energy efficient embedded system for indoor intelligent lighting, air quality monitoring, and ventilation. Internet Things. **11**, 100266 (2020). https://doi.org/10.1016/j.iot.2020.100266

8. Funk, M., Eggen, J.H., Hsu, J.Y.J.: Designing for systems of smart things. Int. J. Des. **12**(1), 1–5 (2018)

9. Schak, M., Bürkner, I., Blum, R., Bomsdorf, B.: Smart home for the elderly - a comparative study on interaction techniques. In: Gao, Q., Zhou, J. (eds.) Human Aspects of IT for the Aged Population, pp. 66–79. Springer, Cham (2023). https://doi.org/10.1007/978-3-031-349 17-1_5

10. Gong, R., Hua, M.: Designing multimodal user interfaces for hybrid collaboration: a user-centered approach. In: Kurosu, M., et al. (eds.) HCI International 2023 – Late Breaking Papers, pp. 67–82. Springer, Cham (2023). https://doi.org/10.1007/978-3-031-48038-6_5

11. Zhao, Y., Zhang, X., Crabtree, J.: Human-computer interaction and user experience in smart home research: a critical analysis. Issues Inf. Syst. **17**, 11–19 (2016). https://doi.org/10.48009/3_iis_2016_11-19

12. Hu, Y., Li, Z.: Research on human-computer interaction control method in the background of Internet of Things. J. Interconnect. Netw. **22**, 2143015 (2022). https://doi.org/10.1142/S02 19265921430155

13. Mao, C., Chang, D.: Review of cross-device interaction for facilitating digital transformation in smart home context: a user-centric perspective. Adv. Eng. Inform. **57**, 102087 (2023). https://doi.org/10.1016/j.aei.2023.102087

14. Edu, J.S., Such, J.M., Suarez-Tangil, G.: Smart home personal assistants: a security and privacy review. ACM Comput. Surv. **53**, 1–36 (2021). https://doi.org/10.1145/3412383

15. Windl, M., Hiesinger, A., Welsch, R., Schmidt, A., Feger, S.S.: SaferHome: interactive physical and digital smart home dashboards for communicating privacy assessments to owners and bystanders. Proc. ACM Hum.-Comput. Interact. **6**, 680–699 (2022). https://doi.org/10.1145/3567739

16. Miaskiewicz, T., Kozar, K.A.: Personas and user-centered design: how can personas benefit product design processes? Des. Stud. **32**, 417–430 (2011). https://doi.org/10.1016/j.destud.2011.03.003

17. Cho, M., Lee, S., Lee, K.-P.: How do people adapt to use of an IoT air purifier?: from low expectation to minimal use. Int. J. Des. **13**, 21–38 (2019)

18. Lallemand, C., Lauret, J., Drouet, L.: Physical journey maps: staging users' experiences to increase stakeholders' empathy towards users. In: CHI Conference on Human Factors in Computing Systems Extended Abstracts, pp. 1–7. ACM, New Orleans (2022)

Use of Service Design Pattern Language to Support Learning and Practice in Design Project

Kaoru Yamamoto[✉], Yuki Taoka, and Momoko Nakatani

Tokyo Institute of Technology, Tokyo, Japan
yamamoto.k.cd@m.titech.ac.jp

Abstract. This research is a practical application of service design combined with Pattern language theory, aimed at assisting individuals who are not design experts in undertaking design projects. Study's aim is to reveal the effects of Pattern Language. In the VUCA society, every individual will be required to address problems that lack a clear solution, so called 'Wicked Problems'. Against this backdrop, designer-like approach is more widespread to respond to such problem.

Since 'Wicked problem' involves many stakeholders, significant aspect of design project is collaboration. Also, in the context of co-design, there is a demand for non-experts to participate in design process to manage with 'Wicked problem'. However, it is difficult for beginners to exhibit design behavior during collaboration in design project without an appropriate guide. Especially in Japan, loss of purpose and inactivation of discussions due to 'lack of knowledge', and 'free riders' problem have been identified as issues in group work tasks. Therefore, there is a demand for support that enables beginners to exhibit design behavior autonomously in design projects. To resolve this issue, this study examines the potential of 'Service Design Pattern Language' as a method to assist non-design experts. The effects brought about by incorporating Pattern Language into collaborative process of design work were thoroughly examined.

Keywords: Service design · Design education · Pattern Language · Workshop

1 Background of the Study

1.1 Problems Without Clear Solutions in the VUCA Era

This study aims to create a tool to support handling 'Wicked Problems' in the complex modern society referred to as VUCA (volatile, uncertain, complex, ambiguous). The term 'Wicked Problems' was proposed in 1973 by the design theorist Rittel and urban planner Webber to refer to problems without clear solutions (Rittel and Webber, 1973). In the VUCA era, everyone, rather than specific experts, should be involved in handling such problems. For example, Manzini, a specialist in social innovation at the Milan Polytechnic University, argued that the ability to deal with such problems is a human quality possessed by everyone, regardless of whether they have received specialized design education, and that something new can be created by combining various

N. A. Streitz and S. Konomi (Eds.): HCII 2024, LNCS 14718, pp. 163–181, 2024.
https://doi.org/10.1007/978-3-031-59988-0_10

unique human abilities (Manzini 2020). Significant aspect of design project is collaboration since 'Wicked problem' involves many stakeholders (Manzini 2020; Stickdorn et al. 2020). Also, it is said that in the coming society, co-design, where non-designers participate in design activities together with designers, will become necessary (Sanders 2008; Kamihira 2020).

However, it is difficult for beginners to exhibit design behavior during collaboration in design project without a complete guide. Especially in Japan, 'loss of purpose' and inactivation of discussions due to 'lack of knowledge', such as prerequisite knowledge and orientation training, and 'free riders' have been identified as issues in group work tasks (Ikariyama et al. 2017). Therefore, there is a demand for education and support during the work that enables beginners to exhibit design behavior autonomously in design projects.

1.2 Popularization of Design Education and Support Tools for Beginners

Against this backdrop that non-designers to participate in design process, design education, or "design thinking" education, is becoming more widespread for cultivating the ability to respond to such problems (e.g., Sanders 2008; Kurokawa 2013). Design thinking, the slogan for the design firm IDEO, is a designer-like approach with three fundamental processes: inspiration (produce new ideas), ideation, and implementation (Brown 2014). Here, design refers not only to material things such as industrial design and design technology but also to activities that create comprehensive new values and services (Kurokawa 2013; Hayashi et al. 2015). In the context of design education, the idea that design thinking is not unique to designers is presented.

In a design project, diverse specialties and experiences is an essential element for success, and such talent development is intended in a design thinking process. From co-design' point of view, Kamihira (2020) states that a design approach which considers many perspectives of stakeholders, is effective when dealing with wicked problems for which there are no correct answers. Thus, design thinking education programs are usually conducted in teams and facilitation is imperative (Kurokawa 2013).

Along with the popularization of design education, the development of methods is also progressing. For instance, Kumar's "101 Design Methods" (Kumar 2012) systematically summarizes techniques. Since methodologies used in service design and design research are intended to be conducted by a team, they often function effectively in a co-creation setting with people of different backgrounds. Referring to specific example, "Graphic recording" which involves combining figures, text, and images to visually record discussions and dialogues in real-time, is said to be particularly powerful when people with different backgrounds try to look at and understand something together. "Customer journey" also yields new insights when created with a variety of stakeholders. (Kamihira 2020)

With such tools, beginners have a better understanding on how to perform their work, and the effect of efficiently creating solutions is observed.

1.3 Importance of Behaviour Toward Design

However, Kamihira (2020) sounds an alarm regarding over-reliance on specific tools that only being taught can lead to a cessation of thinking. It's not the method itself that are important. Co-creation serves not only as a space for designing but also as a place for participants to learn (Stickdorn et al. 2020; Kamihira 2020). One aspect of this learning is adopting a design mindset.

In the Japanese version of 'This Is Service Design Methods,' which catalogues service design methods, Hasegawa (2020) emphasizes 'mindset' as a critical element. Stickdorn et al. (2020) also state that some service design tools are difficult for non-experts to understand. Hence, the goal for beginners should not be mastering specific tools but to adopt the behavior or mindset of a designer. In our study, we use the term 'behavior' to denote the attitude, approach, and mindset necessary for addressing problems without clear solutions, following Hasegawa's advocacy.

One more thing to consider is that in co-creation that involves multiple stakeholders, role of facilitation extremely critical to ensuring effective work. Especially in Japan, specialists of skillful facilitation are necessary in design process, since problems such as the loss of purpose and inactivation of discussions, due to a lack of knowledge, and the presence of 'free riders', have been identified in group work tasks (Ikariyama et al. 2017). Therefore, it is currently crucial for non-designers in the design process to be managed with the help of facilitators who are skilled in design.

Mechanisms that encourage participants to collaborate even without experts proficient in the design process are still in demand, which should work as a "scaffold" (Sayer 2016) for non-designers.

Given the current state of the design process for non-designers, this study explores a method for beginners to learn and demonstrate design behavior even in environments lacking proficient facilitators. To this end, we focused on a supporting method called Pattern Language (PL), which Kamihira (2020) also suggest.

2 Potential of Using Pattern Language

2.1 Patten Language

PL, originally devised by Alexander (1984) in architecture, organises practical experiential knowledge into patterns that can be understood and used by non-experts (Fig. 1). Alexander aimed to create a common language for design and construction, enabling anyone to participate in environmental creation. This approach has been adopted in software development and, more recently, in diverse human activities such as education, collaboration, social change, and even lifestyle. PL in human activities serves as a 'Media of Dialogue' functioning flexibly in different situations and benefiting diverse individuals regardless of their proficiency or experience (Iba 2013). In human activities, each pattern comprises three aspects: situation, problem, and solution (Iba 2013).

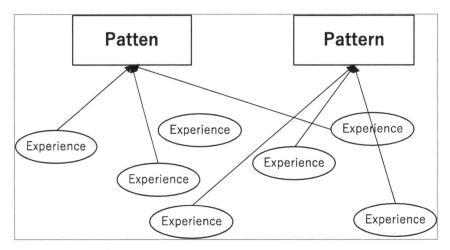

Fig. 1. Image of Pattern Language (Made by Author)

For instance, Iba (2014), an expert in PL in human activities, created "Learning Patterns", which summaries the 'knack' for learning by describing 40 patterns about creative learning.

2.2 Expected Effects of Using Pattern Language

Iba argues that by using PL, an individual can practice a new action that has not been performed before and whose method is unknown, and by practicing it, they can create a positive spiral of 'learning how to do it' and expanding their capabilities (Iba 2019). In addition, he mentions that PL is effective as a tool for promoting 'communication with others', which is important in co-creation.

Notably, PL is not a manual but rather an abstract guide. For example, in "Learning Patterns", pattern named 'Start by grasping the basics', 'Imitate first', 'Play that begins with output', and 'Quantity produces quality' are expressed. These patterns do not immediately allow for blindly following written instructions when conducting an activity; rather, they encourage users to think about the patterns and practice them in their own way. Therefore, using PL is fundamental in learning how to perform tasks through practice, and would not lead to a cessation of thinking.

Moreover, the use of PL enables the implementation and learning of practices but is not limited to the relationship between 'the teacher' and 'the taught' in education (Iba 2019). PL plays a significant role as a starting point for users to practice voluntarily, rather than learning specific methods or transmitting information.

In summary, by using PL, the following effects on participants are expected without guidance from facilitators in general:

- Support for thinking through and practicing activities that they have never performed before to acquire learning for their own practice.
- Promotion of creative communication with others as a common language.

Therefore, if there are PL of design activity, it is believed to be a versatile method for acquiring behavior toward design that suits each beginner to acquire design behavior without relying on specific tools or frameworks and in which all team members actively and purposefully participate.

2.3 Related Case Study

One of the representations of PL in human activities is the Learning Pattern, which summaries the knack for learning by describing 40 patterns about creative learning, described from situation, problem, and solution perspectives. This PL was created by Iba (2014) and was used in a Learning Dialogue Workshop conducted for freshmen at, Shonan Fujisawa Campus (SFC), Keio University. In this workshop, participants used the learning pattern to share their own learning experiences and to plan their future study.

From this study, we extracted following 4 utilization of PL that can be applied to another Project:

1. Establishing guidelines for learning before starting the learning process.
2. Using it as a guide during the work.
3. Promotion of communication with others as a common language.
4. Reflecting on what has been learned.

3 Research Purpose

The research purpose is to clarify the mechanism of using PL in collaborative design process.

As we have seen, the effects of applying PL to human activities in general is to "support for previously unengaged work" and "enhancement of communication among participants."

There are cases where pattern language has been introduced into design projects and tested, leading to a movement to update patterns with high usage effects by evaluating individual patterns (e.g., Teramura et al. 2019; Osada 2021). However, in the design process, how does using PL affects participants and the mechanism of interaction between participants in detail has not been clear; while verification of each individual patterns has been undertaken.

This research examined detail effects of PL from two aspects.

1. Learning: Its effectiveness as a learning tool for beginners to acquire design behavior.
2. Supporting collaboration: Its effectiveness in assisting collaboration within practical work involving diverse stakeholders.

By elucidating this, it is expected that one can select the situations to make use of PL with a clearer purpose and focus within the design process.

4 Method: Service Design Workshop Using Pattern Language

4.1 Procedure

To address this research purpose, we developed the PL to use and designed two workshops in which participants can experience design process using PL. We then verified the effect of using PL in the workshop through interviews with participants after the workshop (Fig. 2).

Experiments were conducted in two types of workshops: one where consisted of only students, and another where multi-generational participants collaborate. The student-only workshop aimed to focus on aspects of learning, while the multi-generational workshop aimed to test the effectiveness of co-design in practice-base as a test for introducing PL into real projects.

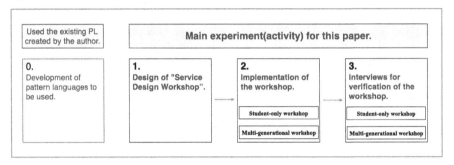

Fig. 2. Steps of the procedure

4.2 Pattern Language Used in this Study

The PL used in this study is an updated version of 'Pattern Language for Design Activities' developed by Yamamoto (2020). This PL was created by compiling 29 patterns with each pattern being created based on the experience of service designers. The actual steps used are as follows.

- **Step1: Unstructured interview:** Interviews were conducted with six service designers using a combination of in-person and online methods via Zoom, with one in-person interview and five online interviews lasting approximately 45 min to 2 h.
- **Step2: Data Classification.** Affinity diagram method was used to classify the data collected. We first used a flipchart and post-it notes, but due to the COVID-19 pandemic and its impact on in-person project progress, we used the online tool Miro.
- **Step3: Pattern Development and Refinement.** The first set of patterns were presented at the international conference. The patterns were then reviewed by experts who provided feedback on their content and structure. Based on this feedback, we refined the PL.

After steps above, patterns were finalized (Fig. 3) and created descriptions for each pattern according to Iba's Learning Pattern (Fig. 4).

29 Pattern
(*Translate original Japanese version into English)

Behavior

1. Be sincere to your excitement.
2. Enjoy exploring the unknown.
3. Welcome what's to come.
4. Beyond the task at hand.
5. Embrace multiple fields.
6. Network feed.
7. Outward reflection.
8. Feedback is treasure.

Co-creation

9. Diverse backgrounds.
10. Team of equallity.
11. Individual expertise.
12. Supporting role player.
13. The power of titles.
14. Tailored Common language
15. Hierarchy of information.
16. Constructive criticism.
17. Share concepts by visual.
18. Explain detail by words

Approach

19. "Correct" is a presumption.
20. Value in the unknown.
21. Grasp the whole picture.
22. Break down processes.
23. Antenna for information sensitivity.
24. The reality on the ground.
25. Hypotheses for the future.
26. Existing combinations over zero.
27. Accumulated patterns.
28. Refine by priority.
29. Spit out what's on your mind.

Fig. 3. A list of Pattern Language for Design Activities.

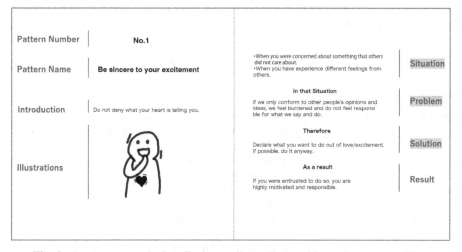

Fig. 4. A pattern example described according to Iba's writing pattern composition.

5 Workshop Procedure

5.1 Workshop 1: Student-Only Workshop

Date/Number of Groups/Location/Participants. The workshop was conducted with three groups in two sessions. The details are presented in Table 2 (Table 1).

Table 1. Design of Student-only workshop

Date	Number of Groups	Location	Number of Participants	Participant socio-demographics
16 August 2022 13:00–16:00	2 groups with 7 people	Tokyo Tech, Suzukakedai Campus	Team A: 4 people	Team A: 3 students and 1 faculty member from Tokyo Tech
			Team B: 3 people	Team B: 2 students and 1 faculty member from Tokyo Tech
18 March 2023 13:00–16:00	1 group with 4 people	Tokyo Tech, Ishikawadai Campus	4 people	3 students and 1 research student from Tokyo Tech

Program Description. Based on the fundamental structure of the workshop (Yamauchi 2013), we designed the detail of the program that utilizes PL for service design experience. The theme of the work was 'Creating a service that makes commuting enjoyable for working people' and included interview sessions with business commuters during the workshop. The detailed program is as follows (Fig. 5):

Table 2. Student-only Workshop Program

Session	Estimated Time	Specific Work	Use of PL
Introduction	30 min	Choose a pattern that you have experienced or are regularly mindful. Choose a pattern that you want to practice or be mindful of during the work. Share 'patterns that you want to practice or put into practice' within the team.	Set a guideline for your own learning before starting the workshop.
User Interview	30 mins	Hold interviews with working people who commute to develop a 'service that makes commuting enjoyable for working people'.	Use as a guide during the workshop.
Idea Creation	60 min	Create idea sketches that are solutions based on the interviews.	Use as a guide during the workshop.

(*continued*)

Table 2. (*continued*)

Session	Estimated Time	Specific Work	Use of PL
Reflection	30 min	Presentations and feedback. Reflect on the process of the workshop while referring to the patterns. Choose 'patterns that were practiced or mindful of' during the workshop and ones that were useful.	Reflect on what was learned.

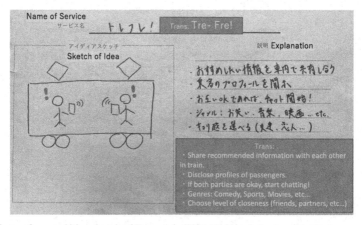

Fig. 5. Photo of created idea sketch of Team A in WS1 (Original sheet written in Japanese. English translation added by author afterwards).

Tools Used. We prepared a simple booklet that describes all 29 patterns, which could be used as a reference tool during icebreakers, workshops, and reflections (Fig. 6). In addition, we created a record sheet for participants to indicate 'patterns they have experience with or are mindful of' and 'patterns they want to practice or be mindful of during the workshop' during the icebreaker session, and 'patterns they practiced or were mindful of during the workshop' and 'patterns that proved to be useful when practiced or mindful of' during the reflection session (Fig. 7).

5.2 Workshop 2: Multi-generational Workshop

Date/Number of Groups/Location/Participants. The workshop was conducted with four groups in two sessions. The details are presented in Table 2.

Program Description. The workshop was intended to be closer to actual social practice than those conducted only by students. For this reason, it was positioned as part of the

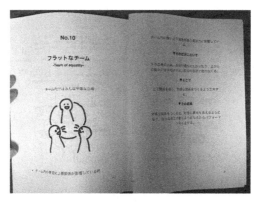

Fig. 6. A booklet used in the workshop (written in Japanese since workshop was held in Japan)

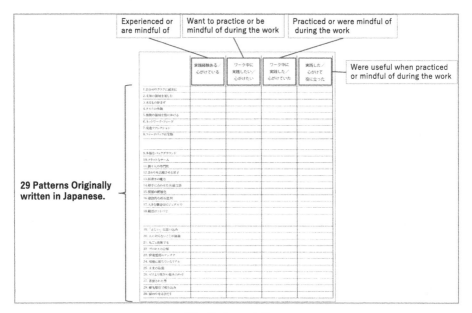

Fig. 7. Record Sheet

'Future Living Lab' project, which has been in progress at Tokyo Institute of Technology since 2022, aimed at creating a better future society together. Concrete theme of the project was to create an idea of "Future working style". Goal of the workshop was to further develop ideas that have emerged from the project through collaboration of students and working adults from multiple generations (Table 4 and Fig. 8).

Tools Used. We prepared a same tool as student-only workshop; that is simple booklet that describes all 29 patterns with record sheet.

Table 3. Design of Student-only workshop

Date	Number of Groups	Location	Number of Participants	Participant socio-demographics
13 December 2024 14:00–17:00	2 groups with 9 people	Tokyo Institute of Technology, Ookayama Campus	Team A: 4 people	2 students and 2 working adult.
			Team B: 5 people	3 students and 2 working adult.
14 December 2024 14:00–17:00	2 group with 8 people	Tokyo Institute of Technology, Ookayama Campus	Team C: 4 people	2 students and 2 working adult.
			Team D: 4 people	2 students and 2 working adult.

Table 4. Multi-generational workshop

Session	Estimated Time	Specific Work	Use of PL
Introduction	30 min	Choose a pattern that you have experienced or are regularly mindful. Choose a pattern that you want to practice or be mindful of during the work. Share 'patterns that you want to practice or put into practice' within the team.	Set a guideline for your practice before starting the workshop.
Macro Data Input	35 min	See some statistical data related to the theme and use it as a reference when considering issues with the team.	Use as a guide during the workshop.
Discuss Idea	55 min	Based on the issues identified by the team, create ideas to solve these problems. In doing so, refer to ideas generated in previous projects.	Use as a guide during the workshop.

(*continued*)

Table 4. (*continued*)

Session	Estimated Time	Specific Work	Use of PL
Presentation and reflection	30 min	Presentations and feedback. Reflect on the process of the workshop. Choose 'patterns that were practiced or mindful of' during the workshop and ones that were useful.	Reflect on what was practiced.

6   Interviews After the Workshop

After the workshop, a semi-structured interview was conducted with eight participants who consented.

6.1   Interview Description

The details of the interviewees and the interview flow are shown in Table 3. Each interview time was approximately 1 h (Tables 5 and 6).

6.2   Analysis: Thematic Analysis

Text excerpts regarding the use and effects of PL during the workshop were extracted from the interview content, and a thematic analysis was conducted (Rosala 2020). The text analysis process was conducted as follows:

- Step 1: Statements related to the use and effects of Pattern Language (PL) were extracted and segmented from the interview records.
- Step 2: Codes were assigned to the segmented statements. Similar segments were grouped together using an affinity diagram before the assignment of codes.
- Step 3: Interpreted themes were created by examining the assigned codes, considering causal relationships, similarities, differences, and contradictions between the codes. It should be noted that not all codes can be incorporated into themes, resulting in some codes not being utilized for theme creation (Fig. 9).

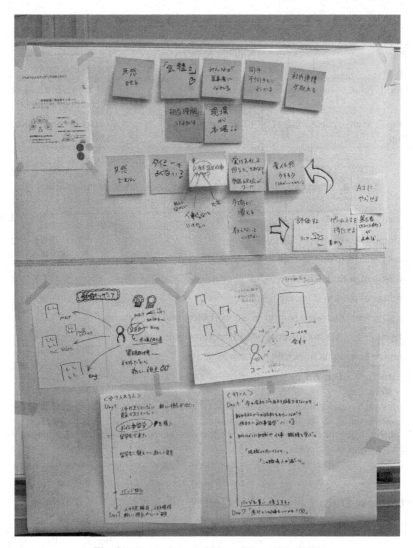

Fig. 8. Photo of created idea of Team B in WS2

Table 5. Interviewee

Workshop	Number of Interviewees	Interviewee socio-demographics
Workshop 1: Student-only workshop	9 people	All Tokyo Institute of Technology students
Workshop 2: Multi-generational workshop	12 people	7 students and 5 working adult

Table 6. Main Questions regarded to PL in Semi-Structured Interview

Questioned items	WS1	WS2
Overall impression of using PL in workshop	O	O
Individual patterns intended to be used during the workshop, and the reason why	O	O
Effectiveness of pattern language for individual	O	O
Effectiveness of pattern language for team	O	O*
Individual patterns that were helpful in the workshop, and the reason why	O	O
If pattern language was not effectively utilized, the reasons why	O	O
New learning or insights from using pattern language	O	

*Particularly focused on WS 2
Interview Notes
- The items are a rough guideline for the interview and the order of questions may have been switched depending on the flow of conversation.
- Additionally, since the maximum interview time was one hour per person, not all items were covered for every participant.

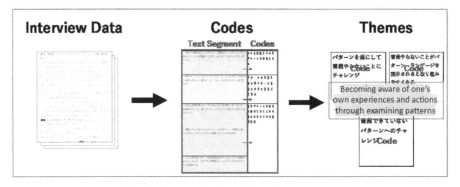

Fig. 9. Image of a thematic analysis process

7   Results

7.1   Extracted Themes

As a result of thematic analysis, extracted themes from each workshop were as follows.

- Confirmation of each theme was recorded for Workshops 1 (WS1) and 2 (WS2). The presence of a circle (○) indicates that the theme was confirmed amongst at least two participants in the workshop.
- The analysis focused on themes directly related to the influence of PL on participants. Themes not aligned with this focus (e.g., such as evaluations of individual patterns or assessments of tool shape usability) were excluded from the current analysis (Table 7).

   Other than the aforementioned themes, many themes related to reasons for not being able to effectively utilize PL during work were identified.

Table 7. Extracted themes.

Themes	Explanation of the theme	WS1	WS2
1. Becoming aware of one's own experience and practice by looking through patterns:	Habitual practice that one is always doing (unconsciously) was recognised, stimulated by patterns, and awareness of something already knew as a pattern name occurred.	○	○
2. Individual practices in the work become clear:	The chosen patterns become a guide for actions in the work.	○	○
3. Try out a practice that you wouldn't normally do:	Use PL as an excuse to try out behaviours that you usually wouldn't practice as a new learning opportunity.	○	
4. Decide one's behavior in the work according to team environment:	The patterns an individual chooses to use and their behaviour during the workshop are influenced by the age and position of other team members, as well as the PL they have indicated a willingness to use.		○
5. Design team's stance toward the work:	By sharing the patterns each member intends to use, a common understanding of the patterns team wants to prioritize and be aware of is established.		○
6. Creating psychological safety for challenges:	Declaration of patterns would be a shield to challenge behaviour that is not usual for an individual.	○	○

(continued)

Table 7. (*continued*)

Themes	Explanation of the theme	WS1	WS2
7.Promoting understanding of other members' actions:	Mutual understanding of each other's stance by declaring patterns to use and could infer the actions of others by PL.	◯	◯
8.Became a common communication language within the team:	PL was used as Vocabulary of communication during work.	◯	◯
9.Enhance an individual's knowledge and skills through patterns:	By reviewing the patterns after workshop, one can recognise the patterns to be used in the future and the actual useful and non-useful pattern for each in this kind of work, whether the use in the work was conscious or not.	◯	
10.Know your strengths and weaknesses through patterns:	Recognise what you could not do by reflecting on patterns, and clarify your strengths by reflecting on patterns too.	◯	◯
11. Bring up when the discussion stuck:	When discussions within the team stall or when opinions diverge to the point where it becomes difficult to move forward, they try to rely on PL if there is a pattern to break the deadlock.		◯

8   Discussion

8.1   Model Diagram that Provides an Overview of the Relationships Between Themes

Based on the results of the thematic analysis, the model was created regarding the themes (Figs. 10, 11). Each theme is numbered.

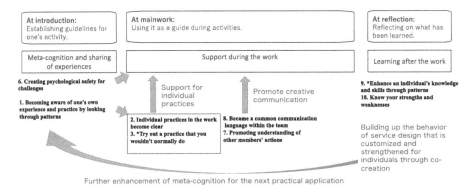

Fig. 10. Model diagram of Relation of Themes in WS 1(*Specific Theme in WS 1)

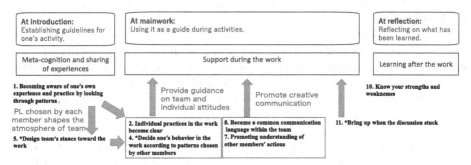

Fig. 11. Model diagram of Relation of Themes in WS 2 (*Specific Theme in WS 2)

8.2   Results in Relation to Research Purpose

In Workshops 1 (WS1) and 2 (WS2), many common themes were identified, indicating a significant overlap in the functioning of Pattern Language (PL). However, differences in participant consciousness due to the nature of the workshops—WS1 being students-only and WS2 involving a multi-generational group with a real project in mind—seem to affect how PL is utilized.

In WS1, students appeared to employ PL from the perspective of acquiring or reinforcing design behavior for the individual. This led to a consciousness of trying patterns previously unused, providing psychological safety during the workshop, and a post-workshop intention to apply useful patterns in the future. It was observed that individuals chose different patterns for the same tasks, influenced by their diverse backgrounds, experience, knowledge, and thinking habits. This lead enhancing design attitudes and mindsets.

In contrast, WS2 participants were more practice-oriented in their use of patterns, which were chosen for their practical applications. Compared to WS1, there was more consideration for other team members, and a cooperative spirit to align personal behavior with the team's stance was evident in the selection of patterns. The effects on team building included:

- Providing guidelines for team activities (acting like loose rules),
- Choosing patterns based on individual strengths for team contribution, and
- Searching for patterns to overcome team challenges in practical situations.

8.3   Challenges and Suggestions

Encouraging active use in practical, multi-generational workshops (WS2) may require additional intervention. From the aspect of tool improvement, more concreteness, such as the usage examples of patterns, might be necessary in PL description. Furthermore, active use of patterns might be fostered through strategic interventions.

9 Conclusion

The experimental outcomes have elucidated, to a certain degree, the mechanisms by which PL is utilized within collaborative design processes. This was observed in two distinct workshop settings: one composed solely of students and the other involving multi-generational collaboration. These findings imply how PL are used by participant, and contribute for applying effectively to both design education and practice-oriented projects.

More specifically, experiment confirmed through what kind of mechanism does the effects of PL manifest within the design process; from learning aspect and from supporting collaboration aspect.

From a learning perspective, it has been confirmed that PL can help individuals to become aware of their mindset. However, in terms of collaboration across generations, the effect was limited. The effectiveness as direct support after the initiation of work was weak, and its main function was to provide guidance to the team. The reasons for the limited work included issues with the usefulness of individual patterns and lack of intervention to promote active use. To utilize design pattern languages in practical settings like co-design, it is necessary to address these challenges.

References

Alexander, C.: A Pattern Language: Towns, Buildings, Construction. (K. Hirata, Trans.). Kashima Publishing, Tokyo (1984). (Original work published 1977)

Brown, T.: Change by Design: How Design Thinking Transforms Organizations and Inspires Innovation. (T. Chiba, Trans.). Hayakawa, Tokyo (2014). (Original work published 2009)

Hayashi, H., Minazuki, A.: An attempt to develop a teacher education system based on a design thinking approach. J. Jpn. Assoc. Social Econ. Syst. Stud. **36**, 99–106 (2015)

Iba, T., Nakano, H., Eto, K., Nakanishi, Y., Takenaka, H., Hanyuda, E.: Pattern Languages: A Language for Creating a Creative Future. (Text in Japanese. Title translated by author). Keio University Press, Minato-ku (2013)

Iba, T.: Pattern languages as media for creative dialogues: a case study on the learning patterns. Keio Sfc J. **14**(1), 82–106 (2014)

Iba, T., Suzuki, K., Iwase, N., Imai, M., Ichikawa, C.: Creative Learning: Learning and Education in a Creative Society. (Text in Japanese. Title translated by author). Keio University Press, Minato-ku (2019)

Ikariyama, K., Kimura, N., Hosokawa, K., Tukakoshi, K., Kikuchi, A.: An examination of supplementary teaching materials designed to improve group work assignments and promote intensive learning. In: Japanese Society for Engineering Education (JSEE) 65th Annual Conference (2017)

Kamihara, T.: Co-Design (Text in Japanese. Title translated by author). NTT Publishing. Co., Shinagawa-ku (2020)

Kumar, V.: 101 Design Methods: A Structured Approach for Driving Innovation in Your Organization. John Wiley & Sons, Hoboken (2012)

Kurokawa, T.: Design thinking education in universities and graduate schools. (Text in Japanese. Title translated by author). Sci. Technol. Trends **131**, 10–23 (2013)

Kusano, K., Ohno, T., Shirasaka, S.: Designing service concept clarifying method based on human centered design. Bull. Human Centered Des. Organ. **10**(1), 17–26 (2015)

Manzini, E.: Politics of the Everyday. (H. Anzai, K. Yaegashi, Trans.). BNN (2020). (Original work published 2019)

METI. FY 2019 Project for Fair Trade and Service Environment Improvement. Research Report on the Effective Introduction and Implementation of Service Design in Japan [Detailed Version] [PDF file] (2019). https://www.meti.go.jp/press/2020/04/20200420002/20200420002-3.pdf

Osada, N.: An ethnographic analysis of a community of practice that appreciates trial and error: through the development of pattern languages that describe experiences in PBL. J. Human Interface Soc. 23(3), 287–302 (2021)

Rittel, H.W., Webber, M.M.: Dilemmas in a general theory of planning. Policy Sci. 4(2), 155–169 (1973)

Rosala, M.: How to Analyze Qualitative Data from UX Research: Thematic Analysis. Nielsen Norman Group (2020). https://www.nngroup.com/articles/thematic-analysis/

Sanders, E.B.N., Stappers, P.J.: Co-creation and the new landscapes of design. CoDesign 4(1), 5–18 (2008)

Sayer, R.K., et al.: The Cambridge Handbook of the Learning Science, 2nd edn. (J.Oshima, et.al., Trans.). Kitaohji Publishing, Kyoto (2016). (Original work published 2014)

Stickdorn, M., Hormess, M., Lawrence, A., Schneider, J.: This Is Service Design Doing. (T. Ando, K. Shirakawabe, Trans. A. Hasegawa, Supervise.). BNN (2020). (Original work published 2018)

Teramura, S., Ando, M., Ohtsuka, A., Okinaga, A., Katsuragi, S., Shimago, M.: The pattern language based on the problems in the case of introducing UX design into company by design support approach. J. Human Interface Soc. 21(4), 335–348 (2019)

Yamamoto, K., Fujita, S., Kugue, M., Hasegawa, A.: Patterns for being creative in uncertain situations. In: Pattern Languages of Programs Conference 2020 Fall 2020 (PLoP 20) (2020)

Yamauchi, Y., Mori, R., Anzai, Y.: Workshop Design Theory: Learning through Creation, 2nd edn. (Text in japanese. Title translated by author). Keio University Press, Minato-ku (2013)

Smart Cities, Smart Industries and Smart Tourism

Enhancing Inclusiveness with Digital Technologies: A Case Study Combining Digital Participation Platforms with Living Lab Programs

Kai Fujii[1]([✉]) [iD], Hiroyuki Kurimoto[1], Atsushi Hassaki[2], Kota Ooyama[3], and Tomoyo Sasao[4]

[1] Liquitous Inc, Minamiaoyama Hy Building 7-3-1, Minamiaoyama, Minato-Ku, Tokyo, Japan
`fujii@liquitous.com`
[2] Urban Design Center, Kashiwa-No-Ha, 148-4, Kashiwanoha-Campus, Kashiwa, Chiba, Japan
[3] UDCK Town Management, 148-2, Kashiwanoha-Campus, Kashiwa, Chiba, Japan
[4] The University of Tokyo, 7-3-1, Hongo, Bunkyo-Ku, Tokyo, Japan

Abstract. Smart cities are being developed throughout Japan. In recent years, living labs have attracted attention as a mechanism for citizen participation in smart cities and have been worked on some municipality. However, conventional Living Labs have been conducted face-to-face, which has resulted in a certain number of citizens unable to participate due to factors such as time and location. In the last couple of years, Digital Participation Platforms are now being recognized as mechanisms to increase the inclusivity of Living Labs and encourage the participation of the silent majority. This research explores the integration of digital participation platforms with Living Lab programs to enhance inclusiveness in smart cities. The study, conducted in the smart city of Kashiwa-no-ha, combines face-to-face Living Lab activities with a digital participation platform developed by the author. Results show increased citizen participation, collection of diverse citizens 'voices, and immediate identification of problems. The digital participation platform accommodates those unable to participate in face-to-face settings and provides anonymity for silent citizens. Additionally, while this platform lacks the dynamism of face-to-face communication, the combination of both methods proves essential for optimal inclusiveness. The study concludes that digital participation platforms contribute to overall inclusiveness by providing continuous feedback and empowering citizens, but sustainability challenges require ongoing promotion and incentives.

Keywords: Citizen Engagement · Living Labs · Digital Participation Platform

1 Introduction

In an age when citizens' needs and local issues have become increasingly diverse and complex, providing services that meet citizens' needs of citizens has become a pressing issue for municipalities across Japan. In recent years, as one of the approaches to address

N. A. Streitz and S. Konomi (Eds.): HCII 2024, LNCS 14718, pp. 185–204, 2024.
https://doi.org/10.1007/978-3-031-59988-0_11

such issues, smart city initiatives, which aim to make cities more livable and sustainable by utilising digital technologies such as ICT, have been paying attention and being encouraged by municipalities across Japan. In Japan, there are approximately 54 [1], smart city-related projects progressing nationwide, with examples such as Kashiwa-no-ha Smart City and Kamakura City Smart City being representative.

Japan's Cabinet Office has set "Being resident-(user-)centric" as one of the basic principles of smart city initiatives. In addition, the "Smart City Guidebook (released on August 10, 2023)" issued by the Cabinet Office explicitly states that "*it is important for citizens to understand smart city initiatives, actively participate in community development, utilise digital technologies, and promptly and carefully grasp the opinions of the community and reflect them in the initiatives.*" Thus, there is a strong emphasis on active citizen participation in smart city projects in Japan [2]. And in Japan, some municipalities have started "Living Labs" as a mechanism for citizen participation in smart cities. "Living Lab" is a co-creation process in which businesses, researchers, government, and citizens enhance mutual understanding, incorporate feedback and ideas from citizens, and implement better services in the city [3]. The implementation of living labs not only expands citizen participation, but also enables the development of services that more accurately reflect the needs of citizens. Additionally, there is previous research indicating that the experience of living labs contributes to increasing citizens' motivation for citizen participation [4]. However, Living Labs also face several challenges. For example, there are some limitations regarding the participation of citizens in Living Lab activities [5], and there are citizens who, although they initially participate, may not be able to continue due to various factors [6]. Ensuring the "inclusiveness" of these activities is critical in efforts to promote citizen participation. That is why we are promoting activities that use digital participation platforms.

This research aims to clarify the usefulness and effective use of digital participation platforms to resolve participant inclusiveness in Living Labs, a function of citizen participation in smart cities in Japan. To achieve the above goals, we will try the usual face-to-face-based Living Lab programs combining a digital participation platform in Kashiwa-no-ha Smart City. The author developed the original digital participation platform to create a mechanism for co-creation of solutions by universities, businesses, government, and citizens and used the field trials in Kashiwa-no-ha. Based on the field trials, we will collect and analyse quantitative data from the digital participation platform and qualitative data from interviews with "MINSTA" staff and participants, on "inclusiveness". Based on the results, we will discuss how the digital participation platform can be used to improve the inclusiveness of Living Lab participants.

2   What is a Digital Participation Platform?

2.1 Digital Participation Platform Background

In the past, municipalities have worked with local communities like neighborhood associations to gather citizens' administrative needs. However, in recent years, issues such as the weakening of relationships within local communities, including the decline of community involvement, have become apparent along with interpersonal relationships among citizens. As a result, it has been pointed out that the relationship between local governments and citizens has become weakened [7]. This has also increased the incentive and momentum for municipalities to better understand the needs of citizens and stakeholders and encouraged them to encourage citizens to participate in the community more than before. In this situation, with the spread of the COVID-19 pandemic, it became challenging for each municipality to organize face-to-face workshops. At the same time, the rapid digitization and advancement of digital transformation (DX) in government tasks has led to the proliferation of digital devices such as smartphones. This has made it easier for municipalities to promote initiatives that actively use digital technologies than in the past. As a result of this situation, the Kakogawa city in Hyogo Prefecture is using the open-source digital participation platform "Decidim," developed in Barcelona, Spain, to encourage citizen participation and engagement and to collect needs from the community. Similarly, the Kamakura city in Kanagawa Prefecture operates a digital participation platform using "Liqlid" developed by Liquitous.

A digital participation platform is a tool that allows citizens and government to work together online to share information and engage in dialogue. Citizens can receive information from the government and submit ideas and opinions. In addition, citizens can provide feedback on draft policies shown by the government and participate in simple voting processes. It is a comprehensive platform for sharing information, collecting opinions, and improving policies. These platforms are mainly used in Western countries. Companies such as "EngagementHQ" by Bang The Table in Australia, "Citizenlab" by Citizenlab in Belgium, and "Raizit" by Raizit in Israel are examples where vendors independently develop and offer platforms. In the Netherlands, the non-profit organization OpenStad, which grew out of a project in the city of Amsterdam, offers the open-source platform "OpenStad". In Finland, Mainio Tech specializes in customizing the open source Decidim platform. as stated above, there are several vendors and approaches in this area. In Japan, "Liquitous" offers a platform called "Liqlid", which they developed independently, to local governments. The "Decidim" is provided to local governments. In addition, there are platforms specialized in collecting opinions, such as "Idea Box" and "PoliPoli Gov".

The use of digital technologies for citizen participation is not an entirely new concept. In the past, many municipalities have implemented citizen engagement initiatives using online tools such as "Electronic Civic Meeting Rooms" and "Community SNS". The "Electronic Civic Meeting Room" is a website operated by a municipality where participants engage in online discussions on topics set by them. This was used by many municipalities in the early 2000s, but most discontinued it due to declining participation and inappropriate comments. And "community SNS" refers to a version of the aforementioned "Electronic Civic Meeting Room" that limits participation to local citizens. By limiting participation to local citizens, there have been successful cases where the number of participants has increased several times compared to the "Electronic Civic Meeting Room". However, especially between 2000 and 2010, many municipalities operated such platforms, but due to a decline in the number of users, they were discontinued [8]. As noted earlier, municipalities have been working on citizen participation using the Internet since the early 2000s. However, at that time, digital technology was not as advanced as it is today, and the essential "user interface" for web services was underdeveloped. In addition, various factors, including the significant administrative burden on municipalities, such as website maintenance, contributed to the discontinuation of many of these initiatives. On the other hand, in contrast to the past, current digital participation platforms have a user-friendly interface for participants and offer a more comprehensive range of features compared to initiatives such as "Electronic Civic Meeting Rooms". Another notable difference from past initiatives is that the companies developing/providing the platform, rather than municipalities, are fully implementing the necessary support for creating citizen participation processes, including maintenance and management of the platform.

3   About the Digital Participation Platform "Liqlid"

"Liqlid" is a digital participation platform developed and provided by Liquitous. Liqlid is based on the concept of "Talk at length and decide firmly" and consists of three phases: the "Information Phase," where the government provides information to citizens about initiatives; the "Idea Phase", where citizens submit ideas and opinions on pre-defined themes; and the "Project Phase", where the government registers policy proposals and citizens provide feedback on these proposals. Liquitous has designed this platform to facilitate more deeper citizen participation as it progresses from the "Information Phase" to the "Project Phase". By providing different phases of participation, citizens can engage with government initiatives in a way that best suits them. In addition, by combining the three phases, the government can flexibly design a citizen participation process that is tailored to the nature of the project. Furthermore, Liquitous has developed "Liqlid" based on the "Spectrum of Public Participation" provided by the International Association for Public Participation (IAP2) [9], and organizes the features of Liqlid as follows: (see Fig. 1).

	INFORM	CONSULT	INVOLVE	COLLABORATE	EMPOWER
PUBLIC PARTICIPATION GOAL (IAP2 Spectrum of Public Participation)	To provide the public with balanced and objective information to assist them in understanding the problem, alternatives, opportunities and/or solutions.	To obtain public feedback on analysis, alternatives and/or decisions.	To work directly with the public throughout the process to ensure that public concerns and aspirations are consistently understood and considered.	To partner with the public in each aspect of the decision including the development of alternatives and the identification of the preferred solution.	To place final decision making in the hands of the public.
PROMISE TO THE PUBLIC (IAP2 Spectrum of Public Participation)	We will keep you informed.	We will keep you informed, listen to and acknowledge concerns and aspirations, and provide feedback on how public input influenced the decision.	We will work with you to ensure that your concerns and aspirations are directly reflected in the alternatives developed and provide feedback on how public input influenced the decision.	We will look to you for advice and innovation in formulating solutions and incorporate your advice and recommendations into the decisions to the maximum extent possible.	We will implement what you decide.
Liqlid's Function	· HOME · Provision of information	· Idea collection · Statistical analysis	Project ├ Idea Acceptance function ├ Publication of draft policies ├ Chat function └ Proposing revisions to draft policies	Project ├ Revision Proposal Acceptance ├ New Policy Draft Registration └ Voting	—
Liqlid's Screen	"HOME" Provision of information	Idea collection Statistical analysis	Project (Chat)	Project (Voting)	—

Fig. 1. Liqlid functions based on a" spectrum of citizen participation" provided by the International Association for Public Participation (IAP2).

Liqlid also has statistical analysis functions such as word clouds, sentiment analysis and co-occurrence networks. It also has notifications, the function to convert Post-it notes used in face-to-face workshops to text and upload them, and the ability to export ideas posted on it. Additionally, it provides official personal authentication through APIs from other companies, integrates the medal function within Liqlid with digital regional payment to provide incentives. It also works with data management and exchange platforms such as FIWARE to display various data on it. Furthermore, since the user interface directly affects the usability of the platform, Liquitous has carefully considered and iteratively improved the Liqlid's interface. For example, in the "Idea Phase", Liqlid adopted a design that resembles post-it notes on a large art paper, making it easy to use for asynchronous discussions. Every month, they conduct user tests with citizens of different demographics, from children to the elderly, aiming to improve and design a user-friendly interface for people of all generations.

By December 2023, around 30 municipality in Japan are using Liqlid for citizen engagement in policy making and co-creation of projects between citizens and government. For example, Kamakura City in Kanagawa Prefecture is using Liqlid as a citizen engagement tool for policy making such as revising human rights promotion policies. At the same time, in an area within the city, residents and the administration are working together using Liqlid to address and solve local issues.

4   Use Cases of the Digital Participation Platform "Liqlid" in Living Labs

This chapter focuses on the use of the digital participation platform "Liqlid" in the Living Lab of Kashiwa-no-ha Smart City. Based on the results of this activity, we discuss the usefulness and effective use of digital participation platforms to resolve participant inclusiveness in Living Labs, a function of citizen participation in smart cities in Japan.

4.1 Overview of Kashiwa-No-Ha Smart City

Kashiwa-no-ha Smart City is in the northwestern part of Kashiwa City, Chiba Prefecture, approximately 25 km from Tokyo Station. Since the opening of the Tsukuba Express Railway in 2005, the city has been developed around the station area of Kashiwanoha Campus. It covers an area of approximately 273 hectares and has a population of approximately 13,000. The citizens are mainly in the 35–45 age group, many of whom are in the child-rearing generation. The "Urban Design Center Kashiwa-no-ha (UDCK)" is a collaborative organization involving the public, private, and academic sectors working on the "Kashiwa-no-ha International Campus Town Initiative" [10]. UDCK is taking the lead in town development activities for the initiative.

Additionally, Kashiwa-no-ha Smart City has initiated the living lab "Minna-no-Machizukuri Studio (MINSTA)" since 2020. It serves as a mechanism for citizens to co-create new services within the community with the aim of solving regional issues and improving the convenience of daily life. UDCK has been actively involved in various Living Lab programs on different themes, such as "Frailty Prevention Using AI" and "Supporting the Pre and Post Childbirth". Typically, these Living Lab programs involve conducting face-to-face workshops.

4.2 Details of Utilising Digital Participation Platforms in Living Labs

In December 2022, UDCK launched "MINSTA ONLINE", a digital participation platform based on "Liqlid" provided by Liquitous. The concept of this platform is to "collect the voices of the community and make them visible", and it is used in the Living Lab programs.

The idea of UDCK to use a digital participation platform in the Living Lab programs originated from the first program of the Living Lab, which was to "Create a mechanism to make the voices of the community visible". In this program, they found that there was a challenge in the Living Lab where there were a certain number of citizens who were interested in town development and wanted to express their opinions. However, there was no effective way to collect and visualize their opinions other than those who participated in face-to-face workshops. This raised an issue of inclusiveness in the Living Lab, which plays a role in citizen participation. This issue was evident not only in the results of the citizen surveys, but also in the fact that the participants in the face-to-face workshops were consistently the same. The project team considered that the challenges related to inclusivity stem from the location and time constraints of face-to-face workshops, which limit the ability to collect a diverse range of citizen voices. In addition, they speculated that there may be barriers to participation for citizens who are not comfortable with face-to-face discussions. To address these issues, the project team recognized the need for a mechanism that would enable participation regardless of location or time limitations and enable asynchronous expression of opinions, as compared to synchronous communication in face-to-face discussions. Furthermore, they identified the potential of digital technology to meet these conditions and to analyze and visualize citizen needs from a quantitative perspective. Based on these considerations, UDCK concluded that a digital participation platform focused on asynchronous communication would be necessary to collect the voices of citizens who cannot participate in face-to-face Living Lab programs which involve synchronous communication and the silent majority. They decided to implement "MINSTA ONLINE" based on Liqlid provided by Liquitous, aiming to address real issues in the community through digital technology integrated into the Living Lab.

4.3 MINSTA ONLINE" Functions (Roles)

"MINSTA ONLINE" has three functions (roles) (see Fig. 2):

- "Collect": Visualizing voices and Identifying issues.

  – Participants post their opinions on various aspects of the town, such as the town's attractions, issues they have noticed and activities they would like to try in the city. The goal is to make these voices visible and pinpoint the challenges or concerns expressed by the community. The opinions and insights collected through this function can be compiled and utilized by various stakeholders, including area management organizations, universities, businesses, and participants, to inform and contribute to town development.

- "Discuss": Discuss the issues in the community.

  - Participants discuss issues and co-create solutions with businesses and l municipality for their city. It is often conducted in combination with face-to-face workshops. And they can participate in both face-to-face workshops and digital participation platforms, whichever is more convenient for them. The themes discussed in this function are based on the voices submitted by the "Collect" function, and in some cases are brought in by businesses and municipality.

- "Connect": Build a local community.

  - Communities are important for citizens to connect with each other. Participants can use this function to share and teach each other what they want to do and what they want to know.

Fig. 2. MINSTA ONLINE" Usage Diagram

In addition, Citizens can do the following on "MINSTA ONLINE":

1. **Receive Information:** Citizens can view information about Living Lab programs. In addition, they can receive notifications by registering an account.
2. **Post "VOICES":** Citizens can post their opinions on the themes solicited in each Living Lab program. These opinions, called "VOICES," can be posted with attached images and location information.
3. **Create "IDEAS":** Based on the posted "VOICES", citizens can brainstorm and register service ideas that they believe would be beneficial to the community. These ideas are then submitted as "IDEAS".
4. **Improve "IDEAS":** Citizens can post feedback on other registered "IDEAS" or engage in dialog via chat. They can also submit revised versions of their own "IDEAS".
5. **Further Consideration for Implementation:** Citizens can continue the iteration of revisions and feedback on "IDEAS" to collaboratively create a better service.

4.4 Activities and Results in Each Living Lab Program

We have been utilizing the digital participation platform "MINSTA ONLINE" in five Living Lab programs since December 2022. Below, we will introduce four use cases of it in each of the three functions ("Collect," "Discuss," "Community") within the Living Lab programs.

"Collect": Visualizing Voices and Identifying Issues

Program 1: "Living and Town Development". This program focuses on "Living and Town Development" and aims to visualize the issues and opinions from the perspective of residents living in Kashiwa-no-ha. When collecting "VOICES", citizens are encouraged to post "VOICES" from four perspectives: "Positive Aspects," "Negative Aspects," "Things you would like to try in the community," and "Others". Community members, including UDCK, UDCK Town Management, Kashiwa City, AIST (National Institute of Advanced Industrial Science and Technology), Mitsui Fudosan, as well as citizens and workers, review the posted "VOICES". They engage in dialogues about community issues and citizen requests and decide how to respond in detail. Additionally, the "MIN-STA" staff office refers to the content posted here when considering the future content of the Living Lab programs. From December 2022 to January 2024, participants have posted a total of 80 "VOICES". These cover a wide range of topics, including the lack of public and private facilities, matters related to transportation, mobility, community, local information, and etiquette in public spaces. To utilize the collected "VOICES" for community development, the "MINSTA" staff office classifies them based on factors such as the time and cost required for implementation, as well as the urgency of the issues. For example, "VOICES" related to the lack of public or private facilities and transportation require a significant amount of time to address. Therefore, the community development organization (UDCK) plans to utilize these insights as themes for future Living Lab programs or as ideas for new businesses. On the other hand, there were cases where immediate action was taken in collaboration with Kashiwa City for "VOICES with high urgency. For example, after reviewing a post about an accident in which a vehicle intruded into a childcare facility, the "MINSTA" staff office worked with

Kashiwa City to immediately install safety poles at the accident site to prevent accidents (see Fig. 3). In this way, the Living Lab program identifies community issues based on opinions posted on "MINSTA ONLINE" and addresses them by considering multiple criteria such as time and cost.

Fig. 3. Posts on MINSTA ONLINE led to the installation of accident prevention poles in front of the nursery.

"Discuss": Discuss the Issues in the Community

Program 2: "Creating a System Supported by the City for Parents in the Anxious Period Before and After Childbirth". In order to create support services for the anxious period experienced by pregnant and postpartum women and their partners, UDCK has conducted a Living Lab program with three key stakeholders: the service users ("pregnant women and their partners"), the service providers ("Kao Corporation", "UDCK City Management"), and the service implementers ("local actors" in the community). In this program, we tried the usual face-to-face-based Living Lab programs, combining "MIN-STA ONLINE" with seven researchers from the project owner, Kao Corporation, and citizens collaborated as project members. They used "MINSTA ONLINE" to collect "VOICES" that could serve as ideas for the service. And participants who did not participate in face-to-face workshops posted 37 "VOICES" on the topic of "Giving birth and raising children in the Kashiwa-no-ha area. Additionally, they not only collected "VOICES" on this platform, but also registered opinions expressed in the face-to-face workshops as "VOICES". Furthermore, the materials used in the face-to-face workshops were published on "MINSTA ONLINE", making it possible to check the contents of the program online (see Fig. 4). Currently, based on the results obtained from "MINSTA ONLINE" and the face-to-face workshops, services are being considered and some have already been implemented in the community, while others are still being discussed for implementation. For example, the "Parents-Cafe", where parents can easily participate and discuss their concerns, has been implemented by local childcare facilities in the community. In addition, the "Kashiwa-no-ha Childcare AI Concierge" is being discussed for implementation with the Kashiwa City Children's Department and the DX Department.

Program 2: "Creating a system supported by the city for parents in the anxious period before and after childbirth"

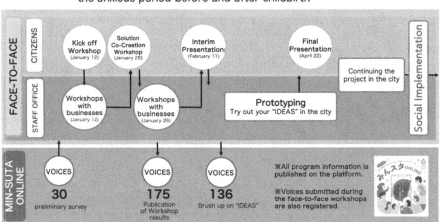

Fig. 4. Prgram2: Living Lab Program Process

Program 3: "Make KOIL 16 Gate a More Appealing Place to Visit!". "KOIL 16 Gate," the commercial facility that opened in 2021 as a roadside store within a 15-min walk of the train station, is facing a situation where fewer customers than expected are visiting, partly due to the impact of the COVID-19 pandemic. In response to this situation, UDCK launched this Living Lab program in October 2023, to address the challenges facing "KOIL 16 Gate" with residents, store owners, and facility managers to find solutions. In this program they also conducted face-to-face workshops while utilizing the digital participation platform. Specifically, they utilized "MINSTA ONLINE" to collect opinions from citizens under the theme "Make KOIL 16 Gate a More Attractive Place to Visit!" to identify issues and collect needs from the community. In collecting opinions, they encouraged submissions under five perspectives: "What kind of shops would you like to visit?", "What is lacking in public spaces?", "What events would you like to participate in?", "How can we make access from the station more enjoyable?", "Other." From October 2023 to January 2024, participants posted a total of 41 "VOICES". Specifically, there are 23 "VOICES" on "What kind of shops would you like to visit?", 6 on "What is lacking in public spaces?", 8 "VOICES" on "How can we make access from the station more enjoyable?", and 4 "VOICES" on "Others". Participants in face-to-face workshops use these posted opinions as the basis for discussing issues and considering solutions to address them. As of January 2024, they are in discussions with the store owners and facility managers to implement the solutions developed through face-to-face workshops and platform utilization into the community.

"Connect":Build a Local Community

Program 4: "Let's Talk About Parenting!". The Kashiwa-no-ha area has a relatively large population of parents with young children. Therefore, UDCK launched this program in December 2023 to create a space where parents can easily discuss and exchange information on parenting-related topics. The program aims to build a community among citizens on "MINSTA ONLINE" and unlike other programs that conduct face-to-face workshops to identify needs and co-create solutions. In addition, efforts have been made to facilitate interaction such as having ambassadors provide useful information in response to citizens' posts.

4.5   Three Strategies to Increase Participation in the Platform

1. Thorough public relations: The first point is to actively promote and raise awareness about the platform. To encourage more citizens to participate, we utilized various tools within the community, such as creating an official LINE account, posting flyers in apartments, and displaying posters to raise awareness about the Living Lab Program using "MINSTA ONLINE". In addition, we continue to promote the activities not only by encouraging new registrations from those who haven't registered on the platform but also by notifying already registered citizens of updates and new information about the activities (such as progress updates) to encourage their continued participation.
2. Establish consistency with the conventional living lab: The next point is to establish consistency with traditional living labs and replicate the culture and methods we have built so far on the platform. The digital participation platform is only a tool utilized within the living lab program and is just one of the participation methods. Therefore, it is necessary to replicate the familiar methods of the living lab program for participants on it. For example, we have made various customizations such as changing the words used on the platform and adjusting the color scheme to adhere to the color codes specified by UDCK. By making these adjustments, we believe that the digital participation platform will become more user-friendly for citizens participating in the living lab program, thereby making it easier for citizens to use the digital participation platform.
3. Show citizens how to utilize the outputs of the platform: We believe it is important to clearly show how to use the outputs of the digital participation platform to encourage more citizens to use it. Therefore, we have provided citizens with information on how the collected opinions are handled and how they contribute to the community. That is why "MINSTA ONLINE" has an "IDEAS" function that allows contributions called "VOICES" to progress to go to the next step. And we showed for citizens the flow from "VOICES" to "IDEAS" to "Implementation in the Town", demonstrating the path from a good contribution to its implementation in the town.

4.6 Evaluation of the Utilization of Digital Participation Platforms

In this chapter, we aim to examine the usefulness of digital participation platforms to resolve participant inclusiveness in Living Labs from both quantitative and qualitative perspectives. First, we examine the usefulness of a digital participation platform to resolve participant inclusiveness in Living Labs from a quantitative perspective. As a result, from December 2022, when the digital participation platform was launched, to January 2024, there were about 2,700 visits and 251 people registered during the 13-month period. In addition, 558 opinions were posted during this period. 60% of account registrants were in their 30s and 40s, followed by those in their 20s and 50s. And 61% of the registrants were male (see Table 1).

Table 1. Number of "MINSTA-ONLINE" participants and posts by Living Lab Program

–	the number of participants			the number of posts
–	male	female	others	–
Total[1]	136	77	9	558
Program 1	47	15	3	80
Program 2	25	10	2	37
Program 3	23	19	–	41
Program 4	12	8	–	10

In addition, the average number of participants in the Living Lab programs conducted only through face-to-face workshops ranges from about 13 to 15 people per program, with the majority in their 30s to 40s. In contrast, an average of 41 citizens participated in each program on the digital participation platform. In addition, this platform attracted citizens with different demographics, including age and gender, compared to the face-to-face workshops. This suggests that the digital participation platform helps increase both the number and diversity of participants in Living Lab programs. As an example of our Living Lab program, we set the theme "Creating a system supported by the city for parents in the anxious period before and after childbirth" and designed face-to-face workshops combined with a digital participation platform. 9 people participated in the workshop, 90% of whom were women and in the age group of 30s-40s. Meanwhile, 37 people participated in the digital participation platform, of whom 67% were men. The volume zone of age groups (62%) was in their 30s–40s, the same as face-to-face workshops, while the number of 20s and 50s increased (see Table 2). In addition, program 3 also found that by using both face-to-face workshops and the digital participation platform, a wider range of citizens could participate (see Table 3). Furthermore, a certain number of contributions were observed in all Living Lab programs between midnight and 3:00 a.m. and in the morning between 6:00 a.m. and 8:00 a.m. (see Fig. 5). It is clear from these observations that participants engage in Living Lab programs through

---

[1] Total number of participants and posts, including programs other than Programs 1–4.

the digital participation platform at times and in places that suit them. This highlights the contribution of the platform as a method of participation that is not constrained by time or place.

Table 2. Comparison of face-to-face and platform participants in Program 2

| | Face-to-face workshop | | | MINSTA ONLINE | | |
age	male	female	others	male	female	others
0–9	–	–	–	–	–	–
10–19	–	–	–	–	–	1
20–29	–	–	–	5	–	–
30–39	–	4	–	7	5	1
40–49	1	4	–	8	3	–
50–59	–	–	–	2	2	–
60–69	–	–	–	2	–	–
70–	–	–	–	–	–	–
				unidentified:1		

Table 3. Comparison of face-to-face and platform participants in Program 3

| | Face-to-face workshop | | | MINSTA ONLINE | | |
age	male	female	others	male	female	others
0–9	–	–	–	–	–	–
10–19	–	–	–	–	–	–
20–29	2	–	–	3	–	–
30–39	3	2	–	7	10	–
40–49	5	2	–	11	6	–
50–59	3	–	–	2	2	–
60–69	1	–	–	–	–	–
70–	–	–	–	–	1	–
				unidentified:0		

Second, we examine the usefulness of digital participation platforms to resolve participant inclusiveness in living labs from a qualitative perspective. We conducted interviews with 3 "MINSTA" staff and citizen who participated in the platform. In addition, we collected opinions within the platform on the use of the digital participation platform in the Living Lab.

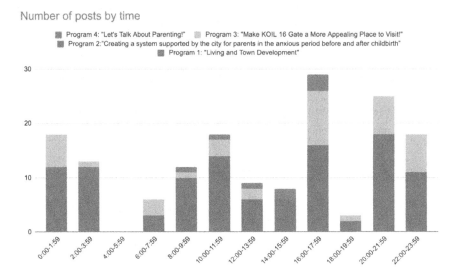

Fig. 5. Number of posts by time

The Interview Results with the "MINSTA" Staff Office are as Follows. The "MIN-STA" staffs evaluated that the digital participation platform was able to attract demographic groups that were not fully reached by the face-to-face workshops, such as different numbers, genders, and age groups in each Living Lab program. They viewed the combination of face-to-face workshops and the online platform as an effective way to address inclusivity in Living Lab. Furthermore, they expected that the participation of diverse citizens in the Living Lab programs would also address the weakening of relationships with citizens due to population growth in the area, as well as enhancing residents' understanding and acceptance of smart cities utilizing technology such as AI and data.

The Interview Results with the Citizen are as Follows. To obtain feedback from citizens about the digital participation platform, we conducted face-to-face interviews and collected opinions about the platform. First, regarding the face-to-face interviews, we conducted interviews with one citizen who participated in both face-to-face workshops and the digital participation platform, focusing on two aspects: (i) the effectiveness of using the platform and (ii) the difference between using the platform and face-to-face activities. For the first aspect(i), the interviewee evaluated two aspects: the ease of understanding the organization of information and the ease of participation. For the former, the interviewee found the platform effective for checking the progress of the program and information about face-to-face workshops, among other details of the Living Lab program. For the latter, the interviewee highlighted the platform's most important effectiveness as being able to participate even with limited time. In addition, the interviewee appreciated the ability to participate online, as it allowed them to introduce these Living Lab programs to family and friends, who could immediately participate and experience them firsthand. Secondly, regarding the aspect of (ii) differentiation between using the platform and face-to-face engagement, the interviewee mentioned using the digital participation platform when they want to participate in their free time or simply express their thoughts about the community. On the other hand, they prefer to participate in face-to-face workshops when they are looking for synchronous and interactive communication or when they want to expand their community by making friends with other citizens in the city. Indeed, the insights of the citizens interviewed reveal a nuanced approach to using both digital participation platforms and face-to-face activities. However, since this interview represents only one individual's perspective, we consider it as a reference rather than a conclusive insight.

We also asked for feedback on the use of the digital participation platform using this platform. While most of the feedback related to suggestions for improving the functionality of this platform, we were able to collect feedback from 6 posts. As shown in Table 4, citizens highly valued the ease of participation offered by the digital participation platform. In addition, citizens expressed particular concern about how opinions posted on the platform are handled, suggesting that clarifying the handling of outputs significantly influences citizens' motivation to participate.

Table 4. Feedback from citizens on the digital participation platform

"MINSTA" staff office's operational approach to this platform is unclear. As it stands, it's uncertain whether the platform will aggregate citizens' requests, leaving users with the feeling that they're talking to a brick wall. Since they can't express themselves directly to the city, this could even have a negative effect. (July 30, 2023)
I think it's wonderful and fun to have a system where you can easily participate in town development. (January 17, 2023)
The number of posts is growing, but it's unclear how they will be acted upon. Will the platform just become a place to vent frustrations, or will there be concrete actions based on these opinions? The future direction is not yet clear. (April 1, 2023)
It's convenient and helpful to be able to participate in my spare time, unlike the ongoing Living Lab programs in Kashiwa-no-ha. I'm happy to contribute to making our city a better place. (December 24, 2022)
It can feel intimidating to voice your opinion to government agencies or businesses, so being able to speak casually is appreciated. (December 24, 2022)

As noted earlier in the quantitative data, it is evident that the digital participation platform enables a greater number of participants, including people of different ages and genders, to participate at any time, including late at night and early in the morning, compared to face-to-face based Living Lab programs. In addition, in the qualitative survey (interviews), "MINSTA" staff evaluated the potential for improved inclusiveness and citizenship development in the Living Lab through increased access for more citizens to participate in the programs. In addition, citizens appreciated the ease of receiving information about Living Lab programs and the convenience of being able to participate easily. From a qualitative perspective, both the office staff and citizens expressed positive attitude towards utilizing the digital participation platform in Living Lab programs. The results of both quantitative and qualitative surveys suggest that the digital participation platform is somewhat effective as a tool for enhancing inclusiveness in the Living Lab. Furthermore, we consider it a significant achievement when cases arise, such as the installation of accident prevention poles in front of the nursery school, where citizen posts on the platform serve as a starting point for collaborative action to address issues. The emergence of cases where community issues which remained unnoticed through face-to-face initiatives alone are visualized and resolved through the platform. We believe these cases are a critical factor in demonstrating the effectiveness of the platform.

5 Considerations for the Effective Operation of Digital Participation Platform

In this section, we outline several considerations for the effective operation of the digital participation platform, based on the experience in Kashiwa-no-ha:

1. Considerations Before Starting Implementation and Operation: In the initial stages of implementation, it is essential to avoid falling into the trap of "solutionism", where the belief that 'introducing the platform will make things more effective" prevails. It is important to understand that the digital participation platform is only a tool and to consider carefully about how to operate it to achieve effective results. Therefore, strategic planning is essential, including selecting themes that meet with citizens' needs, utilizing existing communication channels, and coordinating promotional efforts in collaboration with local organizations and schools. It's also important to understand that the digital participation platform may not yield immediate results at launch. It's necessary to consider operational strategies and maintain a long-term perspective in operations, as the number of participants will gradually increase over time with continued operation. Before implementation, it's effective to have a common understanding that the digital participation platform is not meant to be used for a short period of time but should be continuously operated and improved over time.

2. Accessibility: When considering inclusiveness, accessibility is a crucial aspect to examine. As mentioned in Chapter 4, the platform's participant base primarily ranges from the ages of 20s and 60s, with fewer participants under the age of 10 or over the age of 70. It's especially important to adjust ensure accessibility for children and the elderly. One way to improve accessibility is to improve the user interface of the digital participation platform. Conduct regular user testing to ensure that the platform is user-friendly and iterate improvements to the user-interface and functionality based on feedback. Alternatively, it would be effective to provide opportunities for participation not only through the digital participation platform but also through face-to-face interactions because we consider that some citizens may struggle with digital technology.

3. Hybrid Operation of Face-to-Face Activities and Digital Participation Platforms: Through our experience in Kashiwa-no-ha, we value the combination of face-to-face activities and digital platforms because when the two complement each other, we can get closer to a more favorable process as a citizen empowerment and civic engagement process. The digital participation platform enables citizens to participate

regardless of time and place. In addition, the ability to participate anonymously lowers barriers for citizens who may not be accustomed to face-to-face discussions. And because the interactions are text-based, it is less likely that the strength of arguments will dominate, giving citizens an equal opportunity to make a statement fairly. In addition, because the records are kept online, the platform can serve as an archive and be open, contributing to enhanced transparency in activities. On the other hand, face-to-face activities offer a sense of immediacy in discussions, and discussions tend to be more lively compared to the digital participation platform, which rely on text-based communication. Additionally, face-to-face interactions facilitate the expansion of citizens' social networks, fostering community building related to town development. In this way, we believe that the use of a digital participation platform that enables asynchronous communication, in addition to synchronous communication such as face-to-face workshops, would be effective. Based on the earlier, we think that digital participation platforms are well suited for informing citizens during initiatives and for collecting diverse voices, especially in the brainstorming phase where broad input is needed. On the other hand, face-to-face activities, which facilitate synchronous communication, are considered more suitable for the phase of shaping into ideas (convergence phase). As stated earlier, both face-to-face activities and digital participation platforms have their own advantages and disadvantages. Therefore, it is preferable to design Living Lab programs that utilize both methods, understanding the characteristics of face-to-face initiatives and digital participation platforms (Fig. 6).

4. Effectiveness Verification and Metrics: It is necessary to consider Key Performance Indicators (KPIs) to measure the effectiveness of the digital participation platform. Currently, metrics such as the number of participants and posts on the platform are primarily used as Key Performance Indicators (KPIs), but we believe that these metrics alone are not sufficient. For example, it would be effective to evaluate processes by comparing predictions to outcomes, or by comparing to other cases on similar themes. In addition, it would be valuable to quantitatively assess changes in citizen interest in town development. Furthermore, from an inclusiveness perspective, it would be beneficial to include indicators related to the demographics of platform participants, such as age and gender. In addition, we believe it is critical to integrate the effectiveness verification mechanism as part of the platform's functionality. By having the digital participation platform serve as the user interface for effectiveness verification, operators can improve activities from the citizen's perspective and evaluate activities without feeling burdened, even during the period of platform utilization.

5. Designing Motivation to Participate: To enhance the inclusiveness of Living Lab programs, it is essential to ensure citizens' continuous access to the digital participation platform. For this reason, it is necessary to consider the design of effective motivation strategies to encourage citizen participation. To motivate citizens to participate in the platform, it is important to demonstrate its effectiveness (1) and to select themes of high interest (2). Regarding the first point (1), of course, if there is no effectiveness, meaning that the opinions expressed through the platform are not reflected in the community at all, citizens will not be motivated to participate. As pointed out by the feedback from citizens in the previous chapter, it is crucial for citizens to feel that their opinions are implemented in the community or that their feedback is reflected and beneficial to the community. To demonstrate effectiveness, it would be effective

to "clearly illustrate how outputs are utilized" and "implement citizen feedback in the community". Disclosing information to citizens about how opinions posted on the participation platform are shaped during face-to-face workshops and ultimately reflected in the community can serve as motivation to participate. It is also important to implement ideas from citizens that resonate within the community, rather than simply collecting and visualizing their needs. Regarding the second point (2), it is also effective to select themes that are of high interest to citizens. This will encourage continued participation in the digital participation platform and attract new participants. In the case of Living Labs, it is especially important to consider themes from the perspective of the citizens of the community. Therefore, it would be effective to collect information on topics of interest to participants through surveys conducted at the time of account creation on the platform. However, it is not just a matter of addressing themes that are of high interest to citizens. It's also important to ensure that the themes selected are in line with the objectives of the stakeholders, and that the objectives of the stakeholders are in line with the needs of the citizens.

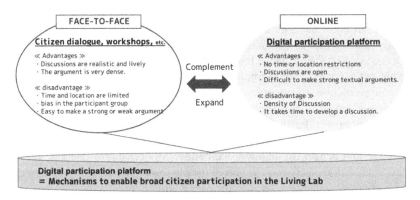

Fig. 6. Hybrid Operation of Face-to-Face Activities and Digital Participation Platform

6 Conclusion - Perspectives for Co-Creation Processes in Living Labs Using Digital Participation Platforms

As noted in Chapter 4, the digital participation platform attracted a larger and more diverse group of citizens than the face-to-face Living Lab programs. There were also a significant number of late night and early morning posts, times when face-to-face workshops were not conducted. In addition, the feedback from citizen interviews regarding the existence of digital pathways to the Living Labs was positive. Based on these findings, it appears that the participation platform is helping to enhance the inclusiveness of Living Lab activities. Additionally, it has become clear that beyond the introduction of the digital participation platform, the way it is operated is crucial. Therefore, to use the platform more effectively, it is necessary to consider how to balance face-to-face activities with the digital participation platform. In this consideration, it is important to recognize the qualitative differences between asynchronous communication on the digital platform and synchronous communication in face-to-face interactions (as discussed in Chapter 4). For example, during the brainstorming phase in Living Lab program, using a digital participation platform rather than face-to-face interactions help collect a greater number of opinions and allow for quantitative analysis. However, during the rapid service refinement phase, face-to-face workshops are more effective. In this way, by considering the roles expected of citizens in each phase of the program, and the qualitative differences between face-to-face and digital interactions, it's possible to strategically design a Living Lab program that ensures inclusivity without simply aiming to increase the number of participants indiscriminately. In addition, reference to the IPA2 spectrum may be beneficial when considering the type of participation expected from citizens at each phase of the Living Lab program.

In addition, participation in the digital participation platform provides citizens with an opportunity to learn about the current state of the community and understand the perspectives of other citizens. In addition, both citizens and officials can experience a positive feedback loop from their participation, which can increase their understanding of town development and their motivation to participate further. Moreover, while traditional citizen engagement activities have largely been conducted in face-to-face settings, the feedback loop within the themes addressed on the platform operates on a shorter cycle compared to stand-alone face-to-face workshops. From this perspective, there is potential to empower citizens through the digital participation platform, which underscores the value of the digital participation platform. In addition, in terms of enabling broader citizen participation and empowerment, living lab programs and digital citizen participation platforms are compatible. Combining the two can create synergies that lead to more effective initiatives.

Acknowledgments. We wish to express our sincere gratitude to the anonymous reviewers and editors for their insightful comments and suggestions. Additionally, we would like to extend our utmost appreciation to the UDCK (Urban Design Center Kashiwa-no-ha) for their invaluable assistance in this study.

Disclosure of Interests. The authors have no competing interests to declare that are relevant to the content of this article.

References

1. Cabinet Office Homepage. https://www8.cao.go.jp/cstp/stmain/20220713smartcity.html. Accessed 20 Jan 2024

2. Cabinet Office / Ministry of Internal Affairs and Communications / Ministry of Economy, Trade and Industry / Ministry of Land, Infrastructure, Transport and Tourism: Smart City Guidebook 2023.08 ver. 2.00. https://www8.cao.go.jp/cstp/society5_0/smartcity/sc-guid-book-0-125-2.html. Accessed 29 Jan 2024

3. Bergvall-Kareborn, B., Stahlbrost, A.: Living Lab: an open and citizen-centric approach for innovation. Int. J. Innov. Reg. Dev. **1**(4), 356–370 (2009). https://doi.org/10.1504/IJIRD.2009.022727

4. Jooho, P., Sayaka, F.: Civic engagement in a citizen-led living lab for smart cities: evidence from South Korea. Urban Plan. **8**(2), 93–107 (2023). ISSN: 2183–7635. https://doi.org/10.17645/up.v8i2.6361

5. Cardullo, P., Kitchin, R., Di Feliciantonio, C.: Living labs and vacancy in the neoliberal city. Cities **73**, 44–50 (2018). https://doi.org/10.1016/j.cities.2017.10.008

6. Habibipour, A., Georges, A., Ståhlbröst, A., Schuurman, D., Bergvall-Kåreborn, B.: A taxonomy of factors influencing drop-out behaviour in living lab field tests. Technol. Innov. Manag. Rev. **8**(5), 5–21 (2018). https://doi.org/10.22215/timreview/1155

7. 山内 一宏: 少子高齢化時代におけるコミュニティの役割 -地域コミュニティの再生-. 立法と調査 / 参議院事務局企画調整室 編 (288), 189–195 (2009). 参議院事務局

8. 中野 邦彦: 官製地域SNSが廃止に至る経緯に関する考察 -自治体職員へのインタビュー調査より-. 社会・経済システム 35 巻 (2014)

9. IAP2 Spectrum of Public Participation. https://iap2.org.au/resources/spectrum/. Accessed 29 Jan 2024

10. Kashiwa City, Chiba:"FutureCity" Inisiative. https://future-city.go.jp/pdf/torikumi_city/kashiwa/futurecity_panel_en.pdf. Accessed 29 Jan 2024

Development of a Prototype for the Monitoring and Management of Telecommunications Network Infrastructure

Leonel Hernandez Collante[1]([envelope]), Hugo Hernandez Palma[2],
Ana Maria Charris Muñoz[3], and Eliana Almarales Torres[3]

[1] Faculty of Engineering, Institución Universitaria de Barranquilla IUB, Barranquilla, Colombia
lhernandezc@unibarranquilla.edu.co
[2] Department of Industrial Engineering, Corporación Universitaria Latinoamericana CUL,
Barranquilla, Colombia
hhernandez@ul.edu.co
[3] Social Communication-Digital Media Program, Universidad de la Costa CUC,
Barranquilla, Colombia
{Acharris29,Atorres74}@cuc.edu.co

Abstract. This research project proposes developing a management system for monitoring the telecommunications network infrastructure at the University Institution of Barranquilla, specifically in the IUB Plaza de la Paz campus in Barranquilla. In this institution, a critical problem related to the network infrastructure has been identified, manifested in various issues and shortcomings that directly impact the operation and quality of communication services at the headquarters. Among the most outstanding problems are the frequent interruption of Internet service, slow data transfer, and the need for an effective network monitoring and management tool. These drawbacks have decreased productivity and the quality of the academic experience for students and staff. The underlying causes of these shortcomings include the need for a comprehensive solution for proactive network infrastructure monitoring, the absence of preventive maintenance policies, and the growing bandwidth demand due to the increased connected devices. The importance of carrying out this project lies in the pressing need to improve the telecommunications network infrastructure at the headquarters, contribute to the technological growth of the institution, and strengthen its capacity to offer efficient and high-quality communication services. This, in turn, will result in a more efficient academic environment and greater satisfaction of the educational community, offering a more reliable network, less downtime, and a greater capacity to adapt to the constantly evolving demands of education and technology. The research methodology is based on a quantitative approach, selected to diagnose the telecommunications infrastructure on the Plaza De La Paz University Institution of Barranquilla (IUB) campus and evaluate its impact on the quality of services. This quantitative method will allow the collection of numerical data, enabling a statistical analysis that measures and quantifies various aspects related to the quality and efficiency of telecommunications services. Along these lines, the research is classified as non-experimental, supported by a solid theoretical basis and the ethics of not intervening directly in the network infrastructure. The project phases follow the top-down methodology for the design of telematics systems. Ultimately,

N. A. Streitz and S. Konomi (Eds.): HCII 2024, LNCS 14718, pp. 205–220, 2024.
https://doi.org/10.1007/978-3-031-59988-0_12

the successful implementation of the prototype will contribute significantly to the continuous improvement of the network infrastructure, ensuring a more efficient academic environment and a satisfying experience for students and staff-

Keywords: Service status · Alert management · Network infrastructure · Monitoring and Servers

1 Introduction

In today's digital world, an entity's efficiency and performance are not only linked to diligent employees and outstanding teams. To ensure smooth operation, it is essential to have a solid, clean, and Secure network infrastructure [1]. The proper network infrastructure can result in poor user experience and security challenges that could impact staff productivity, generate additional costs, and damage the organization's reputation. As such, leaders of higher education institutions must understand the importance of network infrastructure and know its challenges and opportunities, as higher education institutions rely heavily on efficient network infrastructure to facilitate communication, collaboration, and access to essential digital resources. The University Institution of Barranquilla (IUB), specifically in its Plaza de la Paz campus, is no stranger to this reality. This educational environment, increasingly dependent on information technologies, requires a robust and reliable telecommunications infrastructure to effectively support academic, administrative, and research operations and provide quality services to students, teachers, and administrative staff. In this context, there is a pressing need to address the challenges posed by the management of its network infrastructure, affecting the availability and quality of telecommunications services.

This project aims to develop an advanced prototype for monitoring and managing the network infrastructure at the IUB - Plaza de la Paz to address the challenges inherent in managing this infrastructure. The Monitoring and Management System (SMGR) prototype represents a comprehensive and proactive solution to address recurring problems, such as Internet service interruptions, slow data transfer, and an effective monitoring and management tool network. These previously announced shortcomings occur on dates when several users connected to institutional platforms are expected during enrollment and module assignment periods. These inconveniences have decreased productivity and the quality of the academic experience for students and staff. The above is supported given that the network interruption implies that teachers and students need help to adequately access institutional resources or consume the necessary content, which can harm critical processes such as enrollment on the dates established by the institution.

Added to the obsolescence, whether in terms of operating systems or programs, it directly affects the ability of students to participate, which implies setbacks on their part while resolving so as not to harm their learning. The underlying causes of these shortcomings include the need for a comprehensive solution for proactive network infrastructure monitoring, the absence of preventive maintenance policies, and the increasing demand for bandwidth due to the increase in connected devices.

The SMGR seeks to supervise the network infrastructure in real time and analyze and optimize its operation. Through the collection and analysis of data in real-time, this system will allow potential problems to be identified before they affect users, guarantee the availability of services, and facilitate decision-making based on data and alerts. The importance of carrying out this project lies in the pressing need to improve the telecommunications network infrastructure at the headquarters, contribute to the technological growth of the institution, and strengthen its capabilities to offer efficient and high-quality communication services. This, in turn, will result in a more efficient academic environment and greater satisfaction for the educational community, offering a more reliable network, less downtime, and a more remarkable ability to adapt to the constantly evolving demands of education and technology.

2 Materials and Methods

2.1 Monitoring and Management System. Literature Review

The importance of the project lies in the fact that the need for early detection of infrastructure problems is a significant obstacle to effective management. Critical issues are discovered too late without a comprehensive monitoring solution, increasing recovery times and negatively impacting user satisfaction. According to [2], monitoring is crucial in network infrastructure because it allows you to identify and resolve IT problems before they impact critical processes in a company, institution, area, etc.

The literature reviewed highlights the critical importance of implementing monitoring systems in business and educational environments. Technologies are constantly evolving, and it is necessary to adapt to their challenges. The management of systems, especially for medium-sized SMEs that lack efficient solutions, is addressed in the study by [3] that focused on the design of a monitoring tool using CACTI to meet the needs of these companies, offering a solution that provides real-time information about the status of servers and data centers. The waterfall methodology used in this project allowed us to address the identified problems and develop a comprehensive solution sequentially.

On the other hand, [4] highlights automation and virtualization in web infrastructure, using tools such as Ansible and VMWARE. The successful implementation of an automated balancing system and the application of a multi-stage methodology demonstrate the effectiveness of these technologies in improving performance and reducing costs. [5] addresses the centralization of infrastructure management in cloud environments through a unified mechanism and a Command Line Interface (CLI). This approach provides solid foundations for implementing a configurable monitoring system, highlighting the importance of Infrastructure as Code (IaC) and process automation. [6] presented a monitoring system based on ELK Stack to improve IT governance, providing an effective solution to manage outages and anomalies in IT resources. The bibliographic review and conceptual analysis support the effectiveness of this implementation, highlighting the capacity of data collection and analysis for the early detection of incidents.

[7] carried out a study focusing on the needs of a higher education institution lacking a server monitoring system. To achieve this, they used an investigative methodology that focused on collecting information through the structure of the IP packet sent by the Netflow protocol, analyzing elements such as destination address, destination port, source address, source port, packet count, bit counting, and protocol.

In the research developed by [8], a traffic analysis was carried out in a simulated environment with VLANs to offer recommendations for service policies and the design of a UPS network. For this, an analytical application methodology was used, which allowed the evaluation of the different incidents and results of the measurements carried out. In the study developed by [9], the WhatsUp monitoring tool was used to analyze the infrastructure of a large company's network in the mining sector in Colombia, which changed from a centralized infrastructure to a distributed one, optimizing network resources. In the same sense, in the network infrastructure design proposal developed by [10], a detailed study was carried out to implement a monitoring and management tool for the new network. Similar studies were developed by [11] [12, 13] for different companies or even home infrastructure. For example, [14] in their research made an exhaustive monitoring process of the wireless LAN to optimize the infrastructure through an SDN paradigm.

The reviewed literature provides a solid and diverse base of approaches and technologies for infrastructure management and monitoring. These studies offer valuable contributions, from designing specific tools to applying innovative methodologies and technologies. This research will benefit from integrating this knowledge to develop an efficient and adaptable monitoring system for the University Institution of Barranquilla at the Plaza de la Paz campus.

2.2 Network Concepts. Project Components

IT Infrastructure Monitoring. IT infrastructure monitoring (ITIM) monitors critical parameters across various physical and virtual devices in an organization's IT infrastructure. This is an end-to-end activity aimed at ensuring optimal performance of individual elements of the IT infrastructure, eliminating downtime, ensuring faster management of IT failures, and proactive monitoring of IT security. This monitoring is complex since multiple devices and factors are involved, each of which must be given its corresponding importance.

IT infrastructure monitoring can be broken down into five components, as shown in Fig. 1 [15], each aiming to achieve performance optimization, security optimization, downtime reduction, or a combination.

This management is made up of 5 essential components:

- Monitoring of the physical and virtual infrastructure: It is responsible for guaranteeing the excellent condition, availability, and optimal performance of all the critical devices of a network, which is not limited to the devices but extends to the monitoring of the various processes and services that run on those devices.
- Bandwidth Monitoring: Helps optimize the availability and performance of devices in an IT infrastructure. Therefore, it must be done at the infrastructure level (for individual devices based on capacity and criticality) and at the global network level (tracking and defining global traffic patterns).
- Change Monitoring: Planning a clearly defined implementation and change management process is critical to ensuring that your IT infrastructure environment remains well protected from disasters due to configuration errors. Therefore, all changes, regardless of their nature, scope, importance, and implications, must be quantified,

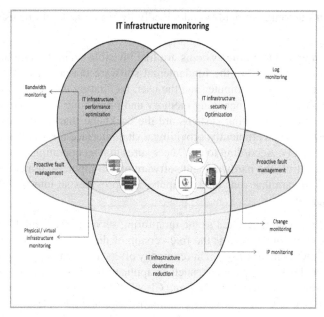

Fig. 1. Components of IT infrastructure monitoring

assigned a well-defined approval hierarchy, and preceded by a backup of existing changes.

- Log monitoring: It is necessary to proactively monitor your organization's IT infrastructure logs to detect and identify critical network failures. Analyzing various types of logs, including syslogs, event logs, and firewall logs, helps optimize performance and detect security threats.
- IP Address Monitoring: Periodically analyzing and monitoring the IP addresses in your IT infrastructure is critical to ensuring that malicious devices do not intrude into your network environment. It also helps avoid network problems such as IP address collision.

Automation. Automation is using technology to perform tasks without the need for a human. By delegating mechanical functions to automated systems, we free up time and resources to focus on more creative and strategic tasks. Plus, it reduces human errors, increases efficiency, and makes everything run like a well-tuned clock. Therefore, automation is the secret recipe for a brighter and smoother workflow.

On the other hand, [16] defines automation as using technology to perform tasks without human intervention. This may include repetitive, dangerous tasks or requiring high precision. Automation can be used in various industries, from manufacturing to healthcare. Mainly, two sectors can be differentiated in the world of automation within technology: automation in IT and automation in business decisions. In the IT sector, automation is used to repeat processes to execute tasks. Regarding the business sector, automation is used to manage business processes and rules. One of the outstanding languages in this automation field is undoubtedly Python, which will be used precisely in this Project.

Operating Systems. Operating systems are like invisible orchestra conductors in the world of computing. They are the fundamental software that acts as an intermediary between the hardware of a computer and the user, facilitating the interaction and coordination of resources. From managing memory and processing to promoting access to files and applications, operating systems are the backbone that allows our devices to function consistently and efficiently, providing a vital interface for users to interact with technology intuitively. According to [17], he assures that an operating system is a set of programs that controls the hardware and software of a computer—remembering that it is the leading software that runs on a computer and provides an interface between the user and the hardware.

The operating system selected as the monitoring server is the CentOS LINUX distribution. This operating system is the free version of the RED HAT operating system from the RED HAT company itself. This company offers its operating system for servers, Workstations, and different products, such as application servers (RED HAT JBOSS). The main difference between RED HAT and CENTOS, ignoring the license, is technical support. In the case of CentOS, a large community supports the operating system, as is the case on other occasions with free software. CentOS is defined as a robust, stable, and easy-to-install system. In addition, it works with basic hardware and can be without great power or great features to use.

Data Visualization. Data visualization is a fundamental part of this, and to achieve this, Grafana, a robust time series analysis and representation tool, will be implemented to make monitoring data more user-friendly and enjoyable. Grafana stands out for its unique approach by providing a single pane of view, allowing the unification of data from various sources without entering it into a specific warehouse or database. Figure 2 shows a dashboard designed in Grafana:

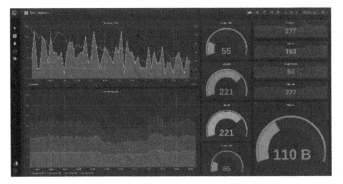

Fig. 2. Dashboard panel designed in Grafana

One of the most notable advantages of Grafana is its ability to access and visualize existing data from various sources, in addition to offering native support for different tools in the field of monitoring. Thus, data visualization is crucial for effectively monitoring and supervising network infrastructure in institutions. Provides a clear and understandable graphical representation of network health and performance. At this point, dynamic graphs and real-time dashboards provide an up-to-date snapshot of data flow, bandwidth utilization, latency, bottlenecks, and other relevant parameters.

Grafana allows you to display specific metrics critical to the network infrastructure. This could include network traffic, server load, and several connected devices, including configuring thresholds and rules to receive immediate notifications when anomalies or problems are detected in the network, allowing quick action.

Virtualization. Virtualization is a technology that allows multiple operating systems to run on a single physical server. This offers several benefits, including reducing costs, improving efficiency, increasing flexibility, and facilitating disaster recovery. [18] defines virtualization as creating a virtual version of a device or resource, such as a server, a storage device, a network, or even an operating system, where the resource is divided into one or more environments. Of execution. This allows multiple operating systems and applications to run on a single physical server, increasing efficiency and flexibility. On the other hand, [18] emphasizes that virtualization creates an abstraction layer between physical resources and their virtual equivalent. This allows physical resources to be securely shared between users or applications. There are several types of virtualization: Server Virtualization, Data Virtualization, Desktop Virtualization, and Network Virtualization.

Each type of virtualization has different functions. Server virtualization is done through a control application known as a Hypervisor so that each virtual machine can function independently as if it were different physical hardware. In addition, each machine can have different operating systems and run other applications. Figure 3 shows a VM architecture:

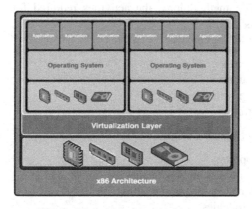

Fig. 3. Virtual Machine Architecture

3   Research Methodology

The research methodology is based on a quantitative approach, selected to diagnose the telecommunications infrastructure on the Plaza De La Paz University Institution of Barranquilla (IUB) campus and evaluate its impact on the quality of services. This quantitative method will allow the collection of numerical data, enabling a statistical analysis that measures and quantifies various aspects related to the quality and efficiency of telecommunications services. Along these lines, the research is classified as non-experimental, supported by a solid theoretical basis and the ethics of not intervening directly in the network infrastructure. This non-experimental approach is considered appropriate for studying the complexity of telecommunications network infrastructure in an educational environment, allowing detailed and accurate information to be obtained without the limitations associated with experimental manipulation. Regarding the research design, a transversal approach focuses on observing phenomena at a specific time. This cross-sectional design, supported by [19], facilitates data collection through surveys, questionnaires, or measurements, offering a snapshot of the current situation of the telecommunications infrastructure on the Plaza De La Paz campus.

By capturing detailed analysis at a specific point in time, this approach is essential for developing a monitoring prototype that adapts to the present needs of the institution. Furthermore, descriptive transversal research is adopted to obtain a thorough overview of the current situation of technological services at the IUB, allowing relevant variables to be described without altering them and facilitating an accurate evaluation of the existing reality. The study population focuses on the IUB community on the Plaza De La Paz campus, encompassing students, professors, and administrative staff.

Therefore, the information collection techniques include the exhaustive review of scientific literature, emphasizing the protocols and tools necessary for managing the data network, and obtaining first-hand information through observation and surveys directed at the university community. To carry out each of the stages of the project, the design methodology for telematic systems was defined, which in this case was TOP-DOWN. Figure 4 shows the phases of the project, following the TOP-DOWN methodology [20]:

Using this exciting methodology, the activities required for each process were identified and established:

Phase 1: Analyze Requirements

- Analyze business goals
- Analyze technical goals
- Analyze existing network
- Analyze existing traffic

  Phase 2: Develop Logical Design

- Design network topology
- Design addressing models and hostnames
- Select protocols for Switching and Routing
- Develop security strategies
- Develop network management strategies

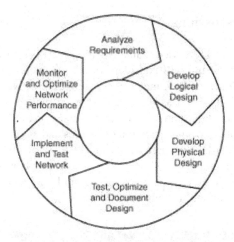

Fig. 4. TOP-DOWN Methodology

Phase 3: Develop Physical Design

- Select technologies and devices for campus networks
- Select technologies and devices for business networks

Phase 4: Test, optimize, and document design

- Test network design
- Optimize network design
- Document the design

Phase 5: Deploy and test the network

- Make an implementation schedule
- Network design implementation (final)
- Perform test stack

Phase 6: Monitor and Optimize the Network

- Network operation in production
- Network monitoring
- Network optimization

4   Results and Discussions

This will seek to monitor IT service management at the operating system and server metrics level. This monitoring will consider critical parameters such as file transfer, operating state, service availability, memory consumption, active services, or running processes. Through an ally such as the Grafana tool, it will be possible to visualize these metrics to understand the status of the service and generate reports from the data, obtaining vital information for the execution of queries and alerts through emails to the staff. IT. You must have a server where the Grafana application is installed, which will be integrated with the monitoring Python scripts. These scripts will feed data from the parameters to generate the graphs; the above results in Fig. 5 where a general panel of statistics in the various services is contemplated:

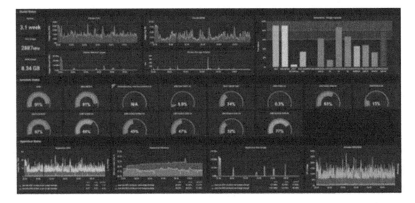

Fig. 5. Grafana Dashboard Metrics

Figure 6 shows the integration with other monitoring tools:

Fig. 6. Systematization of visual design

An alert message schematized as presented in Fig. 7 is expected to notify the personnel in charge of any new developments in the system to promote early response to incidents. Other vital data, such as the location and the computer where it is running, will be included in the configuration of these emails.

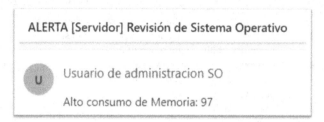

Fig. 7. Alert Message

The basic topology design is presented in Fig. 8. It shows a basic preliminary design of the management of Windows equipment under the monitoring system that will be implemented on the CentOS 7 Server:

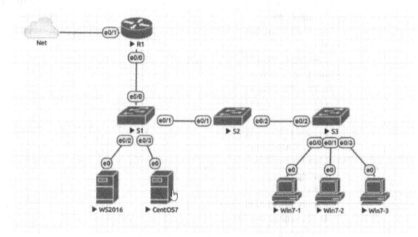

Fig. 8. Physical Network Topological Design

For each of the project phases, the expected result is shown in Table 1:

Table 1. Expected Results by Phases

Phase	Activities	Method	Techniques Used	Expected Results
Diagnose the current state of the IUB regarding equipment, devices, connectivity, security, and management of the telecommunications network infrastructure on the Plaza de la Paz campus	– Carrying out a detailed inventory of all network equipment and devices on the Plaza de la Paz campus, including servers, Wi-Fi access points, routers, and switches – Document each component's technical specifications, location, and operational status – Record of observations of the interaction of users of the IUB community with the information systems provided by the Institution – Quantification of perceptions through a closed survey directed at IUB community staff to analyze patterns and trends related to the state of information services	Non-experimental quantitative approach of a transversal descriptive type	Observation and survey	– Diagnostic report of the different network equipment – Tabulation of the results obtained in the survey – Report on understanding needs that feed the current documentation, including the problem, justification, etc

Table 1. (*continued*)

Phase	Activities	Method	Techniques Used	Expected Results
Consider technologies for monitoring and managing telecommunications networks that allow easy implementation, integration, and compatibility with tools and protocols	– Review of scientific and technical literature related to monitoring technologies, best practices, and network management through the digital library or search engines – Collection of information on the latest innovations, key features, and specific considerations for the educational environment – Annotation of technological suggestions by teachers or experts in telecommunications monitoring solutions – Analysis of case studies of successful monitoring and supervision systems implementations in similar educational institutions	Investigative approach	Digital databases, scientific articles	State of the art, legal, theoretical, and conceptual framework

(*continued*)

Table 1. (*continued*)

Phase	Activities	Method	Techniques Used	Expected Results
Develop scripts and tools that facilitate the visualization of real-time data using system resources, metrics, logs, and sending early alerts in the form of statistics	– Specification of functional and non-functional requirements – Preliminary design of the system architecture – Installation and configuration of the necessary tools and platforms – Implementation of alerts and notifications – Development of system monitoring functionality – Troubleshooting and adjustments based on test results – Preparation of user manuals and technical documentation – Presentation of implementation and results reports	TOP-DOWN network design methodology	Decompose "a problem" into a series of levels or optimization procedures integrated	– Planning graph by phases – Complete and understandable user manuals and technical documentation for end users and maintenance personnel
Perform functional tests on the prototype for monitoring and managing telecommunications networks through a simulated environment	– Analysis of user feedback and evaluation results – Identification of areas of improvement to adjust the prototype – Delivery of the Final project	Non-experimental quantitative approach of a transversal descriptive type	Collection and interpretation of metrics	– Formal delivery of the improved prototype and associated documentation to the interested parties, marking the completion of the project

5   Conclusions and Future Works

The development and implementation of the prototype for the monitoring and management of the telecommunications network infrastructure at the Institución Universitaria de Barranquilla (IUB) Plaza de la Paz campus is crucial to address critical challenges related to frequent Internet interruptions, slow transfer of data, and the lack of practical monitoring tools.

This project will allow early detection of problems and minimize the impact on the operation and user experience. Still, it will also serve as a strategic tool for making informed decisions, optimizing the efficiency of technological resources, and strengthening the institution's competitiveness in the academic field.

Ultimately, the successful implementation of the prototype will contribute significantly to the continuous improvement of the network infrastructure, ensuring a more efficient academic environment and a satisfying experience for students and staff.

As future work, this monitoring system can be implemented in other IUB headquarters, providing comprehensive supervision throughout the University.

References

1. Tanenbaum, A., Wetherall, D.: Redes de Computadoras, 5th edn. Prentice Hall, Naucalpan de Juarez (2012)
2. Murillo, F.M.C.: Desarrollo De Un Prototipo De Red Definida Por Software Sdn Para La Gestión Median Te Recursos De Estándar Abierto (2016). http://repositorio.pucesa.edu.ec/bitstream/123456789/1638/1/76160.pdf
3. Garcia Salas, J., Roa, C.: Diseño de una herramienta de monitoreo y control de servidores utilizando como eje principal Cacti. aplicado a una PYME mediana. Universidad Cooperativa de Colombia (2020)
4. Lladó, R.B.: Proyecto de automatización de una infraestructura web (2020).: http://dspace.uib.es/xmlui/handle/11201/152109
5. Berbel, J.: Automatización de la gestión de la infraestructura en entorno cloud (2021)
6. Barahona Cotarate, A.B., Rodriguez Zevallos, K.V., Escobedo Bailón, F.E.: Sistema de monitoreo basado en ELK Stack para mejorar el gobierno de TI. Revista Investigación Universitaria 11(1), 512–523 (2021). https://doi.org/10.53470/riu.v11i1.14
7. Hernandez, L., Jimenez, G.: Design and validation of a scheme of infrastructure of servers, under the PPDIOO methodology, in the university institution - ITSA. In: Silhavy, R. (ed.) CSOC2018 2018. AISC, vol. 763, pp. 367–379. Springer, Cham (2019). https://doi.org/10.1007/978-3-319-91186-1_38
8. Vallejo, P.: Análisis del Tráfico en un Ambiente Simulado con vlans y Recomendaciones de Políticas de Servicio y Diseño de una red SAI. Escuela Superior Politécnica del Litoral (2019)
9. Hernandez, L.: Distributed infrastructure for efficient management of network services case: large company in the mining sector in Colombia. In: Proceeding - 2016 2nd International Conference on Science in Information Technology, ICSITech 2016: Information Science for Green Society and Environment (2017). https://doi.org/10.1109/ICSITech.2016.7852609
10. Hernandez, L., Villanueva, H., Estrada, S.: Proposal for the design of a new technological infrastructure for the efficient management of network services and applications in a high complexity clinic in Colombia. In: Silhavy, R., Silhavy, P., Prokopova, Z. (eds.) CoMeSySo 2017. AISC, vol. 662, pp. 74–85. Springer, Cham (2018). https://doi.org/10.1007/978-3-319-67621-0_7

11. Untiveros, Y.: Influencia de la Implementación de un Sistema de Monitoreo de Infraestructura TI para Gestionar las Incidencias en la Red LAN de la Universidad Intercultural de la Amazonía. Universidad nacional de Ucayali (2022). http://repositorio.unu.edu.pe/bitstream/handle/UNU/3296/000001326T.pdf?sequence=1&isAllowed=y

12. Palumbo, F., Ullberg, J., Štimec, A., Furfari, F., Karlsson, L., Coradeschi, S.: Sensor network infrastructure for a home care monitoring system. Sensors (Switzerland) **14**(3), 3833–3860 (2014). https://doi.org/10.3390/s140303833

13. Hernantes, J., Gallardo, G., Serrano, N.: IT infrastructure-monitoring tools. IEEE Softw. **32**(4), 88–93 (2015). https://doi.org/10.1109/MS.2015.96

14. Hernandez, L., et al.: Optimization of a Wifi wireless network that maximizes the level of satisfaction of users and allows the use of new technological trends in higher education institutions. In: Streitz, N., Konomi, S. (eds.) HCII 2019. LNCS, vol. 11587, pp. 144–160. Springer, Cham (2019). https://doi.org/10.1007/978-3-030-21935-2_12

15. Monitoreo de infraestructura TI con OpManager Plus. Manage Engine. https://www.manageengine.com/latam/it-operations-management/monitoreo-de-infraestructura-ti.html

16. Hasbi, M., Nurwa, A.R.A., Priambodo, D.F., Putra, W.R.A., Nusantara, S.S., dan Sandi Negara, P.S.: Infrastructure as code for security automation and network infrastructure monitoring. Teknik Informatika dan Rekayasa Komputer **22**(1), 203–217 (2022). https://doi.org/10.30812/matrik.v22i1.2471

17. Stallings, W.: Operating Systems: Internals and Design Principles. Prentice Hall, Upper Saddle River (2011)

18. Moreira, R., da Cunha, H.G.V.O., Moreira, L.F.R., Silva, F.O.: VINEVI: a virtualized network vision architecture for smart monitoring of heterogeneous applications and infrastructures. In: Barolli, L., Hussain, F., Enokido, T. (eds.) AINA 2022. LNNS, vol. 449, pp. 529–541. Springer, Cham (2022). https://doi.org/10.1007/978-3-030-99584-3_46

19. Cvetkovic, J.M., Soto, A.: Cross-sectional studies Estudios transversales. Revista De La Facultad De Medicina Humana **21**(1), 179–185 (2020)

20. Saavedra, J.: Metodología Top-Down para el Diseño de Redes. http://juancarlossaavedra.me/2017/06/infografia-metodologia-top-down-para-el-diseno-de-redes

Factors Influencing Data Completeness in Electronic Records: A Case Study in a Chinese Manufacturing Enterprise

Chaowang Lan[1], Guochao Peng[2], Hui Zhou[1], Lishen Su[1], Yaosheng Huang[1], Dayou Wu[3], and Caihua Liu[1(✉)] [iD]

[1] School of Artificial Intelligence, Guangxi Colleges and Universities Key Laboratory of AI Algorithm Engineering, Guilin University of Electronic Technology, Jinji Road, Guilin 541004, Guangxi, China
Caihua.Liu@guet.edu.cn
[2] Sun Yat-Sen University, Xingang Xi Road, Guangzhou 510275, Guangdong, China
[3] International Institute for Advanced Data Management Study, Hong Kong, China

Abstract. Advance in the information and digital technology demands most industries to transit to fully electronic records management. Addressing data completeness is one of the important challenges that enterprises face when establishing and maintaining electronic records. By conducting a literature review, we identified 14 factors influencing data completeness in electronic records. This was followed by empirically examining and ranking these factors at two stages of the information systems life cycle: (1) system design and implementation; and (2) system use post implementation in a case study of a manufacturing enterprise. In our case study, among these factors, user interface design was identified as the highest rank factor that affects data completeness at the stage of system design and implementation, while training was considered as the most important factor for addressing data completeness at the stage of system use post implementation. The present study identified the factors influencing data completeness in electronic records, in opposite to the factors influencing data quality in general. Furthermore, the study extends the existing literature on data completeness by considering important areas for achieving complete data in electronic records, at each stage of information systems life cycle.

Keywords: Data Completeness · Data Quality · Electronic Records · Ranking

1 Introduction

Advance of the information and digital technology leads to data explosion that has the potential to drive values in business of all sizes [1, 2]. However, enterprises face one of the leading challenges with this large amount of data: data quality problems [3, 4]. As one dimension of data quality, data completeness refers to the extent to which all required data is available for a given task [5–8]. Data completeness has received extensive attention from both academic and practice, because complete data is a key asset for achieving

N. A. Streitz and S. Konomi (Eds.): HCII 2024, LNCS 14718, pp. 221–240, 2024.
https://doi.org/10.1007/978-3-031-59988-0_13

long-term competitive advantages for organizations [7]. Although data completeness has been studied for decades, achieving complete data in electronic records still remains as a significant challenge in industries. It is reported that a forecasting mistake of interests generated from missing data can translate to loss of revenue and even crisis of collapse [34]. Furthermore, incomplete records can post enterprises to the risk of fraud in financial practices and the enterprises have to be confronted with court ordered asset freezes [35]. Recently, digital transformation boosts the process of moving to fully electronic records in most industries [2], and therefore, addressing data completeness in electronic records is put on a high priority for organizations.

The studies addressing the concepts of data quality, the characteristics of data and the processes to ensure data quality began in the 1990s, however, International Organization for Standardization (IOS) published the first part of ISO 8000 data quality standards in 2008 [9]. Thereafter, ISO 8000-140 focusing on completeness was released in 2016 [10]. This part of ISO 8000 specifies the requirements on capture and exchange of complete information in the form of statements and assertions of data completeness [10], however, the identification of the factors influencing data completeness is outside its scope. To date research that identifies and conceptualizes the factors influencing data completeness together with ranking these factors in electronic records is not available in the literature. The identification and ranking of these factors could disclose which areas contribute to addressing data completeness and inform practitioners about which of these factors are more important than the others to achieve complete data.

In the current paper, we aim to (a) identify potential factors influencing data completeness in electronic records from extant literature; and (b) investigative the relative importance of these factors based on two stages related to information systems life cycle: (1) system design and implementation as well as (2) system use post implementation. Because data quality problems could occur from data creation and all the way to its final usage, in this study, we explore these factors at both stages (1) and (2). First, during the stage of system design and implementation, data completeness is needed to address based on users' requirements. Second, after the system implementation, users take advantages of information systems to collect and utilize data. In this process they could encounter various challenges to achieve complete data. Accordingly, the following research question (RQ) guides our study:

RQ: What are the relative ranks (importance) of the factors influencing data completeness in electronic records at different stages of information systems life cycle?

In order to address our RQ, we first conducted a systematic review of empirical studies focusing on data completeness in electronic records to identify and conceptualize the potential factors influencing data completeness. This was followed by collecting data from a manufacturing enterprise through a questionnaire to discover the relative importance of the factors extracted from the literature at each stage of information systems life cycle from the users' perspective in a case study.

This work therefore makes two contributions. First, we conducted a systematic review of empirical studies focusing on data completeness in electronic records that identifies and conceptualizes the factors that influence data completeness, which is not available in the existing literature. This study presents a novel synthesis leading to a categorization of the factors that affect data completeness in electronic records faced by practitioners:

human, managerial, technical, and external perspectives. Furthermore, the empirical results of ranking these factors in our case study reveal that user interface design was identified as the highest rank factor that affects data completeness at the stage of system design and implementation, while training was considered as the most important factor for addressing data completeness at the stage of system use post implementation for the selected enterprise. Second, our findings on these ranks allow practitioners to realize which of these factors are more important to achieve complete data in electronic records and determine which areas should make more efforts to address data completeness at different stages of information systems lifecycle.

The rest of the paper is organized as follows. The next section presents a summary of related studies and the theory of information systems life cycle. Thereafter we outline the factors that influence data completeness in electronic records from the literature review. After that, we describe the research design for our case study and then provide the results from the case study. The last section concludes the paper with limitations of this study and our future work.

2   Literature Review

2.1   Data Completeness as One Dimension of Data Quality

The concepts of data quality were first proposed in the studies on accounting and statistics [11], addressing both "fitness for use" and "conformance to requirements" aspects [12]. In information systems tradition, definitions of data quality are divided into dimensions such as completeness, accuracy and consistency [8]. In this study, we are interested in one dimension of data quality (i.e., completeness).

Data completeness, as one dimension of data quality, is defined as the extent to which all required data is available for a given task [5–8]. In this study, we discuss data completeness in general and we focus on identification and ranking of the factors that influence data completeness in electronic records, providing an initial explanation of this phenomenon. The present work thus could raise the awareness of importance on achieving complete data in organizations and allow practitioners to begin to address data completeness in electronic records.

2.2   Related Studies on Factors Influencing Data Quality

In the recent years contributions have been made to establish an empirical body of knowledge on the factors influencing data quality. Some studies proposed that the factors affecting data quality consist of internal and external factors. These internal factors classified (e.g., completeness and accuracy), in essence, are dimensions in data quality for assessment [8]. These internal factors have not explained the root causes that improve or reduce data quality. A few studies investigated the factors influencing data quality from the perspective of data quality management and examined these factors within enterprises. For example, Xu et al. [13] drew on the theory of critical success factors for Total Quality Management and Just-In-Time to develop a model of factors affecting data quality in accounting information systems. This work establishes a seminal model of factors influencing data quality, because other studies [14–16] then further improved the understanding of the factors affecting data quality based on Xu et al.' model [13]. Similarly, researchers (e.g., [11, 17, 18]) extracted the factors that influence data quality from the literature of data warehousing success and empirically examined these factors within enterprises.

Prior studies of the factors influencing data quality management and improvement have only partially investigated data completeness dimension. However, not every factor that influences data quality could cause data completeness problems. For instance, "measurement and reporting" is considered as a factor influencing data quality [19]. Inappropriate measurements, for example, a sensor placed on the outside of a parcel, could provide inaccurate product temperature due to external conditions, resulting in inaccurate data [20] that reflect data quality problems but not the manifestations of data completeness problems (i.e., missing data [8]). While addressing data completeness in electronic records could present unique challenges [21], the factors influencing data completeness can have an impact on data quality since completeness is one dimension to determine data quality. To date, a systematic review of the factors influencing data completeness in electronic records and ranking these factors is not available in the literature. Our study therefore intends to fill this gap through empirically evaluating the relative importance of the factors influencing data completeness derived from the empirical studies that focus on data completeness in electronic records, and to improve our understanding of these factors at different stages of information systems life cycle.

2.3 Theory of Information Systems Life Cycle

The aim of this study is to identify and rank the factors that influence data completeness at the stages of system design and implementation as well as system use post implementation. Researchers have developed different life cycle models for information systems under the study context (e.g., [22–24]). Because our focus is on the factors that influence data completeness from data creation to its final usage based on users' perspective, we divide information systems life cycle into two stages, including: (1) system design and implementation; and (2) system use post implementation.

System design and implementation describes a process of defining how a computer-based information system is built, installed, and completed in organizations (adapted from [25]). Within the context of addressing data completeness in electronic records, at the stage of system design and implementation, users are likely to focus on whether or not the system under development could meet their data needs.

System use post implementation concerns a process of using, maintaining and enhancing the information system that has been implemented in organizations (adapted from [26]). At this stage, users are likely to concern about whether they could capture, enter and use complete data when using the system.

Based on this analysis, our study could cover the factors influencing data completeness throughout the information systems life cycle, from the perspective of users.

3   Factors from Literature Review

Our research design for this study was a mixed method approach. The investigation of factors that influence data completeness in electronic records was conducted in two phases: (1) systematic review, and (2) case study.

Phase 1 included a systematic review of the literature focusing on data completeness in electronic records to produce a flat list of potential factors that influence data completeness. Thereafter, we separated the list into several relevant groups and gave each group an appropriate name, based on thematic analysis. This phase helped us identify the potential factors that influence data completeness for further ranking. Accordingly, this paper presents the outcomes of the systematic review as well as a research gap that requires an empirical study for ranking these factors. In this section, we present the methods and the results of identifying the factors influencing data completeness in electronic records from the literature in phase 1.

We followed the guidelines of systematic review [27] to search and identify the literature that focuses on data completeness in electronic records. Based on our research topic, the major term is "data completeness". We applied the synonyms of "data" by using "information" and alternative terms of "completeness" by using "availability", "coverage", "presence", "missingness", "omission" and "commission" as our search keywords. Therefore, our search began with those keywords by using the Boolean operator as the following search string: ('data' OR 'information') AND ('completeness' OR 'availability' OR 'coverage' OR 'presence' OR 'missingness' OR 'omission' OR 'commission'). Furthermore, 8 online databases were selected for this SLR, including ACM Digital Library, EBSCOhost, ProQuest, ScienceDirect, Scopus, Springer, IEEE Xplore and Google Scholar. With the search strings, we searched the publications in multiple online databases by title, abstract, and keywords to centralize our search and identified the initial list of papers as shown in Appendix I. We then filtered relevant papers by title, abstract and full-text review based on inclusion and exclusion characteristics. The searched papers were further filtered based on abstract and full-text review within the inclusion and exclusion criteria. The inclusion criteria adopted were: (1) papers published were in English; (2) papers were selected on the publication date from 2000 to 2021 (inclusive); (3) papers were empirical studies focusing on data completeness in electronic records. The articles were removed upon one of the following exclusion criteria: (1) were extended abstracts, editorials, letters, Power-Point presentation, book chapters and theses; (2) were not available online; (3) were duplicate; and (4) did not reveal the root causes of reducing/improving data completeness in electronic records.

By studying the content of the literature addressing data completeness, we reviewed each included study thoroughly and identified and conceptualized a list of potential factors influencing data completeness in electronic records from the reviewed papers as shown in Table 1.

This table is developed by three rounds of thematic analysis: firstly, by analyzing the empirical findings and experience from the literature, we identified a flat list of factors influencing data completeness in electronic records. These factors initially were not listed in a particular order. Secondly, we analyzed and determined the characteristics of these factors by looking at their perspectives to improve or reduce data completeness,

Table 1. Categories of the factors influencing data completeness in electronic records in this review

Category	Factors That Influence Data Completeness
Human factors	F1: Knowledge [S5, S13, S15, S20, S22, S24, S27, S29, S31, S43, S45, S50, S55, S59, S60]
	F2: Experience [S5, S27]
	F3: Training [S3, S27, S28, S47]
	F4: Consciousness [S4, S24, S27, S47, S48]
Managerial factors	F5: Mode of record keeping [S5, S6, S9, S11, S12, S16, S21, S33, S34, S35, S38]
	F6: Workload allocation [S3, S33, S52]
	F7: Man-hour limitation [S6, S27, S37, S46, S47, S52, S55]
	F8: Human resources management [S28, S37, S47, S55]
Technical factors	F9: Data collection methods [S11, S14, S16, S18, S20, S47, S49, S52, S56]
	F10: Data fields design [S2, S16, S18, S19, S24, S27, S39, S42, S52]
	F11: User interface design [S4, S10, S11, S16, S20, S23, S27, S36, S41, S43, S44, S52]
	F12: Data conversion [S24, S55, S57]
	F13: System configuration [S1]
External factors	F14: External environment (i.e., physical [S8, S54, S58], legal [S17], ethical [S16, S17, S19, S24, S27] and cooperative environment [S7, S17, S25, S26, S30, S32, S33, S40, S51, S53])

based on our understanding from the description in the literature as well as our knowledge and past experience. For example, when looking at the factors such as user interface design, data fields design, and physical working environment, obviously, the first two factors concern the technical perspective to improve or reduce data completeness, however, physical working environment refers to an external environment that influences data completeness. Thus, for some of these factors it was easy and relatively obvious to distinguish their perspectives of influencing data completeness such as the aforementioned example, serving as a starting point of grouping. In this light, we assigned all factors identified from the systematic review to groups based on their similarity. Lastly, we gave an appropriate name for each group according to their perspectives. To ensure quality of grouping, two members of the research group assigned the factors into groups independently and compared the results. Any uncertain and inconsistent grouping was discussed further to seek resolution. Hence, our categories of the factors influencing data completeness in electronic records were derived entirely from grouping the factors together. These factors were divided into four categories: human, managerial, technical and external factors. (This link[1] gives the list of included 60 papers in the review labelled by letter S followed by a number.)

3.1 Human Factors

Human factors in this study are defined as individual capability and perception toward addressing data completeness in electronic records, including knowledge, experience, training, and consciousness.

Knowledge. Knowledge refers to individual understanding of data collection and usage within business context. This factor could have an impact on achieving complete data in practices. For example, practitioners selectively capture the information with a bias [S13, S15, S22, S29, S31, S43, S45, S50, S59, S60] or lack sufficient understanding about data entry policy [S5, S20, S24, S27, S55], resulting in incomplete data transcribed into information systems.

Experience. Experience is skills gained from practices of addressing data completeness in electronic records. In data recording tasks, staff members sometimes require specialist's experience to parse and locate the data [S5]. If personnel fail to parse the data, this would introduce the biased data or incomplete data into the dataset. Warsi et al. [S27] evidenced that the omission rate of data fields requiring input by skilled personnel was greater than those requiring data entry by none.

Training. Training in this study emphasizes capability in relation to dealing with data completeness in electronic records acquired by individual that trains. It was reported that general staff with an inappropriate level of training could incur data quality problems in data entry [S3, S27, S28, S47]. Because general staff lacks specialist knowledge, it is difficult for him or her to understand the data content and precisely record the data towards a data field assigned. A training based around terminology could improve staff's capacity of achieving complete data using the system in later practices.

Consciousness. Consciousness concerns individual awareness about the importance of addressing data completeness in electronic records and mental state when conducting relevant activities. If a staff member lacks the awareness about the importance of data recording or reporting tasks, data delays or data omission errors might occur due to human carelessness [S4, S24, S27, S47, S48]. Furthermore, the availability of dedicated time for dealing with data puts practitioners under pressure. The time limitation would cause mental stress or exhaustion that could lead to human errors. As a result, more missing items could emerge that negatively affect data completeness for the data set [S4].

3.2 Managerial Factors

Managerial factors in the present study pertain to standards, procedures, and regulations developed for achieving data completeness in an organization, including model of record keeping, workload allocation, man-hour limitation, and human resources management.

---

[1] https://www.dropbox.com/s/izreqouup1ta4io/Papers.docx?dl=0.

Mode of Record Keeping. Mode of record keeping concerns requirements of data recording formulated by an organization, involving (1) whether the use of paper-based records is adopted, and (2) whether paper-based records are required to document in different departments. If an organization determines the use of hard copy to document original information, personal should locate the required data at first when transcribing information from paper-based records into information systems. At this time, typographical errors [S5] and handwritten inconsistency [S11] may occur, resulting in legibility issues [S5, S9, S38]. This could make practitioners misunderstand the data content and fail to record required data. Further, different departments in an organization are required to acquire information from paper-based records. If some paper-based documents may not arrive at the responsible departments for recording and some of them may be partially or completely missing during the process of electronic scanning [S33], the records are incomplete due to a lack of data sources [S6, S12, S16, S21, S34, S35].

Workload Allocation. Workload allocation addresses the extent to which the workload on dealing with data completeness in electronic records is assigned to an individual. In most organizations, practitioners are playing the role both in their main duties and data recording tasks. Sometimes heavy workload in the main duties detracts person's attention from data recording or reporting tasks [S3, S33, S52]. Consequently, some information could not be recorded in time, thus the data is inevitably incomplete.

Man-hour Limitation. Man-hour limitation emphasizes the time assigned to an individual for completing the tasks related to dealing with data completeness in electronic records. Because the limited time could cause mental stress, personnel would make mistakes in the data recording or report tasks, and thus, the records could have more missing values. It was evident that staff members complained about the availability of time for data entry [S27, S37, S46, S47, S52, S55] or reporting tasks [S6]. However, spending large amounts of time on data recording tasks might impact productivity in organizations [S37].

Human Resources Management. Human resources management addresses how many people are assigned to complete a given task with respect to addressing data completeness in electronic records. It was reported that insufficient human resources have an impact on the amount of data collected [S28, S37, S47, S55]. This could further result in an incomplete data population.

3.3 Technical Factors

Technical factors in this study refer to hard and soft aspects of information systems to support achieving complete data in electronic records, including data collection methods, data fields design, user interface design, data conversion, and system configuration.

Data Collection Methods. Data collection methods focus on how data is collected by using information systems. Data can be recorded either through a machine or via manual input [S11, S56]. If practitioners automatically collect data from information systems or through a monitor (e.g., sensors), the automatic data transfer could improve efficiency in data collection [S49]. While Jang et al. [S47] found that manual entry had better completeness than automatic transfer. However, it was reported that data entry is likely to contribute to the incompleteness if users transform free text into structured data without tools [S14, S16, S18, S20, S52].

Data Fields Design. The design of data fields challenges users to achieve data completeness [S2, S16, S18, S19, S24, S27, S39, S42, S52, S55]. For example, Mohamed et al. [S24] found that: there were some data fields marked as required, however, the value could be null; while some fields were expected to be not null, but they contained empties because those fields were not marked as required. Some fields might not be used anymore in the future and therefore, they would increasingly contain more nulls in those fields that impact data completeness.

User Interface Design. It was reported that complicated design of drop-down menu could be a cause of incomplete records [S4]. Unambiguous design of user interface can be viewed as an outset to address data completeness, since user interface influences users' understandings about the acquired data and users' decision-making [S10, S23, S36, S43, S44]. However, poor interface design could discourage users from inputting complete records such as inconsistence with documentation workflow [S11, S27, S52] and discrepant terminologies for data description [S16, S20, S41, S52].

Data Conversion. Data conversion between versions could generate nulls in incompatible data fields because conversions between different data structures are not guaranteed to be the same [S24]. Poor design of data conversion modules could lead to unnecessary nulls in the data fields that could decrease data completeness for a dataset [S55, S57].

System Configuration. Bardaki et al. [S1] analytically modelled completeness of sensor data derived from product tracking systems under different configurations in supply chain. Because the path of an object's movement was captured by the sensor, results of the measurement of completeness were affected by different distributed capture points and labelling levels in the monitored area [S1]. In other words, configurations of capture points and labelling levels could result in different sets of complete records about the path of object movement.

3.4 External Factors

The external factors refer to external environment in this study, and here we grouped physical, legal and cooperative environment into one sole factor "external environment", since all these three concern the forces outside organizations that could have an impact on data completeness.

For physical working environment, the external interference (e.g., harsh environments) could result in transmission errors and loss of data in sensor networks [S8, S54, S58]. Thus, the data may be missing during the process of transmission that im-pacts completeness of the dataset queried via the network. While legal [S17] and ethical consideration (e.g., personal confidentiality) [S16, S19, S24, S27] restricts the access of the data that could result in the challenges in aggregating sufficient data for the study. In terms of cooperative environment, due to a lack of unified coordination management of data collection, data is scattered in different places and not all the data is freely available for data users [S7, S17, S25, S26, S30, S32, S33, S40, S51, S53]. This increases the difficulty in gathering required data for a given task.

4 Research Design for Ranking Factors

As mentioned, this research was conducted in two phases. In Sect. 3, we have presented the results of phase 1 on identifying the factors influencing data completeness in electronic records from the systematic review. This section provides the research design for phase 2 for examining and ranking these factors.

Phase 2 aims at finding out which of the factors identified in phase 1 are more important for addressing data completeness. We further extended the investigation of these factors at (1) system design and implementation as well as (2) system use post implementation. Additionally, we were also interested in how practitioners look at these factors and reasons that they give their ratings on the factors. Case study was selected that fits for the context of this study, because this research strategy allows an in-depth exploration for the purpose of studying and understanding more about an unknown or poorly understood situation or developing new insights about a phenomenon [36]. In the case study, we developed a questionnaire instrument, distributed and collected questionnaires in a company, and analyzed both qualitative and quantitative data to address our RQ and gain insights into the reasons of the factor ranking from the practitioners' perspective. Appendix II shows our timelines of each stage in the entire study.

4.1 Instrument Development

The questionnaire instrument was developed based on the findings of phase 1 and guidelines of related studies on factors ranking [19, 24]. Thus, all 14 factors that influence data completeness in electronic records identified from our systematic review were used as questionnaire items in the empirical study. All these items were adapted from the relevant included studies as presented in Sect. 3. Furthermore, these questionnaire items were validated both by two professors who are the colleagues of one of the coauthors with expertise in data quality and information systems and by senior managers in the selected enterprise who have been involved in all stages of information systems life cycle for a specific project. Firstly, we invited the two professors as a review group and sent the questionnaire to them. One reviewer did the first-round review, and the other one conducted the second-round review based on the first-round review. Both reviewers gave the comments regarding the descriptions of all 14 factors included in the questionnaire based on their knowledge, experience and judgement. Any inconsistent comments were solved by group discussions. Secondly, we sent the revised questionnaire to the senior managers in order to ascertain whether practitioners can understand the descriptions of the included factors when they read. The managers also gave their feedback according to their understanding and practices and then we revised the questionnaire again and send back to them for confirmation. All these activities assisted in the content validation of the questionnaire.

The instrument used in this study includes two parts. The first part contains a set of questions about the demographic of the participants. The second part has a list of 14 factors that affect data completeness identified from the literature review. Participants were asked to rate the importance of each factor from their opinions and experience, based on a five-point Likert scale ranging from 1 ("not important") to 5 ("extremely important") (see Appendix III). Also, they were required to give reasons of their ratings.

We investigated the implementation of a new information system in a company in China in our case study to identify the relative importance of the factors influencing data completeness in electronic records for two stages related to information systems life cycle. Since the questionnaire instrument was developed originally in English, it was necessary to translate the questionnaire into Chinese. We followed an adequate translation procedure as summarized by Chen and Boore [30]:

1) the authors' native language is Chinese, and therefore, the last author translated the questionnaire from English to Chinese first and another researcher outside the research group who is bilingual in English and Chinese reviewed the translation;
2) thereafter we back-translated the questionnaire from Chinese into English; and
3) we repeated steps (1) and (2) in order to achieve accuracy and consistency of the translation.

4.2 Data Sample and Data Collection

Because questionnaire can be sent to the participants via network and saves expenses for travel and long-distance telephone call, we adopted this data collection method for our case study. We distributed questionnaires in a manufacturing enterprise (XYF[2]). XYF is a government-owned corporation in China. In 2016, XYF introduced a new information system for operation and management (e.g., supply chain management, human resources management, and enterprise asset management). XYF has been making commitment to delivering quality-assured products and services to customers, based on technology and innovation. The upper management level is becoming aware of utilizing high-quality data to enhance the company's competitive advantages.

The targeted subjects were administrative staff who are involved in both stages of information systems lifecycle and employed in a branch company of XYF. The company recruits 92 employees and 16 of them are administrative staff. The administrative staff have the authority to use the information system for routine operation, decision making and planning, while the other 76 staff members who work in the production workshops are only allowed to browse the company's news by using the information system. Hence, the administrative staff are the main users of the information system and were selected as the targeted sample population in this study. We implemented the questionnaire in Chinese version using the wjx.cn platform and sent the link of the questionnaire to the company's senior managers. This link then was distributed among the administrative staff participants in the company. Since our population size was 16 (administrative staff), depending on the 95% confidence level as well as 5% confidence interval and the 90% expected proportion of the population supposed for this study, at least 14 participants should be approached as the sample size (see online sample size calculator[3]). Finally, 14 responses were collected (see Table 2) and all responses were found to be valid for further analysis, achieving the baseline of sample size used in this study.

---

[2] XYF is a fictitious name to maintain its confidentiality.

[3] See https://www.abs.gov.au/websitedbs/D3310114.nsf/home/Sample+Size+Calculator.

Table 2. Demographics of participants in this study.

Characteristics of Participants	Number of Participants
Experience of establishing and/or using the current information system in the company	
<2 years	0
2 - 5 years	14
>5 years	0
Education level	
High school certificate	2
Undergraduate	8
Postgraduate	4
Job position in the company	
Manager	4
Clerical officer	8
System admin	2
Total	**14**

All the questionnaires collected were deidentified, and the data from the questionnaires was arranged, coded, and imported using SPSS for statistical analysis. For the reasons of their ratings for the factors given by the participants in Chinese, we did not translate all texts into English, and only the results of the analysis were written in English. Several important sentences from the respondent's written texts cited in the paper were translated following the same translation procedures presented in Sect. 4.1.

4.3 Data Analysis

The unit of analysis is each questionnaire answered by a participant. The responses were collected from the administrative staff who have been involved in both stages of information system lifecycle in the same branch company of XYF. No differences occurred between the experiences in establishing and using the information system that require further control in the analysis.

Cronbach's Alpha is commonly used to determine the internal consistency of an instrument [31]. For each category of the factors influencing data completeness in electronic records (also a single construct), the internal consistency was computed (human factors: 0.652, managerial factors: 0.841, technical factors: 0.846, and external factors: 0.752). According to [31], an acceptable reliability score should be 0.6 or higher. Our results were well above the recommended limits, presenting a high reliability for each construct. Appendix IV provides the descriptive statistics of the factors rated in this study.

The instrument of this study was developed based on 5-point Likert scale where the middle value is 3 that indicates a medium degree, and when the mean of a factor rated by participants is higher than 3, this factor can be considered as an average important factor. T-test was thus used to determine whether or not the identified factors have significant impacts on data completeness in electronic records from the perspective of participants, and 3 became the test value for these tests. Our null hypothesis (H_0) pertained to that the factor has no significant impacts on data completeness, and the alternative hypothesis (H_1) referred to the factor that has a significant impact on data completeness. If the mean of gained scores is higher than 3, we should reject the null hypothesis and accept the alternative hypothesis. Otherwise, we should accept the null hypothesis. The test for the hypothesis was conducted by evaluating the general pattern of the identified factors for each stage of the information systems life cycle, with a 5 percent level of significance for the T-test. The 5 percent level is to draw 95 percent accuracy from the dataset results. By using the T-test, we identified the essential factors that influence data completeness for each stage of the information systems life cycle. These results are presented in Sect. 5.

Since we intended to rank the identified factors for both stages of information systems life cycle, the two datasets in relation to the measurements of the factors for system design and implementation and system use post implementation were collected and computed for their ranks. Recent research on ranking the factors of the topic of interests most often found in information systems management based on the mean of the participants' responses (e.g., [28, 37]) and this ranking method is simple and easy to carry out. The method thus is utilized in this study to rank the data.

5   Results and Discussion

Table 3 outlines the results of the T-test, showing that all 14 factors played important roles in addressing data completeness both at the stages of system design and implementation as well as system use post implementation because all these sig. Values were at least significant at 0.01 levels in our case study.

As mentioned, ranking the factors that influence data completeness in electronic records could help researchers and decision makers to better understand these factors and provide valuable information for making decisions in relation to addressing data completeness (e.g., give information for practitioners to allocate resources and determine which areas should receive more attention). Table 4 gives the rank for each factor at each stage of information systems life cycle, based on the calculated mean of each factor.

In our case study, we observed that user interface design was ranked as the most essential factor influencing data completeness at the stage of system design and implementation based on the viewpoints of the administrative staff. Two keywords *"save time"* and *"improve communication between machine and human"* were frequently mentioned by participants when they gave the reasons of their ratings. User interface design was more important for participants to address data completeness, as an unambiguous and friendly user interface that aligns with the workflow could motivate staff members to further participate in the task related to addressing data completeness when using the information system. 12 papers from the literature review also highlight the importance of user interface design in addressing data completeness. Our results confirm this at the stage of system design and implementation. In the meantime, this factor was ranked as the fourth important factor for the administrative staff to address data completeness in electronic records at the stage of system use post implementation.

Table 3. The T-test results in this study.

Factors influencing data completeness in electronic records	Sig.(two-tailed)	
	SDI	SUI
Knowledge	0.000	0.000
Experience	0.000	0.000
Training	0.000	0.000
Cursoriness	0.001	0.000
Model of record keeping	0.001	0.000
Workload allocation	0.001	0.003
Man-hour limitation	0.000	0.002
Human resource management	0.000	0.001
Data collection methods	0.000	0.000
Data field design	0.000	0.000
User interface design	0.000	0.000
Data conversion	0.000	0.001
System configuration	0.000	0.001
External environment	0.000	0.006

SDI: system design and implementation; SUI: system use post implementation

Training was ranked as the most important factor that influences data completeness at the stage of system use post implementation. When the information system has been implemented in the company, training *"significantly improves the knowledge, skills and capability"* of staffs in the tasks of achieving complete data. In the reviewed papers, only 4 studies concern the training based around data content and use of information systems for achieving complete data. Specifically, researchers found that the lack of training in using information systems for data documentation could limit users to record the data in time [S3, S27, S28, S47]. In this study, the administrative staff highlighted the role of training in achieving complete data at the stage of system use post implementation, because they had received a formal training when using the information system for the first time. This training could help staff members in the enterprise improve the understanding of using the system to achieve complete data. One respondent directly pointed out that *"without training the enterprise cannot meet the requirements of rapid development in the era of Big Data"*. Training can help the company aggregate complete data, and further the use of this high-quality data for delivering quality-assured services and products. This complete data can be viewed as the enabler of achieving and sustaining competitive advantages for enterprises [7]. However, at the stage of system design and implementation, training is less important, as the system is not ready to put into use and a training is not needed at this stage. It is worth mentioning here that the factor "training" is high in the importance of ranking in this study but is low in the frequency of the reviewed studies, indicating that this factor may have more research space.

Table 4. Comparison of the factors in each stage of the information system life cycle in this study.

Factors influencing data completeness in electronic records	Frequency in the literature review	SDI		SUI	
		Mean	Rank	Mean	Rank
Knowledge	15	4.00	5	4.43	3
Experience	2	4.00	5	4.50	2
Training	4	3.93	6	**4.64**	**1**
Consciousness	5	3.93	6	4.43	3
Model of record keeping	11	3.93	6	4.21	4
Workload allocation	3	4.00	5	3.86	6
Man-hour limitation	7	**3.86**	7	3.93	5
Human resource management	4	4.00	5	3.93	5
Data collection methods	9	4.36	2	4.21	4
Data field design	9	4.29	3	4.21	4
User interface design	12	**4.43**	**1**	4.21	4
Data conversion	3	4.29	3	3.93	5
System configuration	1	4.21	4	3.86	6
External environment	19	4.21	4	**3.79**	7

External environment takes a less important place that influence data completeness among these factors at both stages of information systems life cycle (e.g., the fourth important factor at system design and implementation and the last important factor at system use post implementation that affects data completeness). A manager indicated: *"the support of external environment to the data collection could determine whether the system can be successfully installed and utilized"*. In other words, the *"cooperation between branch companies"* (cooperative environment) contributes to *"data sharing"* in the entire enterprise and reveals the great potential of having complete data for further use. Furthermore, *"the system design must follow relevant legal requirements (of data management)"*. With the consideration of *"business confidentiality"*, not all data is available for users. The system only displays the corresponding information products based on different user roles. Thus, developers should take this into account and address various data needs at the stage of system design and implementation. At the stage of system use post implementation, *"external environment that contributes to ensuring routine data collection"* may not have intense changes, and therefore it may not have much impact as other factors on achieving complete data. Since we grouped physical, legal, and cooperative environment into the external factors, this aggregated a great number of relevant papers (n = 19) in our review. Although the results of this study showed that external environment plays a less important role in influencing data completeness in electronic records, our findings confirm the influence of external environment on data completeness, which is similar with the results reported by related studies.

6   Conclusion

In this work, we identified and conceptualized 14 factors that influence data completeness in electronic records and classified these into four main groups: human, managerial, technical, and external factors. Furthermore, we sought the opinions of IS users in a manufacturing company and empirically examined and ranked these factors from the viewpoints of administrative staff by using a questionnaire. We have the following findings to our RQ.

RQ. What are the relative ranks (importance) of the factors influencing data completeness in electronic records at different stages of information systems life cycle?

Findings. 14 factors influencing data completeness in electronic records were identified in this study, including: (1) Knowledge, (2) Experience, (3) Training, (4) Consciousness, (5) Model of record keeping, (6) Workload allocation, (7) Man-hour limitation, (8) Human resource management, (9) Data collection methods, (10) Data field design, (11) User interface design, (12) Data conversion, (13) System configuration, and (14) External environment. The ranks of each factor at each stage of the information systems life cycle in our case study are summarized in Table 4.

6.1   Academic Implications

This paper contributes to the literature in at least three ways. First, we conducted a systematic review to identify and conceptualize the factors that influence data completeness in electronic records, which is not available in the existing literature. Focusing on the empirical studies on data completeness in electronic records, we extracted specific 14 factors toward data completeness from the literature through thematic analysis and gave an initial explanation of these factors, in opposite to the factors influencing data quality in general. Second, we extend the existing literature on data completeness by empirically examining and ranking the factors that influence data completeness in electronic records. Our study is the first to consider the ranks of these factors at both stages of information systems life cycle, from the users' perspective in a case study. Our findings of the case study reveal that user interface design was identified as the highest rank factor that influences data completeness at the stage of system design and implementation, while training was considered as the most important factor for addressing data completeness at the stage of system use post implementation, from the perspective of administrative staff users, in the selected company. These findings may offer interesting possibilities for improving or furthering these core areas for addressing data completeness. Last, this work also extends the existing literature of data completeness in the following way: our study is the first to consider the reasons of ratings given by the participants. Our findings point to a previously undocumented examination and analysis on the relative importance of the factors influencing data completeness in electronic records grouped from human, managerial, technical and environmental perspectives. Our empirical results show that the groups of these factors have the potential to exacerbate or mitigate their role in influencing data completeness at different stages of information systems life cycle.

6.2 Practical Implications

This study uncovered that most factors have received attention from the users in the selected company. At the stage of system design and implementation, user interface design that guilds users' behavior to record data could determine how "good" is the data captured and entered, and therefore, this factor takes the first place in addressing data completeness based on the viewpoints of the participants in our case study. Furthermore, technical factors took a relatively important place than human and managerial factors at this stage, as discussed in Sect. 5. While at the stage of system use post implementation, an appropriate training is a significant enabler to help users address data completeness when using the information system in the selected company. At the same time, human factors were considered as more important factors than managerial and technical factors. Hence, similarly, decision makers should take the ranks of these factors into account at each stage and make the corresponding efforts for addressing data completeness in the context of their organizations. An appreciation of this topic also can be of practical use as practitioners increasingly use information systems and supporting technologies to improve their data practices for addressing data completeness in electronic records.

6.3 Limitations and Future Work

This study has several limitations. First, since our case study was limited to a single company, future work could survey a broader range of organizations and individuals or data quality experts to improve the generalization of findings of the study. However, our findings of this study also allow other companies to raise the awareness of data completeness problems and begin to address data completeness in electronic records. Our study allows practitioners to consider some core areas uncovered in this paper for achieving complete data in electronic records, at each stage of information systems life cycle. Second, the participant's responses were based on their perception, experience, and memory. Although in the instrument development we described each factor in a simple way that could help the participants better understand these factors, in order to make sure the collected data that reflects the participants' actual perceptions and experience, the responses from the participants may have been affected by recall bias. That is to say, the participants may not be able to accurately recall the experience of addressing data completeness that happened over time. Furthermore, to reduce the risk of losing the data context, the reasons of their ratings were not translated into English, and only the results of the analysis were written in English that may be affected by the researcher's background and assumptions. Thus, further verification and clarification of the results should be sought from the participants. Third, although T-test for determining whether or not the identified factors from the literature significantly influence data completeness in electronic records as has traditionally been done in prior studies of identifying important factors (e.g., [24, 32]), there is a concern regarding the use of T-test for Likert-like data. However, as noted in Kang [33, p.3], "*although the small sample size might cause some violations in the normality assumption, the use of t test was appropriate as it is robust against small to moderate deviations from the normality assumption. The assumptions would still be checked to ensure no major violations.*" Hence, this limitation does not pose a significant concern for this study. Fourth, we faithfully used the terms precisely described in the literature to name the most factors through content analysis, grouped these factors according to their perspectives to improve or reduce data completeness, and gave them an appropriate name, based on our understanding from the description in the literature as well as our knowledge and past experience. The original authors may or may not agree our classification. However, we assigned these factors independently and these assignments achieved a relatively high level of reliability (86%). Further surveys or questionnaires with respect to the classification of these factors are encouraged to compare the results from the present study that may open an interesting area to reexamine and see whether or not some of these factors could be combined or reassigned (e.g., human factors). Last, this study only focuses on the relative ranks of the factors influencing data completeness in electronic records, our future work intends to investigate the relationships between these factors that could help explain the underlying mechanisms to achieve complete data, assisting in the tasks of potentially preserving data completeness or systematically reducing missing data at an early stage.

Acknowledgement. This research was supported and funded by the Humanities and Social Sciences Youth Foundation, Ministry of Education of the People's Republic of China (Grant No.21YJC870009).

Appendix I. An Overview of Literature Review in This Study

Appendix I is available at: https://www.dropbox.com/s/mpmnd8kfhzwxsgj/Appendix%20I.docx?dl=0

Appendix II. Timelines of Each Stage in This Study

Appendix II is available at:
    https://www.dropbox.com/s/oehvqhh28xr3m0w/Appendix%20II.docx?dl=0.

Appendix III. Questionnaire Example of This Study

Appendix III is available at:
    https://www.dropbox.com/s/nqaulcmlye8rapw/Appendix%20III.docx?dl=0.

Appendix IV. Descriptive Statistics for the Factors Rated in This Study

Appendix IV is available at:
    https://www.dropbox.com/s/hr14vdfj70ujpcn/Appendix%20IV.docx?dl=0.

References

1. Dublino, J.: Reinventing business intelligence: 10 ways big data is changing business. https://www.business.com/articles/reinventing-business-intelligence-ways-big-data-is-changing-business/. Accessed 15 Oct 2023
2. Ferris, R.: Digital transformation – What's next for business' biggest buzzword? https://www.information-age.com/digital-transformation-buzzword-10204/. Accessed 15 Oct 2023
3. Carmody, B.: Biggest Problem with Big Data Management in 2016. https://www.inc.com/bill-carmody/biggest-problem-with-big-data-management-in-2016.html. Accessed 15 Oct 2023
4. Cai, L., Zhu, Y.: The challenges of data quality and data quality assessment in the big data era. Data Sci. J. **14**, 2 (2015)
5. Pipino, L.L., Lee, Y.W., Wang, R.Y.: Data quality assessment. Commun. ACM. ACM **45**(4), 211–218 (2002)
6. Batini, C., Cappiello, C., Francalanci, C., Maurino, A.: Methodologies for data quality assessment and improvement. ACM Comput. Surv.Comput. Surv. **41**(3), 1–52 (2009)
7. Kwon, O., Lee, N., Shin, B.: Data quality management, data usage experience and acquisition intention of big data analytics. Int. J. Inf. Manage. **34**(3), 387–394 (2014)
8. Wang, R.Y., Strong, D.M.: Beyond accuracy: What data quality means to data consumers. J. Manag. Inf. Syst.Manag. Inf. Syst. **12**(4), 5–33 (1996)
9. Benson, P.: ISO 8000 - A New International Standard for Data Quality. https://www.dataqualitypro.com/iso-8000-new-international-standard-data-quality/. Accessed 15 Oct 2023
10. ISO.: Data quality – Part 140: Master data: Exchange of characteristic data: Completeness (2016). https://www.iso.org/standard/62395.html/. Accessed 15 Oct 2023
11. Xiao, J-h, Xie, K., Wan, X-w.: Factors influencing enterprise to improve data quality in information systems application – An empirical research on 185 enterprises through field study. In: Proceedings of 16th International Conference on Management Science and Engineering, pp. 23–33. IEEE, Moscow, Russia (2009)
12. De Feo, J.A., Juran, J.M.: Juran's Quality Handbook: The Complete Guide to Performance Excellence, 7th edn. McGraw-Hill, New York (2017)
13. Xu, H., Koronius, A., Brown, N.: Managing data quality in accounting information systems. IT-Based Management: Challenges and Solutions, pp. 277–299 (2003)
14. Xu, H.: Data quality issues for accounting information systems' implementation: systems, stakeholders, and organizational factors. J. Technol. Res. **1**, 1–11 (2009)
15. Xu, H., Lu, D.: The critical success factors for data quality in accounting information system–Different industries' perspective. Issues Inf. Syst. **4**, 762–768 (2003)
16. Nord, G.D., Nord, J.H., Xu, H.: An investigation of the impact of organization size on data quality issues. J. Database Manage. **16**(3), 58–71 (2005)
17. Kokemueller, J.: An empirical investigation of factors influencing data quality improvement success. In: Proceeding of the 17th Americas Conference on Information Systems, pp. 1–10. Association for Information Systems, Detroit, Michigan, USA (2011)
18. Tee, S.W., Bowen, P.L., Doyle, P., Rohde, F.H.: Factors influencing organizations to improve data quality in their information systems. Accoun. Financ. **47**(2), 335–355 (2007)
19. Xu, H.: What are the most important factors for accounting information quality and their impact on ais data quality outcomes? J. Data Inf. Qual. **5**(4), 1–22 (2015)
20. Haan, G.H., Hillegersberg, J.V., De Jong, E., Sikkel, K.: Adoption of wireless sensors in supply chains: a process view analysis of a pharmaceutical cold chain. J. Theor. Appl. Electron. Commer. Res.Theor. Appl. Electron. Commer. Res. **8**(2), 138–154 (2013)
21. Kadhim-Saleh, A., Green, M., Williamson, T., Hunter, D., Birtwhistle, R.: Validation of the diagnostic algorithms for 5 chronic conditions in the Canadian Primary Care Sentinel Surveillance Network (CPCSSN): A Kingston Practice-based Research Network (PBRN) report. J. Am. Board Family Med. **26**(2), 159–167 (2013)

22. Alter, S.: The work system method for understanding information systems and information systems research. Commun. Assoc. Inf. Syst.. Assoc. Inf. Syst. **9**, 90–104 (2002)
23. Costa, C.J., Aparício, M.: Information system life cycle: applications in construction and manufacturing. Int. J. Ind. Manuf. Eng. **1**(8), 424–429 (2007)
24. Ashja, M., Hadizadeh Moghadam, A., Bidram, H.: Comparative study of large information systems' CSFs during their life cycle. Inf. Syst. Front. **17**, 619–628 (2015)
25. Maxie Burns, O., Turnipseed, D., Riggs, W.E.: Critical success factors in manufacturing resource planning implementation. Int. J. Oper. Prod. Manag.Oper. Prod. Manag. **11**(4), 5–19 (1991)
26. Arvidsson, V., Holmström, J., Lyytinen, K.: Information systems use as strategy practice: a multi-dimensional view of strategic information system implementation and use. J. Strateg. Inf. Syst.Strateg. Inf. Syst. **23**(1), 45–61 (2014)
27. Wolfswinkel, J.F., Furtmueller, E., Wilderom, C.P.M.: Using grounded theory as a method for rigorously reviewing literature. Eur. J. Inf. Syst. **22**(1), 45–55 (2013)
28. Richardson, D.A., De Leeuw, S., Dullaert, W.: Factors affecting global inventory prepositioning locations in humanitarian operations – a Delphi study. J. Bus. Logist.Logist. **37**(1), 59–74 (2016)
29. Tilly, R., Posegga, O., Fischbach, K., Schoder, D.: Towards a conceptualization of data and information quality in social information systems. Bus. Inf. Syst. Eng. **59**, 3–21 (2017)
30. Chen, H.-Y., Boore, J.R.: Translation and back-translation in qualitative nursing research: methodological review. J. Clin. Nurs.Nurs. **19**, 234–239 (2010)
31. Nunnally, J.: Psychometric methods. McGraw-Hill, New York (1978)
32. Tayeh, B.A., Maqsoom, A., Aisheh, Y.I.A., Almanassra, M., Salahuddin, H., Qureshi, M.I.: Factors affecting defects occurrence in the construction stage of residential buildings in Gaza Strip. SN Appl. Sci. **2**, 167 (2020)
33. Kang, M.L., Wong, C.M.J., Tan, H., Bohari, A., Han, T.O., Soon, Y.: A secondary learning curve in 3D versus 2D imaging in laparoscopic training of surgical novices. Surg. Endosc.Endosc. **35**, 1046–1051 (2021)
34. Freedman, A.: The coronavirus pandemic and loss of aircraft data takes toll on weather forecasting. https://www.boston.com/news/coronavirus/2020/05/13/aircraft-data-weather-foreca sting-coronavirus. Accessed 15 Oct 2023
35. Coulson, S.: Combatting civil fraud against businesses in the age of COVID-19. https://www. lexology.com/library/detail.aspx?g=d759c150-b1ed-4c14-ab26-e91e9f0b94ea. Accessed 15 Oct 2023
36. Leedy, P.D., Ormrod, J.: Practical research: Planning and design, 12th edn. Pearson Merril Prentice Hall, New Jersey (2019)
37. Sony, M., Antony, J., Mc Dermott, O., Garza-Reyes, J.A.: An empirical examination of benefits, challenges, and critical success factors of industry 4.0 in manufacturing and service sector. Technol. Soc. **67**, 101754 (2021)

AI Virtual Travel Assistant Based on Smart City - An Application Interface Design Study

Ying Liu and Xueying Niu[✉]

Tsinghua University, Beijing 100084, People's Republic of China
Xueying_n@163.com

Abstract. The construction of smart cities provides more convenient and efficient services and facilities for the tourism industry, and together with the continuous advancement of AI technology, it can support the intelligent development and digital transformation of the tourism industry in terms of data analysis and prediction, automation and intelligence, personalization and customization, intelligent decision support, and exploration. The implementation of digital technology in various industries, the establishment of large-scale data systems, and the development of modern urban areas lay the groundwork for the intelligent evolution of the tourism sector. This study aims to examine the current state of transforming tourism consumption through the use of data processing, specifically by performing a literature survey on the existing applications of artificial intelligence and big data in the tourism industry. By conducting questionnaire surveys and in-depth interviews, we investigate how tourists utilize tourism application from an audience analysis standpoint. We also consider the use and satisfaction theory to plan the design of application, incorporating the benefits of artificial intelligence to speculate on the design of tourism application. This study seeks to examine the impact of AI on the conventional framework of the tourism industry and its role in facilitating the intelligent evolution of the industry within smart cities. Additionally, it aims to investigate how AI can be leveraged as a significant competitive edge for the advancement of the tourism sector.

Keywords: Tourist Behaviour · Artificial Intelligence · Smart Tourism

1 Introduction

1.1 Smart Cities and the Transformation of Tourism Industry

The tourist industry and its associated activities have undergone substantial transformations as a result of scientific and technological breakthroughs, as well as the convergence of industries. The emergence of digital platforms and the integration of artificial intelligence have resulted in the swift advancement of smart cities. These cities strive to optimize human connection, enhance the convenience of people's lives, and augment the effectiveness of city governance. Arroub and Zahi define smart cities as urban environments that leverage electronic tools and sensors to collect data, which is then used to efficiently manage assets, resources, and services [1]. This refers to the collection of

© The Author(s), under exclusive license to Springer Nature Switzerland AG 2024
N. A. Streitz and S. Konomi (Eds.): HCII 2024, LNCS 14718, pp. 241–254, 2024.
https://doi.org/10.1007/978-3-031-59988-0_14

information from individuals, devices, structures, and resources. Subsequently, this data is processed and scrutinized to oversee and regulate diverse systems, including traffic and transportation, power plants, utilities, and water supply networks [1, 2]. Through the utilization of information and communication technology, in conjunction with the incorporation of physical items that are connected to the network, smart cities are able to enhance the effectiveness of city operations and services, as well as provide inhabitants with communication. [2, 3]. Smart city technology allows for immediate contact among city officials, the community, and city infrastructure, enabling real-time monitoring of city activities and development. Smart city applications are specifically developed to effectively manage and govern urban activities, facilitating prompt responses [4]. The concept of smart cities is currently undergoing development and has not yet achieved global adoption due to technological, economic, and governance challenges.

The intelligent evolution of the tourism industry is becoming an increasingly important topic of discussion within the context of smart cities. Smart tourism cities are a concept that is gaining popularity and involves the incorporation of sophisticated technology into destinations, which are often cities, with the goal of enhancing tourism experiences and improving the competitiveness of the destination [5]. This concept is founded on the notion that intelligent technologies erode the boundaries between residential regions and tourism districts, necessitating cities to discover more intelligent methods of management [6]. Smart tourist towns strive to maximize sustainable surroundings and provide urban areas that both residents and visitors can collectively appreciate. "Utilizing information and communication technology (ICT), mobile communication, cloud computing, artificial intelligence, and virtual reality" is essential in creating creative tools and methods to enhance the tourism industry [7]. The core tenets of smart tourism involve boosting the quality of tourism experiences, optimizing the management of resources, and maximizing the competitiveness of destinations, with a particular focus on sustainability [8]. The transformation of tourism in smart cities requires improvements to be made on the basis of applied technology and infrastructure.

Moreover, with the ongoing sustainable growth of the tourism industry, along with the expanding variety of consumer preferences and the widespread adoption of smartphones, individuals are increasingly drawn to self-reliant and personalized types of tourism. Due to the growing popularity of the internet and the vast amount of information accessible, more and more people are opting for independent travel instead of typical group tours. This choice allows them greater autonomy and adaptability in their experiences. Therefore, the evolution and improvement of the conventional tourism model into the intelligent tourism model is an inevitable progression from the perspective of tourism clients. The extensive integration of mobile applications in the tourism sector has bestowed travelers with enhanced independence and authority in managing their trip experiences. This has disturbed the conventional limitations placed on travelers throughout their trips, while simultaneously accommodating their progressively personalized and varied needs.

1.2 The Application of Mobile App and Artificial Intelligent in Tourism

Mobile applications have emerged as a primary means via which individuals communicate, make purchases, manage their daily activities, engage in recreational activities, and even do professional tasks. China's Apple App Store and different Android App Stores offer a diverse range of apps pertaining to tourism and travel. Individuals commonly utilize travel apps to streamline their travel arrangements [9]. This is an opportunity for tourist attractions to enhance the convenience of their services for tourists through the mobile application platform. Additionally, these applications can give up-to-date content pertaining to the newest travel information, popular attractions, and promotions from various service providers [10]. Several studies have examined the influence of travel mobile apps on tourists' travels, namely through audience analysis using surveys [11, 12]. According to Kamboji and Joshi, the results of the study suggest that the use of travel application affects the behavioral outcomes of tourists [12].

Several studies have highlighted the significant impact of information and communication technologies on the tourism and hospitality industry. This is particularly evident in the intricate decision-making process associated with travel. Intelligent systems are well-suited for the tourism industry, and travel websites that facilitate the sharing of information have been widely used for a considerable period of time. The study asserts that the integration of artificial intelligence into service automation presents significant prospects for tourism enterprises and organizations. As Inanc-Demir and Kozak concluded, "artificial intelligence systems, particularly those powered by machine technology, can achieve significant results through the rapid elimination of large data sets" [14]. Consequently, the use of these kinds of automations may make it possible for tourism organizations to reap the benefits of marketing operations with the assistance of various algorithmic solutions that are founded on big data [14]. The results of a number of studies indicated that artificial intelligence will be the most important factor in ensuring continued competitiveness in the future. An artificial intelligence framework for internet destination picture images recognition has been developed by one study, it identifies 25 image classification categories that encompass all tourism scenes [15]. The study on the advancement and prospective of e-ecotourism for the purpose of sustainability also revealed that artificial intelligence might have a significant impact [16]. The study seeks to develop a dynamic model to enhance the performance of tourism in ecotourism destinations, and it proposes the use of artificial intelligence (AI) and big data to analyze ecotourism features and implement various scenarios [16]. The advent of the digital era of artificial intelligence signifies the swift advancement of tourism engineering and the steady enhancement of intelligent management theory [16]. According to Hou, Artificial intelligence systems can "solve the problems of low efficiency of dynamic relationship analysis and low data utilization in the traditional intelligent management methods of tourism engineering" [17]. Hou also observed that the travel and tourism industry is expected to undergo significant advancements in smart automation in the future, driven by the progress in artificial intelligence (AI) and its associated technologies [17].

1.3 Human-Computer Interaction and the Intelligent Tourism

The development of smart cities in the tourism industry will play a crucial role in driving future innovation and facilitating the intelligent transformation of the tourism sector. The interactive design of smart cities can improve the tourism experience and service quality by utilizing intelligent technology and methods. This allows for the exchange of information and common services, ultimately enhancing the city's appeal and competitiveness. Initially, by utilizing the intelligent guide system, tourists may effortlessly acquire information about attractions, tour itineraries, audio narrations, and other services to enhance their overall tourism experience. Furthermore, the implementation of information sharing enables both tourists and city managers to access up-to-date tourism information and data. This not only helps tourists to engage in more automated and intelligent consultations regarding tourism information, but also assists city managers in enhancing tourism management and services through data analysis. Furthermore, the incorporation of diverse services, amenities, attractions, and other components of the city can enhance the consistency and entirety of tourism services. By employing sophisticated management systems, it can facilitate the alignment of hotels, transportation, and tourist sites, thereby offering tourists tailored and personalized tourism services. Furthermore, the integration of large-scale data and the application of algorithmic modeling can assist tourist cities in analyzing popular tourist destinations, thereby improving the city's appeal and competitiveness in the tourism industry.

2   Methodology

2.1   The Questionnaire and In-Depth Interview

A survey was distributed to Chinese tourists, with a sample size of 151. Upon gathering the outcomes of the questionnaire, we proceeded to conduct in-depth interviews with specific respondent cohorts. There were a total of 15 interviews conducted to assess the extent of dissatisfaction with the current travel application. The inquiry on the acceptance of AI intelligent application involved a sample size of 10 individuals who were interviewed.

Demographic Characteristics of Respondents. The study conducted a descriptive statistical analysis to characterize the respondents based on their gender, annual household income, and educational qualifications. The study results revealed a favorable correlation between the annual household income of the interviewees and their annual frequency of travel, as determined using cross-tabulation analysis. 50% of individuals with annual household earnings exceeding ¥1 million reported an annual travel frequency of more than five visits. Half of those with annual household incomes above ¥1 million responded that the annual frequency of traveling was more than five or more times. Those with annual household incomes of less than ¥30,000 per year and those with annual household incomes between ¥30,000 and ¥80,000 mostly traveled with an annual frequency of less than one or two trips. Those in the middle of the spectrum, with annual household incomes of ¥80,000 to ¥150,000 and ¥150,000 to ¥300,000, focused their choices on two to three times a year (Tables 1 and 2).

By doing regression analysis, we see that there is no significant correlation between education level and travel frequency or travel spending. However, we do find a positive correlation between yearly household income and both travel frequency and travel spending.

Table 1. Cross analysis of income and frequency of tourism.

Annual household income/Annual frequency of tourism	None(Last year)	Once or twice a year	Three to five times a year	More than five times a year	Sum
Less than 30k(yuan)	4(44.44%)	4(44.44%)	0(0.00%)	1(11.11%)	9
30k- 80k(yuan)	2(66.67%)	1(33.33%)	0(0.00%)	0(0.00%)	3
80k-150k(yuan)	1(5.56%)	11(61.11%)	5(27.78%)	1(5.56%)	18
150k-300k(yuan)	8(16.33%)	30(61.22%)	10(20.41%)	1(2.04%)	49
300k - 1million(yuan)	4(7.27%)	28(50.91%)	18(32.73%)	5(9.09%)	55
More than 1 million yuan	0(0.00%)	3(37.5%)	1(12.5%)	4(50%)	8

Table 2. Regression analysis of frequency of tourism.

Item	Regression coefficient	t	p	VIF
Constant	1.37	4.54	0.000**	-
Annual household income	0.20	3.63	0.000**	1.15
Education level	0.02	0.17	0.864	1.15

Current Status of Tourists' use of Travel Application. The questionnaire survey results indicate a movement among tourists from the conventional group tour model to self-driving tours and independent trips, and the overwhelming majority of individuals using travel applications on their mobile devices for the purpose of organizing trips and have expended (Table 3, 4 and 5).

Table 3. Tourist Travel Mode.

	Self driving tour	Independent tour	Group tour	Sum
Travel mode	67	77	7	151
(Percentages)	44.37%	50.99%	4.64%	

By doing cross-tabulation analysis, we discovered that different travel companions have a significant impact on the planning of trip itineraries. Individuals typically meticulously plan their excursions, particularly when traveling with their lover. Individuals who

Table 4. Frequency of use of travel application

	Always	Occasionally	Barely	Sum
Frequency of using app	103	38	10	151
(Percentages)	68.21%	25.17%	6.62%	

Table 5. Cross analysis of travel partners and frequency of making travel plans.

Travel partners/ Do you make travel plans	Always	Occasionally	Barely	Sum
Family	75(79.79%)	16(17.02%)	3(3.19%)	94
Friends	23(62.16%)	10(27.03%)	4(10.81%)	37
Lover	7(87.5%)	0(0.00%)	1(12.5%)	8
Alone	3(25%)	3(25%)	6(50%)	12

opt to travel solo are more likely to travel according to their own preferences, without the need to make specific travel arrangements.

This will serve as a valuable source of inspiration for our application design, which will incorporate many types of transportation.

Tourists' Motivations for Using Travel Application. Our regression research revealed a significant correlation between the decision to create a travel plan prior to traveling and the impact it has on travel application. The findings indicate that individuals are primarily driven to utilize travel application for the purpose of trip planning (Table 6).

Table 6. Regression analysis of frequency of tourism application usage.

Item	Regression coefficient	t	p	VIF
Constant	1.18	12.48	0.000**	-
Do you make travel plans	0.11	2.17	0.031*	1.00
Education level	0.02	0.17	0.864	1.15

Subsequently, we conducted an in-depth investigation of the visitors' reasons for using a variety of application programs, taking into account the use and gratification theory. This allowed us to investigate the manner in which visitors utilize these applications. Use and gratification theory refers to the fundamental motivations behind visitor behavior and satisfaction. Studies have shown that visitors share photographs on social media sites to seek social approval, have a sense of achievement, communicate personal information, and engage in a habitual leisure activity [18]. Moreover, e-tourists extensively employ cellphones for socializing, entertainment, gaining knowledge, and ease, so significantly influencing their degree of satisfaction [19]. Furthermore, the user's perception of a fan page for a tourist site is shaped by the gratifications they receive, including entertainment, knowledge, and social interaction [20]. Consequently, this impacts their desire to visit the site. By categorizing visitors' motives based on their purpose and level of satisfaction, we may examine the distinct requirements of tourists and their reasons for utilizing travel application (Table 7).

Table 7. Cross analysis of travel tool usage and application categories.

Travel tool usage/application categories	Social media application (Red, Weibo)	Friends' opinion reference	Travel application(Qunaer, Feizhu)	Search engine (Baidu, Google, etc.)	Others subtotal	Sum
Convenience: hotel, transportation, attraction booking	75(55.15%)	61(44.85%)	91(66.91%)	53(38.97%)	19(13.97%)	136
Getting information: others' travel sharing, official introduction	74(72.55%)	63(61.76%)	52(50.98%)	41(40.20%)	12(11.76%)	102
Socializing: Sharing self-travel and interacting with friends	16(84.21%)	8(42.11%)	13(68.42%)	9(47.37%)	2(10.53%)	19
Other reasons	2(28.57%)	4(57.14%)	2(28.57%)	1(14.29%)	3(42.86%)	7

According to the Uses and Satisfaction Theory, we classified tourists' motives into three primary categories. Additionally, we discovered that tourists' motivations are linked to the instruments they employ to personalize their trip arrangements. Tourists select travel application for booking purposes when they have a need for convenience. On the other hand, when it comes to requests for information and social sharing, a greater number of visitors opt to utilize social media application to fulfill their needs.

Thus, it can be inferred that travelers must utilize several resources to fulfill their requirements when engaging in vacation planning, as there is a lack of a comprehensive platform that can cater to all their demands.

Deficiencies of Existing Travel Application. During our investigation into individuals' discontent with current travel application, We discovered that convenience remains the primary criterion for selection. First, we conducted a study with the individuals who do not enjoy using travel application. More than half of those individuals stated that the primary reason they do not enjoy using travel application is because they do not have a sufficient understanding of the functionalities that are available in the travel application that is currently available. Furthermore, respondents believed that they could not perform all of the operations of their trip through a single travel application, and they suggested that services a single application provided cannot satisfied all their need. This was discovered through follow-up interviews, which revealed that respondents indicated that the existing application required cumbersome operations, and as a result, they did not find it to be convenient enough (Table 8).

Table 8. Regression analysis of satisfaction with the use of travel application.

Item	Regression coefficient	t	p	VIF
Constant	1.82	8.00	0.000**	-
Traveling companion	0.17	2.44	0.016*	1.03
Travel Expenses	−0.10	−2.11	0.036*	1.03

Subsequently, our regression study revealed a significant correlation between trip expenditure and the level of satisfaction among travel companions with the travel application. The variation in travel companions and trip expenses suggests the difference in travel needs and travel modes, therefore it can be found that the existing travel application cannot suit all travel needs (Table 9).

Table 9. Requirements that are not satisfied by travel application

Dissatisfaction	Amount	Percentages
Price comparison of travel expenses	71	47.02%
Travel booking to avoid queues	95	62.91%
Attractions real-time navigation	54	35.76%
Virtual scenic experience	52	34.44%
Travel enthusiast community sharing	28	18.54%

Then, we studied the needs that visitors were unable to satisfy when using travel application, with convenience being a significant role in the investigation. The most major concerns that tourists wished to solve were the ability to quickly compare prices and the avoidance of waiting in lines that took a significant amount of time.

Through the use of questionnaires and in-depth interviews, we came to the conclusion that the currently available travel application is unable to cater to the varied requirements of tourists, even when considering the convenience factor.

Attitudes Toward Artificial Intelligence in Tourism. Our regression research revealed a correlation between educational parameters, travel mode, and the acceptability of AI travel application.The level of education directly correlates with one's knowledge of AI, thereby increasing their openness to AI travel application. Conversely, independent travelers prefer to create their own travel itineraries and have a reduced reliance on instant, automated navigation (Table 10).

Subsequently, we examined the current inadequacy of travel application in fulfilling the requirements of visitors and the level of acceptance of AI application using cross-tabulation analysis. In general, individuals who perceive the application as difficult to use and struggle to comprehend its functions, along with other inconveniences encountered while using it, will prefer utilizing AI to generate a travel plan with a single click.

Table 10. Regression analysis of acceptance of AI application.

Item	Regression coefficient	t	p	VIF
Constant	1.60	8.67	0.000**	-
Travel mode	−0.13	−2.50	0.014*	1.00
education level	0.11	2.71	0.007**	1.00

Conversely, those who harbor doubts about the accuracy of the application's information are more inclined to independently create their own travel plans (Table 11).

Table 11. Cross analysis of application dissatisfaction and acceptance of AI application in tourism.

Application dissatisfaction	Yes, I prefer AI	No, I prefer make the plan by myself
Memory consumption	9(100%)	0(0.00%)
Don't understand its function	45(83.33%)	9(16.67%)
Incomplete and inaccurate information	3(23.08%)	10(76.92%)
Too many advertisements	9(33.33%)	18(66.67%)
Payment methods are not convenient	9(100%)	0(0.00%)
Fewer services provided	18(66.67%)	9(33.33%)
Don't know about mobile travel application	45(83.33%)	9(16.67%)
Others	9(50%)	9(50%)

By doing a cross-analysis of the frequency of trips and the use of artificial intelligence (AI) travel application, we discovered that tourists who have more leisure time tend to prefer the autonomy of creating their own travel itineraries (Table 12).

Table 12. Cross analysis of travel frequency and the use of AI application in tourism.

Heading level	Yes, I prefer AI	No, I prefer make the plan by myself
None (last year)	12(60%)	8(40%)
Once or twice a year	53(63.86%)	30(36.14%)
Three to five times a year	26(72.22%)	10(27.78%)
More than five times a year	5(41.67%)	7(58.33%)

Then we involved conducting extensive interviews with individuals who chose to independently plan their own trips. We discovered that these individuals had greater flexibility with their time, which reduced their reliance on AI smart application to save time. They also expressed a preference for creating personalized travel itineraries on their own.

2.2 Results

Therefore, the major objective of the application is is to fulfill the requirement for convenience, to save time for visitors in terms of planning travel arrangements, and to save time in lineups during tourists' journeys by means of massive data retrieval. At the same time, tourists' diverse traveling partners will make their demands for traveling and the needs offered by the application different, therefore the design of the program should take into account the configuration of travel modes.

3   Application Design

By developing an application that incorporates an AI-powered virtual assistant, virtual picture, and social media platform features, it is possible to seamlessly combine AI technology with human-computer interaction, information exchange, and common service functions. The program is specifically built to execute three primary duties, encompassing tour planning, real-time navigation of the tour process, and information sharing and VR tour simulation within a virtual community.

3.1 Intelligent Generation of Travel Plans

Through the utilization of large amounts of data and computational models, the artificial intelligence virtual assistant is able to provide intelligent and individualized recommendations, as well as streamline and automate the service process. Tourists have the option to utilize either voice or text commands to instruct the AI to make hotel reservations, purchase tickets, or even have the AI autonomously design a travel itinerary by establishing a specific travel pattern (see Fig. 1). This eliminates the need to deal with complicated procedures, thus enhancing efficiency. Through the analysis of the previous questionnaire survey, we have discovered that various travel requirements, such as modes of transportation, are influenced by factors such as travel companions and expenses. By providing concise information about travel modes and estimated expenses, the AI tour guide can efficiently generate suitable travel plans with just one click. It will be necessary to analyze data from past trip platforms and using algorithms to suggest suitable travel plans. Parent-child travel in the context of tourism prioritizes recommending appropriate attractions for children to enjoy, whilst couples traveling tend to prefer destinations with a romantic ambiance. Simultaneously, the selection of hotels will be suggested based on factors such as proximity to attractions, travel companions, and travel costs.

According to the findings of the questionnaire survey, we discovered that tourists use travel application that is inconvenient for the purpose of price comparison. Furthermore, according to the statistics of big data, artificial intelligence assistants have the potential to be directly involved in the selection of tourists within the scope of tourism expenditures. This is done in accordance with the evaluation system and various booking platforms for price comparison. This allows tourists to select the most cost-effective hotels and modes of transportation, thereby eliminating the need for the third platform, which is responsible for the intermediary costs, and tourists in the price of comparisons in the amount of time wasted.

Fig. 1. AI virtual assistant generates travel plans

3.2 Intelligent Travel Real-Time Navigation

The AI virtual assistant also offers intelligent navigation and tour guide systems, allowing tourists to track attraction crowds in real-time and gather travel time statistics (see Fig. 2). Additionally, it helps tourists locate facilities such as attractions, restaurants, and restrooms, saving them time and effort.

Based on the questionnaire survey, we found out that the primary issue that tourists need to address is the challenge of accessing offline sites and dealing with transportation queues. By continuously monitoring the current flow of people, the AI assistant can accurately estimate the waiting time for attractions and transit. It can also provide real-time navigation guidance to users. For instance, if there are two attractions and attraction A currently has a higher volume of visitors compared to attraction B, while both attractions have the same expected traffic time, the AI assistant will prioritize guiding users to attraction A. During the later phase of constructing the smart city, the AI system will be integrated with the scenic spot supervision system. This would enable online pre-queuing, allowing the system to intelligently manage the flow of people in batches, effectively eliminating the need for tourists to wait in line.

Fig. 2. AI virtual assistant for real-time travel navigation.

The AI system has the capability to examine data from visitors who are within the area and can offer augmented reality explanations of popular landmarks. After the system determines the location, it will display detailed explanations and introductions of various attractions and special features in the surrounding area. These explanations will include historical information about the attractions, as well as detailed backstories of special buildings in the scenic area.

3.3 Virtual Community

It is possible for the virtual community to serve as a social and communication platform for travelers. Additionally, tourists can pre-tour a variety of tourist destinations and experience diverse cultures and flavors in a virtual environment by utilizing virtual reality technology, which makes it easier for tourists to organize their trips. At the same time, tourists have the opportunity to meet other travelers in a virtual environment, discuss their feelings and experiences related to travel, or organize events that take place outside of the virtual world. The kind of social contact that is described here not only improves the overall travel experience for visitors, but it also makes it simpler for artificial intelligence to collect and evaluate the information data that is generated by social interaction.

4 Discussion

In this study, questionnaires and in-depth interviews are used to investigate the use of existing tourism application from the point of view of audience analysis. Additionally, the study examines the requirements of tourists and investigates the possibilities of using artificial intelligence to the tourism business. This study investigates the potential of integrating AI with tourism by developing a model for the interface of an application that utilizes a future AI virtual assistant. This smartphone application has the capacity to stimulate inventive progress and transform smart tourism by enhancing the effectiveness and excellence of services offered by the tourism sector, while also heightening guests' feeling of involvement and interactivity. To foster social progress, urban economic development, and new industrial technology, one might establish a positive feedback loop by enhancing the efficiency of the tourism industry.

A limitation of this study is the small sample size of the questionnaire. In future research, we will utilize the findings from current questionnaires and refer to the scales used in prior studies to develop more reliable questionnaires that can facilitate regression analysis.

References

1. Arroub, A., Zahi, B., Sabir, E., et al.: A literature review on Smart Cities: Paradigms, opportunities and open problems. In: 2016 International conference on wireless networks and mobile communications (WINCOM). IEEE, pp. 180–186 (2016)
2. Silva, B.N., Khan, M., Han, K.: Towards sustainable smart cities: a review of trends, architectures, components, and open challenges in smart cities. Sustain. Cities Soc. **38**, 697–713 (2018)
3. Ismagilova, E., Hughes, L., Dwivedi, Y.K., et al.: Smart cities: advances in research' an information systems perspective. Int. J. Inf. Manage. **47**, 88–100 (2019)
4. Lai, C.S., Jia, Y., Dong, Z., et al.: A review of technical standards for smart cities. Clean Technol. **2**(3), 290–310 (2020)
5. Gretzel, U., Koo, C.: Smart tourism cities: a duality of place where technology supports the convergence of touristic and residential experiences. Asia Pacific J. Tourism Res. **26**(4), 352–364 (2021)
6. Della Corte, V., D'Andrea, C., Savastano, I., et al.: Smart cities and destination management: impacts and opportunities for tourism competitiveness. Europ. J. Tourism Res. **17**, 7–27 (2017)
7. Lee, P., Hunter, W.C., Chung, N.: Smart tourism city: Developments and transformations. Sustainability **12**(10), 3958 (2020)
8. Habeeb, N.J., Weli, S.T.: Relationship of smart cities and smart tourism: an overview. HighTech Innov. J. **1**(4), 194–202 (2020)

9. Jia, Z., Li, D., He, F.: Analysis and reviews on tourism and travel mobile apps of China. In: International Conference on Electronics, Mechanics, Culture and Medicine, pp. 62–66. Atlantis Press (2016)

10. Tobing, R.D.H.: Mobile tourism application for samosir regency on android platform. In: 2015 International Symposium On Technology Management And Emerging Technologies (ISTMET), (IF: 3) (2015)

11. Lim, T.Y., Tan, T.L., Jnr Nwonwu, G.E: Mobile in-app advertising for tourism: a case study. In: Stephanidis, C. (eds) HCI International 2013 - Posters' Extended Abstracts. HCI 2013. Communications in Computer and Information Science, vol. 373. Springer, Heidelberg. https://doi.org/10.1007/978-3-642-39473-7_138

12. Kamboj, S., Joshi, R.: Examining the factors influencing smartphone apps use at tourism destinations: a UTAUT model perspective. Int. J. Tourism Cities 7(1), 135–157 (2021). https://doi.org/10.1108/IJTC-05-2020-0094

13. Zlatanov, S., Popesku, J.: Current Applications of Artificial Intelligence in Tourism and Hospitality. Paper presented at Sinteza 2019 - International Scientific Conference on Information Technology and Data Related Research (2019). https://doi.org/10.15308/Sinteza-2019-84-90

14. Inanc–Demir, M., Kozak, M.: Big data and its supporting elements: implications for tourism and hospitality marketing. In: Sigala, M., Rahimi, R., Thelwall, M. (eds.) Big Data and Innovation in Tourism, Travel, and Hospitality. Springer, Singapore (2019). https://doi.org/10.1007/978-981-13-6339-9_13

15. Wang, R., Luo, J., Huang, S.S.: Developing an artificial intelligence framework for online destination image photos identification. J. Destin. Mark. Manag.Manag. 18, 100512 (2020)

16. Eddyono, F., Darusman, D., Sumarwan, U., et al.: Optimization model: the innovation and future of e-ecotourism for sustainability. J. Tourism Futures (2021)

17. Hou, T.: Research on Management Efficiency and Dynamic Relationship in Intelligent Management of Tourism Engineering Based on Industry 4.0. Computational Intelligence and Neuroscience (2022)

18. Liao, J.C., Wang, Y.C., Tsai, C.H., et al.: Gratifications of travel photo sharing (GTPS) on social media: scale development and cross-cultural validation. Tour. Anal. 26(4), 265–277 (2021)

19. Moon, J.W., An, Y.: Uses and gratifications motivations and their effects on attitude and e-tourist satisfaction: a multilevel approach. Tourism Hospitality 3(1), 116–136 (2022)

20. Ho, K.K.W., See-To, E.W.K.: The impact of the uses and gratifications of tourist attraction fan page. Internet Res. 28(3), 587–603 (2018)

Policy Research in the Metaverse Technologies Enabled Publishing Industry in China (2016–2023)

Xinze Liu[1] ⓘ, Haobing Liu[2] ⓘ, Qiongpei Kong[3] ⓘ, and Ning Zhang[1(✉)] ⓘ

[1] Beijing Normal University at Zhuhai, Zhuhai 519087, China
ningzhang@bnu.edu.cn
[2] Beijing Normal University Publishing Group, Beijing 100875, China
[3] King's College London, Strand London WC2R 2LS, UK

Abstract. Chinese publishing industry enters the era of metaverse publishing in 2021. This study analyzes the metaverse publishing policy attributes and evolutionary trajectories in order to propose useful recommendations for the advancement of publishing sector in China. This research collected a corpus of 83 policy documents issued by Chinese governments from 2016 to 2023. It adopted social network analysis, co-word analysis, and multidimensional scaling, a TNP (Policy Tools, Interdepartmental Relations Network, Policy Focus) as research methods to explore the policy characteristics and evolutionary trends driving the integration of Metaverse technologies into publishing. This research reached the conclusion that a concentration of policy tool utilization primarily on the supply and environmental aspects, with comparatively limited emphasis on the demand aspect, alongside loose interdepartmental relations. Moreover, the policy focus highly lies on cloud computing and artificial intelligence. The digital publishing empowerment primarily focused on public cultural services, the digital cultural industry and education. A number of critical research suggestions can be put forward to steer the development of the metaverse technology-supported publishing industry in a positive direction: a) analysis of policy effectiveness and impact; b) investigation into technological progress and infrastructure; c) examination of consumer behavior and market demands; d) development of a regulatory framework and legal considerations for works published with metaverse technology; e) promotion of cross-sector collaboration and intergovernmental cooperation; f) establishment of standards for policymaking in Metaverse publishing works.

Keywords: Metaverse · digital publishing · Policy research · Virtual reality · Policy bibliometric analysis · culture digitization

1 Introduction

The Metaverse is composed of six core foundational technologies: blockchain, interactivity, gaming, artificial intelligence, networking, and the Internet of Things. Virtual Reality (VR) and Augmented Reality (AR), as interactive technologies, are often regarded as the

N. A. Streitz and S. Konomi (Eds.): HCII 2024, LNCS 14718, pp. 255–271, 2024.
https://doi.org/10.1007/978-3-031-59988-0_15

embodiment of the Metaverse [1]. VR/AR devices, which act as terminals, serve as the gateway for individuals to enter the Metaverse. The actual realization of the Metaverse depends on the widespread adoption and advancement of VR/AR devices.

Metaverse technology has underwent significant development since 2016. It was referred to as the Year of VR, signifying the rise of VR/AR in Chinese national-level policies in 2016. Roblox, often called the first stock of the Metaverse, made its debut on the New York Stock Exchange in March of 2021, achieving a valuation ten times higher than initially estimated [2]. This event showcased the Metaverse's potential to the world. Following that, there was a notable increase in interest in the Metaverse both domestically and internationally, leading to 2021 being referred to as the inaugural year of the Metaverse. In the same year, the State Council of the People's Republic of China issued the Outline of the 14th Five-Year Plan for the National Economic and Social Development of the People's Republic of China and the Long-Range Objectives Through the Year 2035 in 2021, following the introduction of the first national-level guidance on the Metaverse, titled Three-Year Action Plan for Innovative Development of the Metaverse Industry (2023–2025), provinces across the nation responded by implementing Metaverse industry policies.

Given this context, this paper conducts a systematic review and quantitative analysis of China's Metaverse-related policies spanning the years. The study specifically concentrates on Metaverse technology policies released between 2016 and 2023. Its goal is to analyze and summarize the key areas of focus and evolutionary patterns, especially regarding digital publishing technology. Ultimately, the aim is to provide reference-based recommendations for the high-quality development, talent cultivation, and policy formulation within the Chinese publishing industry.

2 Literature Review

The publishing industry has experienced multidimensional transformations, and the future convergence of Publishing 4.0 will bring together traditional and Metaverse publishing, with digital twinning technology playing a crucial role. Even though this integration is not fully realized yet, simulations can be conducted within the Metaverse when needed. The standardization of Metaverse publishing has found numerous applications in various contexts [3].

Existing research has primarily focused on qualitative studies related to the Metaverse and its application scenarios. The research of Wang et al. offers a comprehensive overview of the Metaverse, covering its characteristics, technological framework, social aspects, and challenges [4]. From a bibliometric perspective, Feng et al. systematically outline the current status, knowledge structure, and popular topics in Metaverse research, thereby providing thematic guidelines for the field [5], demonstrating the current status, knowledge structure, and hot topics in Metaverse research, providing thematic axes for the field [5].

Existing research predominantly consists of qualitative studies on the Metaverse and its application scenarios. They discussed characteristics, technological framework, and sociality of Metaverse, Metaverse applications [6], and also the challenges of Metaverse [4].

A conducive policy environment is crucial for Metaverse development. However, existing research on Metaverse policies is mostly qualitative, with limited quantitative analysis. Zhang et al. employ a combination of bibliometrics and content analysis to construct a three-dimensional TNP (Tool, Network, Point) model, analyzing interdepartmental relations, policy tools, hotspots, and policy clustering to delineate the characteristics and evolutionary trends of China's 5G policies [7]. Yang and Huang explore policy evolution using a literature-based quantitative research framework, focusing on China's information technology policies [8].

3 Data Collection and Analysis

3.1 Policy Collection and Selection

To comprehensively gather and organize Metaverse policy documents issued by central and local governments, this study utilizes official websites of relevant departments such as The State Council of the People's Republic of China, Ministry of Industry and Information Technology of the People's Republic of China (MIIT), Ministry of Science and Technology of the People's Republic of China (MOST), and National Development and Reform Commission of the People's Republic of China (NDRC). It also leverages legal and policy information retrieval platforms like PKULaw (https://en.pkulaw.cn/Sea rch/SearchLaw.aspx) and China National Knowledge Infrastructure (CNKI)(https:// www.cnki.net/). Keywords such as "Metaverse", "next-generation information technology", "VR", "virtual reality", "artificial intelligence", "cloud computing" and "cultural digitization" are employed for policy document retrieval.

The collected documents are categorized by type and issuing authority into departmental regulatory documents, administrative regulations, legal documents, and government work reports. The study focuses on policy themes related to public cultural services, cultural institutions, cultural industries, and education. It organizes relevant information such as document titles, release dates, and issuing authorities.

Through these procedures, a total of 83 documents are obtained, comprising 1 constitution, 42 departmental regulatory documents, 26 administrative regulations, 10 legal documents, 2 judicial interpretations, and 2 intra-party regulations. The data retrieval period extends to 30th of September in 2023.

Figure 1 illustrates the policy retrieval process through keyword searches, with all policy titles compiled and stored in a WPS spreadsheet for further filtering. Duplicate policy entries are first eliminated, followed by the removal of policies unrelated to Metaverse foundational technologies, cultural services, or cultural digitization. A detailed review of policies is then conducted, and inaccessible entries are excluded from the study. The final selection of policy documents is determined through full-text filtering, considering inclusion and exclusion criteria.

3.2 Research Methods

This study employs a policy bibliometric approach, utilizing Policy Instrument Analysis, social network analysis, and multi-dimensional scaling analysis as frameworks to

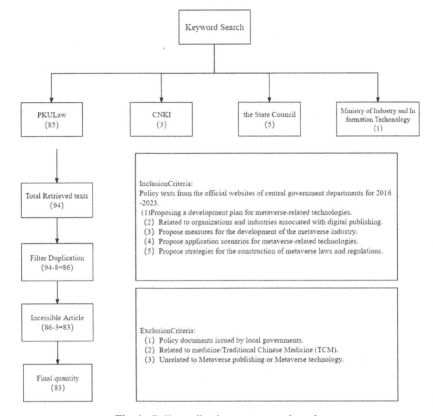

Fig. 1. Policy collection strategy and results

analyze China's Metaverse publishing policies from the perspectives of policy tools, intergovernmental relations, and policy hotspots.

Policy bibliometrics involves applying bibliometric methods to policy texts. In this context, time-series analysis includes examining trends in the number of policy documents over time, analyzing changes in the roles of policy subjects, tracking shifts in policy themes based on keywords, and evaluating fluctuations and sustainability of policy influence based on citation counts. Co-word analysis focuses on exploring policy themes based on keywords. Additionally, network analysis methods, such as citation networks, cooperation networks, and co-occurrence networks, are used to analyze the associative characteristics and relationships among various elements within the policy document system [9].

Policy tools refer to the methods and means employed by the government to achieve policy objectives. Drawing from Rothwell and Zegveld, this study categorizes policy tools into three types: demand-side tools, supply-side tools, and environmental tools [10]. Demand-side tools exert a pulling force on the cultural Metaverse, supply-side tools exert a pushing force, and environmental tools exert an influencing force on the cultural Metaverse. This study records the frequency of appearances of these tools in policy texts without quantifying the extent of their usage. The frequency of tool usage is measured separately for various aspects of Metaverse publishing, such as Metaverse foundational technologies, cultural services, and big data in cultural area.

4 Findings and Discussion

4.1 Policy Data Analysis

Over the past eight years, there has been a consistent upward trend in the quantity of policy texts related to Metaverse publishing technology. Figure 2 illustrates the distribution of relevant policy quantities from March of 2016 to September of 2023. This timeframe covers the release of the "13th Five-Year Plan" in 2016 to the issuance of the first national-level Metaverse guidance in 2023.

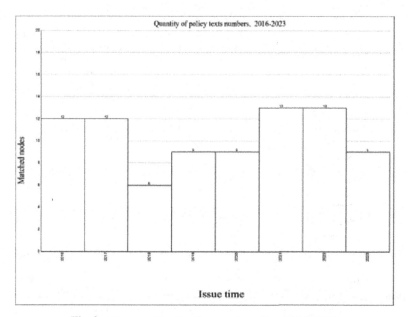

Fig. 2. The quantity of policy numbers from 2016–2023

It is evident that the number of policy texts related to cultural Metaverse and the digitization of classic literature has generally increased over the past eight years. From 2016 to 2021, the quantity of relevant policy texts remained relatively consistent and low, primarily focusing on project initiation and planning. However, there was a significant surge in Metaverse policy publications in 2022, indicating a period of substantial policy development in the Metaverse domain.

The encoding analysis of policy texts has provided insights into the distribution of various types of policy tools in the context of digitizing classic literature (as shown in Table 1). It becomes evident that policy instruments related to Metaverse publishing predominantly fall into the supply aspect and the environmental aspect, and this distribution pattern is consistent across all three types of policy texts shown in Table 1.

Further calculations reveal the ratio of each sub-tool within the total number of policy tools in this type of text. It is found that strategic measures in the environmental aspect, goal planning, and technological investment within the supply aspect have the highest proportions, accounting for 22.70%, 8.28%, and 9.82% respectively. This suggests that in the development of Metaverse enabled publishing works, policies emphasize the creation of a conducive development environment for Metaverse through goal planning and the formulation of corresponding strategic measures in cultural area. Additionally, there is a focus on promoting innovation through support for technological investment. It is noteworthy that strategic measures and technological investments emerge as the predominant policy sub-tools across different categories of policy texts.

Table 1. The utilization of policy instruments

Types	Sub-tool	Totality	The proportion of policy sub-tools			
			Departmental policies (%)	Administrative policies (%)	Constitution, laws, intra-party regulations, and judicial interpretations (%)	In total (%)
Demand-side	Funding support	6	1.24	2.44	2.86	1.84
	Talent team development	19	8.70	1.22	5.71	5.83
	Results transformation and entrepreneurial incubation	15	5.59	3.66	4.29	4.60
	Public services	17	6.21	3.66	5.71	5.21
	Infrastructure	26	6.83	10.98	8.57	7.98
	Scientific investment	32	11.18	10.98	7.14	9.82
	Total	**115**	**37.27**	**32.93**	**28.57**	**35.28**
Environmental	Standard design	15	6.21	3.66	2.86	4.60
	Target planning	27	6.83	13.41	7.14	8.28
	Strategic measures	74	22.36	26.83	22.86	22.70
	Financial support	11	3.73	2.44	4.29	3.37
	Tax incentives	3	0.62	1.22	0.62	0.92
	Regulatory measures	16	3.11	3.66	11.43	4.91
	Intellectual property rights	13	1.86	4.88	8.57	3.99
	Total	**159**	**44.72**	**56.10**	**58.57**	**48.77**
Supply-side	Government procurement	7	1.86	3.66	1.43	2.15

(continued)

Table 1. (*continued*)

Types	Sub-tool	Totality	The proportion of policy sub-tools			
			Departmental policies (%)	Administrative policies (%)	Constitution, laws, intra-party regulations, and judicial interpretations (%)	In total (%)
	Demonstration	20	8.07	4.88	4.29	6.13
	Consumer subsidies	1	0.62	0	0	0.31
	International exchanges	9	4.35	2.76	1.43	2.76
	Outsourcing	8	3.10	0	4.28	2.45
	Overseas institutions	7	3.11	1.22	1.43	2.15
	Total	**52**	**18.01**	**10.98**	**12.86**	**15.95**

4.2 Intergovernmental Relations Analysis

The interaction and reference relationships among policy entities play a crucial role in understanding interdepartmental dynamics. In this study, focusing on national-level policies, network analysis is employed to examine interdepartmental relations. Joint publications serve as significant indicators of collaboration and cooperation levels among government entities, offering valuable insights into interdepartmental relations [11]. The quantity of cultural Metaverse-related policies issued jointly has fluctuated and increased between 2016 and 2023. The enthusiasm for digitization, sparked by the "*The First Year of Virtual Reality*" in 2016, gradually decreased over time but was reignited during the " *The First Year of Metaverse* " in 2021. However, the proportion of joint publications to total policy documents does not show a discernible trend, suggesting that interdepartmental relations do not necessarily dominate the issuance of policies related to the digitization of classic literature.

Using UCINET software and drawing upon government departmental collaborative publishing relationships and social network theory, the degree centrality of each department was computed. Figure 4 visualizes the interdepartmental relations network, with node size representing degree centrality, and line thickness indicating the strength of their relationships.

The computation results reveal that there are a total of 40 institutions issuing policies related to the digitization of classic literature. Among them, the NDRC exhibits the highest frequency of publications and the highest centrality, making it the focal point of the entire Metaverse publishing technology policy network. Entities such as the Ministry of Finance of the People's Republic of China (MOF) and the Ministry of Education of the People's Republic of China (MOE) also hold prominent positions in the publishing network due to their high centrality. While the State Council of the People's Republic of China and the MIIT issue policies frequently, their joint publication frequency is relatively low, resulting in lower centrality compared to the NDRC, positioning them as independent publishing entities alongside the NDRC.

Furthermore, the degree centrality reflects the overall concentration of the network, with the Metaverse policy interdepartmental relations network demonstrating a 23.25% centrality, indicating a relatively decentralized structure (Fig. 3).

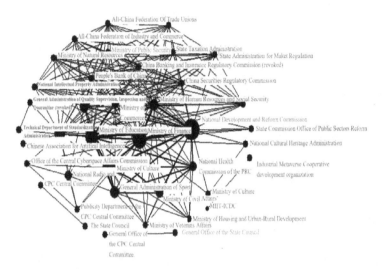

Fig. 3. Visualization of intergovernmental network

In conclusion, the network of institutions responsible for Metaverse publishing technology policies has gravitated towards the core role of the NDRC. Several other departments, including the MOF, the MOE, Ministry of Human Resources and Social Security of the People's Republic of China (MORHSS), the MOST, and Ministry of Culture and Tourism of the People's Republic of China (MCT), actively engage in interdepartmental relations within this network. These collaborations and relationships highlight the concerted efforts of multiple government entities in shaping and implementing policies related to Metaverse publishing technology.

4.3 Policy Hotspots Analysis

Keywords and Co-occurrence Matrix. The process of extracting key words from each policy document and aggregating them for each stage involves a meticulous examination of the core content of each document. Typically, 1 to 10 key terms are extracted from each document, and these terms are then combined and refined to eliminate overlaps and streamline synonymous terms. For example, terms like "cloud computing","5G" and "artificial intelligence" may be consolidated under the broader category of "Next-Generation Information Technology". Similarly, terms such as "digital public culture" and "digital cultural services" can be unified as "digitalized public cultural services". Additionally, terms such as "copyright" and "intellectual property rights" or "financial support" and "funding support" may be combined into more general terms, such as "financial support".

The selection of key terms is based on the vocabulary encountered within each respective stage of policy documents. This process culminates in the creation of a "Policy Text - Keywords" table for the specific stage under consideration. To further analyze the relationships among these key terms, an Excel spreadsheet is used to construct a key term co-occurrence matrix. This matrix provides insights into the associations and patterns of terminology within the policy documents (Table 2).

Table 2. Keywords extracted from selected policies.

Development stage	Keywords of hotspots
The first stage(03/2016–03/2021)	Technology application, internet, open sharing of resources, Internet Plus, digitalization of public cultural services, digital culture, digitalization of cultural resources, technological innovation, innovation-driven development, new infrastructure, financial support, artificial intelligence, technology research and development, industrial integration, virtual reality and augmented reality
The second stage(03/2021–09/2023)	Metaverse, integrated innovation development, artificial intelligence, intelligentization of public cultural services, technology research and development, application of metaverse technology, standard construction, industrial digitalization, cultural industry digitalization, metaverse technology research and development, big data

Multidimensional Scaling Analysis Based on Clusters. Co-occurrence analysis offers a point-based summary of policy hotspots, while multidimensional scaling analysis takes it a step further by grouping statistically correlated keywords into clusters through dimension reduction. This transformation from individual points to clusters provides a new perspective for systematically summarizing policy hotspots at a particular stage of policy evolution. In multidimensional scaling analysis, the keyword co-occurrence matrix is imported into SPSS software, and the Ochiia method is used to calculate the similarity matrix of keywords. This similarity matrix helps identify how closely related keywords are to each other [12].

Additionally, the Euclidean distance model is applied in multidimensional scaling analysis to delineate small groups of keywords based on their distances from each other. This clustering analysis of keywords builds upon the keyword co-occurrence matrix and the multidimensional scaling analysis, resulting in the identification of two major stages in the policy evolution towards the digitization of classic literature [13].

Overall, multidimensional scaling analysis provides a more holistic view of policy hotspots by grouping related keywords into clusters, making it a valuable tool for understanding the evolving landscape of policy priorities in the context of digitizing classic literature.

The first stage: Preparatory Phase of Cultural Metaverse Development (March of 2016 - March of 2021). In the first stage, a total of 49 relevant policy documents were identified, resulting in 55 extracted keywords. After applying a frequency criterion of at least 3 occurrences, the keywords were merged and filtered, resulting in 33 keywords. The keyword list and co-occurrence matrix for this stage are obtained, and the co-occurrence matrix was analyzed using UCINET software.

The analysis reveals that during this stage, several keywords such as technology application, the Internet, open and shared resources, Internet Plus, digitalization of public cultural services, digital culture, and digitalization of cultural resources had higher frequencies and centrality. These keywords signify their crucial roles within the policy network. Notably, technology application emerged as the central theme with both high frequency and centrality, making it the focal point of the network. However, the concept of "Metaverse" did not appear in policy texts during this stage. Policies during this phase were less directly related to the Metaverse, instead focusing more on the application of Internet technology, open resource sharing, digitalization of public cultural services, digital culture, and cultural resource digitalization. The association with the Metaverse was relatively low, and the fusion of technology and humanities was primarily concentrated in the domain of public cultural services. During this period, national efforts primarily aimed at establishing a digital public cultural service system, with the development and application of other core Metaverse technologies remaining on the periphery of policy directions.

Additionally, the co-occurrence matrix was imported into SPSS to compute the similarity matrix of keyword co-occurrences during this stage, enabling multidimensional scaling analysis [13]. Through clustering, four small groups of keywords were identified (refer to Fig. 4). This clustering analysis helps provide a more nuanced understanding of the relationships among keywords and their relevance within this policy stage [14].

Cluster A primarily focuses on information technology research and application. Most of the keywords in this group are situated in the first quadrant, with a small portion in the second quadrant. Technologies like cloud computing, artificial intelligence, and 5G, which hold strategic positions across multiple domains, along with the application of Internet technology in education, exhibit high centrality and density. This signifies their significant importance in policy focus during this stage. On the other hand, VR and AR technologies, located in the second quadrant, as well as research and application of new-generation information technologies, show low density and high centrality, indicating the potential for interconnectivity among core Metaverse technologies.

Cluster B encompasses keywords related to emerging industries, the Internet, intellectual property rights, laws and regulations, new infrastructure, and outcome transformation. The Internet industry serves as a crucial cornerstone for the digitization of classic literature and is a fundamental component of the cultural Metaverse. Policies in this cluster emphasize creating an environment conducive to technological innovation and industrial integration by providing support. This group is situated in the third quadrant and is relatively mature in terms of policy development.

Cluster C includes policies related to cultural digitization, such as the digitalization of cultural industries, digitalization of public cultural services, digital culture, and digitalization of cultural resources. This cluster is located in the fourth quadrant, representing a marginalized direction. It indicates that during this stage, the integration of Metaverse technology with humanities is not closely aligned, and the direction of Metaverse-enabled publishing is relatively marginalized in policy focus.

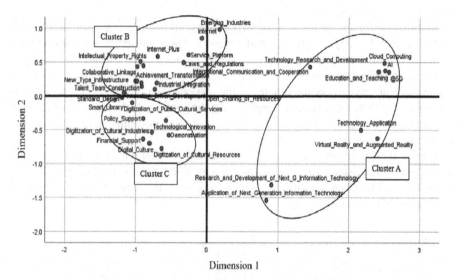

Fig. 4. Multi-dimensional scaling analysis of the Stage 1

These clusters and their positions on the multidimensional scaling analysis provide a comprehensive view of the policy landscape during this particular stage of the digitization of classic literature, highlighting areas of emphasis and potential connectivity among key technologies and themes.

The Second Stage: Metaverse Exploration and Expansion Phase (April of 2021-September of 2023). A final set of 25 keywords remained in this research after screening and merging of the selected policies. A similarity matrix was created and analyzed for centrality by using the keyword co-occurrence matrix. It is evident that Metaverse technology continues to be a focal point of policy attention in this stage. Compared to the previous stage, regulatory measures such as laws, regulations, standard construction, and technical standards play a more prominent role, indicating the establishment of an environment conducive to the development of Metaverse technology as a core focus of policies.

Cultural digitization, which was previously marginalized, tends to stabilize and mature in this stage. The emergence of "smart public cultural services" indicates further development of the digital public service system, progressing towards the Metaverse. Key areas of focus, such as cloud adoption, numerical utilization, and intelligence empowerment, provide strategic guidance for the digitalization of public cultural services and cultural industries. The concept of the Metaverse becomes a central point of attention, while the research, application, interconnectivity, and integrated innovation of Metaverse technology remain relatively marginalized in the policy landscape.

Overall, this stage reflects a shift towards regulatory measures and a more mature approach to cultural digitization. The Metaverse emerges as a focal point of attention, with strategic guidance for the digitalization of public cultural services and industries. However, there is still room for further development and integration of Metaverse technology within the policy landscape.

Multidimensional scaling analysis of keywords in this stage reveals four distinct clusters, each exhibiting a high degree of cohesion. These clusters provide insights into the policy priorities and areas of emphasis during this stage, as illustrated in Fig. 5 [15].

Cluster A includes keywords such as big data, cloud computing, laws and regulations, and intellectual property rights, situated in the first quadrant. This cluster represents the core focus of policies in this stage, emphasizing the continued advancement of strategic Metaverse technologies and the implementation of regulatory measures to standardize the technological development environment.

Cluster B encompasses keywords like Metaverse, virtual reality applications, technical standards, and standard construction, positioned in the second quadrant. This suggests that the Metaverse and its technologies, along with standardization efforts, are focal points of policy emphasis.

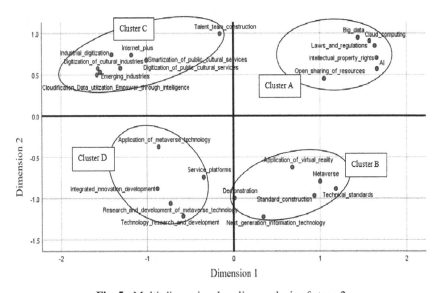

Fig. 5. Multi-dimensional scaling analysis of stage 2

Cluster C comprises keywords related to industrial digitization, smart public cultural services, digitalization of public cultural services, cloud-based intelligence for cultural revitalization, and digitalization of cultural industries. This cluster indicates that China's Metaverse-enabled classic literature policies are maturing, with a closer integration of "smart" concepts with Metaverse technologies, reflecting a more holistic perspective on cultural Metaverse policies.

Cluster D, located in the fourth quadrant, consists of keywords such as Metaverse technology research and application, integrated innovation and development, and technology research and service platforms. This cluster indicates lower levels of attention to these specific areas during this stage of policy development.

When analyzing the policy hotspots in both stages, it becomes evident that China's Metaverse publishing technology policy development has evolved from primarily providing guidance to a combination of guidance and regulation, as depicted in Fig. 6. This shift in policy focus reflects the growing maturity and strategic importance of the Metaverse within the context of classic literature digitization. It signifies the government's efforts to both promote the development of Metaverse technologies and establish a regulatory framework to ensure their effective and responsible use. This evolution highlights the dynamic nature of policy development in the rapidly evolving field of Metaverse technology. These clusters help provide a structured view of the policy landscape during this stage, highlighting key areas of focus and interrelated policy priorities within the digitization of classic literature and the development of the Metaverse.

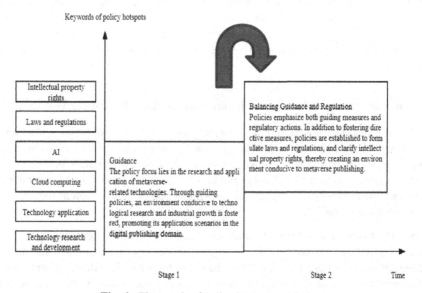

Fig. 6. The trends of policy hotspots evolution

5 Conclusions and Suggestions

5.1 Conclusions

The findings from the descriptive statistical analysis indicate that in recent years, the issuance of policy documents pertaining to the Metaverse has been fluctuating at a comparatively low level. The predominant focus of these policies has been on the supply side and environmental factors, with less emphasis on policies targeting the demand side. It is notable that within the environmental aspect of these policy tools, strategic actions, goal-setting, and investment in technology hold the highest significance. In terms of intergovernmental relations, the collaborative publication of government documents demonstrates a weak concentration.

From the standpoint of policy evolution, there has been a shift from prioritizing guidance on technological development to a focus on directive policies and an increase in regulatory actions. This shift coincides with the gradual maturation of key Metaverse technologies and the expansion of their application in the field of digital publishing. These changes are intended to foster a conducive environment for the growth of Metaverse publishing.

In summary, from the Metaverse perspective, between 2016 and 2023, the trends in China's digital publishing policies have been characterized by weak intergovernmental relations in terms of issuing authorities, a sustained focus on guiding measures for research and application of Metaverse technology, and an escalating attention to regulatory aspects, particularly in terms of laws and regulations. The evolution of Metaverse publishing policies is aligned with the overall development stages of Metaverse technology."

5.2 The Suggestions to Metaverse Technology Enabled Publishing Works

Based on the aforementioned findings regarding the current state of China's Metaverse-enabled publishing policies, several key research suggestions can be proposed. These suggestions aim to guide policymakers, stakeholders, and researchers in understanding and enhancing the effectiveness of policies to foster the growth of Metaverse publishing in China. The research suggestions are categorized into different themes for a comprehensive approach.

Policy Effectiveness and Impact Analysis. Research should be conducted to evaluate the effectiveness of existing Metaverse publishing policies in China. This includes assessing how well these policies have supported technological development, digital publishing platforms, and content creators within the Metaverse framework. A comparative analysis with international standards and practices can provide insights into the global competitiveness of China's Metaverse publishing sector. Additionally, the impact of these policies on related industries and the overall digital economy should be examined to identify synergies and potential areas of improvement.

Technological Advancements and Infrastructure. Investigating the role of emerging technologies in shaping the future of Metaverse publishing is crucial. This research should focus on identifying key technologies that require further development and investment. It should also explore the infrastructure needed to support large-scale adoption of Metaverse publishing, such as high-speed internet, data security, and interoperability standards. Understanding the technological needs and challenges can guide policymakers in allocating resources and formulating targeted support measures.

Consumer Behavior and Market Demand. Given the lesser emphasis on demand-side policy tools, there is a need to study consumer behavior and market demand within the Metaverse publishing realm. Research should focus on identifying consumer preferences, trends, and potential barriers to adoption. This would provide valuable insights for tailoring policies to stimulate consumer interest and participation in Metaverse publishing, ensuring that the sector develops in line with market needs.

Regulatory Framework and Legal Considerations. As the Metaverse evolves, new legal and regulatory challenges will emerge. Research in this area should focus on developing a comprehensive legal framework that addresses issues such as intellectual property rights, privacy, content regulation, and cyber security within the Metaverse. This research should also consider international best practices to ensure that China's regulatory framework is robust and globally aligned.

Cross-sector Collaboration and Intergovernmental Cooperation. Given the weak intergovernmental relations in policy issuance, research should explore ways to enhance collaboration between different government departments and sectors. This includes identifying best practices for multi-departmental cooperation and developing strategies for effective cross-sector collaboration. Such research could lead to more cohesive and comprehensive policy frameworks that leverage the strengths of various government entities.

Establishing Standards for Metaverse Publishing Policy-Making. It is crucial to focus on creating a framework that is adaptive, inclusive, and forward-looking. This framework should encompass technological advancement, intellectual property rights, user privacy, content regulation, and ethical considerations. Technological innovation should be at the core of policy-making. Policies must encourage research and development in Metaverse technologies, ensuring that they are scalable, secure, and interoperable. This approach will facilitate a robust infrastructure that can support a wide range of digital publishing activities within the Metaverse. Intellectual property rights need to be clearly defined and protected in the Metaverse. Policies should establish guidelines for content creation, distribution, and consumption that respect creators' rights while promoting creativity and innovation. This balance is critical in maintaining a vibrant and fair digital publishing environment. Privacy and data security are also paramount. Policies must enforce stringent data protection standards to safeguard user information. This includes ensuring that personal data is collected, stored, and used responsibly, with transparent user consent mechanisms. Lastly, ethical considerations should be embedded in policy-making. This includes addressing potential societal impacts, such as digital divide issues and the psychological effects of prolonged Metaverse engagement. Policies should promote responsible usage and ensure that the Metaverse contributes positively to society.

Overall, these research suggestions aim to provide a multidimensional analysis of the challenges and opportunities within China's Metaverse-enabled publishing sector. By addressing these key areas, the research can inform policymakers and stakeholders in developing more effective, inclusive, and forward-looking policies that not only support the growth of the Metaverse in China but also ensure its sustainable and responsible development in the digital age.

Acknowledgments. This study was funded by The 2023 Guangdong Province Philosophy and Social Science Planning Academic co-development Project entitled *'Research on the Pathways for Revitalization and Dissemination of Classic Readings Enabled by the Metaverse - A Case Study of Guangdong Province '*(number GDGD23XTS01), and also The 2022 Guangdong Provincial Department of Education Planning Fund: *'Research on the Model and Practice of VR Ancient Books Gamification System for university Students' Traditional Cultural Education'* (number 2022GXJK416).

Disclosure of Interests.   The authors have no competing interests to declare that are relevant to the content of this article.

References

1. Liu, M., Fang, S., Dong, H., Xu, C.: Review of digital twin about concepts, technologies, and industrial applications. J. Manuf. Syst. **58**, 346–361 (2021)
2. Mystakidis, S.: Metaverse. Encyclopedia **2**(1), 486–497 (2022)
3. Zhang, X.X., Xia, C.J., Xiao, P., Li, B.Y., Li, X.R., Wang, Y.X.: Creating meta-universes: theoretical and applied disciplinary scenarios. J. Inf. Resources Manage. **5**, 139–148 (2022)
4. Ning, H., et al.: A survey on the metaverse: the state-of-the-art, technologies, applications, and challenges. IEEE Internet Things J. (2023)
5. Feng, X., Wang, X., Su, Y.: An analysis of the current status of metaverse research based on bibliometrics. Library Hi Tech. (2022)
6. Chong, H.T., Lim, C.K., Rafi, A., Tan, K.L., Mokhtar, M.: Correction: comprehensive systematic review on virtual reality for cultural heritage practices: coherent taxonomy and motivations. Multimed. Syst. **29**(6), 3973 (2023)
7. Zhang, Y.R., Jiang, K., Meng, Q.S.: A research on china's 5g policy characteristics and evolution trends based on multi-dimensional quantitative analysis of policy documents. Forum Sci. Technol. China **11**, 125–137 (2022)
8. Yang, C., Huang, C., Su, J.: A bibliometrics-based research framework for exploring policy evolution: a case study of China's information technology policies. Technological Forecasting and Social Change, 157 (2020)
9. Li, J., Liu, Y.H., Huang, C., Su, J.: Reshaping policy text data analysis through bibliometric research: origins, migration, and methodological innovations in policy literature metrics. J. Public Manage. (2),138–144+159 (2015)
10. Zhou, N., Yang, Z., Zhao, X.X., Chen, P.: Co-evolution of science and technology innovation policies in the Beijing-Tianjin-Hebei region: 2011–2021. Forum Sci. Technol. China **8**, 27–38 (2023)
11. Rothwell, R.O.Y., Zegveld, W.: An assessment of government innovation policies. Rev. Policy Res. **3**(3–4), 436–444 (1984)
12. Zhang, X.N.: Quantitative analysis: a novel approach to policy text research. J. Shanxi Provincial Committee Party School of C.P.C(3),119–123 (2019)

13. Feng, L., Leng, F.H.: Development of theoretical studies of co—word analysis. J. Library Sci. China **2**, 88–92 (2006)
14. Zhong, W.J., Li, J.: A research on co-occurrence analysis (II) - cluster analysis. J. Inf. **6**, 141–143 (2008)
15. Chen, X.L., Lu, R.Y.: Hot spots research on China's policy of "mass entrepreneurship and innovation" based on co-word analysis. J. UESTC (Soc. Sci. Edition) **2**, 9–17 (2019)

Toward Facilitating Going Out:on the Relationship Between Residents' Outing Behavior and Cognitive Distance in Suburbs

So Makita[1(✉)] and Kenro Aihara[1,2,3]

[1] Tokyo Metropolitan University, Hachioji, Tokyo 192-0397, Japan
makita-so@ed.tmu.ac.jp, kenro.aihara@tmu.ac.jp
[2] National Institute of Informatics, Tokyo, Japan
[3] Joint Support-Center for Data Science Research, Research Organization of Information and Systems, Tokyo, Japan
https://behavior.ues.tmu.ac.jp/

Abstract. It is known that there are various factors that influence people's intention to go out.

In this study, the effects of each of these factors on the going-out behavior of residents in urban and suburban areas by the range of going out were analyzed and compared. This study focuses on Saitama City. Saitama City is a suburb in the Tokyo Metropolitan area and the convenience of going out varies greatly within the region.

Data of 1,000 respondents to a web-based questionnaire survey are prepared on a variety of factors thought to explain going-out behavior, such as basic attributes, impressions of public transportation, cognitive distance and preferences. And then a random forest classifier was trained by using collected data.

As a result, the study revealed two key findings on the relationship between various factors and intention to go out. Firstly, cognitive distance significantly influences the intention to go out, confirming prior studies. Secondly, two main patterns of going-out behavior emerge: general intention to go out and intention for leisure activities, versus intention to go outside the city or district. Increase of age influences the former pattern, while preferences for longer outings directly impact the latter. This detailed breakdown offers practical insights for local governments to enhance residents' intention to go out.

Keywords: going-out behavior · intention to go out · cognitive distance · lack of public transportation

1 Introduction

In recent years, public transportation has been rapidly declining. The circumstances may differ from country to country, but in Japan, for example, the reasons for these declines are a decrease in the number of users and labor shortages [7]. This trend is also observed in relatively populated suburban areas, and the number of areas where public transportation is inconvenient is on the increase [2].

According to the 6th Tokyo Metropolitan Area Person Trip Survey [5], residents in areas where public transportation is inconvenient generally have a lower rate of going out than residents in areas where it is not inconvenient. On the other hand, the rate of going out is higher among residents who have free access to a car than among those who do not, regardless of whether public transportation is inconvenient or not. These results suggest that more than one factor, rather than a single factor, influences people's intention to go out. This study aims to analyze how the various factors that residents in suburban areas individually possess affect their intention to go out, and to clarify the relationship between these factors and their intentions.

2   Going-Out Behavior

Going-out behavior is one of the most universally performed actions in our lives. In deciding whether or not to perform this behavior, people is unconsciously influenced by various factors. For example, according to Ueno et al. [9], the number, duration, and distance of going-out behaviors decreased when people felt that their outing behavior was at risk. In addition, more people visited nearby green spaces and took walks to maintain health and refresh themselves. Pocock also argued that there exists a tendency, named the 'reward hypothesis', that the more attractive a destination is, the shorter the sense of distance to that destination will be relative to the destination [6].

On the other hand, factors independent of the destination of an outing are also thought to influence behavioral decisions. Hansen et al. revealed that driving cessation can be a particularly challenging and troublesome transition in older adulthood that can lead to social isolation. This research also shows that lack of transportation options in rural areas, changes in driving behaviors, the lack of planning for driving cessation, and the social isolation that comes from the loss (or potential loss) of one's driver's license are one of the most important factors in our lives [3].

In addition, the survey that asked about their awareness of their home province as a tourist destination and their sense of proximity and distance in relation to their preferred vacation destination by Jeuring et al. [4]. This showed that the groups that preferred 'proximity' and 'remoteness' had a positive effect on the preference for proximity tourism and remote tourism, respectively. The results show a positive effect of 'proximity' and 'remoteness' on the preference for proximity and remoteness tourism, respectively. This suggests that proximity and distance are used as push and pull factors to motivate destination preference.

Parra Vargas et al. conducted a study aimed at identifying the lifestyle-based tourism profile of national tourists and analyzing the influence of personality traits on tourism segmentation [10]. The results suggest that lifestyle is an appropriate indicator for this market segmentation and that analyzing its

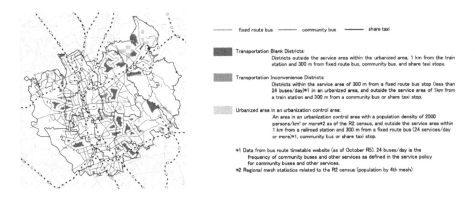

Fig. 1. Map of public transportation gaps in Saitama City

relationship with personality provides a deeper understanding of the profiles obtained. This indicates that preferences in an individual's lifestyle also have a significant impact on going-out behavior.

Thus, a great number of factors are considered to be potentially involved in going-out behavior. However, most of these studies are limited to specific types of people, such as the elderly or disabled, who generally have difficulty going out.

Due to very few studies which have been conducted on more general group, what factors influence many people's willingness to go out remains one of open issues. Therefore, this study will conduct the analysis presented in the next chapter to derive factors that may be important in explaining the intention to go out.

3   Methodological Framework

3.1   Selection of the Research Field

Saitama City is one of the designated cities by government ordinance and the capital of Saitama Prefecture of Japan with a population of approximately 1.3 million, located in the Tokyo metropolitan area. The city has developed around transportation nodes in the city, such as Omiya and Urawa stations, due to the convenience of being able to reach the city center of Tokyo in about 20 min. On the other hand, even within the city, public transportation networks have been withdrawn from areas far from the public, and the number of 'Transportation Blank Districts' is increasing (Fig. 1).

In addition, in the "Saitama City Questionnaire on Public Transportation" conducted by Saitama City in the 2023 fiscal year, in the summary of the questionnaire results, it was stated that "in areas with inconvenient public transportation, the public transportation sharing ratio and frequency of outings by the elderly and women tend to be low, and support for outings is required" and this issue is set as a "priority issue regarding public transportation".

Thus, in Saitama City, there are both developed and declining areas of public transportation in the suburbs of the city, and the difference in transportation mobility, which is largely manifested in the degree of transportation adequacy, greatly affects residents' intention to go out, which is a serious issue for the municipality. Therefore, Saitama City was judged to be an appropriate field to conduct research on the intention to go out and cognitive distance, and was selected as a candidate site for this study.

3.2   A Preliminary Survey in Saitama City

Preliminary interviews were conducted with residents in Saitama City as a preliminary study in cooperation with the Urban Affairs Division and the Transportation Policy Division of the Saitama City Office. At regular meetings between officials of the city hall and residents' associations of two districts; one is of Miyuki-cho; the other is of Kashiwazaki-cho; in Iwatsuki Ward of Saitama City, group discussions and interviews regarding people's intentions to go out and cognitive distance were held. Both areas are classified as "transportation blank districts" by the Saitama City. It should be noted that the average age of the participants on the day of the meeting was over 70 years old, and the opinions of the participants were generally from elderly groups. The opinions obtained there included the followings:

Reasons for Going Out

- The reason for going out depends not only on age but also on the situation and living environment.
- Shopping and medical visits are the most common reasons for going out.
- Surrounding environment and situation have more influence on the decision to go out than factors like age or gender.
- There are situations where going out is necessary due to the presence or absence of chronic illnesses or elderly care.

Frequency and Range of Going out

- If you can drive a car, you can move around relatively freely.
- Conversely, if you cannot drive, you feel more constrained, and your cognitive distance increases.
- Due to the difficulty of matching factors such as time of day and frequency of service, the use of demand-responsive transportation services is limited.
- Currently, whether or not a car is available strongly influences the intention to go out.
- If a car is not available, you need to arrange for a taxi to go shopping nearby.

Means of Going Out

- In recent years, there are many people in their 70s and older who are still working, so excluding those who find it difficult to go out due to illness or disability, the frequency of going out itself is higher than intuition might suggest.

- If you go to a nearby home center, you can find anything you need, so you basically don't go out of town.
- I haven't been on a train for over 10 years.

Through this interview, it was obtained that there may be several other major factors that influence people's decision to go out, such as the ownership of a car and the presence of someone living with them who can drive, in addition to cognitive distance.

3.3   Data Collection

In order to reveal the intention to go out from multiple perspectives, an Internet survey to collect a wide range of data was conducted. The questionnaire survey targeted 1,000 men and women aged 15 to 99 who currently reside in Saitama City. The survey was conducted from December 22 (Friday) to December 26 (Tuesday), 2023.

The survey included the following questions:

- personal attributes: such as age, gender, occupation, and annual income;
- transportation-related attributes: such as main means of transportation, distance to the nearest station or bus stop, number of cars owned, and frequency of driving;
- satisfaction with the current public transportation system;
- preference for going out;
- actual number of outings per month;
- qualitative cognitive distance to go out to 50 various destinations in Saitama City;
- the means of transportation used at that time;
- the number of intention to go out per a month.

For the qualitative cognitive distance, respondents were asked to indicate their means of transportation when visiting a total of 50 destinations in Saitama City, and to select one from seven options ranging from 1. fairly close to 7. fairly far away, assuming that they would take that means of transportation. The data obtained from these questions will be analyzed assuming that they are factors explaining the intention to go out.

The target variable of this analysis is the number of times the respondents would like to go out in a month. Target variables includes these four types of intention to go out, such as:

- all outing intentions
- intention to go out for leisure activities

- intention to go out outside the district
- intention to go out outside the city

Since the preliminary survey revealed that a certain number of respondents were reluctant to go outside the district or outside Saitama City, it is focused on analyzing the range of going out. In contrast, it also showed that enjoying leisure activities can be a reason which they want to go out, so it is also focused. These outing intentions are used as objective variables for comparison with "all outing intentions".

After pre-processing, including the removal of missing values, the data for 828 respondents was finally obtained. Table 1 summarizes the attributes of the surveyed subjects to be used in subsequent analyses.

4   Analysis

4.1   Explanatory and Target Variables

Explanatory variables consists of several types of factor groups. Most of variables are categorical ones, for example, for "walk," which is one element of the Major transportation methods group, the data is based on the respondents' answers on a 5-point scale from 1: Very often to 5: Never used. Also, trans_XX is the impression of the public transportation system that the respondents usually use, and style_XX is a factor representing the nature and preferences of each respondent. Furthermore, cognitive distance information are defined respectively like these;

sum_time_values: The sum of the time taken to reach the 50 destinations in the city by the means of transportation that the respondents would like to use. In general, the larger the value, the further away from any destination in terms of time on average.

sum_cognitive_dist: The sum of qualitative cognitive distance ratings for 50 destinations in the city. In general, the larger the value, the more distant the destination is perceived to be on average. These two may be regarded as general barometer which express residents' sense of cognitive distance.

Target variables are already introduced on Sect. 3.3. Please look at Table 2 for more details.

4.2   Method of Analysis

To predict and classify the classes of the intention to go out, the RandomForest-Classifier, an implementation of random forest classifier in scikit-learn library[1] for Python environment, was used. Of the data set of 828 respondents used in the analysis, 621 (75%), or training data, and 207 (25%), or validation data,

---

[1] https://scikit-learn.org/.

Table 1. Respondent attributes in the questionnaire survey

Attribute	Number (N = 828)	Percentage (%)
Gender		
Male	395	47.7
Female	433	52.3
Age Group		
15 to 29 years	109	13.2
30 to 39 years	211	25.5
40 to 49 years	170	20.5
50 to 59 years	158	19.1
60 to 99 years	180	21.7
Administrative District of Residence		
Nishi Ward, Saitama City	55	6.6
Kita Ward, Saitama City	84	10.1
Omiya Ward, Saitama City	100	12.0
Minuma Ward, Saitama City	78	9.4
Chuo Ward, Saitama City	80	9.7
Sakura Ward, Saitama City	47	5.7
Urawa Ward, Saitama City	138	16.7
Minami Ward, Saitama City	124	15.0
Midori Ward, Saitama City	68	8.2
Iwatsuki Ward, Saitama City	54	6.5
Years of Residence		
Less than 5 years	170	20.5
5 to less than 10 years	120	14.5
10 to less than 20 years	218	26.3
20 to less than 30 years	141	17.0
31 years and above	179	21.6
Household Income		
Less than 2 million yen	97	11.7
2 million yen to less than 4 million yen	197	23.8
4 million yen to less than 6 million yen	180	21.7
6 million yen to less than 8 million yen	131	15.8
8 million yen to less than 10 million yen	101	12.2
10 million yen and above	122	14.7
Family Composition		
Living alone	165	19.9
Living with spouse	195	23.6
Living with spouse and children	244	29.5
Living with children	18	2.2
Living with parents/spouse	75	9.1
Living with parents/spouse and children	14	1.7
Living with parents/children	25	3.0
Other	92	11.1
Occupation, etc.		
Self-employed	32	3.9
Regular employee	365	44.1
Corporate officer	15	1.8
Dispatched worker	30	3.6
Family worker	0	0.0
Part-time/Temporary worker	119	14.3
Student	27	3.3
Homemaker	131	15.8
Unemployed	92	11.1
Other	17	2.1

Table 2. Explanatory and target variables

Explanatory variables	
Basic attributes	
sex	categorical (1: Male, 2: Female)
age	continuous (Integer value, unit: years)
years_of_residence	continuous (Integer value, unit: years)
income	categorical (1: Less than 2 million yen to 6: 10 million yen or more)
family_type	categorical (1: Living alone to 8: Other)
profession	categorical (1: Self-employed to 10: Other)
Major transportation methods	
walk	categorical (1: Very often used to 5: Never used)
bicycle	categorical (1: Very often used to 5: Never used)
driving_car	categorical (1: Very often used to 5: Never used)
courtesy_car	categorical (1: Very often used to 5: Never used)
motorbike	categorical (1: Very often used to 5: Never used)
com_bus	categorical (1: Very often used to 5: Never used)
bus	categorical (1: Very often used to 5: Never used)
railway	categorical (1: Very often used to 5: Never used)
taxi	categorical (1: Very often used to 5: Never used)
other_transport	categorical (1: Very often used to 5: Never used)
Attributes related to transportation	
mobility_anytime	categorical (1: Think it's sufficient to 5: Think it's insufficient)
numbers_of_cars	continuous (Integer value, unit: number of cars)
driving_licence	categorical (1: Can drive without inconvenience, 2: Can drive short distances or times without problem, 3: Don't have a license and can't drive, 4: Have a license but can't drive)
courtesy_car_request	categorical (1: Can request without problems, 2: Can't request depending on the time, 3: Can't request at all)
mobility_freely	categorical (1: Can use without inconvenience to 5: Can't use basically)
nearest_stat	categorical (1: Iwatsuki to 31: Yono-Hommachi, 32: Not among these, 33: Don't usually use stations)
nearest_stat_dist	categorical (1: less than 500 m to 5: 2000 m+, 6: usually used but not sure)
nearest_busstop_dist	categorical (1: less than 300 m to 5: 1000 m+ , 6: usually used but not sure, 7: don't usually use and not sure)
Impressions of public transportation	
trans_access	categorical (1: Think so to 5: Don't think so at all)
trans_anytime	categorical (1: Think so to 5: Don't think so at all)
trans_comfort	categorical (1: Think so to 5: Don't think so at all)
trans_economy	categorical (1: Think so to 5: Don't think so at all)
trans_satisfaction	categorical (1: Think so to 5: Don't think so at all)
trans_buy_household	categorical (1: Think so to 5: Don't think so at all)
trans_commuting	categorical (1: Think so to 5: Don't think so at all)
trans_entertainment	categorical (1: Think so to 5: Don't think so at all)
trans_hospital	categorical (1: Think so to 5: Don't think so at all)
trans_shopping	categorical (1: Think so to 5: Don't think so at all)

(continued)

Table 2. (*continued*)

Preference in daily lives	
style_economy	categorical (1: Think so to 5: Don't think so at all)
style_outing	categorical (1: Think so to 5: Don't think so at all)
style_paying	categorical (1: Think so to 5: Don't think so at all)
style_saitama	categorical (1: Think so to 5: Don't think so at all)
style_entertainment	categorical (1: Think so to 5: Don't think so at all)
style_outing_faraway	categorical (1: Think so to 5: Don't think so at all)
style_outing_longtime	categorical (1: Think so to 5: Don't think so at all)
style_tokyo	categorical (1: Think so to 5: Don't think so at all)
style_driving	categorical (1: Think so to 5: Don't think so at all)
style_mind_timeloss	categorical (1: Think so to 5: Don't think so at all)
Recent outing performance in a month	
meet_friends	categorical (1: 15+ times/month to 7: none per month (never going out))
entertainment	categorical (1: 15+ times/month to 7: none per month (never going out))
concert	categorical (1: 15+ times/month to 7: none per month (never going out))
shopping	categorical (1: 15+ times/month to 7: none per month (never going out))
buy_household	categorical (1: 15+ times/month to 7: none per month (never going out))
restaurant	categorical (1: 15+ times/month to 7: none per month (never going out))
walking	categorical (1: 15+ times/month to 7: none per month (never going out))
commuting	categorical (1: 15+ times/month to 7: none per month (never going out))
hospital	categorical (1: 15+ times/month to 7: none per month (never going out))
other_reason	categorical (1: 15+ times/month to 7: none per month (never going out))
Cognitive distance information	
sum_time_values	continuous (Integer value, unit: minutes)
sum_cognitive_dist	continuous (Integer value, unitless)
Target variables (going-out intention in a month)	
outing_all	categorical (0: less than 3, 1: 3–10, 2: 10+ (times/month))
outing_entertainment	categorical (0: less than 3, 1: 3–10, 2: 10+ (times/month))
outing_from_ward	categorical (0: less than 3, 1: 3–10, 2: 10+ (times/month))
outing_from_saitama	categorical (0: less than 3, 1: 3–10, 2: 10+ (times/month))

were randomly split for training and testing the models. Next, the hyperparameters were tuned by random search using the training and validation data. The model was trained by tuning the main hyperparameters of RandomForestClassifier, such as n_estimators (the number of decision trees to create), max_depth (the depth of each decision tree), and max_features (the number of features to select when splitting nodes). Finally, the confusion matrix and the graph showing the top 10 most important factors that served as the basis for classifying the validation data were generated.

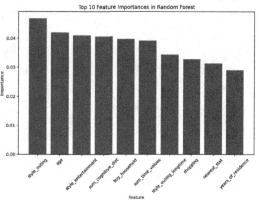

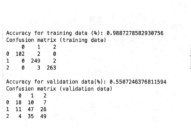

```
Accuracy for training data (%): 0.9887278582930756
Confusion matrix (training data)
        0    1    2
0     102    2    0
1       0  249    2
2       0    3  263

Accuracy for validation data(%): 0.5507246376811594
Confusion matrix (validation data)
        0    1    2
0      18   10    7
1      11   47   26
2       4   35   49
```

Fig. 2. All outing intentions

5 Result

Figure 2 shows that style_outing (whether or not you like going out) has a big impact on classification. Age, style_entertainment (whether they like to go out for leisure activities), sum_cognitive_dist (total qualitative cognitive distance) are also important. Figure 3 expresses that sum_time_values (total route time per individual), sum_cognitive_dist, age and style_entertainment (whether they like to go out for leisure activities) are more significant than any other factor in this analysis. Figure 4 indicates that style_outing_longtime (whether they like to go out for a long time), buy_household (outing performance of buying household goods), age and sum_time_values are important. Figure 5 shows that sum_time_values, age, style_outing_longtime and years_of_residence play a role as significant factors of this analysis.

6 Discussion

Comparing the analysis results for each of the four types of outing intentions, there are some similarities and some differences. First, as a whole, cognitive distance information, such as sum_time_values and sum_cognitive_dist, had a significant impact on the classification. This result confirms Tanaka's findings that human spatial behavior in urban areas is largely influenced by qualitative cognitive distance [8].

It can also be seen that age has a significant impact on this analysis. When a partial-dependence graph was created to examine which class a person was classified into when age was taken, a characteristic trend was observed when the target was 2 (when going-out intention was 10+ (times/month)). Figures 6 and 7 indicate that there are two types of graph shapes; monotonically increasing and non-monotonically changing. The former is found in outing_all and outing_entertainment, indicating that the expected value of being judged as having a high intention to go out increases with increasing age. The latter is seen

Accuracy for training data (%): 0.9694041867954911
Confusion matrix (training data)
```
     0   1   2
0  149  11   0
1    1 360   0
2    0   7  93
```

Accuracy for validation data(%): 0.6086956521739131
Confusion matrix (validation data)
```
    0   1  2
0  18  36  0
1  10 104  6
2   2  27  4
```

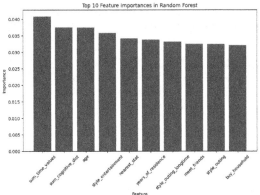

Fig. 3. Intention to go out for leisure activities

Accuracy for training data (%): 0.9892008639308856
Confusion matrix (training data)
```
     0   1   2
0  165   2   0
1    1 217   0
2    1   1  76
```

Accuracy for validation data(%): 0.608433734939759
Confusion matrix (validation data)
```
    0   1  2
0  36  16  2
1  19  59  9
2   3  16  6
```

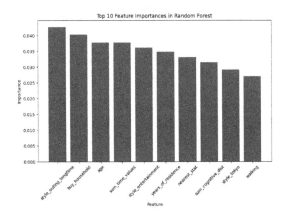

Fig. 4. Intention to go out outside the district

Accuracy for training data (%): 0.9838969404186796
Confusion matrix (training data)
```
     0   1   2
0  242   3   0
1    1 278   0
2    2   4  91
```

Accuracy for validation data(%): 0.5507246376811594
Confusion matrix (validation data)
```
    0   1  2
0  46  34  1
1  24  64  5
2   4  25  4
```

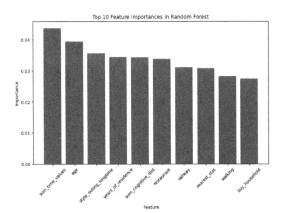

Fig. 5. Intention to go out outside the city

in outing_from_ward and outing_from_saitama, indicating that the relationship between age and high intention to go out is small. This may be due to the fact that all generations feel that it is a chore to go out all the way from their residential area.

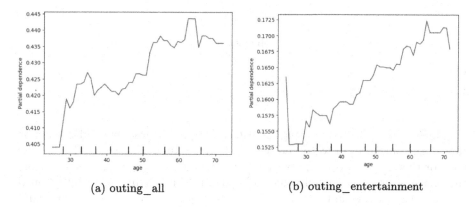

(a) outing_all   (b) outing_entertainment

Fig. 6. Partial dependency plot for age, outing_all and outing_entertainment (class: 2)

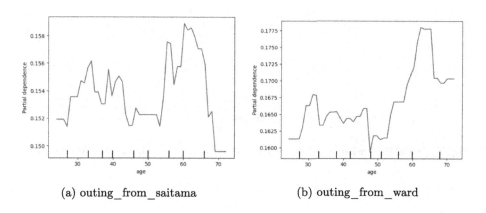

(a) outing_from_saitama   (b) outing_from_ward

Fig. 7. Partial dependency plot for age, outing_from_ward and outing_from_saitama (class: 2)

Furthermore, according to Crombie et al., the most powerful deterrent for not going out for leisure activities was lack of interest, and the other facotrs were lack of daily access to a car, lack of energy, not belonging to a group, and so on [1]. Figure 3 shows that sum_cognitive_dist (related not to belong to a group), style_entertainment (related to lack of interests), nearest_stat (related to lack of daily access to a car), and style_outing (related to lack of energy) were selected as highly important factors, which is consistent with the findings of Crombie et al.

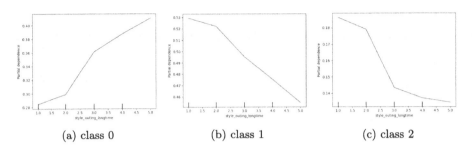

(a) class 0   (b) class 1   (c) class 2

Fig. 8. Partial dependency plot for style_outing_longtime, outing_from_ward (class: 0, 1, 2)

Finally, note the style_outing_longtime. This factor was particularly important in the outing_from_ward and outing_from_saitama. The partial dependency plot for this factor also suggests that those who do not like to go out for a long time have a higher expected value to be classified as having a low intention to go out (class: 0), while those who like to go out for a long time have a higher possibility to be classified as having a relatively high intention to go out (class: 1, 2) (Figs. 8 and 9).

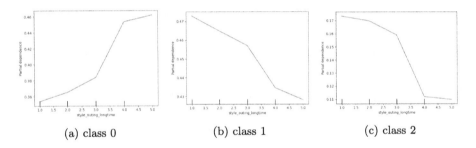

(a) class 0   (b) class 1   (c) class 2

Fig. 9. Partial dependency plot for style_outing_longtime, outing_from_saitama (class: 0, 1, 2)

7   Conclusion

The aim of this study was to analyse how the various factors that suburban dwellers have individually affect their intention to go out, and to determine the relationship between these factors and their intention to go out.

The authors illuminated two findings of this relationship. At first, cognitive distance information has a big influence on intention to go out. Same as the former study, it is confirmed that (qualitative) cognitive distance is related to going-out behavior. Second, the main going-out behavior is captured in two patterns: general going-out intention and going-out behavior for leisure activities, and going-out intention to go outside the city and going-out intention to go outside the district. For the former, the probability of being classified as having a high intention to go out increases with increasing age. In the latter pattern, there is little relationship between the change in age and the classification rate of high intention to go out, but on the other hand, it is suggested that the factor of preference for going out for a long time has a direct influence on the intention to go out.

In addition, as a practical contribution, this study was able to explain going out intention after breaking it down into more detailed factors than conventional analyses of going out behavior, such as PT surveys. Moreover, the fact that this study clarified in detail a group of factors closely related to the intention to go out will enable local governments, for example, to effectively consider what factors they should address in order to increase the intention to go out among local residents.

Acknowledgments. The authors would like to thank Saitama City Office and KPMG Consulting Co., Ltd. for their cooperation with this research.

This work was supported by JSPS KAKENHI Grant Number JP22H03856.

References

1. Crombie, I.K.: Why older people do not participate in leisure time physical activity: a survey of activity levels, beliefs and deterrents. Age Ageing **33**, 287–292 (2004). https://doi.org/10.1093/ageing/afh089
2. Erhardt, G.D., Hoque, J.M., Goyal, V., Berrebi, S., Brakewood, C., Watkins, K.E.: Why has public transit ridership declined in the united states? Transport. Res. Part A Policy Pract. **161**, 68–87 (2022). https://doi.org/10.1016/j.tra.2022.04.006
3. Hansen, S., Newbold, K.B., Scott, D.M., Vrkljan, B., Grenier, A.: To drive or not to drive: Driving cessation amongst older adults in rural and small towns in canada. J. Transp. Geogr. **86**, 102773 (2020). https://doi.org/10.1016/j.jtrangeo.2020.102773
4. Jeuring, J., Haartsen, T.: The challenge of proximity: the (un) attractiveness of near-home tourism destinations. In: Proximity and Intraregional Aspects of Tourism, pp. 115–138. Routledge, Abingdon (2018)
5. Ministry of Land, Infrastructure, T., Tourism: Tokyo metropolitan area person trip survey homepage. https://www.tokyopt.jp/static/hp/file/publicity/toshikoutsu_1.pdf. Accessed 13 Feb 2024
6. Pocock, D.: The cognition of intra-urban distance: a summary. Scottish Geogr. Maga. **94**, 31–35 (1978). https://doi.org/10.1080/00369227808736385
7. Sueyoshi, C., Takagi, H., Uchibayashi, T., Inenaga, K.: Employee management support application for regional public transportation service in Japan, pp. 71–81 (2022). https://doi.org/10.1007/978-3-030-84913-9_7
8. Tanaka, M.: Qualitative aspects of cognitive distance in urban space in relation to daily movement behavior: a case study of university students in Kanazawa. Jpn. J. Hum. Geogr. **65**, 47–62 (2013). https://doi.org/10.4200/jjhg.65.1_47

9. Ueno, Y., Kato, S., Mase, T., Funamoto, Y., Hasegawa, K.: Changes in the use of green spaces by citizens before and during the First COVID-19 pandemic: a big data analysis using mobile-tracking GPS data in Kanazawa, Japan, pp. 257–270 (2022). https://doi.org/10.1007/978-981-16-6791-6_16

10. Vargas, E.P., de Juan-Ripoll, C., Panadero, M.B., Alcañiz, M.: Lifestyle segmentation of tourists: the role of personality. Heliyon **7**, e07579 (2021). https://doi.org/10.1016/j.heliyon.2021.e07579

Building a Sustainable Local Community Through Collaborative Creation Between Global Talents and Local Residents: A Model of Human Network Transformation in the INOW and Its Impacts

Takuya Matsumoto[1,2]([⊠]) and Takuya Yabe[1,2]

[1] Center for Community Engagement and Lifelong Learning, The University of Tokushima, Tokushima, Japan
{tmatsumoto,yabe.takuya}@tokushima-u.ac.jp
[2] Institute of Socio-Arts and Sciences, The University of Tokushima, Tokushima, Japan

Abstract. This paper examines the transformative impact of global talents on local communities through the case study of the "INOW" Project in Kamikatsu, Tokushima Prefecture. As the local community declines due to population decline, this study proposes the integration of foreign human resources to sustain the local community. A case study highlights the successes and challenges of integrating foreign human resources and the positive impact on local community development. The study aims to understand the human network changes resulting from the interaction between local residents and immigrants, and presents a model of human network change. The paper discusses in detail the language and cultural barriers, the role of technology, and the need for connectors to bridge global and local perspectives. The paper concludes by emphasizing the importance of ongoing research on the dynamics of global human resource integration in local areas.

Keywords: Sustainable community development · Global Talents · Collaborative creation · Human network transformation

1 Introduction

1.1 Background and Problem Statement

The population of Japan reached a peak in 2008 at 128.08 million people; since then, the population has steadily declined [1]. The country faces several challenges, including economic stagnation caused by labor shortages due to the decline in the working-age population and an increased welfare burden due to the rising rate of aging. The impact of this trend is particularly noticeable in rural communities, where local populations continue to decline at faster rates due to the migration of young people to urban areas and a shrinking local economy resulting from an aging population and falling birth rates. Against this social background, there is a need for new kinds of communities that include people living outside the local community, rather than closed communities based on traditional territorial ties to help sustain such rural areas.

N. A. Streitz and S. Konomi (Eds.): HCII 2024, LNCS 14718, pp. 287–297, 2024.
https://doi.org/10.1007/978-3-031-59988-0_17

This paper discusses how local communities can be sustained through the integration of foreign human resources. The impact of internationalization and the global economy on local communities is inevitable. Developing local resource-based businesses, such as within the tourism sector, requires human resources familiar with different cultures and languages. By increasing the diversity of local communities through foreign human resources with different backgrounds and experiences has the potential to create new perspectives and solutions to the problems faced by local communities, not only economically but also socially. In fact, the Japanese government's policy of relocation of the domestic population from cities to regions is a zero-sum game for domestic human resources. This is why it is important to examine the extent to which foreign human resources are accepted by local communities and what they bring to the table, and to explore the possibilities for such integration into rural areas.

1.2 Objectives of the Study

This research is based on a case study of the sustainable tourism project "INOW" in Kamikatsu, Tokushima, Japan. Kamikatsu is a typical Japanese rural area in the middle of a mountainous region, that has attracted attention in Japan and abroad for its advanced efforts in regional development. New businesses ventures such as" "Irodori" and the local governmental policies related to "zero-waste" are key initiatives that have been carried out over 20 years ago. However, the city in recent years is faced with a succession problem that ensures the future viability of these initiatives due to a lack of human resources. In addition, many projects depend on public funding, and the private sector has not yet established a mechanism for reinvestment and reproduction. In order to sustain local communities in the future, it will be necessary to create businesses based on new local values and community management that is not based on conventional processes.

In this case study, researchers are trying to understand how the interaction and integration between local residents and immigrants, born and raised outside of Japan, play a central role in Sustaining a new community and developing new businesses that are connected to a global network while situated in a locality. This study aims to: (1) clarify the changes in human networks through the introduction of foreign human resources and (2) clarify the successes and challenges that the emerging human networks have brought to the local communities. Finally, the study then examines the importance of global human resources in the formation of sustainable local communities in depopulated rural areas of Japan as new partners for co-creation, rather than "immigrants" as labor.

1.3 Literature Review

This paper does not focus on foreign human resources such as technical trainees or foreign students. Nor will it be considered as a creative class of class theory. Rather, the research attempts to provide insight into the potential of foreign human resources from a regional planning perspective.

In the field of regional planning in Japan, there have been numerous studies highlighting the possibility of community development through the co-creation of external human resources and local residents. For instance, Maeda et al. (2015) clarified the process of acquiring neighborhood residents as operators in local festivals and described the role of festivals in the formation of resilient communities [2]. However, they do not address the diversity of external actors that can potentially influence the impact. Similar to this research, Togashi et al. (2019) present a case study on a twenty-two year collaboration project with a British architecture school in a small community in Niigata Prefecture that focused on integrating foreign human resources [3]. The study clarifies how foreign students' participation in local festivals fosters a common awareness among residents and students and deepens the collaborative relationship. It is evident that the local community experiences a transformation from the temporary involvement of an external entity in a traditional local festival. This paper does not focus on foreign human resources such as technical trainees or foreign students. This paper provides insight into the changes in the local network and the impact on the community during the establishment of a community business co-created by foreign human resources and local residents.

1.4 Research Methodology

This study is based on the authors' participant observation in the "INOW". The author moved to Kamikatsu Town in 2011 and have been involved with INOW as an advisor since its beginning. This study employed the ethnographic approach to gain an in-depth understanding of the INOW and behavioral patterns through detailed on-site investigation and participant observation. The researcher resided in Kamikatsu, establishing close interactions with local residents to collect information on daily life, events, and the social structure of the community. In addition, this study gathered deeper insights by conducting semi-structured interviews with INOW project members, referring to the author's participatory observation results.

1.5 Research Structure

The chapter is structured as follows. First, Sect. 1 describes the research background, objectives, literature review, and methodology. Section 2 provides an overview of the case study, including the region, project, and project members of INOW that are interviewee of the study. Section 3 outlines the process of the case study project from its inception to the present day. The project underwent qualitative changes in phases, which were identified as turning points based on the results of participant observation and interviews with those involved in the project. Section 4 models the expansion of the global network developed around the INOW project as a process of network building in the local community. Section 5 discusses the integration of foreign human resources and the co-creation of local communities based on the points clarified in this study.

2 Case Study

2.1 Kamikatsu

Kamikatsu is a small town located in Tokushima Prefecture, less than an hour's drive from Tokushima City. The town area is divided into five districts. According to 2020 Census data, the town covers an area of 109.63 km^2 and has a population of 1,380.

The population has decreased rapidly since the period of high economic growth, with the current population being only 22% of what it was in 1950. Additionally, the aging rate has reached 55.9%. Fifty-five villages of varying sizes are dispersed at elevations ranging from approximately 100 to 700 m above sea level. These villages experience high rates of population decline and aging, resulting in weakened communities and smaller households. The number of foreign residents is 5.

Table 1. Research participants

Name/ID	Position	Birth	Background
Terumi Azuma/T	CEO of RDND, LLC	Kamikatsu, Japan	Born and raised in Kamikatsu, Terumi is the chef and owner of Cafe polestar, a Zero Waste accredited business in Kamikatsu
Linda Ding/L	Co-founder, supporter	Canada	Linda moved to Kamikatsu in 2019 and co-founded INOW in 2020. In 2023, Linda moved to Tokyo and continues to support INOW
Kana Lauren Chan/K	Co-founder, program organizer and interpreter (English ⇔ Japanese), guide	Canada	Kana was born and raised in Canada. Kana has diverse experiences studying and working across Europe and Asia. She moved to Kamikatsu in 2020
Sil Van de Velde/S	Program organizer and guide	Belgium	Sil was born and raised in Belgium. Previously he worked in education, communications, and research with a focus on conservation and development

2.2 Distinctive Town Initiatives

Over the past two decades, Kamikatsu has steadily gained national and international recognition for two regional activities: first, Irodori is an agribusiness that produces the leaves used in Japanese cuisine. Elderly people, with an average age of over 70, produce and sell the leaves while making full use of computers and reading market conditions [4]. The second notable initiative implemented by the town municipality is a 'Zero Waste Declaration,' which was created with the aim to divert all household waste from landfill and incineration. Kamikatsu was the first town in all of Japan to make such a declaration. The town has implemented a 45-separation recycling system and has achieved an impressive recycling rate of 80%. These efforts have gained the town an international reputation as an environmentally advanced region. In 2019, the then president of the Zero Waste Academy, a non-profit organization responsible for promoting zero-waste policies, was elected as co-chair at the 2019 Davos meeting held by the World Economic Forum [4].

2.3 INOW

This case study focuses on the INOW, a sustainable tourism initiative run by RDND.LLC, a community development company in the region. The program invites guests to stay in the village and experience life in Kamikatsu by engaging with local residents through various activities. In 2021, the program was awarded the 'Good Life Award' at the crQlr Awards, which recognize projects that promote a circular economy [5]. In 2023, the project received a special award in the transformative travel category of the JAPAN TRAVEL AWARDS [6]. The project is based in a community with a population of less than 1,400 people and is developed within a global network of local residents and members with international backgrounds (Table 1).

3   Results

3.1   Survey Summary

In this paper, an overview of the subject from the launch of the INOW to the present is described in phases, with qualitative changes in the business as the turning point, according to the results of the survey shown in Table 2.

3.2   Results

The following section describes the results of the participant observation and in-view analysis, with a focus on the changes in the human network observed in this case study.

Table 2. Survey Summary

Duration	Methodology and Objectives	Questionnaire
2019-	The author's observation and analysis of the impact of global talents on the local community	

(continued)

Table 2. (*continued*)

Duration	Methodology and Objectives	Questionnaire
2023.12–2024.1	Questionnaire survey referring to Baker (2001) to measure the personal networks of program participants and analyze changes in human networks within the local community centered on the project [7]	1) Most people discuss important matters with those around them from time to time. Looking back over the past 6 months, who are the people with whom you have had discussions about matters of importance to you? 2) Who are the people you need to communicate with to get your work done? (By your work, we mean your main activity.) Of all the people with whom you communicated during the past 6 months, who was the most important person to complete your work? 3) Now consider the important new projects you are currently promoting or working on. Think about who you can influence to get approval for the project or to secure the people, money, or other resources you need. Who will you talk to gain support for your project? 4) What kind of people do you socialize with? Socializing includes spending time together after work, visiting each other's homes, going to events together, having dinner, etc. In the past 6 months, who is the most central person you have socialized with on a daily basis?
2023.12–2024.1	Semi-structured interviews based on three questions to analyze the impact of global talents on and received from the community	1) What value did the connection with the local community have for you? 2) What value have you provided to the local community? 3) What changes are needed for the local community in Kamikatsu to accept global talent?

3.2.1 Phase I. Meeting the Founders (May 2019-)

The INOW started when L visited Kamikatsu in May 2019 and met T at a local cafe. Impressed by the beautiful scenery and the zero-waste spirit of the locals, L expressed her desire to live in Kamikatsu to T, who agreed to host her as a homestay guest. T saw this as an opportunity to broaden her horizons and improve her English skills through interaction with L.

Around the same time that L began her stay, T received inquiries from people who wanted to experience the initiatives and lifestyle of Kamikatsu while staying in Kamikatsu.

T considered how to match those needs for people from diverse backgrounds, especially those living abroad, to learn about Kamikatsu with the town's labor shortage. In consultation with L, she thought about the possibility of accepting additional applicants as homestay families. In October, the program was launched as the 'Try Kamikatsu Program' and publicized through a web page. Through the 'Try Kamikatsu Program,' T and L gained an understanding of the global demand for a more comprehensive zero-waste lifestyle experience in Kamikatsu, including the global market. The participants, many of whom were city residents, experienced a lifestyle in Kamikatsu that was very different from their usual lifestyle and gained a new sense of values through self-reflection. As a result of this experience, T and L were inspired to create the INOW as a community business. Despite the impact of the Covid-19 disaster, the project was still attended by foreigners residing in urban areas of Japan and university students who were unable to study abroad due to the pandemic. In September 2020, K, who had a Master's in Sustainability and Tourism Management joined the project.

3.2.2 Phase II. Global Network Expansion and Business Start-Up (October 2019-)

Around the same time that L began her stay, T received inquiries from people who wanted to experience the initiatives and lifestyle of Kamikatsu while staying in Kamikatsu. T considered how to match those needs for people from diverse backgrounds, especially those living abroad, to learn about Kamikatsu with the town's labor shortage. In consultation with L, she thought about the possibility of accepting additional applicants as homestay families. In October, the program was launched as the 'Try Kamikatsu Program' and publicized through a web page. Through the 'Try Kamikatsu Program,' T and L gained an understanding of the global demand for a more comprehensive zero-waste lifestyle experience in Kamikatsu Town, including the global market. The participants, many of whom were city residents, experienced a lifestyle in Kamikatsu that was 180° different from their usual lifestyle and gained a new sense of values through self-reflection. As a result of this experience, T and L were inspired to create the INOW project as a community business. Despite the impact of the Covid-19 disaster, the project was still attended by foreigners residing in urban areas of Japan and university students who were unable to study abroad due to the pandemic. In December 2020, K, who had studied sustainability and tourism management at university, joined the project.

3.2.3 Phase III. Expansion of Local Network with Business Diffusion (August 2021-)

Despite the challenges posed by the COVID-19 pandemic, the INOW persevered and underwent a process of trial and error, resulting in gradual improvements. In September 2020, K, a graduate of Sustainability and Tourism Management, joined the program, contributing to its expansion. Along with the increase in the number of participants accepted, the number of local farmers, chefs, community activists, and creators who participated as teachers to share the lifestyle and ideas of Kamikatsu with the participants increased (24 organizations and individuals participated as teachers in 2023). This increase in local stakeholders has also raised awareness within the local community. Towards the end of 2022, local events that were canceled due to the pandemic were gradually restarted, and by participating in such activities, L and K have directly expanded their network with the local community without the need for T.

L and K have gradually had the opportunity not only to participate in community activities, but also to take responsibility for their own activities. In April 2022, L moved to Tokyo for personal reasons, and K's partner, S, joined INOW as a member in Kamikatsu. The impact of COVID-19 has significantly diminished. INOW's media exposure has increased, and the business has entered a growth phase with 152 participants throughout the year 2023. During the growth phase, the focus was on sharing and growing guests being welcomed in 2023, which is about two-fold from the previous year. For instance, a community meeting was set up to discuss the management of the INOW program with the residents who participated as instructors, so that it was not just a consuming guided tour, but also the needs of the local side and the pricing of the actual instructor fees paid. At the December 2023 Christmas market, led by S and K with the aim of benefiting the local community, new developments were observed, including the reestablishment of the net.

4 Conclusion

4.1 Model of Human Network Change in the Case Study

Based on the results of participant observation and interviews, this paper clarifies the changes in human networks in the case study project. As shown in Fig. 1, in this case study, a chance encounter between local human resources T and L led to the development of a global network and the establishment of a new community business. Later, L, K, and S, who are foreign human resources, built a relationship of trust with local residents through cooperation in local festivals and farming on abandoned land, and became integrated into the local community.

Recently, a young organic farmer who is a teacher in the INOW program contacted a Singaporean chef who was a participant in the INOW program to learn about farming overseas. In this way, local stakeholders are beginning to directly connect with INOW's global network to gain new knowledge and business ideas.

In this way, it is clear that the expansion of the network around the case studies offered new opportunities for the maintenance and development of the local community, both economically and socially.

4.2 The Successes and Challenges that the Changes in Human Networks Have Brought to the Local Communities

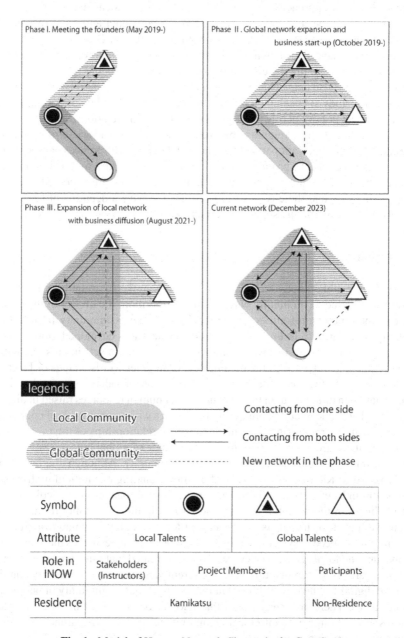

Fig. 1. Model of Human Network Change in the Case Study

One of the outcomes of the human network change is a change in the mindset of the local community. Through interaction with foreigners who immigrated to Kamikatsu, the host community was given the opportunity to rethink their own perspectives and seek new ideas and approaches. INOW is one of the new ideas and approaches that have emerged from the interaction between foreign personnel and local residen. The impact of the project has the potential to expand in the future, as local residents in the surrounding areas have also shown a willingness to incorporate foreign knowledge and experience. However, while the change in human networks has brought such results to the region, there are also many challenges. For example, language barriers are significant, and in this case study it became clear that the presence of K, who speaks English and Japanese, plays an important role in the process of deepening relationships with the local community. Although the foreigners observed in the study use a variety of digital tools to communicate with relevant parties, language and cultural differences caused varying conflicts. It is necessary to promote multicultural understanding to aid in minimizing misunderstanding. In reality, even if these human resources are accepted, there is a shortage of housing and the city government does not have a department to deal with them, so strengthening public support is a major issue.

5   Discussion

In this study, the human network that developed in Kamikatsu around the INOW was expanded and the local community was sustain. Furthermore the impact of the network involving global human resources on the local society and community in a declining community was clarified. In this case, while the project was developed globally based on neoliberal values, the project was promoted not in pursuit of self-interest but with an emphasis on shared values with the community, or in other words, values of Degrowth Communism [9]. Rather than the unilateral imposition of values by outsiders in the region, as has been pointed out in the past, the global human resources raised in different cultures have been able to build community businesses with a perspective of cooperation and sharing with the region and with an emphasis on relationships of trust.

However, there are many barriers to the acceptance of global human resources. T's presence in this case study is rare in the local community. Although she herself was born and raised in Kamikatsu, she has had an understanding of multiculturalism since childhood through zero-waste activities and internships abroad during her college years, and she believes in the potential to create new value in the community through global connections. It is clear that she is a connector of local and global human resources, and local communities need to systematically develop such human resources that can connect the global and the local. The interview results also revealed that miscommunication due to language barriers, different cultures and different values create unnecessary conflicts. The role of digital technology is important in creating a local community of people with different values. There are many issues that need to be addressed in order for global human resources to integrate into local communities, such as transparency in decision making and information sharing processes.

Furthermore, while it will be a future concern in the case study, the potential contribution of technology to the local community is a significant point of debate. This includes the maintenance of the expanding global network and the digital community, which utilizes DAOs as reported in Yabe (2023) [10].

Since this article focuses on business professionals, further investigation is necessary to examine the changes in local communities that have interacted with global talent and have expanded from local to global networks. It is clear that global talent plays a significant role in local communities that are facing depopulation and stagnation. It is important to continue researching the possibility of networks in rural areas.

Acknowledgments. This work was supported by JSPS KAKENHI Grant Number 22H03853.

References

1. Ministry of Land, Infrastructure, Transport and Tourism HP. https://www.mlit.go.jp/hakusyo/mlit/r01/hakusho/r02/html/n1111000.html. Accessed 31 Jan 2024
2. Maeda, M., Takada, M., Morishige, H., Nishino, K.: Actual condition of Jizo-bon management and diversity of the participants in the central area of Kyoto - a study on roles of Jizo-bon in the resilient formation of the local community. J. Archit. Plann. **80**(714), 1833–1842 (2015)
3. Togashi, R., Goto, H., Morita, R., Yamachika, Y., Yamazaki, Y.: Transformation of activity and consciousness of the British Architecture School and Residents through the Past 22 years in Koshirakura Village Niigata Prefecture. J. Archit. Plann. **54**(3), 1460–1467 (2019)
4. Irodori HP. https://irodori.co.jp. Accessed 31 Jan 2024
5. The Government of Japan HP. https://www.japan.go.jp/tomodachi/2019/spring2019/young_global_leader_focuses.html. Accessed 31 Jan 2024
6. crQlr HP. https://crqlr.com/2021/ja/announce/. Accessed 31 Jan 2024
7. JAPAN TRAVEL AWARDS HP. https://japantravelawards.com/jta-2024-jp. Accessed 31 Jan 2024
8. Baker, W.E.: Achieving Success Through Social Capital: Tapping Hidden Resources in Your Personal and Business Networks, kindle edn, Jossey-Bass, San Francisco (2007)
9. Saito, K.: Marx in the Anthropocene: Towards the Idea of Degrowth Communism, kindle edn, Cambridge University Press, Cambridge (2023)
10. Takuya, Y.: A consideration of how to solve social issues while maintaining traditional communities in local cities. The case study of KITTAMU, a general incorporated association in Yoshinogawa City, Tokushima Prefecture, which has expanded its activities under the COVID-19 disaster. City Plann. Rev. **72**(5), 38–41 (2023)

Conversing with Our Cars and the Drive for More Aware Experiences, Applying Ambient Theory to Mobile Design

H. Patricia McKenna[✉]

AmbientEase, Victoria, BC V8V 4Y9, Canada

Abstract. This paper considers the application of ambient theory for smart cities to vehicles as an approach to contributing greater understanding to increasingly more aware mobile environments. A review of the research and practice literature for people and car interactions is provided as well as for the use of theory in smart cities, environments, and mobile spaces, enabling formulation of a conceptual framework for more aware driving experiences aided by ambient theory. Methodologically, an exploratory case study approach is employed combined with an explanatory correlational design in operationalizing the conceptual framework formulated for use in this paper. Variables of interest such as sharing and access to public data are identified and assessed in relation to awareness, in search of patterns and relationships. Findings also emerge for awareness through online conference polling and in relation to the everyday driving experience, employed to gain insight into vehicular conversing and interacting. Limitations, challenges, and opportunities are identified giving rise to rich spaces for debate and exploration among vehicle manufactures; software developers; urban researchers, practitioners, and planners; and community members going forward.

Keywords: Ambient Theory · Attention · Attuning · Awareness · Conversational AI · Data Access · Data Sharing · Design · Mobile Spaces · Privacy · Smart Cities

1 Introduction

This paper is motivated by the need for developing more awareness about evolving data and information systems in everyday life, particularly in the vehicles we drive. While Suplee (2016) [1] highlights the importance of behavioral science for learning about "how drivers interact with their vehicles" and in turn influencing design changes for improved safety and trust, there seems to be less discussion of the notion of awareness and aware environments. For example, regarding privacy, Bajak (2023) [2], referring to work by the Mozilla Foundation (Caltrider, Rykov, and MacDonald, 2023) [3], points to the "failure" on the part of vehicle manufacturers where owners are said to "have little or no control over data collected" in that, personal information – think vehicles with many data collecting sensors, microphones, cameras – is being sold with few details about buyers and 50% of manufacturers are said to have indicated "they would share" such information "with the government or law enforcement without a court order." Given the pervasiveness of data and information systems, ambient theory for smart cities (McKenna, 2021) [4] is explored in this paper as a way of understanding such systems and gaining greater awareness while acknowledging that various other theories have been advanced in support of increasing the understanding of smart cities, spaces, and environments.

To the extent that ambient theory for smart cities is concerned with awareness in relation to people and technologies in smart environments (McKenna, 2023) [5], it would seem to be particularly appropriate for this exploration. Guided by the literature review, and the components and characteristics of the conceptual framework for ambient theory in smart cities [4], a way forward is advanced for smarter and more aware driving experiences. Methodologically, the experience of everyday use is employed, through an exploratory case study approach combined with an explanatory correlational design, to provide insight into conversing and interacting with our car as part of the driving process/episode.

As such, the main objective of this paper is to explore application of ambient theory for smart cities to mobile in-car environments.

2 Background

Streitz (2021) [6] points to concerns with privacy associated with "smart cars" as "a design challenge" since "[t]he explosion of surveillance, monitoring, and data harvesting systems shows that privacy and control of data about our personal behavior in public spaces is not possible." In response to the "design challenge" of "how to communicate the actions and interactions possible in smart environments" where "people are not aware how their behavior is being tracked" with AI (artificial intelligence) and other technologies, the need arises for "new types of affordances" in the form of "hybrid affordances" accommodating real and virtual world experiences that "provide guidance in understanding the specific situation" (Streitz, 2021) [6]. Heineke, Laverty, Möller, and Ziegler (2023) [7], in a recent McKinsey report, indicate that "private cars are still the most popular mobility mode" when compared with walking, public transport, ride hailing and taxi, micromobility (e.g., scooters, bikes, etc.), and robotaxis, although this is projected to shift by 2030 and 2035 to lesser and greater degrees globally in cities and surrounding areas. In this evolving landscape, the importance of awareness in mobile environments and the experience of people-technology interactions is one of many urban spaces to understand. In an interview with Azeem Azhar (Azhar, 2023) [8], Alex Kendall, CEO of Wayve, an autonomous driving startup, speaks of version 2 of autonomous vehicles (AV2.0) and the importance of "an industry-first vision-language action model" that enables AI technologies to "see and act, drive a car" and crucially, "ground it in language" that in turn enables potentials "to interact and talk to our car and literally ask it questions" about "why and what its doing to prompt it to drive in a certain way" as in, a "model lingo" (LINGO-1) and with such "capability" we can begin "to understand why it made decisions, debug and interpret the system and get it to explain its actions and text." For Kendall [8] such interaction capability "just democratizes access to understanding it and opens up a whole new range of possibilities and trust and interoperability."

2.1 Definitions

Definitions for key terms used in this paper are provided here based on the practice and research literature.

Ambient. McCullough (2015) [9] describes ambient in a variety of ways including "that which surround but does not distract" and "an awareness of continuum and continuum of awareness."

Ambient Computing. Ambient computing is described by Business Insider (2023) [10] as "a world where there is no need for conscious interaction as billions of devices will work invisibly in the background and only come to the fore when necessary."

What follows is a theoretical perspective providing a review of the research and practice literature; the methodology; results and discussion; limitations and future directions; and the conclusion.

3 Theoretical Perspective

This paper provides a review of the research and practice literature focusing on the evolving designs of 21st century vehicles in support of people and car interactions on the one hand, and the use of theory in smart cities, environments, and mobile spaces, on the other.

3.1 People and Car Interactions

Kouatli (2015) [11] advances the notion of "computing with words (CWW)" drawing on the work of Zadeh (2002) [12] as a way to "talk" or converse with our cars. As such, CWW is said to provide a way of augmenting, rather than replacing "computing with numbers to give machines a human like intelligence" in order to "communicate with vehicles using the same linguistic variables we use" with each other such as "closest", "Highest speed", "extreme left" and the like (Kouatli, 2015) [11]. Lee and Kim (2017) [13] claim that automobiles are undergoing a transformation into "smart cars" which they describe as "a prosthesis that assists the driver" and this is "enhancing the original function of the car" giving way to "a new place environment to the driver" consisting of "a hybrid space where information space and actual space are fused." Categories of technology are said to include safety, convenience, and sensibility where speech recognition and AR (augmented reality in the real world) display appear in the sensibility category [13]. Lee and Kim (2017) [13] found that "the degree of use, ease of use, and user satisfaction were low in [the] case of sensibility technology such as speech recognition" and this is perhaps not surprising given the year of the study, the ongoing evolving of technologies for cars, and the presence of complementary technologies for cars enabled through smartphones and Apple's CarPlay and the use of Siri and the like. Townsend (2020) [14] speaks in terms of "attention" in the context of autonomous vehicles and the need for "a far more cautious approach" suggesting that "our eyes, ears, and minds must be managed as carefully as torque, throttle, and traction." Townsend (2020) [14] claims that "Kia built a concept car that uses facial scans to identify and read its occupants' emotions to fine-tune content recommendations" and suggests that "[o]ne likely business model for the self-driving age" may be "the capture and monetization of our attention" going so far as to speak of "an infrastructure of attention" and an "attention machine" with the capability to "scan, study, and steer." We need only think of conversational AI chatbots such as Siri, Alexa, and so on "marking a shift toward more conversational data interactions" and this, according to Hazel (2023) [15], "turns data interaction into a casual conversation." It is worth noting that Derakhshan et al. (2022) [16] identify a decline in trust in autonomous vehicles even though in virtual reality (VR) explorations, "a self-explaining car has a positive impact on trust and perceived usefulness." According to Business Insider (2023) [10], ambient computing is heavily reliant on sensors and smartphones and their enabling of contextual awareness, in support of various applications, including "transforming the driving experience" focusing on the personal "needs and preferences of the driver and occupants."

McCullough (2023) [17] calls for a revisiting of the notion of ambient information in the city in the contextualizing of AI. Blum (Thompson, 2023) [18] highlights the challenges of building AI driven machines, noting that "[h]umans and machines don't speak the same language" using the example of instructing "your automated car" to "park in the shady spot under the tree", a big ask since "the vehicle needs to look at its image of the surrounding area and find the right spot" as well as "understand the words tree and shade and translate them into bits and bytes" not to mention "figure out that you mean the tree on the right, not the one on the other side of the street." Evans (2023) [19] describes the argument by GM that the use of smartphones in cars is a safety issue, promoting instead the use of in car systems for navigation, audio, and so on. And yet, customers are said to prefer CarPlay and other products that seem to work well with smartphones for navigation rather than "sub-par in house navigation systems" often found in vehicles where "[v]oice controls in cars are nothing new, but they've long been even worse than automaker navigation systems." Also of note is the issue of having "full access to the vehicle's systems" (Evans, 2023) [19] so as to "handle calls and texting through any Bluetooth-paired phone" but also to "control the audio, navigation, climate, and more all while the driver keeps their hands on the wheel and their eyes on the road" yet, despite increased capabilities over time of applications such as CarPlay and Android Auto, it is said they "still don't have access to most of those systems." The issues of "money and data" are also highlighted by Evans (2023) [19] regarding "access to, control over, and ownership of data generated in the vehicle." Evans [19] stresses that "[r]egardless of whose software the driver is using, enormous amounts of data are being collected on how they drive, where they go, the apps they use while driving, and more" and this is important because such "data is valuable to the automakers and tech companies both for customer research as well as to be anonymized, packaged, and sold to third parties."

Table 1 provides an overview by author from 2015 to 2023 of people and car interactions highlighting a range of elements. In summary, elements emerging from this review of the literature for people and car interactions pertain to computing with words [11], smart cars [13], infrastructure of attention [14], trust and autonomous vehicles [16], context awareness [10], safety [19], conversational data interactions [15], and ambient information and AI [17].

Table 1. People and car interactions.

Author	Year	People and car interactions
Kouatli	2015	Computing with words for talking to cars
Lee & Kim	2017	Smart cars
Townsend	2020	Infrastructure of attention
Derakhshan et al.	2022	Autonomous cars and declining trust
Business Insider	2023	Ambient computing and contextual awareness
Evans	2023	Safety and car system interactions
Hazel	2023	Conversational data interaction
McCullough	2023	Ambient information revisited, contextualizing AI

3.2 Theory and Smart Cities, Environments, and Spaces

Harrison and Abbott Donnelly (2011) [20] advanced the need for developing a theory of smart cities enabled by instrumentation and the use of information technologies, in making "the invisible visible." Camacho, Foth, Rakotonirainy, and Rittenbruch (2017) [21] employ activity theory, said to be "concerned with the notion of human activity and the historical, cultural, and contextual elements that shape activity and consciousness", to the study of urban rail in-vehicle activities in terms of needs and behaviors in an effort to provide a "depiction of what defines, shapes, and restricts in-vehicle activities in the context of public transport." By contrast to technology-driven foundational approaches to smart cities, Streitz (2019) [22] offers the perspective of moving "beyond 'smart-only' cities towards humane, cooperative hybrid cities." Batty (2020) [23] speaks of high frequency and low frequency cities where the former refers to changes in very brief time intervals such as seconds, minutes, hours, or days and the latter refers to years, decades, centuries, and the like, requiring a rethinking and "reinvigorating" of theory to assist in understanding "complexity, simulation, and new forms of data mining and perhaps artificial intelligence (AI)." McKenna (2021) [4] advances ambient theory for smart cities focusing on awareness and the interplay of one or more elements such as adaptive, dynamic, emergent, interactive, and pervasive "involving people and technologies, contributing to smart environments, and new action potentials." Ammara, Rasheed, Mansoor, Al-Fuqaha, and Qadir (2022) [24] provide a review of the research literature pertaining to systems theory as an approach for understanding smart cities, offering a system of sub-systems (SoS) approach. Christou (2023) [25] undertakes to investigate the potential of AI in the building or advancing of theory. According to Christou (2023) [25], "the researcher's cognitive input and evaluative skills are essential to the progress of theory development" while AI provides "a valuable means and tool" but does not "generate theory." It is worth noting that Christou (2023) [25] identifies several dynamics and benefits of AI for theory building, one of which is "stimulation and awareness dynamics" that seem to encompass inspiration and insight.

Table 2 provides an overview by author from 2011 to 2023 for theories pertaining to smart cities, environments, and spaces. In summary, elements emerging from this review of the literature for theory advanced for smart cities, environments, and spaces pertain to smart cities and information technology [20]; activity theory and human activity [21]; a moving beyond 'smart-only' cities towards humane, cooperative hybrid cities [22]; high and low frequency cities theory for understanding complexity, simulation, and data/AI [23]; ambient theory [4] focusing on awareness for understanding people and technology interactions in dynamic, adaptive, and emergent environments; systems theory [24] as a system of sub-systems for understanding smart cities; and the possible use AI in the building or advancing of theory [25], drawing on "stimulation and awareness dynamics" among other dynamics.

Table 2. Theory and smart cities, environments, and spaces.

Author	Year	Theories
Harrison & Abbott Donnelly	2011	Theory of smart cities
Camanco et al.	2017	Activity theory and human activity
Streitz	2019	Beyond 'smart-only' cities towards humane, cooperative hybrid cities
Batty	2020	High and low frequency cities
McKenna	2021	Ambient theory
Ammara et al.	2022	Systems theory
Christou	2023	AI potential in theory building or advancing of theory

3.3 Conceptualizing Ambient Theory for More Aware Driving Experiences

As shown in Fig. 1, ambient theory for smart cities in the image on the left, as advanced by McKenna (2021) [4], consists of three propositions involving 1) *awareness* in relation to the two key components of – technologies and people; 2) awareness-based spaces, that foster an evolving interplay of one or more elements, such as – adaptive, dynamic, emergent, interactive, pervasive; and 3) *meaningfully* involving people in action. It is worth noting that "awareness, sensing, and meaningful involvement" are said to "denote conditions indicative of when and where ambient theory will hold in the context of smart cities, environments and regions" (McKenna, 2021) [4]. As such, it would seem that the adaptive, dynamic, emergent, interactive space of a car with many sensors, cameras, and the like would be indicative of a space accommodating ambient theory and to this end, the image on the right in Fig. 1 shows an application of ambient theory to the design of mobile spaces, in this case, the car environment and the interactive, conversational activities occurring as part of the driving experience.

Among the activities coming into play as the driver and car engage in interaction are destination choice, route planning, pattern detection and learning, data generation, data access, awareness of other vehicles, and the like. Operationalization of the framework for use in this paper is described in the Methodology section.

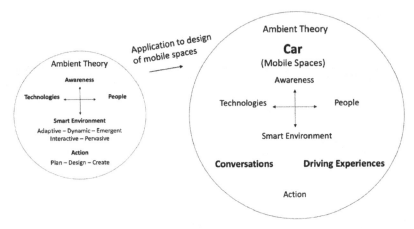

Fig. 1. Conceptual framework for more aware driving experiences with ambient theory.

4   Methodology

This paper uses an exploratory case study approach, said to be particularly important (Yin, 2017) [26] for the study of contemporary phenomena, everyday car use in this case, combined with an explanatory correlational design, where the former is used to assist in explaining the latter [26]. Ambient theory for smart cities is used to guide the exploration in mobile environments in this paper using *awareness* and other variables emerging from the literature review. Through an online webspace, people were invited to participate in the study and during sign up, demographic data were gathered including age range, gender, location, and self-categorization (e.g., educator, student, community member, to name a few). Study participants span the geographic areas of North America, Europe, and the Middle East. Data collection methods included use of a pre-tested survey instrument with closed and open-ended questions pertaining to smart cities and in-depth interviews using a pre-tested interview protocol. As an exploratory study, questions pertaining to awareness, trust, privacy, and so on were not defined or described but simply included as options for selection in relation to smart cities. Results provided in Sect. 5 include the questions as posed in the survey. In parallel with this study, data were also gathered systematically through individual and group discussions across a range of sectors in Canadian cities (e.g., Toronto, Vancouver, and Victoria). Overall, an analysis was conducted for n = 79 consisting of 42% females and 58% males for people ranging in age from their 20s to their 70s.

Additionally, online conference poll spaces across sectors involving human computer interaction (HCI) (McKenna, 2022) [27] and future technologies (Chauncey and McKenna, 2023) [28] are explored as a way of gathering data in the real-world networking spaces of researchers, students, practitioners, and other interested attendees.

5   Results and Discussion

As shown in Table 3, when asked to assess the extent to which factors such as awareness contribute to the making of smart cities, on a Likert type scale where 1 = Not at all and 7 = Absolutely, 25% of survey participants responded at position 5 (Sort of), 25% at position 6 (Sure) and 50% at position 7. Noting that social media and other aware technologies give rise to many possibilities, when asked to assess elements such as sharing for such possibilities, 25% responded at position 6 (Sure) and 75% at position 7.

Table 3. Correlation between assessments of awareness and sharing.

Variables	Assessments	Correlation
Awareness	5 (25%); 6 (25%); 7 (50%)	.27
Sharing	6 (25%); 7 (75%)	

Using the Real Statistics add in for Microsoft Excel (Zaiontz, 2023) [29], a Spearman correlation coefficient for ordinal data of .27 emerges between the variables of *awareness* and *sharing* (Table 3) and, according to Creswell (2018) [30], for correlations in the .20 to .35 range "there is only a slight relationship."

As shown in Table 4, when asked to assess the extent to which factors such as *trust* contribute to increased value for data in smart cities, 25% of participants selected position 6 on the scale; and 75% selected position 7.

Table 4. Correlation between assessments of awareness and trust.

Variables	Assessments	Correlation
Awareness	5 (25%); 6 (25%); 7 (50%)	.27
Trust	6 (25%); 7 (75%)	

Using the Real Statistics add in for Microsoft Excel (Zaiontz, 2023) [29], a Spearman correlation coefficient for ordinal data of .27 emerges between *awareness* and *trust* (Table 4).

As shown in Table 5, when asked to assess the extent to which factors such as *privacy* contribute to increased value for data in smart cities, 50% of participants selected position 6 on the scale and 50% selected position 7.

Using the Real Statistics add in for Microsoft Excel (Zaiontz, 2023) [29], a Spearman correlation coefficient for ordinal data of −.23 emerges between *awareness* and *privacy*, revealing an inverse or negative relationship such that as one variable increases the other decreases (Creswell, 2018) [30].

In Table 6, using *attuning to urban spaces* as a proxy for context awareness in mobile environments (automobiles), when asked to assess the extent to which factors

Table 5. Correlation between assessments of awareness and privacy.

Variables	Assessments	Correlation
Awareness	5 (25%); 6 (25%); 7 (50%)	-.23
Privacy	6 (50%); 7 (50%)	

such as *attuning to urban spaces* contribute to the making of smart cities, 25% of survey participants responded at position 5 (Sort of), 25% at position 6 (Sure) and 50% at position 7. When asked to assess the extent to which factors such as *access to public data* contribute to the livability of a smart cities, 25% of participants selected position 4 (neutral) on the scale; 25% of participants selected position 5 on the scale; 25% of participants selected position 6 on the scale; and 25% selected position 7.

Table 6. Correlation between assessments of attuning and access to public data.

Variables	Assessments	Correlation
Attuning to urban spaces	5 (25%); 6 (25%); 7 (50%)	.63
Access to public data	4 (25%); 5 (25%); 6 (25%); 7 (25%)	

Using the Real Statistics add in for Microsoft Excel (Zaiontz, 2023) [29], a Spearman correlation coefficient for ordinal data of .63 emerges between *attuning* and *access to public data* and, according to Creswell (2018) [30], correlations in the .35 to .65 range "are useful for limited prediction." A wide spread of responses occurred for access to public data including 25% neutrality at position 4.

In summary, while findings from this exploration shed light on the importance of awareness in relation to people and technologies in smart environments and the degree of correlation with other variables pertaining to interactions, such as sharing and access to public data, the nature of the relationships that emerged suggest the need for further, larger studies involving additional variables and perhaps more direct variables. Also, in view of the work by various researchers on neutral responses to survey questions (Fakhrhosseini and Jeon, 2017; Nadler, Weston, and Voyles, 2015) [31, 32], an avenue for further exploration emerges for the *access to public data* variable. Also, the inverse correlation between *awareness* and *privacy* gives rise to questions about the coexistence of awareness and privacy in smart environments, perhaps confirming the need identified by Streitz [6] for "hybrid affordances" accommodating virtual and physical spaces, attentive to specific situations involving say – awareness by city administration about the mobility behavior of citizens (e.g., tracking traffic data); or citizens being aware of changes in the urban space (e.g., new buildings, new streets, new routings of traffic on streets or change of one-way streets, street lights); or the reporting of potholes in city streets.

Additionally, through online polls conducted on the Whova platform during two separate conference events, the following findings emerged. First, in response to a poll conducted at the Future Technologies Conference in 2021 (Table 7) on *heightened awareness,* from a total of 16 responses, 44% of respondents selected a) Cultural events; 19% selected b) Economy; 31% selected the c) Urban mobility option; and 6% selected d) Other.

Table 7. FTC2021 poll 1 pertaining to awareness. Poll 1 (FTC2021): Where do you notice 'the ambient', as in, 'heightened awareness' in your city?

Options	Responses (n = 16)
a) Cultural events	44%
b) Economy (e.g., smart products, recommending of products, etc.)	19%
c) Urban mobility options	31%
d) Other	6%

Secondly, as shown in Table 8, during the Future Technologies Conference in 2023 (Chauncey and McKenna, 2023) [28], the poll poses a question pertaining to *awareness* while driving which sheds light on the importance of smart products, urban mobility options, and other factors such as data privacy, distraction, and the augmenting of human capabilities.

Table 8. FTC2023 poll pertaining to 'awareness' in mobile spaces. Poll (FTC2023): Considering use of AI in mobile environments, such as the cars we drive, identify how conversational AI may, or may not, assist us to improve our awareness?

Poll Options	Responses (n = 9)
a) Augments our driving capabilities (e.g., navigation, etc.)	11%
b) Uses data collected to improve navigation and other driving assistance	56%
c) May cause distraction, affecting our awareness and driving capabilities	11%
d) Leaves us unaware of all or any data being collected	11%
e) May compromise our privacy if data collected are shared with unknown third parties	11%
f) Other	0%

In response to this poll (Table 8), from a total of 9 responses, 11% of respondents selected a); 56% selected b); 11% selected c); 11% selected d); and 11% selected e), with no responses for the "Other" category.

In summary, poll findings in 2021 (Table 7) show the relative importance of urban mobility options in relation to "heightened awareness" at 31%. Poll findings in 2023 (Table 7) pertaining to awareness aided by AI show the importance of data collected to improve navigation and other driving assistance at 56% while all other concerns pertaining to augmenting capabilities, distraction, data collection, and privacy show equal importance at 11%.

Overall, it would seem that awareness is a key element in mobile smart environments, the importance of which could perhaps be better understood with the aid of ambient theory for smart cities, environments, and spaces (McKenna, 2024) [33] in accommodating the emergent, dynamic, interactive, and pervasive nature of such environments while allowing for action, in the form of variables explored, including conversations and experiences, involving people and technologies.

6   Limitations and Future Directions

Limitations of this work pertain to the small sample size for the explorations conducted, and this is mitigated by the opening of opportunities for researchers and practitioners going forward to further explore the variables used in this paper as well as other variables (e.g., learning, etc.) in other mobile venues (e.g., such as autonomous vehicles) and geographic areas.

Caution is urged in the interpretation of conference poll results since it should be noted that participation in online conference polling and other activities on the Whova platform is perhaps motivated in part as a way of garnering leaderboard points, yet participants did choose to respond to our polls on the questions posed (Table 7 and Table 8), among the many other polls to choose from.

While the variable *access to public data* was explored in this paper, going forward it may be important to explore questions such as whether the private vehicle data being generated becomes essentially public data if sold to, or shared with, third parties.

7   Conclusion

In conclusion, this exploration of awareness and aware environments through application of ambient theory to the design of mobile environments, focusing on the interactions between people and their in-car driving experiences in increasingly technology-pervasive spaces, highlights the importance of data on the one hand, and the challenges in learning more about the nature of relationships with variables such as trust and privacy in smart environments, on the other hand. This paper is significant in that a relatively new, real-world theory [4] in the evolving domain of smart environments is being applied and further tested and validated, in relation to mobile environments. Additionally, focusing on data and information sharing and access to public data, ambient theory for smart cities is being generative possibly of new approaches to awareness in support of trust, pertaining to urban mobile design while contributing to ongoing understandings of smart cities and environments and associated potentials. As such, this paper encourages uptake and ongoing use of theories for smart cities through exploration, testing, and discussion, while also highlighting the critical importance of enabling and increasing our human awareness capabilities.

Disclosure of Interests. The Author Has no Competing Interests to Declare that Are Relevant to the Content of This Article.

References

1. Suplee, C.: Social science studies the most hazardous thing on the road: You. From Research to Reward: A National Academy of Sciences Series about Scientific Discovery and Human Benefit (2016). https://nap.nationalacademies.org/read/23673/
2. Bajak, F.: Carmakers are Failing the Privacy Test: Owners Have Little or no Control Over Data Collected. The Associated Press, CityNews Everywhere (2023). https://toronto.cit ynews.ca/2023/09/06/carmakers-fail-privacy-test-give-owners-little-or-no-control-on-per sonal-data-they-collect/. Accessed 24 Sept 2023
3. Caltrider, J., Rykov, M., MacDonald, Z.: It's official: Cars are the worst product category we have ever reviewed for privacy. Mozilla Foundation Blog, 6 September (2023). Accessed 25 September 2023 from https://foundation.mozilla.org/en/privacynotincluded/articles/its-official-cars-are-the-worst-product-category-we-have-ever-reviewed-for-privacy/
4. McKenna, H.P.: The importance of theory for understanding smart cities: making a case for ambient theory. In: Streitz, N., Konomi, S. (eds.) HCII 2021. LNCS, vol. 12782, pp. 41–54. Springer, Cham (2021). https://doi.org/10.1007/978-3-030-77015-0_4
5. McKenna, H.P.: Urban Life and Ambient in Smart Cities, Learning Cities, and Future Cities. IGI Global, Hershey (2023)
6. Streitz, N.A.: From smart-only cities towards humane and cooperative hybrid cities. Technology ‖ Architecture + Design **5**(2), 127–133 (2021). https://doi.org/10.1080/24751448.2021.1967050
7. Heineke, K., Laverty, N., Möller, T., Ziegler, F.: The Future of Mobility. McKinsey Quarterly (2023). https://www.mckinsey.com/industries/automotive-and-assembly/our-insights/the-fut ure-of-mobility-mobility-evolves. Accessed 12 Dec 2023
8. Azhar, A.: AI takes the wheel: new advances in autonomous driving. Harvard Business Review (HBR) Transcript of a podcast, Exponential View, Session 6, Episode 56, 27 December (2023). https://hbr.org/podcast/2023/12/ai-takes-the-wheel-new-advances-in-aut onomous-driving?ab=HP-hero-latest-text-1. Accessed 28 Dec 2023
9. McCullough, M.: Ambient Commons: Attention in the Age of Embodied Information. MIT Press, Cambridge (2015)
10. Business Insider: The rise of AI is fueling a seamless technology evolution called ambient computing: Here's what that could mean for us. Business Insider, 28 November (2023). https://www.businessinsider.com/sc/how-arm-is-taking-leading-role-rise-of-amb ient-computing. Accessed 28 Nov 2023
11. Kouatli, I.: Computing with words: are we ready to "talk" to our cars? In: 2015 International Conference on Connected Vehicles and Expo (ICCVE), Shenzhen, China, pp. 212–213 (2015). https://doi.org/10.1109/ICCVE.2015.14
12. Zadeh, L.: From computing with numbers to computing with words: from manipulation of measurements to manipulation of perceptions. Int. J. Appl. Math. Comput. Sci. **12**(3), 307–324 (2002)
13. Lee, S.-E.; Kim, S.: The influence of smart car technologies on drivers' perceived control and attachment. In: 14th Asia-Pacific Regional Conference of the International Telecommunications Society (ITS): "Mapping ICT into Transformation for the Next Information Society", Kyoto, Japan, 24th–27th June (2017)
14. Townsend, A.M.: Ghost Road: Beyond the Driverless Car. W. W. Norton & Company (2020)
15. Hazel, T.: Understanding the impact and driving factors of conversation AI. Forbes, 7 August (2023). https://www.forbes.com/sites/forbestechcouncil/2023/08/07/understanding-the-impact-and-driving-factors-of-conversation-ai/?sh=393b154dd442#:~:text=Conversat ion%20AI%20harnesses%20the%20potential,and%20innovation%20across%20various% 20fields. Accessed 3 Oct 2023

16. Derakhshan, S., et al.: Talking cars, doubtful users—a populations study in virtual reality. IEEE Trans. Hum.-Mach. Syst. **52**(4), 602–612 (2022). https://doi.org/10.1109/THMS.2022. 3168437

17. McCullough, M.: Active city reading – a walk in urban technology. Personal Blog, University of Michigan (http://www-personal.umich.edu/~mmmc/) (2023). http://www-personal.umich. edu/%7Emmmc/ActiveCityReading_1page.pdf. Accessed 29 Nov 2023

18. Thompson, N.: Dialogues: On AI, Society, and What Comes Next. Atlantic Re:think, The Atlantic (2023). https://cdn.theatlantic.com/assets/marketing/prod/misc-files/2023/12/Atlant icRethink_Google_Dialogues_2023-mobile.pdf. Accessed 6 Dec 2023

19. Evans, S.: GM says it's ditching apple CarPlay and android auto for your safety: GM claims people won't stop looking at their phones and it wants to minimize that danger inside its cars. Motortrend (2023). https://www.motortrend.com/news/general-motors-removing-apple-car play-android-auto-for-safety-tim-babbitt/. Accessed 12 Dec 2023

20. Harrison, C., Donnelly, I.A.: A theory of smart cities. In: Proceedings of the 55th Annual Meeting of the ISSS - 2011, Hull, UK, vol. 55, no. 1 (2011). https://journals.isss.org/index. php/proceedings55th/article/view/1703

21. Camacho, T., Foth, M., Rakotonirainy, A., Rittenbruch, M.: Understanding urban rail in-vehicle activities: an activity theory approach. Transp. Res. Part F: Traffic Psychol. Beh. **46**(Part A), 70–86 (2017). https://doi.org/10.1016/j.trf.2017.01.010

22. Streitz, N.: Beyond 'smart only' cities: Redefining the 'smart-everything' paradigm. J. Ambi-ent Intell. Humanized Comput. **10**(2), 791–812 (2019). https://doi.org/10.1007/s12652-018-0824-1

23. Batty, M.: Defining smart cities: high and low frequency cities, big data and urban theory. In: Willis, K.S., Aurigi, A. (eds.) The Routledge Companion to Smart Cities, pp. 51–60. Routledge (2020). https://doi.org/10.4324/9781315178387-5

24. Ammara, U., Rasheed, K., Mansoor, A., Al-Fuqaha, A., Qadir, J.: Smart cities from the perspective of systems. Systems **10**(3), 77 (2022). https://doi.org/10.3390/systems10030077

25. Christou, P.A.: The use of artificial intelligence (AI) in qualitative research for theory devel-opment. Qual. Rep. **28**(9), 2739–2755 (2023). https://doi.org/10.46743/2160-3715/2023. 6536

26. Yin, R.K.: Case Study Research: Design and Methods, 6th edn. Sage, Thousand Oaks (2017)

27. McKenna, H.P.: Is ambient theory for smart cities even a theory? An affirmative assessment. In: Arai, K. (ed.) FTC 2021. LNNS, vol. 359, pp. 550–558. Springer, Cham (2022).https:// doi.org/10.1007/978-3-030-89880-9_41

28. Chauncey, S.A., McKenna, H.P.: An exploration of the potential of large language models to enable cognitive flexibility in AI-augmented learning environments. In: Arai, K. (ed.) FTC 2023. LNN S, vol. 816. Springer, Cham (2023). https://doi.org/10.1007/978-3-031-47448-4_11

29. Zaiontz, C.: Real statistics using excel (2023). www.real-statistics.com. Accessed 20 Dec 2023

30. Creswell, J.W.: Educational Research: Planning, Conducting, and Evaluating Quantitative and Qualitative Research, 6th edn. Pearson, Boston (2018)

31. Fakhrhosseini, S.M., Jeon, M.: Affect/emotion induction methods. In: Emotion and Affect in Human Factors and Human-Computer Interaction, pp. 235–253. Elsevier, The Netherlands (2017). https://doi.org/10.1016/B978-0-12-801851-4.00010-0

32. Nadler, J.T., Weston, R., Voyles, E.C.: Stuck in the middle: the use and interpretation of midpoints in items on questionnaires. J. Gen. Psychol. **142**(2), 71–89 (2015). https://doi.org/ 10.1080/00221309.2014.994590

33. McKenna, H.P.: An exploration of theory for smart spaces in everyday life: enriching ambient theory for smart cities. In: Lyu, Z. (ed.) Smart Spaces. Elsevier (2024)

Balancing Excitement and Environmental Conservation in Information Dissemination for Safari Game Drives

Kaiya Shimura[iD], Shin Katayama[iD], Kenta Urano[iD], Emanuel Leleito[iD],
Takuro Yonezawa[iD], and Nobuo Kawaguchi[(✉)][iD]

Nagoya University, Furo-cho Chikusa-ku, Nagoya 464-8601, Japan
kawaguti@nagoya-u.jp

Abstract. In the context of Kenyan Safari Game Drives, which traditionally rely on visual scouting and intermittent communication, challenges arise regarding the effectiveness of animal detection and environmental conservation. Consequently, animals experience stress, and tourists encounter difficulties in observation due to obstruction by other visitors. Addressing these challenges involves maintaining animal welfare while enhancing tourist satisfaction. To revitalize post-pandemic tourism and enrich safari experiences, this study proposes a wildlife spotting and sharing system. The proposed method integrates wildlife detection and sharing technologies guided by three core principles: preserving encounter serendipity, regulating information access, and promoting environmental conservation. The system architecture incorporates sensors, GPS, and tablet terminals to facilitate real-time data collection, animal identification, and information dissemination. This approach aims to foster an engaging, efficient, and environmentally conscious wildlife spotting and sharing experience, potentially establishing a model for sustainable wildlife tourism in comparable wildlife-rich regions.

Keywords: Wildlife Spotting · Game drive · Navigation System · Animal protection · Entertainment

1 Introduction

Kenya's wildlife tourism sector heavily depends on game drives as a central attraction, offering visitors a unique chance to engage with the natural environment and witness a diverse range of wildlife. Game drives, symbolic of Kenyan tourism, occur in natural wildlife habitats like nature reserves and wildlife sanctuaries. During these excursions, tourists embark on specially-designed vehicles to observe wildlife in their natural habitat, accompanied by experienced guides who explain the behaviors and habits of the animals. These expeditions, often lasting several hours or days, offer visitors the chance to witness a spectacular variety of wildlife, including lions, elephants, zebras, giraffes, and others, while appreciating the natural beauty and biodiversity of the ecosystem. The appeal

N. A. Streitz and S. Konomi (Eds.): HCII 2024, LNCS 14718, pp. 311–323, 2024.
https://doi.org/10.1007/978-3-031-59988-0_19

of game drives in safari is often enhanced by unexpected wildlife encounters, which typically rely on visual scouting by guides and the occasional exchange of sightings information between tourism vehicles.

The global tourism industry, including Kenya, has experienced a notable decline in the wake of the COVID-19 pandemic. As part of the efforts to rejuvenate Kenya's tourism sector, the revitalization of game drives has emerged as a pivotal strategy. However, the existing manual practices of animal spotting and information exchange during game drives are plagued by inefficiencies. Instances arise where tourists spend extended periods on drives with few wildlife sightings. On the other hands, the clustering of multiple vehicles around sighted animals may cause stress to the wildlife, highlighting the necessity for a more structured information-sharing mechanism that prioritizes animal welfare.

As Ranaweerage et al. [8] argue, the presence of tourists during elephant-watching activities in protected areas of Sri Lanka significantly increases the frequency and duration of alertness, fear, stress, and aggressive behaviors among different age and sex groups of elephants. Additionally, Kays et al. [5] mention the potential for tourist behavior to decrease the population of wild animals and disrupt the activity patterns of these animals. Balancing the improvement of animal sighting detection and sharing, while preserving the thrill of unexpected wildlife encounters, poses a complex challenge to be solved.

The objective of this study is to conceptualize, construct, and assess a wildlife spotting and sharing system tailored for Kenyan game drives. This system, named SafariCast, aims to investigate its effectiveness within safari game drives. Moreover, the study seeks to examine how SafariCast could integrate the improvement of animal detection and information dissemination among tourists while maintaining the integrity of the genuine safari experience characterized by unexpected wildlife encounters. In the context of the post-pandemic landscape, characterized by the imperative of revitalizing tourism as a cornerstone of Kenya's economic recovery, this study assumes a distinct and pivotal role. The forthcoming insights have the potential to outline a framework for integrating technology into wildlife conservation endeavors, tourist engagement strategies, and the sustainable management of game drives. Such a framework could establish a precedent not only for Kenya but also for other nations abundant in wildlife, offering a sustainable approach to enhancing wildlife tourism experiences.

In summary, our key contributions are the following.

- We identified inefficiencies in current wildlife spotting and information sharing practices during game drives in Kenya, such as prolonged periods with few wildlife sightings and stress caused to animals by clustering vehicles.
- We introduced SafariCast, a system designed to enhance wildlife spotting and sharing experiences during Kenyan game drives. SafariCast aims to improve effectiveness, efficiency, and tourist engagement while maintaining the authenticity of the safari experience.

– We developed SafariCast as a solution, addressing discussions on sustainable tourism and wildlife conservation by balancing economic benefits with environmental and wildlife welfare considerations.

2 Related Works

The intersection of animal detection and location-sharing systems presents an innovative interdisciplinary approach to enriching wildlife spotting experiences during game drives. Exploring relevant research in these fields sheds light on the progression of methodologies and technologies, laying a sturdy groundwork for the proposed study. For instance, Kim et al. [6] argue that monitoring and predicting tourists' spatial movement patterns from mobile phone data hold promise in contributing to biodiversity management in protected areas. Additionally, Barros et al. [1] forecasted peak visitation periods by tourists using geotag data and validated the potential utility of visitors' time patterns as surrogate indicators for visitation rates.

2.1 Animal Detection

Park et al. [7] explore a cloud-based system used in a Smart Farm environment for real-time animal monitoring and detection. This system is designed to oversee the health and behavior of animals, providing alerts in case of abnormalities, ultimately ensuring the welfare of livestock. Karlsson et al. [4] focus on the tracking and identification of animals within a digital zoo context. The study is geared towards monitoring the location and behavior of animals, with a digital platform developed to disseminate information to visitors, thereby enriching their zoo experience.

2.2 Wildlife Communication Systems

The ZebraNet project [3], as explored by Jones et al., investigates energy-efficient computing techniques for wildlife tracking. This research outlines the design tradeoffs entailed in developing a system that optimizes energy efficiency while effectively tracking wildlife, offering early experiences and lessons from the ZebraNet deployment. Nisrine et al. [2] delve into a smart system for the collection and sharing of real-time vehicular mobility traces. Although the context differs, the methodologies and technologies explored could be relevant to devising an information-sharing system between vehicles during safari drives, ensuring efficient communication about wildlife sightings while minimizing environmental impact.

These studies collectively constitute a mosaic of methodologies, technologies, and experiences that could inform the design, development, and evaluation of SafariCast in the distinctive setting of Kenyan Game Drives. The gleaned insights from these studies could potentially steer the harmonization of animal detection enhancements with the preservation of authentic safari experiences, aiming towards a sustainable and engaging wildlife spotting and sharing endeavor.

3   SafariCast

Our proposed system, SafariCast, aims to reconcile environmental conservation with tourist satisfaction. This approach has centered around three core elements: maintaining the serendipity of encounters, restricting crowding, and equalizing opportunities for encounters.

3.1   Requirements

Encountering wildlife during a game drive is inherently thrilling. Our approach aims to implement a structured information-sharing system while maintaining this excitement and considering stress on the animals.

Equalizing Opportunities for Encounters. Currently, one-to-one information sharing among local guides is the primary means of communication during game drives, which is not an efficient method of information sharing. Our proposed approach seeks to collect, distribute, and maximize participant satisfaction with location information of animals from all participants.

Maintaining the Serendipity of Encounters. Providing excessive information to tourists may diminish the element of surprise and could potentially impact the habitat of animals. We will establish a system that limits tourist access to information. The priority of shared location information is determined by the encounter history of vehicles with animals and the distance from the animals. Additionally, shared location information will be displayed as an ambiguous circle rather than pinpointed locations. This preserves the excitement of finding animals, makes animals easier to find, and prevents vehicles from clustering around animals. Furthermore, by limiting information disclosure, we maintain situations where vehicles are less likely to become overcrowded.

Restricting Crowding. Due to the tendency for vehicles to cluster around spectacular events such as sightings of the Big Five (elephant, buffalo, lion, leopard, and rhinoceros) or crossings of the Mara River, mechanisms will be introduced to regulate vehicle approaches when the threshold number of vehicles is near target animals or areas. This prioritizes animal welfare and minimizes impacts on habitats.

3.2   Implementation

To facilitate information sharing on SafariCast, it is necessary to have equipment for capturing animals and software for processing information. Below, we enumerate the equipment to be installed on each vehicle and the software used for exchanging information. The system architecture is shown in Fig. 1.

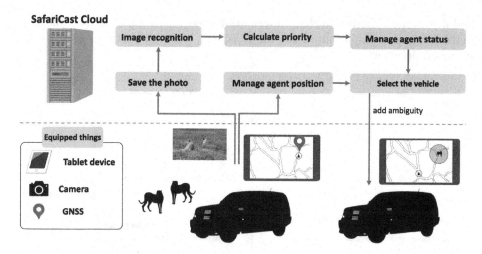

Fig. 1. The system architecture of SafariCast consists of both hardware and software components, with data being processed on the SafariCast Cloud.

Hardware Components. Each vehicle is equipped with a tablet device that displays the safari map, current location, vegetation, and the probability range of animal presence based on previous encounters. Sensors utilized by the device include:

– GPS: To acquire precise location data of vehicles and potential sighted animals.
– Camera: To capture images.

We presume that internet connectivity is available within the safari area. In fact, we have already verified that the mobile network (LTE network) covers a broad expanse of the safari.

Software Components.

– Image Analysis: To identify animals from captured photos by deep learning models.
– Navigation Map: Provides users with real-time visual surroundings.
– Wildlife Location Acquisition Function: Obtains and displays precise wildlife coordinates nearby.

3.3   Information Sharing Procedure of SafariCast

The details of SafariCast's information-sharing procedure are explained here. The flow of information sharing in SafariCast is depicted in Fig. 2, where Safari-Cast calculates priorities based on the number and rarity of encountered animals and determines whether to share information accordingly. Once shared, the animal's location is displayed on the tablet screen, allowing participants to make informed decisions.

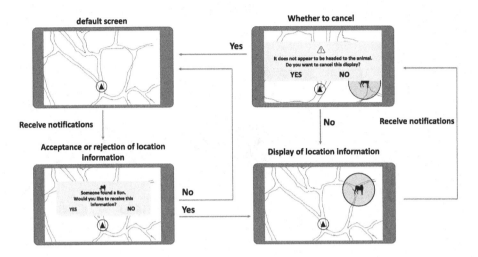

Fig. 2. This represents the flow of information that is notified to tourist vehicles. Tourists can choose whether to receive information about animals. Also, if tourists are clearly not heading towards their destination, they can turn off the display.

Animal Discovery. Animal discovery is conducted through cameras installed in vehicles. The camera is not continuously recording but is assumed to start recording when the vehicle stops. Upon animal discovery, a few frames of recorded video are uploaded to SafariCast. From these uploaded images, the species, total count, and estimated distance to the animal are inferred. Based on the information obtained from the images, SafariCast updates the encounter history of the discovering vehicle. It also evaluates the impact of the images on other individuals and shares the information. In the example of Fig. 2, Vehicle 0 has discovered animals.

Conditions for Receiving Notifications. In SafariCast, information is shared among vehicles based on their priority rankings. When delivering information, the priority of all vehicles is compared, and information is distributed in descending order of priority values. From the perspective of wildlife conservation, an entry restriction of up to 5 vehicles within a 1km radius of the animal is implemented. In the example depicted in Fig. 3, since there are already 2 vehicles within a 1km radius of the animal, the next 3 vehicles will receive the information.

Delivery Restrictions. When the total number of vehicles receiving animal location information and the total number of vehicles within a 1km radius of the target animals (restricted entry zone in Fig. 3) reach the capacity (5 vehicles), notification delivery stops. Once the capacity limit is below, notification delivery resumes. When counting the capacity limit, the vehicle that first discovered the animals is also included. If a rarer animal is found within a 1km radius of animals already discovered, notifications are updated to inform about the rarer one. If there are no updates in observation information within the same zone, notification delivery stops 15 min later.

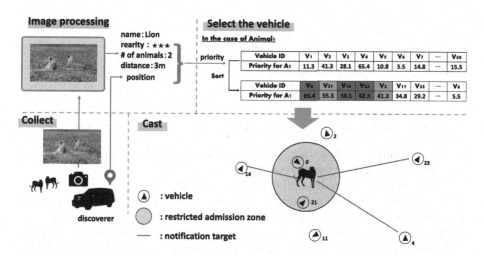

Fig. 3. This diagram illustrates the flow of information sharing related to animal A1. The location information of animal A1 is disseminated to vehicles with high priority values. However, vehicles that have already encountered the same animal as A1 or vehicles within the restricted area do not receive information sharing.

Notifications. Figure 2 illustrates the screen transitions of the tablet devices in each vehicle. Each vehicle's tablet device receives a notification: "Lion sighting. Do you want to acquire this information?" This notification can be declined. If declined, it is forwarded to the next participant. Once received, the vehicle cannot freely cancel the notification until it enters the zone of the target animals. If the receiving vehicle is evidently not heading towards the zone of the target animals, a message is sent to the participant: "It seems you are not heading towards the target animals. Do you want to cancel?" The user is notified and can choose whether to cancel or not. If the search is interrupted in this manner, no cooldown period is imposed.

3.4   Process of SafariCast

In the previous version of SafariCast, satisfaction was used as a metric. [9] However, incorporating the subjective notion of satisfaction led to ambiguity. Therefore, this paper introduces a new metric called priority. Priority is the criterion used to determine which vehicle to share information with when an animal is discovered. It is calculated based on the vehicle's encounter history with animals, the rarity of the animal, and the distance to the animal.

Priority Calculation Formula.

$$P = \frac{(S_a \times S_v)}{(L_a - L_v)^2}$$

where S_a is status of the animal, S_v is status of the vehicle, L_a is location of the animal and L_v is location of the vehicle.

Procedure for Determining Delivery Targets.

1. For each animal, calculate the priority for all vehicles and store it in the dictionary `animal.priority[vehicle]`.
2. Sort the dictionary in descending order of priority.
3. Remove vehicles close to the target animal and vehicles that have already encountered the target animal from the dictionary.
4. Cast information to the top vehicles in the dictionary. The number of vehicles that can receive information varies depending on the number of vehicles within the restricted area of the animal.
5. Each vehicle receives the information with the highest priority from the animal.

Algorithm for Selecting Notification Targets. Algorithm 1 defines a function that computes priority values for vehicles based on various factors including the status of animals, the status of vehicles, and the distance between animals and vehicles. Algorithm 2 then generates a dictionary to hold these priorities, calculating them for each vehicle in relation to all animals. Additionally, it identifies vehicles that are adjacent to animals based on a specific threshold distance. Afterward, the priorities are sorted in descending order to facilitate subsequent processing. In Algorithm 3, certain elements are removed from the dictionary, such as vehicles that have already been associated with an animal and vehicles

Algorithm 1. Algorithm for calculating priority

1: **procedure** CALC_PRIORITY(L_a, L_v, S_a, S_v)
2:     Input:
3:         L_a: animal's Location
4:         L_v: vehicle's Location
5:         S_a: animal's state
6:         S_v: vehicle's state
7:     Output:
8:         P_{av}: priority
9:     $r^2 = (L_a.x - L_v.x)^2 + (L_a.y - L_v.y)^2$
10:     $P_{av} = \frac{S_a \times S_v}{r^2}$
11:     **return** P_{av}
12: **end procedure**

Algorithm 2. Priority Calculation and Sorting

1: **for** each animal in all_animals **do**
2:     **for** each vehicle in all_vehicles **do**
3:         calculate *priority* for *animal* with *vehicle*: *animal.priority[vehicle]* ←
         calc_priority(*animal, vehicle*)
4:         **if** (*animal.location − vehicle.location*) < restricted_distance **then**
5:             *animal.neighbors* ← *vehicle*
6:         **end if**
7:     **end for**
8:     Sort *animal.priority* in descending order
9: **end for**

Algorithm 3. Selecting

1: **for** each animal in all_animals **do**
2:     *tmp_dict* ← animal.priority
3:     **for** each vehicle in all_vehicles **do**
4:         **if** (*vehicle* ∈ *animal.neighbors*) **or** (*animal* ∈ *vehicle.encounted_list*)
         then
5:             *tmp_dict*.pop(*vehicle*)
6:         **end if**
7:         *animal.cast_member*   ←   *tmp_dict*[:   restricted_number   −
         (length of animal.neighbors)]
8:     **end for**
9: **end for**

---

that are too close to an animal. Finally, Algorithm 4 ensures that each vehicle is assigned the position information of the animal with the highest priority, setting this information as the vehicle's vehicle.goalposition.

Algorithm 4. Receiving

1: **for** each animal in all_animals **do**
2:     **for** each vehicle in animal.cast_member **do**
3:         $vehicle.candidate \leftarrow animal$
4:     **end for**
5:     **for** each vehicle in all_vehicles **do**
6:         **for** each animal in vehicle.candidate **do**
7:             $max\_priority \leftarrow 0$
8:             **if** $max\_priority < animal.priority[vehicle]$ **then**
9:                 $max\_animal \leftarrow animal$
10:                $max\_priority \leftarrow animal.priority[vehicle]$
11:            **end if**
12:        **end for**
13:        **if** $max\_priority \neq 0$ **then**
14:            $vehicle.goal\_location \leftarrow animal.location$
15:        **end if**
16:    **end for**
17: **end for**

Algorithm 5. Spotting

1: **for** each vehicle in all_vehicles **do**
2:     **if** $(animal.goal_location - vehicle.location) <$ spotting_distance **then**
3:         $vehicle.encounted\_list \leftarrow animal$
4:     **end if**
5: **end for**

4   Simulation

To validate the efficacy of SafariCast, a experiment is conducted. In this context, a simulation is employed to assess the impact before installing equipment on actual vehicles.

4.1   Condition

We conducted simulations assuming 50 tourist vehicles would engage in a 60-minute game drive in a 10km × 10km safari area. When controlled by SafariCast, we delimited a range of 1km from the animal sighting position as the restricted area. We set the total number of vehicles within the restricted area and the number of vehicles receiving information to be 5. Additionally, the prioritization of receiving information by vehicles was determined by their priority values. Conversely, when not controlled by SafariCast, there were no restrictions on the number of people in the restricted area, and casting was done in order of proximity. We conducted simulations for each case described above. By comparing the fluctuations in the number of vehicles in the restricted area during the simulations, we evaluated the effectiveness of SafariCast.

4.2 Result

Figure 4 shows the numbers of vehicles within the restricted areas with and without SafariCast. From the figure, the introduction of SafariCast reduced the number of vehicles within the restricted area. Compared to the without control, SafariCast proved to be an effective way to control how vehicles move in animal habitat areas.

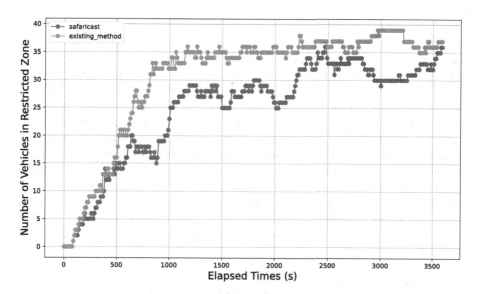

Fig. 4. Simulation result with and without SafariCast. This indicates the number of vehicles within the restricted area over time. The orange line represents the scenario without control, while the blue line represents the scenario with the proposed method. It is evident that employing the proposed method results in fewer vehicles within the restricted area. (Color figure online)

5 Discussion

The simulation result, as depicted in Fig. 4, confirms that SafariCast reduces the number of vehicles near animals, thereby potentially alleviating stress on the animals. Moreover, this study indicates the potential contribution of SafariCast not only to animal conservation but also to enhancing the quality of tourism experiences. The decrease in vehicle density within the restricted area is expected to enrich the opportunity of wildlife observation and natural experiences. However, in real game drives, animal positions are sometimes identified through visual scouting and communication among guides. These elements were not considered in the simulation, and their impact remains unclear. Furthermore, the outcome may vary depending on the extent to which the rarity of animals and encounter history are prioritized. Future research should explore the optimization of these parameters. Additionally, in this simulation, vehicles are set to move linearly toward the location of the animals. However, in actual game drives, there are geographical constraints such as roads and rivers, which should be considered. Conducting simulations under conditions closer to real-world settings, accounting for these constraints, is desirable.

6   Conclusion

SafariCast embodies an approach aimed at revitalizing the wildlife spotting and sharing experience on Kenyan safari drives. By intertwining real-time detection and information sharing technologies, it seeks to overcome the inefficiencies of traditional spotting methods while preserving the thrilling unpredictability of wildlife encounters. Based on the simulation results, we confirmed that controlling information with SafariCast can alleviate vehicle congestion near animals. However, in this simulation, we could not verify the equalization of tourist encounters with animals. In the next study, we aim to evaluate the effectiveness of simulations in animal encounter opportunities and flexibly address these elements in a trade-off relationship. Furthermore, following the evaluation of SafariCast through simulation, our aim is to pursue its practical application. In the future, we are considering extending the application beyond Kenya to other regions abundant in wildlife, thereby broadening the horizons for sustainable wildlife tourism.

Acknowledgments. This research is supported by
JST CREST JPMJCR22M4 and JSPS KAKENHI Grant Number 22H03580.

References

1. Barros, C., Moya-Gómez, B., García-Palomares, J.C.: Identifying temporal patterns of visitors to national parks through geotagged photographs. Sustainability **11**(24) (2019). https://doi.org/10.3390/su11246983, https://www.mdpi.com/2071-1050/11/24/6983
2. Ibadah, N., Minaoui, K., Rziza, M., Oumsis, M., Benavente-Peces, C.: Smart collection of real-time vehicular mobility traces (2018)
3. Juang, P., Oki, H., Wang, Y., Martonosi, M., Peh, L.S., Rubenstein, D.: Energy-efficient computing for wildlife tracking: design tradeoffs and early experiences with zebranet. SIGOPS Oper. Syst. Rev. **36**(5), 96–107 (2002). https://doi.org/10.1145/635508.605408
4. Karlsson, J., Ren, K., Li, H.: Tracking and identification of animals for a digital zoo. In: 2010 IEEE/ACM International Conference on Green Computing and Communications and International Conference on Cyber, Physical and Social Computing, pp. 510–515 (2010). https://doi.org/10.1109/GreenCom-CPSCom.2010.69
5. Kays, R., et al.: Does hunting or hiking affect wildlife communities in protected areas? J. Appl. Ecol. **54**(1), 242–252 (2017). https://doi.org/10.1111/1365-2664.12700, https://besjournals.onlinelibrary.wiley.com/doi/abs/10.1111/1365-2664.12700

6. Kim, Y.J., Lee, D.K., Kim, C.K.: Spatial tradeoff between biodiversity and nature-based tourism: Considering mobile phone-driven visitation pattern. Global Ecol. Conserv. **21**, e00899 (2020). https://doi.org/10.1016/j.gecco.2019.e00899, https://www.sciencedirect.com/science/article/pii/S2351989419305220
7. Park, J.K., Park, E.Y.: Animal monitoring scheme in smart farm using cloud-based system. ECTI Trans. Comput. Inf. Technol. (ECTI-CIT) **15**(1), 24–33 (2021)
8. Ranaweerage, E., Ranjeewa, A.D., Sugimoto, K.: Tourism-induced disturbance of wildlife in protected areas: a case study of free ranging elephants in Sri Lanka. Global Ecol. Conser. **4**, 625–631 (2015). https://doi.org/10.1016/j.gecco.2015.10.013, https://www.sciencedirect.com/science/article/pii/S2351989415001067
9. Shimura, K., Katayama, S., Urano, K., Leleito, E., Yonezawa, T., Kawaguchi, N.: Balancing excitement and environmental conservation in information dissemination for safari game drives. In: 2023 The 13th International Conference on the Internet of Things (2023)

The Impact of Road and Urban Infrastructure Variances on Electric Kick Scooter Travel

Ami Tsuruoka[1]([✉]), Hiroyuki Kadokura[2][iD], Tetsuo Shimizu[1,3][iD], and Kenro Aihara[1,4,5][iD]

[1] Tokyo Metropolitan University, Hachioji, Tokyo 192-0397, Japan
tsuruoka-ami@ed.tmu.ac.jp, {t-sim,kenro.aihara}@tmu.ac.jp
[2] Tohoku Gakuin University, Miyagi, Japan
kadokura@mail.tohoku-gakuin.ac.jp
[3] Kanazawa University, Ishikawa, Japan
[4] National Institute of Informatics, Tokyo, Japan
[5] Joint Support-Center for Data Science Research, Research Organization of Information and Systems, Tokyo, Japan
https://behavior.ues.tmu.ac.jp/

Abstract. Electric kick scooters are currently used in many countries, mainly in Europe and the United States. However, the route guidance of electric scooters is used as a substitute for that of bicycles, and it is possible that the routes are not easy to ride. In addition, studies on ride comfort have shown that vertical swaying of a vehicle in relation to the ground has a negative effect on ride comfort, and it is possible that the unevenness of the road surface has an effect on ride comfort for electric scooters as well.

This study, therefore, aims to clarify the relations between users and routes from the perspective of being able to ride ultra-compact mobility, such as electric kick scooters, safely and comfortably and to propose new options for route selection. As route physical conditions, the visibility by axial analysis and the pavement condition by the International Roughness Index (IRI) are used. Then, driving experiments were conducted to compare which routes are easier to drive. As a result, it was found that the route with less uneven surfaces and fewer traffic signals was more likely to be perceived as easier to drive, regardless of the attributes of the route selected. The visibility was found to have no effect on the ease of travel. In addition, since the respondents supported not only the shortest route but also the route guidance that is easy to travel, it is considered necessary to develop a route guidance service that actively adopts routes with less uneven road surfaces and fewer traffic signals.

Keywords: Micromobility · Behavior change · MaaS · Roughness of road · Space syntax

1 Introduction

Electric kick scooters have been rapidly gaining popularity in recent years as a convenient means of transportation, especially in Europe and the United States.

N. A. Streitz and S. Konomi (Eds.): HCII 2024, LNCS 14718, pp. 324–338, 2024.
https://doi.org/10.1007/978-3-031-59988-0_20

They are also positioned as a part of MaaS as a form of ultra-compact mobility, and are expected to continue to spread in the future as a means of solving the last mile problem. In Japan, the number of users is increasing due to the revision of the law to allow vehicles to drive without a driver's license in July 2023. However, research on electric kick scooters is scarce and needs extensive consideration from the research community to integrate political developments (e.g., financial support and regulation) with research and practice to evaluate and improve the e-scooter user experience [8].

Moreover, there is currently no route guidance specifically for electric kick scooters, and only routes that are legally allowed to be traveled are provided. Therefore, the current route guidance route is not an easy route for users to travel.

The purpose of this research is to clarify relations between users and routes from the perspective of being able to ride ultra-compact mobility, such as electric kick scooters, safely and comfortably and to propose new options for route selection. It is expected that this will reduce users' resistance against such mobility services. Expanding the popularity of such services may also contribute to improving the last mile problem.

2   Background

2.1   Electric Kick Scooters in Urban Area

Standing electric kick scooters are electrically powered vehicles with a handlebar, deck, and wheels. Usually only one person can ride it and travel at a relatively low speed [3]. Since the launch of the first shared e-scooter schemes in late 2017, e-scooters have become an increasingly popular means of transport for urban residents [5].

"The Promise and Pitfalls of E-Scooter Sharing", a 2019 report on the electric kick scooters market by the Boston Consulting Group, estimates that the electric kick scooters sharing market is growing rapidly and the global market will reach approximately The global market for electric kick scooter sharing is growing rapidly and is estimated to reach approximately 40–50 billion dollar by 2025 [2]. The website of the New Urban Mobility Alliance (NUMO)[1], a research institute on micromobility in the U.S., shows a map of the introduction of shared micromobility (electric bikes, electric kick scooters, and electric bicycles) in cities around the world. According to NUMO, as of April 2022, electric kick scooters have been introduced as a sharing service in a total of 64 countries and 1026 cities. Electric kick scooters are expected to be a solution for the "last mile" in urban areas, a means of transportation for seamless mobility services in Mobility as a Service (MaaS), and a new means of transportation in tourist areas.

Bird[2] is one of major sharing service providers and currently used in more than 300 cities around the world, and according to data compiled by Social Systems Corporation based on NUMO data

---

[1] https://www.numo.global/.
[2] https://www.bird.co/.

In a survey conducted mainly among Bird users, 94% of respondents reported feeling unsafe while riding. In addition to vehicle and pedestrian-related items, the survey also found that respondents felt danger in the areas of road surface and visibility.

2.2 Ride Comfort

Malone et al. summarized that the comfort in mobility effects that were assessed in the VRUITS, which was sponsored by the European Commission DG MOVE[3], are workload related to travel; stress related to travel; uncertainty related to travel; travelling in adverse conditions (weather etc.); and feeling of safety in relation to traffic [10].

Cano-Moreno et al. showed that a speed of 16 km/h is a threshold of being uncomfortable for a regular e-scooter rider in a very good pavement condition, while 23 km/h speed is harmful to riders [4]. This finding needs further exploration and could be discussed within the importance of speed limit and dedicated facilities for e-scooters [8].

Berg showed that it is necessary to develop a combination of both soft and hard measures for the vehicle-sharing system to be successful [1].

In existing research, vertical sway is related to ride comfort in several vehicles [11,12] and, that routes with good sight lines have higher pedestrian traffic volumes [7,14].

3   Methodology

3.1   Overview of the Plan

BRJ Corporation, which is developing the electric kick scooter Bird, is cooperating with us in this research[4]. At first a questionnaire survey to Bird users was conducted. In preparation for the driving experiment, the authors drove a vehicle throughout the area, measured IRI and acceleration, which are indicators of unevenness, and mapped them. For visibility, an axial analysis of the area to be analyzed based on SS theory [6,13] was used. Then, driving experiments and questionnaire surveys based on this information were conducted to obtain actual driving date and to analyze them.

3.2   Location

This study site is located south of Tachikawa Station. This is the area where the Bird service, which cooperated in this study, is deployed. Tachikawa station is located in Tokyo, Japan. On the north side of the station, there are commercial facilities, a national park, a disaster prevention base, and large-scale commercial facilities. The south side is mainly residential area, dotted with parks and schools.

---

[3] https://www.polisnetwork.eu/project/vruits/.
[4] Bird service in Japan is operated by BRJ, Inc.

3.3   Road Indices

The authors used SS theory and IRI to analyze the urban and road structures of the target area. For IRI, smartphones were installed in a car and an electric kick scooter, and acceleration and position data were measured. Then, the obtained acceleration values in the X, Y and Z axes were squared and added together, and color scaled on the map. Based on the analysis results, six travel routes with different characteristics were created. Subjects who answered the pre-running survey are asked to run along these routes, and acceleration and brain waves are measured and a questionnaire survey is conducted. Based on the analysis results of SS theory and IRI before and after the driving experiment, and the results of the questionnaire, the characteristics of the routes that are easy to drive with an electric kick scooter are determined.

4   Experimental Settings

4.1   Experiment Period

Experiments were conducted in four days in November and December of 2023. There were two sessions in one day and each session had up to five subjects and spent about three hours including instructions.

4.2   Subjects

Call for participation in the experiment was sent to registrants of Bird service in Japan by BRJ, Inc. In addition, students of the experimenter's department also participated. A total of 24 people participated in the experiment. Three of them only drove on a part of the route.

4.3   Experimental Equipment

Electric Kick Scooter. In this experiment, the electric kick scooters of the Bird service were used. On the day of the experiment, the required number of kick scooters were prepared in advance at a port near site 1, and the subjects themselves borrowed the kick scooters to secure a car body. The subjects were provided with coupons by BRJ Corporation, which they could use without having to pay the service fee, and each subject applied the coupons.

Smartphone. Smartphones (Apple iPhone XR) were prepared for the experiment to measure positional information, speed and direction of the vehicle, and acceleration and rotation of the vehicle body. These smartphones were used with necessary applications to record data and to support driving. The application for measurement was installed and used. In addition, the application Mind Monitor[5] was installed and used to record electroencephalograph quickly. The Google Maps application[6] was used to check the route and the user's location during the run. These applications were set to start recording before the start of the first run, and were used to record constantly during the experiment.

---

[5] https://apps.apple.com/jp/app/mind-monitor/id988527143.
[6] https://apps.apple.com/us/app/google-maps/id585027354.

Simple Electroencephalograph. In this experiment, Interaxo's "Muse2"[7] were used to capture electroencephalograph (EEG) data while riding. The data measured by Muse2 is sent to Mind Monitor on a smartphone via Bluetooth and recorded by the application.

4.4 Procedure

1. After gathering at the meeting point, participants will borrow a kick scooter and move to the starting point (Site 1) for a brief explanation of the experiment, confirmation of their willingness to participate, and explanation of the following procedures
   - Traveling along a specified route
   - If the driver is not comfortable driving on a roadway where vehicles are running side by side, he/she may move on the sidewalk and push the vehicle by hand.
   - Before the start of the ride, the specified route is read out on the map app of the smartphone attached to the kick scooter, so that the user can confirm his/her own position and route at the time of the ride.
   - After each run, they must answer a web-based question about the run.
2. After each run, answer the web-based questions about the run.
3. Subjects who agreed to the protocol were fitted with Muse2, a smart headband including EEG brain sensors.
4. They traveled the six routes in the specified order and answered the driving questions.
5. After completing the entire route, they answered a series of questions and interviews about the whole
6. Administrative procedures such as gratuities, etc.
7. Dissolution

4.5 Routes Traveled

Figure 1 shows the six routes traveled that day. In addition to the shortest route, these routes were set up so that the unevenness and visibility of the road surface measured in advance would be varied.

5 Experimental Results

5.1 Questionnaire Results for All Driving Routes

Figure 2 shows the results of the questionnaire after all the routes were traveled. Route 3 was selected most frequently, followed by Routes 2 and 4. Route 1 was the shortest route displayed in the Google route search, but it was the second least selected route after route 6. Figure 3 shows the result of asking the respondents whether they would like to see the "easiest route" or route 1 (the shortest route) displayed in the route guidance system. No one preferred to have

Fig. 1. Routes traveled

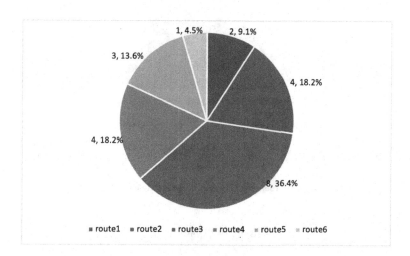

Fig. 2. Easiest route to travel

the "shortest route" displayed, and more than 50% of the respondents preferred to be able to select one.

Figure 4 compares the running time of each route for the subjects who answered that each route was easy to drive. The subject (user 5) who selected route 5 as the easiest route to travel has a longer travel time for the first run of route 4, since this is the first run on the electric kick scooter. The subjects (user 6) who selected route 6 as the easiest route to travel have some missing data because they deviated from the route significantly when they traveled route 5. Figure 5 shows the difference between the maximum and minimum values of the running time in Fig. 4, and the difference between the running time of the easiest route to drive and the minimum value. The difference between the maximum and the minimum travel time of the easiest route is within 3 min for the five participants. Table 1 shows the preliminary survey of the six participants in Fig. 4, in which they were asked what route they would choose when riding an electric kick scooter. All of the subjects preferred the route that arrived at the destination faster, but none of the subjects actually chose the route that arrived the fastest.

5.2   Characteristics for Each Route

Figure 6 is a box-and-whisker plot of acceleration obtained for all subjects during their runs. Figure 7 is the result of focusing on those acceleration values greater than 100. The acceleration for route 2 was the largest and route 3 the smallest. However, all data did not differ significantly up to the third quartile.

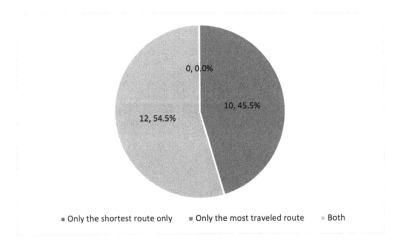

Fig. 3. Routing guide

---

[7] https://choosemuse.com/products/muse-2.

Table 1. Easiest route and route selection preferences

Subject	Easiest route	What route to choose when traveling on an electric kick scooter
user 1	route1	Routes that arrive at the destination faster Routes with fewer cars and pedestrians Routes with smooth road surface
user 2	route2	Routes that arrive at the destination faster Routes that allow you to arrive at your destination at a lower cost Routes that include bicycle ways
user 3	route3	Routes that arrive at the destination faste
user 4	route4	Routes that arrive at the destination faster Scenic routes Routes with smooth road surface
user 5	route5	Routes that arrive at the destination faster
user 6	route6	Routes that arrive at the destination faster Routes with fewer cars and pedestrians

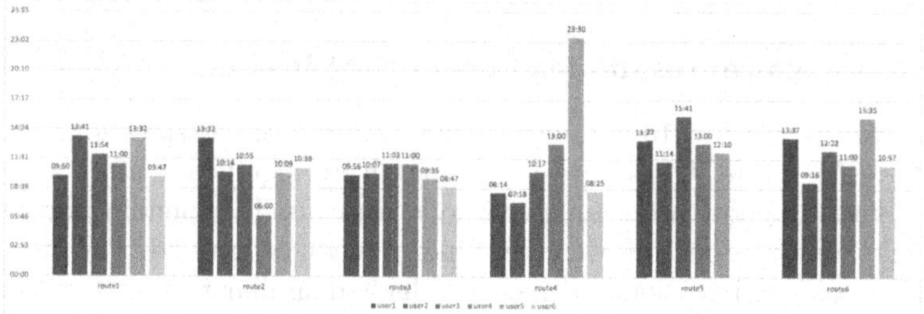

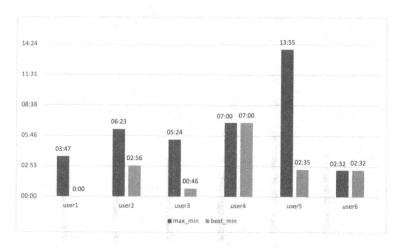

Fig. 4. Running time of each route

Fig. 5. Differences between the maximum and minimum values in Fig. 4

Figure 8 shows the product of the integration value and the distance for each travel route, expressed as a function of the distance. There is no significant difference among the routes, but the integration values of routes 2 and 4 are

Table 2. Number of right/left turns and traffic lights

route	right turns	left turns	traffic lights
1	1	1	14
2	2	2	11
3	2	2	8
4	2	2	8
5	2	2	11
6	2	2	12

high and those of routes 3 and 5 are relatively small. Table 2 shows the number of right/left turns and the number of traffic signals for each route. The route with the highest number of signals is route 1, and the routes with the lowest number of signals are routes 3 and 4.

5.3 Questionnaire Results for Each Travel Route

Figure 9, 10, 11, 12, and 13 summarize the averages of the questionnaires conducted for each route. These are those that were significant after analysis of variance. Two different processing methods were used, depending on whether the missing values in the data were kept in the mean or ignored. The "fewer cars and pedestrians" and "easier to drive" graphs had similar relationships between the routes.

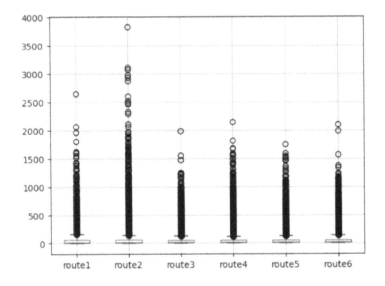

Fig. 6. Acceleration

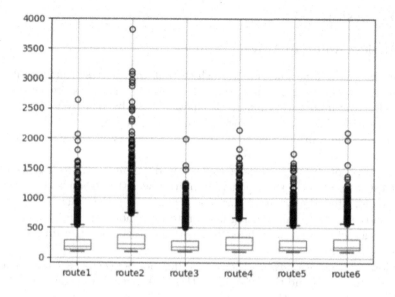

Fig. 7. Acceleration focusing on values greater than 100

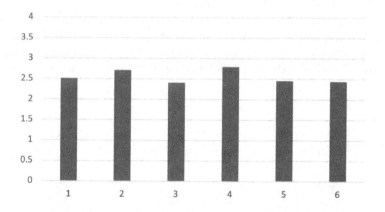

Fig. 8. Integration value

5.4 Characteristics of Each Attribute

In this experiment, most of the subjects were male and had a driver's license, and there was a bias in the attributes of the subjects. In addition, most of the subjects felt danger when driving in terms of vehicles, pedestrians, and road surfaces, and there was no difference in the number of subjects who felt danger.

6 Discussion

6.1 Easiest Route to Travel

The results of the final questionnaire show that the shortest route (route 1) is not necessarily the easiest route to travel. Route 3, which was the easiest route to travel in the final questionnaire, is characterized by relatively low acceleration, suggesting that the route with the above characteristics may be preferred. Furthermore, the route tended to be selected as the easiest route to travel when the number of traffic signals was small.

The "Ease of driving" of each route was different from the results of the final questionnaire, with the result that route 1 was the easiest to travel. Many subjects indicated that route 1 had fewer cars and pedestrians. According to Kim's study [9], stress values using heart rate were more stressful than the same traffic mode, which may be related to the ease of driving when different traffic modes are mixed.

As for the integration value, there is a difference between the value calculated by the axial analysis and the "visibility" (Fig. 12) perceived by the subjects, and both graphs do not show the same tendency as the graphs of the "Ease of driving" (Fig. 9) and the "Easiest route to drive" (Fig. 2) . In this experiment, it is not necessary to provide route guidance that is tailored to the user's attributes, because the result shows that the route that is easy to travel is independent of the user's attributes.

The "Ease of driving" of each route differed from the results of the final questionnaire. They could not make a relative evaluation because the subjects were answered and sent after each run, and could not be viewed after it was sent. The final questionnaire was answered while showing the route to the subjects, and it is considered that the subjects will choose the route that is easy to drive

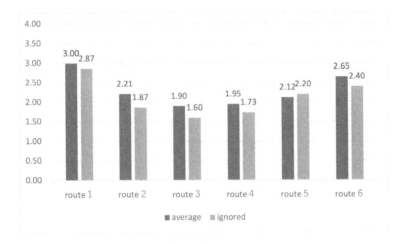

Fig. 9. Easier to drive

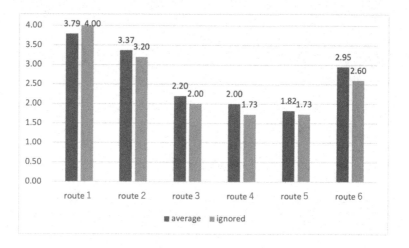

Fig. 10. Fewer cars and pedestrians

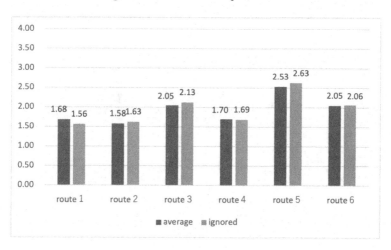

Fig. 11. Fast to arrive

from their memory again next time, but unfortunately, it is still a matter of speculation. In this study, the authors give priority to the results of the final questionnaire and treat route 3 as the easiest route to drive.

6.2   Route Guidance

In this study, routes with low acceleration and few traffic signals were characterized as easy to travel. In the following discussion, a route with the above characteristics is defined as a route that is easy to travel. As for the route guidance, all subjects were positive about the display of the easiest route to drive.

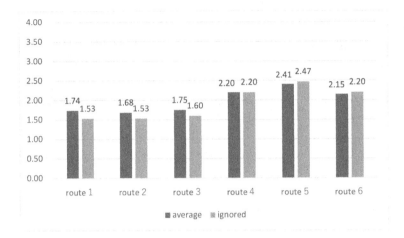

Fig. 12. Visibility

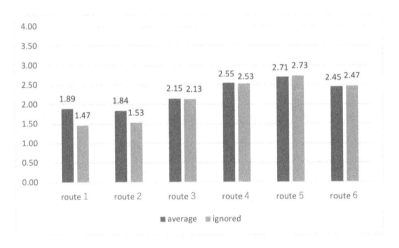

Fig. 13. Wide road

Therefore, a flexible service such as displaying not only the currently displayed shortest route but also the easiest route to drive would be preferred.

In the comparison of some subjects, while they preferred the route that arrived at the destination earlier, none of the subjects actually chose the route that arrived the fastest. In this study, since the route guidance was provided by a smart phone, it was possible to know the travel time. However, it is unlikely that the subjects knew the travel time for each route, since they were not informed of the travel time. This indicates that the characteristics of routes that are preferred before driving and those that are perceived to be easy to drive after driving are different. It is also possible that there are features that are more important than the feature of early arrival. Furthermore, it is possible that the differences in time for each travel route were too small to be perceived.

7   Conclusion

This paper analyzed the relationship between the results of the analysis of urban structure and road structure using SS theory and acceleration, and the users' psychology. Based on the results of the analysis, the paper showed a possibility of new options for route selection in order to reduce the fear of electric scooters users. The pre-run survey revealed that many users were concerned not only about vehicles and pedestrians, but also about the road surface. In the driving experiment, the subjects were asked to randomly drive on six routes, and questionnaires and acceleration measurements were conducted.

It was found that electric kick scooters, regardless of their attributes, were more likely to find routes with less uneven road surfaces and fewer traffic signals easier to travel. In addition, the electric kick scooters supported not only the shortest route but also the route guidance that is easy to travel. Therefore, it is necessary to develop a route guidance service that actively adopts routes with less uneven road surfaces and fewer traffic lights. However, the tires of an electric scooters are thinner than those of a car, and the acceleration rate of the scooters tends to vary depending on the place where the scooters is traveling. Therefore, it is necessary to develop a wide range of uneven road surfaces, such as bicycle lanes.

Acknowledgments. The authors would like to thank BRJ Inc. to support the surveys and the experiments of this research.

This work was supported by JSPS KAKENHI Grant Number JP22H03856.

References

1. Berg, J., Henriksson, M., Ihlström, J.: Comfort first! vehicle-sharing systems in urban residential areas: the importance for everyday mobility and reduction of car use among pilot users. Sustainability **11**(9), 2521 (2019). https://doi.org/10.3390/su11092521
2. Boston Consulting Group: The promise and pitfalls of e-scooter sharing (2019). https://www.bcg.com/ja-jp/publications/2019/promise-pitfalls-e-scooter-sharing
3. Bozzi, A.D., Aguilera, A.: Shared E-scooters: a review of uses, health and environmental impacts, and policy implications of a new micro-mobility service. Sustainability **13**(16), 8676 (2021). https://doi.org/10.3390/su13168676
4. Cano-Moreno, J.D., Islán, M.E., Blaya, F., D'Amato, R., Juanes, J.A., Soriano, E.: E-scooter vibration impact on driver comfort and health. J. Vibr. Eng. Technol. **9**(6), 1023–1037 (2021). https://doi.org/10.1007/s42417-021-00280-3
5. Fitt, H., Curl, A.: The early days of shared micromobility: a social practices approach. J. Transp. Geogr. **86**, 102779 (2020). https://doi.org/10.1016/J.JTRANGEO.2020.102779
6. Hillier, B.: Space is the Machine. Cambridge University Press, Cambridge (2007). https://spaceisthemachine.com/

7. Inohae, T., Hokao, K., Nagaie, T.: An analysis of urban configurations by using space syntax theory and the development trend. In: Papers and proceedings of the Geographic Information Systems Association, vol. 17, pp. 111–114 (2008). https://cir.nii.ac.jp/crid/1571135650848014592. (in Japanese)

8. Kazemzadeh, K., Sprei, F.: Towards an electric scooter level of service: a review and framework. Travel Behav. Soc. **29**, 149–164 (2022). https://doi.org/10.1016/J.TBS.2022.06.005

9. Kin, T., Shibuya, D.: Study on the Biological Stress Measurement of Cyclist. Japan Society of Civil Engineers. (in Japanese)

10. Malone, K., Silla, A., Johanssen, C., Bell, D.: Safety, mobility and comfort assessment methodologies of intelligent transport systems for vulnerable road users. Eur. Transp. Res. Rev. **9**(2), 21 (2017). https://doi.org/10.1007/s12544-017-0235-y

11. Okabe, M., Takahashi, K., Tomiyama, K., Hagiwara, T., Moriishi, K.: Construction of evaluation index for road surface roughness based on the bicycle vibration model. J. Jpn. Soc. Civil Engineers Ser. E1 (Pavement Eng.) **75**, L67–L75 (2019). https://doi.org/10.2208/jscejpe.75.2_L67. https://www.jstage.jst.go.jp/article/jscejpe/75/2/75_L67/_article/-char/ja/. (in Japanese)

12. Ono, T., Yoshimura, S., Shimizu, Y.: Route selection of an ambulance considering the disease or injury of a patient. Trans. JSME **advpub**, 20–00223 (2020). https://doi.org/10.1299/transjsme.20-00223. (in Japanese)

13. Ota, A.: A Study on Factors of Prosperity in Nagoya CBD by Using Space Syntax Measures. Nagoya Institute of Technology (2016). (in Japanese)

14. Ueno, J., Kishimoto, T.: An analysis of pedestrian movement in multilevel complex by space syntax theory. J. City Plan. Inst. Jpn. **43**(3), 49–54 (2008). https://doi.org/10.11361/journalcpij.43.3.49

Factors Influencing Continuance Usage of Smart City Apps: A Mixed Study Based on Behavioral Reasoning Theory

Siyuan Wu[1](✉), Ruizhi Wang[1], Qing Zhang[1], Xuzheng Zhang[1], Dayou Wu[2], and Guochao Peng[1](✉)

[1] School of Information Management, Sun Yat-Sen University, Guangzhou 510006, Guangdong, China
wusy28@mail2.sysu.edu.cn, penggch@mail.sysu.edu.cn
[2] International Institute for Advanced Data Management Study, Guangzhou, China

Abstract. The continuous usage behavior of Smart City App users is pivotal to the success of smart technologies and the realization of smart cities. A mixed-method was used to construct a theoretical model of users' continuous usage behavior of Smart City App based on qualitative findings, and an extended model of continuous use of Smart City App users was constructed and the model was empirically investigated through questionnaires. The findings underscore the applicability of behavioral reasoning theory in elucidating the inherent mechanisms underlying users' sustained engagement with the Smart City App. The behavioral rationality (adoption/rejection) of users jointly contributes to the intention of continuous use of Smart City App users. Among them, referent network size and perceived government support constitute the main reasons for users to adopt Smart City App. However, usage barriers, tradition barriers, and value barriers are important reasons for users to reject Smart City App. This study not only expands the purview of behavioral reasoning theory and bridges the divide with traditional frameworks in examining users' continuous usage patterns but also sheds light on the challenges and motivational factors users encounter in navigating the Smart City App. The insights gained offer valuable guidance to app developers and managers in enhancing user engagement and fostering the app's overall success.

Keywords: Smart City App · Continuance Usage Intention · Behavioral Reasoning Theory · Innovation Resistance Theory · Mixed-method

1 Introduction

As one of the technical elements supporting smart city initiatives, Smart City Apps have become an important channel for cities to achieve smart governance. Smart City Apps is a core component of the urban ecosystem [1], which connects urban infrastructure, public service departments, city brain's computing

N. A. Streitz and S. Konomi (Eds.): HCII 2024, LNCS 14718, pp. 339–355, 2024.
https://doi.org/10.1007/978-3-031-59988-0_21

platforms and resident users to achieve data interaction, service interoperability, and collaborative governance among entities [2]. It mainly uses mobile phones as a carrier to provide urban residents with necessary medical appointments, government approvals, living payments, transportation and other services, such as *iShenzhen, Jinxin Office, Smart Ningbo* etc. In 2022, the number of registered and active Smart City Apps in various regions has grown repeatedly [3]. And smart apps have gradually become an important way for local governments to explore new modes of urban governance and improve governance efficiency.

Smart City App has enormous development value and prospects. However, it still faces problems such as low public penetration rate [7], low satisfaction [2,4], low willingness to use [5,6] and other practical problems. Consequently, strategizing ways to enhance the sustained engagement of smart city app users and broaden the user base for ongoing utilization emerges as a critical challenge requiring immediate resolution. Furthermore, it is pivotal in realizing the full potential and value maximization of smart city applications.

Previous research have applied Expectation Confirmation Model [8], Unified Theory of Acceptance and Use of Technology [9], Cognitive Theory of Emotion [10] to conduct extensive and in-depth research on users' continuous use behavior. According to these traditional theories and models, the relationship between factors such as users' attitude, satisfaction, perceived usefulness, and usage intentions has been extensively studied. However, research on continued usage is still lacking, particularly in the context of considering both user adoption and rejection reasons. Behavioral Reasoning Theory suggests that individuals frequently search for a set of reasons(i.e. specific adoption and rejection reasons) in memory to defend their intentions or actions. Those reasons of adoption and rejection be called behavioral rationality(reason set), which is a more direct and critical factor that influences people's behavioral intentions and decisions [11]. Therefore, it is crucial to refine the reasons for continuous use from the perspective of behavioral rationality in order to gain a deeper understanding of the behavioral mechanisms of users' continuous use.

Consequently, in order to provide a new and possible explanatory path for the continuous usage behavior of Smart City App users, this study intends to use a mixed-method combining qualitative and quantitative research, introduce behavioral rationality, use Behavioral Reasoning Theory and Innovation Resistance Theory as theoretical foundations to deeply explore the factors influencing continuance usage of Smart City App users. This study adopts a multifaceted approach to examine user interactions with Smart City Apps. Initially, employing a qualitative research framework, it delves into the intricacies of user adoption and rejection of these apps through comprehensive interviews. This phase aims to discern and catalog the precise factors that either impede or facilitate continued user engagement. Subsequently, the study transitions to a quantitative phase, employing meticulously structured surveys to empirically validate the continuous usage model, which was initially conceptualized and expanded upon through qualitative insights.

2   Literature Review

Smart City App is an effective tool to promote smart cities and an important channel for citizens to directly participate in urban public life [12]. In the early days, many smart app applications with different functions were born in different fields, such as smart bus [13], handheld medical [14], and smart parking [15]. Since the rise of the "City-as-a-Platform" concept [16], local governments are more inclined to create one-stop Smart City Apps [17], which means to integrate various single smart service systems into one terminal, simultaneously covering multiple fields such as healthcare, transportation, elderly care [18] and so on. These apps benefit the business collaboration and data sharing among various systems, as well as enhance the comprehensive operation and management capabilities of cities. Famous one-stop Smart City Apps include Tianjin's "Jinxin Office" and Guangzhou's "Suihao Office" one-stop Smart City Apps. We focus on the one-stop Smart City App in this study, explore the impact mechanism of continuous user use, and providing valuable policy suggestions for Smart City App's development and management personnel.

Previous research primarily studied three aspects of smart city technology and relative applications: 1) Technique. Scholars focus on hardware or system design for applications, such as improving sensors [19], embedded positioning and tracking systems [20], and algorithm development [21]. 2) Implementation barriers. Peng (2017) [1]found that government promotion and public awareness are two important factors that can affect the use of smart parking apps by citizens; McGrath (2016) [22] found that mandatory government policies and users' privacy concerns are the determining factors hindering the promotion of smart services through case studies in different countries. 3) Behavior intentions of users. Research on the behavioral intention of smart applications mostly focuses on user satisfaction [4], adoption [23], and usage [24], with relatively few studies on the continuous usage of users after adoption [6,25].

In the information system domain, it is widely acknowledged that the success of a system depends on users' continuous usage rather than their initial adoption [25,26]. In recent years, the interests of scholars in this domain have gradually shifted from users' adoption research to their continuous use research. Scholars mainly empirically investigated the factors that influence the sustained use of Smart City App users based on classical theoretical models, such as Expectation Confirmation Theory (ECM), Technology Acceptance Model (TAM), and System Success Model (Delone and Mclean Theory, D&M). Bhattacherjee [26] proposed the Information System Continuous Use Model (ECM-ISC) after integrating ECM and TAM model. He found that perceived usefulness, expected confirmation, and satisfaction affect users' willingness to continue using. Wang [25] drew on the theory of task-technology matching and the ECM-ISC model to verify that perceived matching, perceived usefulness, and user satisfaction all have the positive impact on user willingness to continue using. Based on trust theory, Xu et al. [27] confirmed that confirmed that public trust, perceived quality, and public satisfaction have a positive impact on sustained use basing on trust theory. Research above mainly explains the continuous usage of smart systems from users' adoption reasons(such as perceived usefulness, usability, perceived quality, satisfaction, trust, etc.). Nevertheless, the underlying factors influencing users' reluctance to apply Smart City Apps have not been thoroughly examined. Regarding the Smart City App, behavioral rationality of users' continuance usage encompasses the reasons behind adopting and rejecting the app. Both factors interact in distinct ways that collectively influence users' continued usage of the app.

In summary, there are still the following issues in current research on the continuous use of Smart City App users: Firstly, most existing studies construct user sustained use models from a single perspective of users' positive support, without considering the negative impact of their opposition reasons. Second, previous research has not comprehensively studied users' sustained use from the perspective of behavioral rationality. In addition, current literature mostly uses questionnaire data to study the factors that influence users' sustained use, but the specific adoption and rejection reasons for deep sustained use by users have not been fully understood. To fill the research gaps, this study builds upon Behavioral Reasoning Theory and employs a mixed-method approach using a sequential design (QUAL→QUAN) to explore the impact mechanism of sustained use among Smart City Apps users. We would like to address the following questions: 1) What are the core elements that constitute the adoption and rejection reasons for users to continue using the Smart City Apps? 2) How do users' adoption and rejection reasons affect their willingness to continue using the Smart City Apps?

3   Theoretical Framework and Hypotheses

This article uses Behavioral Reasoning Theory (BRT) to understand the continuous use behavior of Smart City Apps users. The BRT theory was proposed by Westaby [28], introducing behavioral rationality into traditional rational behavior theory, and it has been widely applied in the fields of behavioral science and leadership decision-making.

The BRT theory recognizes the importance of behavioral rationality in behavior and suggests that a complete understanding of human decision-making and behavior should include individual reasons for supporting and opposing a given behavior [29]. Behavioral rationality refers to the specific reasons that individuals use to justify their expected behavior. These are considered antecedent variables that contribute to their attitudes and intentions. The BRT theory suggests that the causes of behavior are reinforced and can be used to support, distort, or rationalize individuals' actual behavior [28]. Therefore, behavioral rationality can influence an individual's attitude and overall motivation. Building on this, to provide a comprehensive understanding of the sustained use of Smart City Apps users, this study proposes a framework based on the BRT theory that connects the rationality, attitude, and intention of user behavior (as shown in Fig. 1).

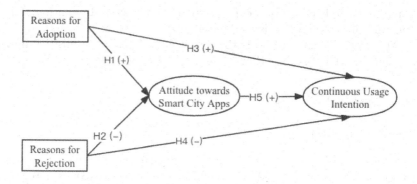

Fig. 1. The initial theoretical framework for the continuance usage of Smart City Apps base on Behavioral Reasoning Theory

According to BRT theory, behavioral rationality predicts attitudes and behaviors. Individuals rationalize their attitudes and intentions through justification, promoting their intended behavior. In the context of using the Smart City App, behavioral rationality specifically refers to the reasons why users adopt and reject the Smart City Apps. Users may strongly perceive the benefits of adoption. However, due to rejection reasons such as value barriers and usage barriers, they may choose not to continue using it. Therefore, the rationality of behavior will shape individual attitudes in this context. Therefore, the following assumptions are proposed:

H1: The reasons why users adopt Smart City Apps have a positive impact on their attitude towards Smart City Apps.

H2: The rejection reasons of users towards the Smart City Apps have a negative impact on their attitude towards the Smart City Apps.

Westaby [30,31] found that behavioral rationality can also directly affect one's intention, meaning that both sub dimensions of reason contribute to behavior prediction. This has been supported by various studies. The field of social psychology has also confirmed that rational performance alone explains behavior beyond attitude [32]. As Wu et al. [33] found, although consumers hold a positive attitude towards products, they still refuse to purchase due to price. Therefore, the following assumptions are proposed:

H3: The reasons for the adoption of Smart City Apps by users have a positive impact on their continuous usage intention.

H4: The reasons for the rejection of Smart City Apps by users have a negative impact on their continuous usage intention.

Attitude refers to an individual's perception of specific things, concepts, or behaviors; that is, their evaluation or stance on things. The relationship between attitude, intention, and behavior has been extensively explored by scholars, and many have also demonstrated a significant correlation between attitude and intention [30,31,34]. Ajzen proposed the Theory of Planned Behavior, which

states that attitude is the most robust predictor of behavioral intention. Therefore, the following assumption is proposed:

H5: The user's attitude towards the Smart City Apps has a positive impact
on their continuous usage intention.

4   Research Methods

4.1   Mixed-Method

Mixed research methods can provide more comprehensive insights than single
qualitative or quantitative methods, while addressing both confirmatory and
exploratory research questions [35], thus offering a multi-level understanding of
the phenomenon being studied [36]. This study adopts a mixed research method
of sequential exploration [37], which is divided into two stages.

At the first stage, we conducted semi-structured interviews. Open coding was
applied to analyze the interview data. We also referred to innovation resistance
theory and Network Externalities Theory to identify and extract relevant topics
on the rationality of respondent behaviors. Experiments at this stage were to
determine the specific reasons for users' adoption and rejection of the Smart City
Apps. And, building on this research, we conducted experiments at the second
stage. To be specific, we collected data through questionnaires to validate our
proposed user continuous usage model.

4.2   Interview

Collection of Interview Data. Due to the fact that this study targets post-
adoption users, who are aware of and have used the Smart City Apps, two screening questions were used to screen interviewees, and ultimately we interviewed 20
interviewees. In order to ensure the quality of interview data, we used a combination of convenience and purposive sampling strategies to select respondents.
Meanwhile, to overcome geographical limitations, this study adopted a combination of online and offline interview formats, with an average interview duration
of approximately 10–25 min for respondents. The demographic information of
the interviewees is shown in Table 1.

Analysis Procedures. After the interview, we followed Braun and Clarke's [38]
method to conduct thematic analysis of the interview text. The thematic analysis
is divided into four steps: firstly, two researchers proofread and repeatedly read
all interview texts. Secondly, to facilitate the determination of data saturation,
20 interviewees were grouped into 4 groups for encoding. During the encoding
process of the last group, if there were no new codes appeared, the data was
indicated to reach saturation. Finally, we rechecked and ensured that the allocation to the core theme and subtopics follows a consistent pattern, then we
determined the final naming. Thirdly, based on the research objectives, the two
researchers classified the codes mentioned by more than half of the respondents

Table 1. Information of Interview Samples (N = 20)

Respondent	Sex	Age	Education Level	Occupation
P1	Female	27	Doctor	Civil Servant
P2	Female	25	Postgraduate	Middle School Teachers
P3	Female	25	Postgraduate	Freelancer
P4	Female	24	Undergraduate	Enterprise employees
P5	Male	31	Undergraduate	State- owned enterprise employees
P6	Female	32	Doctor	Student
P7	Male	21	Undergraduate	Student
P8	Male	29	Doctor	Middle School Teachers
P9	Male	30	Doctor	Student
P10	Female	29	Postgraduate	State- owned enterprise employees
P11	Male	18	Undergraduate	Student
P12	Male	22	Undergraduate	Unemployment
P13	Female	32	Doctor	College Teacher
P14	Male	21	Undergraduate	Student
P15	Female	30	Doctor	Enterprise Postdoctoral
P16	Female	27	Undergraduate	Civil Servant
P17	Male	32	Undergraduate	Enterprise employees
P18	Male	29	Undergraduate	Enterprise employees
P19	Male	24	Undergraduate	Freelancer
P20	Female	33	Doctor	College Teacher

as sub-themes, and similar sub-themes as core themes, dividing them into users' adoption reasons and rejection reasons. Finally, we rechecked and ensured that the allocation to the core theme and sub-themes follows a consistent pattern, then we determined the final naming of themes and sub-themes.

4.3 Questionnaire

Data Collection and Samples. We used a questionnaire survey with probability sampling and convenience sampling methods, and finally collected a total of 396 questionnaires. After excluding questionnaires with a short answer time. To ensure the accuracy and scientific nature of the questionnaire sample, we excluded questionnaires with a short completion time and deleted questionnaires from users who had never used the smart city application, resulting in 348 valid questionnaires. Table 2 shows the basic information.

Data Analysis. We applied the Partial Least Squares (PLS) method in this study. To confirm whether the sample data falls within the applicable range of

Table 2. Population characteristic information statistics of Questionnaire Data (N = 348)

Variable	Option	Number	Proportion\%	Variable	Option	Number	Proportion\%
Sex	Male	133	38.2	Age	<=22	90	25.9
	Female	215	61.8		23-32	229	65.80
Living Area	Capital, Municipalities Directly Under The Central Government, And Provincial Capital Cities	243	70		33-42	22	6.3
	Other Small And Medium-Sized Enterprises City	59	17		43-52	23	6.6
	County Town	34	9.7		>=53	6	1.7
	Township	4	1.1	Education Level	Junior high school and below	4	1.1
	Countryside	1	0.3		High school	22	6.3
	Other Regions (such As Overseas)	3	0.9		College/ Under-graduate	157	45.1
					Graduate and above	155	44.5
					Others	10	2.9

PLS-SEM, we checked the multivariate characteristics of the data before formal analysis. The skewness and kurtosis values [46] fall within the range of -2 to 2, indicating a normal distribution of the data. The VIF value (2.16–4.088) indicates the absence of multicollinearity [47].

5   Results

5.1   Qualitative Study

Thematic Analysis Results and Model Expansion. According to the thematic analysis, we identified Referent Network Size (RNS) and Perceived Government Support as sub-themes of "adoption reasons" for core theme users; identified usage barriers, value barriers, and tradition barriers as sub-themes of the core theme of "rejection reasons" for users (as shown in Table 3).

Referent network size is one of the key concepts in Network Externalities Theory (NET) [39], which is the user's perception of the number of participants in a given network [40]. The Network Externalities Theory(NET) suggests that the value technology gives to users increases with the number of users [41], and referent network size play an important role in the diffusion of technology. Therefore, the referent network size is the reason why users adopt Smart

City Apps. Perceived government support refers to the subjective evaluation of user support for administrative agencies (government departments). According to Resource Dependence Theory (RDT), resource support from the external environment will increase users' confidence in the technology or system to some extent. Thereby affecting individual's sustained investment [43]. Therefore, perceived government support is also the reason why users continue to adopt Smart City Apps.

The core theme of "rejection reasons" is also consistent with the findings from Ram and Shetch [45]. The Innovation Resistance Theory (IRT) divides barriers into value barriers, risk barriers, usage barriers, tradition barriers, and image barriers [45]. According to qualitative analysis, usage barriers, value barriers, and tradition barriers are the main reasons for Smart City App users to reject. The extended theoretical model constructed based on this is shown in Fig. 2.

Table 3. Qualitative analysis results

Core Theme	Sub Theme	Excerpt from Interview Text	Supporting Theories
Adoption Reasons	Referent Network Size	"My colleague told me that she pays the water and electricity bills directly on the app, and I also feel that it's more convenient." (P3)	Network Externalities Theory [39]
		"Many people around me are using this APP"(P16)	
	Perceived Government Support	"Many places in the government hall have posted tutorials on using apps to process approvals" (P8)	Perceived Government Support [43]
		"I feel that the government has provided promotion and publicity for this app" (P11)	
Rejection Reasons	Value Barrier	"I think it's useless, so I uninstalled it" (P14)	Innovation Resistance Theory [44]
		"Its push content doesn't help me at all, but rather makes me very annoyed" (P11)	
	Tradition Barrier	"I don't trust APP's technology."(P11)	
		"I am still used to handling transactions offline" (P8)	
	Usage Barrier	"This app is quite complex to use" (P6)	
		"I found that my phone burns when using this app" (P11)	
		"For older people, it can be difficult to use, just like my dad thinks it's difficult, so he doesn't use it" (P20)	

5.2 Quantitative Study

Reliability Analysis. We used Cronbach's Alpha (internal consistency) and CR (composite reliability) to test reliability. As shown in Table 4, all constructed latent variables' Cronbach's Alpha values and CR values are higher than the threshold of 0.7 [47,48], indicating that the scale used in this study has internal consistency and good reliability.

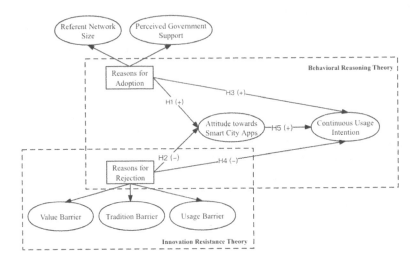

Fig. 2. An Extended Research Model for the Continuous Use of Smart City App Users

Table 4. Reliability and Validity Index Coefficients

Variable	Item	Factor Loading	Composite Reliability	Cronbach's Alpha	AVE
Attitude, (ATT) (Yadav, Panda & Kumar,2022 [51])	ATT1	0.869	0.938	0.901	0.834
	ATT2	0.933			
	ATT3	0.936			
Continuous Use Intention, (CUI) (Xiong et al.,2022 [52])	CUI1	0.942	0.945	0.912	0.851
	CUI2	0.886			
	CUI3	0.938			
Adoption Reasons					
Referent Network Size, (RNS) (Cheng, Lee & Choi,2019 [53])	RNS1	0.890	0.937	0.899	0.832
	RNS2	0.928			
	RNS3	0.917			
Perceived government support, (PGS) (Li and Atuahene-Gima,2001 [54])	PGS1	0.894	0.920	0.870	0.794
	PGS2	0.900			
	PGS3	0.878			
Rejection Reasons					
Usage Barrier, (UB) (Ram and Sheth,1989 [45])	UB1	0.904	0.943	0.908	0.845
	UB2	0.932			
	UB3	0.922			
Value Barrier, (VB) (Ram and Sheth,1989 [45])	VB1	0.919	0.944	0.912	0.850
	VB2	0.939			
	VB3	0.908			
Tradition Barrier, (TB) (Ram and Sheth,1989 [45])	TB1	0.926	0.943	0.910	0.847
	TB2	0.930			
	TB3	0.906			

Validity Analysis. Convergent validity was tested by mean variance extraction (AVE) and factor loading tests. The results showed that the factor loading values of all items are higher than the critical value of 0.7 [49], and the AVE values of all constructs were greater than 0.5 [47], indicating that the scale of this study has good validity. In addition, as shown in Table 5, the correlation coefficients between each variable are smaller than the arithmetic square root of the variable AVE [50], thus, the data achieve discriminant validity.

Table 5. AVE Square Root and Factor Correlation Coefficient

	RNS	PGS	VB	TB	UB	ATT	CUI
Referent Network Size	0.912						
Perceived Government Support	0.609	0.891					
Value Barriers	−0.449	−0.411	0.922				
Tradition Barriers	−0.342	−0.418	0.192	0.920			
Usage Barriers	−0.478	−0.477	0.625	0.236	0.919		
Altitude towards Smart City App	0.487	0.388	−0.443	−0.386	−0.552	0.913	
continuous use intention	0.508	0.398	−0.410	−0.295	−0.576	0.601	0.922

* The values in bold on the diagonal are the square root of the AVE value.

Test of Goodness for Fit. We used AMOS 28.0 to evaluate the overall fitness of the model. The goodness of fit indicators for the model are $X2/df = 1.887$, $RMSEA = 0.051$, $GFI = 0.914$, $SRMR = 0.0635$, $NFI = 0.944$, $CFI = 0.973$, $IFI = 0.973$, $TLI = 0.968$, all of which are within the recommended range. The model has good goodness of fit.

Hypothesis Test. As shown in Table 6, the five path relationships of the two formative constructs (adoption reasons and rejection reasons) in this article are significant; that is, the variables of the second order exhibit a significantly positive correlation with those of the first order. This suggests that factors such as Referent Network Size and Perceived Government Support are driving forces behind user adoption of Smart City Apps. Conversely, obstacles related to usage, value, and tradition serve as deterrents, dissuading users from engaging with these applications.

Table 6. Path relationship testing of second-order model

	Path coefficient-β	t-value	p-value	Accept/Not
Adoption Reasons→ Referent Network Size	0.909	96.257	0.000	Accept
Adoption Reasons→ Perceived Government Support	0.885	56.936	0.000	Accept
Rejection Reasons→ Usage Barriers	0.876	50.653	0.000	Accept
Rejection Reasons→ Value Barriers	0.847	36.953	0.000	Accept
Rejection Reasons→ Tradition Barriers	0.511	7.001	0.000	Accept

We generated the standardized path coefficient graph (Fig. 3) and assessed the second-order model assumptions based on the PLS analysis. The results indicate that the adoption reasons have a significant positive impact on users' attitudes towards Smart City Apps (H1: $\beta = 0.183$, t $= 3.006$, p < 0.01) and continuous use intention (H3: $\beta = 0.176$, t $= 3.170$, p < 0.01). In contrast, the rejection reasons have a significantly negative impact on attitude (H2: $\beta = -0.492$,

$t = 7.985$, $p < 0.001$) and continuous use intention (H4: $\beta = -0.243$, $t = 3.560$, $p < 0.001$). Finally, attitude has a significantly positive impact on user's continuous use intention (H5: $\beta = 0.353$, $t = 5.462$, $p < 0.001$).

In addition, statistical results indicate that gender ($\beta = 0.156$, $t = 0.156$, $p > 0.05$), age ($\beta = 0.003$, $t = 0.086$, $p > 0.05$), education level ($\beta = 0.051$, $t = 1.181$, $p > 0.05$), and living area ($\beta = 0.030$, $t = 0.827$, $p > 0.05$) do not have significant impacts on users' continuous use intention.

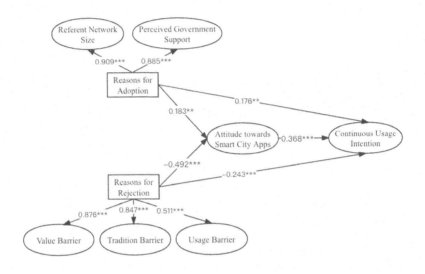

Fig. 3. Standardized path coefficient diagram

6   Conclusions and Contributions

6.1   Discussion and Conclusions

In this study, we applied a mixed research approach, based on the theories of BRT, NET, and IRT, to explore the impact of users' adoption and rejection reasons on attitude towards Smart City Apps, and further explored their post effects on continuous use intention. The following conclusions are drawn from this study:

(1) The rationality of user behavior (adoption reasons and rejection reasons) jointly affects the continuous use intention of Smart City App users. At present, the academic community mainly explores the impact of users' adoption reasons on their continuous use intention, with less attention paid to the impact of users' rejection reasons on their continuous use intention. This paper found that the reasons for adoption and rejection of Smart City App users are not symmetrically related, but both together constitute the antecedent factors of

users' attitude and intention. Specifically, people will decide whether to continue using Smart City Apps by evaluating their adoption and rejection reasons. This is consistent with the previous research findings [30] and also extends the previous research argument, indicating that the rationality of individual behavior also affects their continuous use intention. Among these, the adoption reasons positively influence users' attitude and behavioral intention while the rejection reasons negatively influence users' attitude and behavioral intention, which confirms previous research [30], too.

Furthermore, it is worth noting that compared to adoption reasons, the rejection reasons of users have a greater impact on their attitude and continuous use intention. This suggests that individual's behavioral intention is more susceptible to negative reasons. To sum up, this study found that the users' adoption and rejection reasons jointly affect the overall motivation and behavioral intention of them, which is viewed from the perspective of behavior and rationality (support-opposition), supplementing and improving the single understanding of user's continuous use intention.

(2) The referent network size and perceived government support constitute the main reasons for users to adopt Smart City Apps. The main reasons for users' rejection of smart city apps include usage barriers, tradition barriers, and value barriers. This study finds that usage barriers, tradition barriers, and value barriers can serve as important indicators for users to reject Smart City Apps. Among these, usage barriers and value barriers have the strongest impact. This suggests that in the absence of user experience, users' perception of the difficulty and value from app usage is more important than habit or trust. This is consistent with the conclusion of Agag et al. [55].

In addition, the referent network size and perceived government support are important factors for users to adopt Smart City Apps, indicating that the group's acceptance of new technologies and the user's perceived support for the external environment will guide individual attitude and behavioral intention, which is particularly evident in collectivist culture [56]. This conclusion provides additional confirmation to the beneficial supplement of traditional continuous use models and smart application research by highlighting the asymmetric relationship between users' adoption and rejection reasons.

(3) Behavioral Reasoning Theory is applicable to analyzing the continuous use mechanism of Smart City App users. This article verifies that both adoption reasons and rejection reasons have a significant impact on users' attitude and continuous use intention. In this study, we found that individuals with more comprehensive reasons for adoption have a more positive attitude towards the Smart City App, leading to a more comprehensive willingness to continue using it. Conversely, individuals with more comprehensive reasons for rejection tend to have a more negative attitude towards Smart City Apps, and users with a negative attitude tend to have a lower willingness to continue using them.

In addition, this study also found that users' attitude towards Smart City Apps directly affects their continuous use intention, which confirms the planned behavior theory and indicates that attitudes towards specific things are the primary antecedent of users' behavioral intention [34,57]. Therefore, the prereq- uisite for driving individuals to continue a certain behavior is to provide them with diverse adoption reasons, so that they will have a positive attitude towards the product or thing. It can be seen that this article applies the BRT theo- retical framework to organically integrate behavioral rationality, attitude, and behavioral intention, comprehensively and systematically explaining the continu- ous use mechanism of users towards Smart City Apps. By introducing behavioral rationality into traditional planned behavior theory, it compensates for the short- comings of expectancy confirmation theory, information system's continuous use model, and planned behavior theory.

6.2   Contributions and Limmitations

Based on behavioral reasoning theory, innovation hindrance theory, and network externality theory, this study explores and enriches the behavioral mechanisms of continuous use of Smart City App users, and expands the application scope of behavioral reasoning theory. From a theoretical perspective, our study proves that behavioral reasoning theory is applicable to analyzing the mechanism of continuous use of Smart City App users, filling the gaps of traditional theories such as rational behavior theory and planned behavior theory in user behavior research by means of mixed research. On the other hand, this study enriches the behavioral rationality in BRT theory, which is the sub-dimension of users' adoption and rejection reasons in the context of Smart City Apps. It provides an overall analysis perspective of adoption and rejection dimensions, compre- hensively explores the mechanism of users' continuous use, thus filling the gap of previous single-dimension research.

Our work also offer several practical implications. Firstly, this study explores the specific reasons why users adopt and reject Smart City Apps from five sub- dimensions, which can provide a reference for application developers and man- agers, and also help future researchers understand the challenges and behavioral motivations users face when using Smart City Apps. Our findings suggest that the developers of Smart City Apps pay more attention to the rejection reasons, in order to improve the user experience. On the other hand, government depart- ments or city managers should focus on the adoption reasons, to strengthen the promotion and guidance policies of the positive image of the Smart City App. Such measures are instrumental in boosting user confidence and enticing a broader user base.

There are several limitations to our work that should be noted. Firstly, this study focuses on continuous use intention rather than actual user behavior. Although considering willingness is widely accepted in social science field, future research can also take the true use behaviors of uses into consideration. In addi- tion, the quantitative part of this study applied questionnaire data, which may lead to social desirability bias. In the future, experimental methods and other research methods would be considered for exploration.

References

1. Peng, G., Nunes, M., Zheng, L.: Impacts of low citizen awareness and usage in smart city services: the case of London's smart parking system. IseB **15**(4), 845–876 (2017)
2. Liang, T., Peng, G., Xing, F.: Research on the status and problems of mobile application of smart city in China. Libr. Inf. Serv. **63**(8), 65 (2019)
3. China Internet Network Information Center: The 50th Statistical Report on the Development of China's Internet. https://www.cnnic.net.cn/n4/2022/0916/c38-10594.html. Accessed 02 Feb 2024
4. Zhu, D., Guo, J.: Research on users' satisfaction of mobile government based on TAM model. Inf. Sci. **34**(7), 141–146 (2016)
5. Misuraca, G.C.: e-Government 2015: exploring m-government scenarios, between ICT-driven experiments and citizen-centric implications. In: Foresight for Dynamic Organisations in Unstable Environments. Routledge (2013)
6. Li, Y., Xie, L., Chen, J.: Research on the behavior of public's continuous use of mobile government services. J. Hefei Univ. Technol. (Soc. Sci.) **32**(06), 40–49 (2018)
7. Wang, C., Teo, S.H., Dwivedi, Y., et al.: Mobile services use and citizen satisfaction in government: integrating social benefits and uses and gratifications theory. Inf. Technol. People **34**(4), 1313–1337 (2021)
8. Khan, M., Loh, J., Hossain, A., Talukder, M.: Cynicism as strength: privacy cynicism, satisfaction and trust among social media users. Comput. Hum. Behav. **142**, 107638 (2023)
9. Purohit, S., Arora, R., Paul, J.: The bright side of online consumer behavior: continuance intention for mobile payments. J. Consum. Behav. **22**(3), 523–542 (2022)
10. Chen, Y., Yang, L., Zhang, M., et al.: Central or peripheral? Cognition elaboration cues' effect on users' continuance intention of mobile health applications in the developing markets. Int. J. Med. Informatics **116**(8), 33–45 (2018)
11. Westaby, J., Versenyi, A., Hausmann, R.: Intentions to work during terminal illness: an exploratory study of antecedent conditions. J. Appl. Psychol. **90**(6), 1297 (2005)
12. Sharma, S., Al-Badi, A., Rana, N., et al.: Mobile Applications in government services (mG-App) from user's perspectives: a predictive modelling Approach. Gov. Inf. Q. **35**(4), 557–568 (2018)
13. Kumar, T., Rajmohan, R., Pavithra, M., et al.: Automatic face mask detection system in public transportation in smart cities using IOT and deep learning. Electronics **11**(6), 904 (2022)
14. Ge, X., Guo, L., Liu, X., Xue, Y.: Information security policy and practice of palmtop hospital based on mobile internet. China Digit. Med. **10**(6), 12–14 (2015)
15. Geng, Y., Cassandras, C.G.: A new "smart parking" system infrastructure and implementation. Procedia-Soc. Behav. Sci. **54**, 1278–1287 (2012)
16. Repette, P., Sabatini-Marques, J., Yigitcanlar, T., et al.: The evolution of city-as-a-platform: smart urban development governance with collective knowledge-based platform urbanism. Land **10**(1), 33 (2021)
17. Zhang, B., Peng, G., Liu, C., et al.: Adaptation behaviour in using one-stop smart governance apps: an exploratory study between digital immigrants and digital natives. Electron. Mark. **32**(4), 1971–1991 (2022)
18. Johnson, P., Robinson, P., Philpot, S.: Type, tweet, tap, and pass: how smart city technology is creating a transactional citizen. Gov. Inf. Q. **37**(1), 101414 (2020)

19. Minoli, D., Sohraby, K., Occhiogrosso, B.: IoT considerations, requirements, and architectures for smart buildings-energy optimization and next-generation building management systems. IEEE Internet Things J. **4**(1), 269–283 (2017)

20. Abbas, R., Michael, K.: COVID-19 contact trace app deployments: learnings from Australia and Singapore. IEEE Consum. Electron. Mag. **9**(5), 65–70 (2020)

21. Shafiq, M., Tian, Z., Sun, Y., et al.: Selection of effective machine learning algorithm and Bot-IoT attacks traffic identification for internet of things in smart city. Futur. Gener. Comput. Syst. **107**, 433–442 (2020)

22. Mcgrath, K.J.: Identity verification and societal challenges. MIS Q. **40**(2), 485–500 (2016)

23. Loo, W., Yeow, P., Chong, S.: User acceptance of Malaysian government multipurpose smartcard applications. Gov. Inf. Q. **26**(2), 358–367 (2009)

24. Sheng, N.: Research on the influencing factors model of sustainable use of mobile e-government by the public. Sci. Technol. Vis. **09**, 138–139 (2018)

25. Wang, C., Lu, Z., Feng, Y., Fang, R.: M-government continuance use in the post-adoption stage-an empirical research on task-technology fit theory. J. Intell. **30**(10), 189–193 (2011)

26. Bhattacherjee, A.: Understanding information systems continuance: an expectation–confirmation model. MIS Q. **25**(3), 351–370 (2001)

27. Xu, X.L., Zhang, Z.Y., Ming, C.G.: Public trust, government service quality and continuous use intention: an empirical study based on PLS-SEM. Adm. Tribune **26**(03), 5–11 (2019)

28. Westaby, J.: Behavioral reasoning theory: identifying new linkages underlying intentions and behavior. Organ. Behav. Hum. Decis. Process. **98**(2), 97–120 (2005)

29. Westaby, J., Probst, T., Lee, B.: Leadership decision-making: a behavioral reasoning theory analysis. Leadersh. Q. **21**(3), 481–495 (2010)

30. Dhir, A., Koshta, N., Goyal, R., et al.: Behavioral reasoning theory (BRT) perspectives on E-waste recycling and management. J. Clean. Prod. **280**, 124269 (2021)

31. Claudy, M., Garcia, R., O'Driscoll, A.: Leadership decision-making: consumer resistance to innovation-a behavioral reasoning perspective. J. Acad. Mark. Sci. **43**(4), 528–544 (2015)

32. Kunda, Z.: The case for motivated reasoning. Psychol. Bull. **108**(3), 480 (1990)

33. Wu, S., Chen, J.: A model of green consumption behavior constructed by the theory of planned behavior. Int. J. Mark. Stud. **6**(5), 119 (2014)

34. Ajzen, I.: The theory of planned behavior. Organ. Behav. Hum. Decis. Process. **50**(2), 179–211 (1991)

35. Venkatesh, V., Brown, S., Bala, H.: Bridging the qualitative-quantitative divide: guidelines for conducting mixed methods research in information systems. MIS Q. **2013**, 21–54 (2013)

36. Mele, V., Belardinelli, P.: Mixed methods in public administration research: selecting, sequencing, and connecting. J. Public Adm. Res. Theory **29**(2), 334–347 (2019)

37. Cameron, R.: A sequential mixed model research design: design, analytical and display issues. Int. J. Multiple Res. Approaches **3**(2), 140–152 (2009)

38. Braun, V., Clarke, V.: Using thematic analysis in psychology. Qual. Res. Psychol. **3**(2), 77–101 (2006)

39. Lin, C., Bhattacherjee, A.: Elucidating individual intention to use interactive information technologies: the role of network externalities. Int. J. Electron. Commer. **13**(1), 85–108 (2008)

40. Wang, C., Hsu, Y., Fang, W.: Acceptance of technology with network externalities: an empirical study of internet instant messaging services. J. Inf. Technol. Theory Appl. (JITTA) **6**(4), 4 (2005)

41. Hsu, C., Lu, H.: Why do people play on-line games? An extended TAM with social influences and flow experience. Inf. Manag. **41**(7), 853–868 (2004)
42. Lin, K., Lu, H.: Why people use social networking sites: an empirical study integrating network externalities and motivation theory. Comput. Hum. Behav. **27**(3), 1152–1161 (2011)
43. Lavergne, K., Sharp, E., Pelletier, L., Holtby, A.: The role of perceived government style in the facilitation of self-determined andnon self-determined motivation for pro-environmental behavior. J. Environ. Psychol. **30**(2), 169–177 (2010)
44. Kaur, P., Dhir, A., Ray, A., et al.: Innovation resistance theory perspective on the use of food delivery applications. J. Enterp. Inf. Manag. **34**(6), 1746–1768 (2020)
45. Ram, S., Sheth, J.: Consumer resistance to innovations: the marketing problem and its solutions. J. Consum. Mark. **6**(2), 5–14 (1989)
46. George, D.: SPSS for windows step by step: a simple study guide and reference, 17.0 update, 10/e. Pearson Education India (2011)
47. Hair, J., Risher, J., Sarstedt, M., et al.: When to use and how to report the results of PLS-SEM. Eur. Bus. Rev. **2019**(1), 2–24 (2019)
48. Fornell, C., Larcker, D.F.: Structural equation models with unobservable variables and measurement error: algebra and statistics. J. Mark. Res. **18**(3), 382–388 (1981)
49. Bagozzi, R., Yi, Y.: On the evaluation of structural equation models. J. Acad. Mark. Sci. **16**, 74–94 (1988)
50. Fornell, C., Larcker, D.: Evaluating structure equations models with unobservable variables and measurement error. J. Mark. Res. **18**(1), 39–50 (1981)
51. Yadav, R., Panda, D., Kumar, S.: Understanding the individuals' motivators and barriers of e-waste recycling: a mixed-method Approach. J. Environ. Manage. **324**, 116303 (2022)
52. Xiong, L., Wang, H., Wang, C.: Predicting mobile government service continuance: a two-stage structural equation modeling-artificial neural network Approach. Gov. Inf. Q. **39**(1), 101654 (2022)
53. Cheng, S., Lee, S., Choi, B.: An empirical investigation of users' voluntary switching intention for mobile personal cloud storage services based on the push-pull-mooring framework. Comput. Hum. Behav. **92**, 198–215 (2019)
54. Li, H., Atuahene-gima, K.: Product innovation strategy and the performance of new technology ventures in China. Acad. Manag. J. **44**(6), 1123–1134 (2001)
55. Agag, G., El-Masry, A.: Why do consumers trust online travel websites? Drivers and outcomes of consumer trust toward online travel websites. J. Travel Res. **56**(3), 347–369 (2017)
56. Kumar, S., Baishya, K., Sadarangani, P., et al.: Cultural influence on egovernment development. Electron. J. Inf. Syst. Eval. **23**(1), 17–33 (2020)
57. Ajzen, I., Madden, T., Ajzen, I., Madden, T.J.: Prediction of goal-directed behavior: attitudes, intentions, and perceived behavioral control. J. Exp. Soc. Psychol. **22**(5), 453–474 (1986)

Research on Interaction Design of Smart Scenic Spots Based on User Needs

Lei Xu and Wei Feng[✉]

Shandong College of Tourism and Hospitality, East Jingshi Road, Jinan 3556, Shandong, China
13964076217@163.com

Abstract. This paper first expounds the concept and significance of smart city, and points out that human-computer interaction design plays an important role in smart city as a bridge connecting technology and people. The paper introduces the related concepts of smart scenic spots and user needs in detail. Next, the paper puts forward the problems existing in the human-computer interaction design of smart scenic spots, and analyzes the smart ticketing system and smart navigation system as examples. Finally, this paper proposes the optimization strategy of human-computer interaction design in smart scenic spots, and discusses the challenges and prospects of human-computer interaction design in smart cities.

Keywords: smart city · human-computer interaction design · Smart Scenic Area

1 Introduction

With the rapid development of science and technology, the concept of smart city has gradually penetrated into the public. Smart city is a highly integrated city in various fields through information technology and Internet technology, so as to achieve intelligent, efficient and sustainable development in urban management, social services and economic operation. The construction of smart city is of great significance for improving the quality of life of urban residents, promoting urban economic development and enhancing urban competitiveness. At the same time, smart city is also one of the important ways to achieve sustainable and green development of cities. In the process of urban smartization, human-computer interaction design plays a crucial role as a bridge connecting technology and people, and is a key link to achieve the goal of smart city. Excellent human-computer interaction design can make the services of smart city more close to the needs of the public, and improve the convenience and comfort of urban life.

In smart cities, human-computer interaction design is widely used, covering urban management, social services, economic operation and other fields, such as urban smart transportation, urban smart environmental protection, smart healthcare, smart security, smart energy management, smart scenic spots, smart education, etc., and the services of these fields need to be presented to users through human-computer interaction design. Human-computer interaction design not only considers the aesthetics and usability of the interface, but also delves into the actual needs and behavior habits of users to ensure that the service can truly meet the expectations of users, providing more convenient, efficient and safe services for the development of the city and the lives of residents. In the application of intelligent transportation, human-computer interaction technology can help realize the management and scheduling of intelligent transportation, including traffic monitoring and control, traffic signal optimization, intelligent transportation navigation, intelligent parking, etc. Through the intelligent transportation system, urban traffic congestion can be alleviated, traffic efficiency can be improved, and traffic accidents can be reduced. In the urban intelligent environmental protection, human-computer interaction technology can realize real-time monitoring, protection and early warning of the urban environment through environmental monitoring equipment, intelligent garbage classification and processing system, timely detection and treatment of environmental problems, improve the efficiency of urban management, improve the quality of urban living environment, improve the quality of life of urban residents, and ensure the health and safety of urban residents. In the application of intelligent security, intelligent monitoring system, face recognition technology, etc. can be used to achieve accurate monitoring of various parts of the city, and timely detection and prevention of security accidents. In the application of smart healthcare, remote diagnosis and treatment, smart medical devices and other technical means are used to improve the convenience and efficiency of medical services and improve the health status of residents. In the application of smart education, online education platforms and virtual reality technology are used to provide more abundant teaching resources and means to improve students' learning efficiency and creativity. Smart scenic spots are an indispensable part of smart cities, covering tourism, culture, ecology and other aspects, providing city residents and tourists with more convenient, comfortable and safe tourism experience. Smart scenic spots help to improve the image and competitiveness of cities. A smart and humanized scenic spot can attract more tourists to visit and improve the popularity and reputation of the city. At the same time, smart scenic spots can also promote the protection and inheritance of culture, history, nature and other aspects of the city, and improve the cultural soft power of the city.

2 Related Concepts and Status Quo of Smart Scenic Spots

2.1 Concept of Smart Scenic Spots

Smart scenic spots are comprehensive, thorough and timely perception of geographical features, natural resources, tourist behavior, staff tracks, scenic spots infrastructure and service facilities through intelligent networks, which can more effectively protect the ecological environment, provide tourists with better services, and create greater value for society.[1]

2.2 Status Quo of Smart Scenic Spots

In recent years, China's construction of smart scenic spots has made remarkable progress. The comprehensive tourism platform of smart scenic spots of Chuangshi Technology has

---

[1] Baidu Encyclopedia: Smart Scenic Area [EB/OL]. https://baike.baidu.com.

been put into use in many well-known scenic spots in China. This platform provides a perfect tourism management system for scenic spots, a perfect tourism service system for tourists, and a perfect tourism marketing system for enterprises. The Fujian Provincial Department of Culture and Tourism recently announced the second batch of smart scenic spots in 2023, with a total of 14 scenic spots selected. In addition, at the Smart Tourism Development Conference held in Nanjing, various innovative smart tourism projects attracted many audiences. Many tourist attractions are transforming into smart scenic spots, with tourism resources and facilities upgraded and management level improved. However, the construction of smart scenic spots also faces some challenges, such as high technology investment and maintenance costs, data security and privacy protection, difficulty in technology update and upgrade, poor tourist experience and lack of unified standards and regulations.

2.3 Concept of Human-Computer Interaction Design

Human-computer interaction design, abbreviated as HCI (Human Computer Interface), is a science and technology that studies the interaction between users and computer systems. Human-computer interaction functions mainly rely on external devices that can input and output and corresponding software to complete. The devices available for human-computer interaction mainly include keyboard, mouse, various modes and recognition devices.[2] Human-computer interaction design focuses on user experience, emphasizing the user-centered design concept. The main goal is to improve the usability of products and the comfort of user experience. First of all, human-computer interaction designers will study and understand user behavior, needs and preferences, and then design interaction methods that meet user habits and expectations to meet user needs, so that users can use products more conveniently and efficiently. Human-computer interaction design also focuses on the visual design and information architecture of products to ensure that users can quickly and accurately find the information and functions they need. As products and operating systems become more and more complex, users need to master more new skills, so designers are faced with the challenge of how to help users improve their efficiency. Interaction design attempts to ensure the function of products while shortening the learning time of users and improving the accuracy and efficiency of tasks.

3 The Concept of User Needs

User needs are the core driving force of product design and development. It refers to the expectations and needs of users for the function, performance, experience and other aspects of products or services in a specific scenario, or the state that users hope to achieve or solve when using products or services. Understanding and analyzing user needs is an important prerequisite for product design and service provision, which can make products better meet user expectations and improve user experience and satisfaction.

---

[2] Liu Xing: The application of multimedia interactive devices in science museums, [J]Technology Communication, 2017 9(19), pp:102–103.

User needs can be divided into multiple levels, functional needs, performance needs, experience needs, emotional needs, etc. There are many ways to understand user needs, such as user research, observation, interview, questionnaire survey, etc. By collecting and analyzing user feedback, product design and service provision can be constantly optimized to meet the ever-changing needs of users.

3.1 Functional Needs

The functional needs of users refer to the specific functions or operations that users hope to achieve when using products or services. These needs are the functional characteristics that users hope products to have in order to solve problems or meet their desires. Functional needs usually describe in detail what products should do and how users interact with products to achieve these goals. In the process of product design and development, the definition and realization of functional needs is a very critical step. First of all, users can communicate with users through user research, user interviews and other means to understand their needs and pain points, and systematically collect and analyze user needs. Secondly, the product team can also analyze the products of competitors to understand the functions they provide and learn from them what needs to be improved. Finally, we should pay attention to market dynamics and trends in order to timely grasp the changes in user needs. Functional requirements are important inputs for product design. They help the user product team to understand the goals of users and guide the development of products. By constantly collecting and realizing the functional requirements of users, the product can better meet the needs of users and provide better user experience.

3.2 Performance Requirements

The performance requirements of users refer to the expectations and requirements of users on the performance of various aspects of the product when using the product. These requirements usually come from the user's experience of using the existing product, their understanding of the competitors' products, and their expectations of the new product's functions. The performance requirements of users mainly include the following aspects. First, users expect the product to respond quickly to their operations, process tasks efficiently, and provide a smooth user experience without too long waiting time, such as page loading, data processing and other common problems. Second, users expect the product to maintain stable operation in the process of use, without frequent lags, crashes or errors, and without interrupting their work or entertainment due to technical problems; Third, users expect the product to run normally on different devices, operating systems and browsers; Fourth, users expect the product to have a good user interface and operation process, easy to learn and use; Fifth, users expect the product to be extended with the growth of user needs, and to add new functions and features; Sixth, users expect the product to have a strong security mechanism, which can protect their privacy and data security in the process of using the product, and prevent unauthorized access and data leakage.

3.3 Experience Needs

The experience needs of users for the product mainly involve the overall satisfaction and comfort they feel in the process of using the product. First, users expect the product to have clear functions, intuitive operation, simple and easy to use, and to be able to complete tasks quickly, without spending a lot of time and energy to learn and adapt to the product. Second, users expect the product's appearance and interface design to be attractive, and the product's color, layout, icon and other visual elements to be coordinated and consistent, in line with the user's aesthetic standards, and bring them a pleasant feeling. Thirdly, users expect products to provide personalized settings and options according to their preferences, habits and needs. Finally, users expect products to provide good interactive experience, natural communication with the product, clear feedback, and help users complete tasks efficiently.

3.4 Emotional Needs

The emotional needs of users for products are the emotional satisfaction or resonance they expect to obtain when using the product. First of all, users need to obtain a sense of identity. Users hope that the product can conform to their personal values and lifestyle, so that they feel a sense of resonance and connection between themselves and the product. This sense of identity can come from the brand, design, function and other aspects of the product. Secondly, the sense of pleasure, users expect to obtain pleasure and enjoyment in the process of using the product. This can come from the product's ease of use, aesthetics, interaction and other aspects, so that users feel relaxed, happy and satisfied in the process of using the product. Thirdly, the sense of belonging, users hope to feel a sense of belonging and community when using the product. This can be achieved through the product's social functions, user communities, customized services and other aspects, so that users feel that they are part of the product and have common interests and goals with other users. Finally, the sense of respect, users expect products to respect their personal preferences, needs and habits. This requires products to have a certain degree of flexibility and customizability in design and function, which can adapt to the needs and preferences of different users, and make users feel respected and valued. To sum up, users' emotional needs for products include identity, pleasure, belonging and respect. These emotional needs largely affect users' overall satisfaction and loyalty to products. Understanding and meeting these emotional needs is crucial to improving user experience and satisfaction, and helps to establish long-term user loyalty and brand image.

4 The Status Quo and Problems of Human-Computer Interaction in Smart Scenic Spots

Human-machine interaction design of smart scenic spots refers to the use of advanced information technology, such as the Internet of Things, cloud computing, big data analysis, artificial intelligence and other information technology means, so that tourists can more conveniently and quickly obtain information and complete operations, so as to improve the experience sense and satisfaction of tourists in the scenic spot. In the construction of smart scenic spot, human-computer interaction design is the key link, which covers all the interactive interfaces and interaction processes that visitors may come into contact with in the scenic spot, including mobile applications, intelligent navigation devices, websites, self-service terminals, etc. Through intelligent human-computer interaction design, tourists can more easily visit the scenic spot, get a more comfortable and pleasant travel experience, and the scenic spot can realize intelligent management and improve operational efficiency. Human-computer interaction design is applied to all aspects of scenic spots. Here, only the most important intelligent ticketing system and intelligent navigation system in smart scenic spots are analyzed as examples.

4.1 Smart Ticketing System

Tourists can purchase tickets in advance through online channels such as the scenic site website, mini program, and mobile phone application, without queuing up at the ticket office of the scenic spot. (see Fig. 1) After the purchase of the ticket in electronic form, tourists can use the two-dimensional code or ID card, through face recognition technology, tourists arrive at the scenic area, without manual ticket verification can achieve rapid entry, entertainment reservation and other functions, greatly reducing the waiting time of tourists. If visitors are unable to enter the park for personal reasons, they only need to refund their tickets on the platform, and some platforms also support the "outdated return" function, that is, if visitors do not enter the park after the agreed time, the platform will automatically handle the refund procedure, without the need for tourists to handle it themselves. To sum up, smart ticketing does optimize ticket purchase and refund functions for tourists, but the smart ticketing system can achieve far more than that. For example, when tourists purchase tickets online, through facial recognition technology, voice recognition technology and other technical means, the first time to identify and identify special tourists, collect their physical conditions, contact information, emergency contacts and other data information, to develop personalized park plans for them, such as suitable entertainment activities, barrier-free park access, priority queuing system, etc. And sent to visitors in the form of text messages. When the tourists arrive at the scenic spot, the intelligent gate system recognizes the identity of the tourists and reminds the scenic spot personnel to provide convenient services for special tourists. With the increase of international tourists, the intelligent ticketing system will also integrate multi-language intelligent customer service to provide convenient services for tourists with different language backgrounds.

4.2 Smart Navigation System

The scenic intelligent navigation system integrates self-service systems such as touch screen, Internet of Things, artificial intelligence, voice recognition and other technologies. Through the smart terminal or mobile APP, tourists can obtain real-time positioning services, and through the touch screen or the electronic map on the mobile phone screen, view the layout of the scenic spot and the distribution of tourists, reasonable planning of the tour route, to help tourists save time, avoid unnecessary queuing and travel and other situations. To sum up, the function of the smart tour guide system is only to inform

Fig. 1. Universal BeiJing Resort Smart ticketing system (source: Universal BeiJing Resort APP)

tourists of the geographical location of each scenic spot or project and the current number of visitors and queues, and it cannot scientifically and effectively issue a feasible tour plan for tourists, and the tour plan formulated by tourists completely depends on personal subjective judgment. (see Fig. 2) However, the accuracy of tourists' subjective judgment cannot be guaranteed, or most tourists flock to the browsing items with a small number of people at the same time, so it is very likely to lead to crowded traffic and other situations. The intelligent tour needs to automatically generate a tour route for tourists according to the geographical layout of the scenic spot, the distribution of tourists, the time of tourists entering the park, the pace of tourists and other data, including the total time consumed by the day to play, the walking time to the entertainment project, the waiting time in line, the time consumed by a single play project, the lunch break, the restaurant, the bathroom and other convenient facilities reminder services. According to the past consumption habits of tourists collected by the smart ticket system, the smart guide system will also recommend scenic restaurants for tourists according to their tastes.

Fig. 2. Universal BeiJing Resort Smart navigation system (source: Universal BeiJing Resort APP)

5 Human-Computer Interaction Design Optimization Strategy of Smart Scenic Spots

5.1 Smart Ticketing System

The optimization scheme of the scenic spot smart ticketing system can be carried out from the following aspects. First, system scalability and flexibility are enhanced. The ticketing system can be customized according to the needs of the scenic area and function expansion, while supporting the integration of other systems with the scenic area, such as the navigation system, security system, etc., to achieve information sharing and collaborative work. For example, the ticketing system collects the face recognition information of special groups over the age of 70, and wears a scenic bracelet for real-time positioning when entering the park. The smart camera in the scenic area is used to capture the activity information of tourists, determine the image information under their normal posture, and set its status to "1". Once the tourist falls and other abnormal circumstances, the smart camera will obtain the abnormal image information in time, and its status will be automatically set to "0", triggering the bracelet worn by the tourist to issue an alarm and send real-time positioning information, so as to facilitate the scenic spot managers to arrive at the scene in time for rescue.

5.2 Intelligent Navigation System Based on Myoelectric Interaction Technology

After decades of development, human-computer interaction technology has produced a variety of new interaction methods, common voice interaction, user interface interaction, somatosensory interaction, myoelectric interaction, EEG interaction, virtual-real interaction and so on. There are also many human-computer interaction devices, including Oculus Rift, HTC vive and other VR devices, infrared Motion capture system, invasive/non-invasive brain computer interface, myoelectric sensor, Leap Motion, Kinect visual motion sensor and so on.[3] Myoelectric interaction technology (see Fig. 3), as a new way of human-computer interaction, mainly captures and analyzes the human muscle electrical activity to identify the user's actions and intentions, and then controls the device or performs a specific function. In a smart scenic navigation system, myoelectric interaction can provide an innovative and in-depth experience that makes the visitor's visit more interactive and interesting.

Through myoelectric interaction technology, visitors can experience a more immersive tour service. For example, when watching the reproduction of historical scenes, visitors can interact with virtual characters through specific myoelectric interactive devices, such as sensors on gloves or clothes, such as simulating sword movements in ancient wars, which triggers corresponding virtual scene changes and enhances the sense of reality of the experience. For visitors with mobility difficulties or visual and hearing impairments, myoelectric interaction can provide auxiliary tour functions. Through the specific myoelectric equipment, these visitors can feel the detailed description of the scenic spot, and even control the movement of the guide equipment through the myoelectric signal, to achieve independent tour.

The combination of myoelectric interaction technology and AR/VR technology can also create a new way of viewing. For example, when visitors visit cultural relics, through gesture control, they can watch the three-dimensional model of cultural relics, understand their historical background and production process, and even simulate the use of cultural relics to provide more abundant display content.

5.3 AIGC+AR Provides an Immersive Gaming Experience

The full name of AIGC is Artificial Intelligence Generated Content, translated as Generative Artificial Intelligence, which interacts and collaborates with humans in a behavior that is close to human behavior. AIGC technology utilizes artificial intelligence algorithms to generate content with certain creativity and quality. By training models and learning from a large amount of data, AIGC can generate relevant content based on input conditions or guidance. For example, by entering keywords, descriptions, or samples, AIGC can generate articles, images, audio, videos, etc. that match them.[4]

From June 15th to July 8th, 2023, the first Rural Children's Art Carnival was held in Guangshan County, Xinyang City, Henan Province, the birthplace of the traditional Chinese story "Sima Guang Smashing the Jar". AIGC technology was combined with traditional stories to create the "Sima Gang" AIGC cultural and creative IP. (see Fig. 4) Due

---

[3] Xu Ruishuo, Research on Visual Based Remote Human Computer Interaction Technology, [d] Master's thesis in engineering, hebei university of engineering.

[4] Baidu Encyclopedia:AIGC [EB/OL]. https://baike.baidu.com

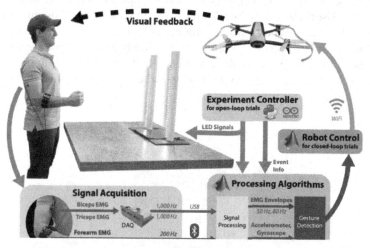

Fig. 3. Myoelectric interaction technology (source: Baidu)

Fig. 4. 'Sim Gang' AIGC Creative IP Design Competition (source: Wujie Community mixlab)

to the fact that AIGC painting does not require professional painting techniques, creators only need sufficient imagination to create exquisite works, which has attracted the active participation of many teenagers and children. Through this event, Guangshan County increased its local exposure while also receiving a large number of works. Among them, the image of the first prize winning work "Sima Gang's Little Companion Ganggang" (see Fig. 5) was selected as the Guangshan Cultural and Tourism IP image. Guangshan County has turned some award-winning works into digital collectibles, empowering local scenic spot tickets and strengthening interaction between tourists and scenic spots. The digital works created by AIGC can also be directly transformed into virtual reality games for scenic spots. (see Fig. 6) When tourists switch from online to offline and arrive at the scenic spot, the scenic spot adopts LBS positioning technology+AR inter-active games. Users can use mobile AR programs to scan specific buildings or items to capture "Sima Gang". When a certain number of "Sima Gang" are captured, they can be exchanged for hotel accommodation, transportation and other preferential benefits. Guangshan County has successfully integrated AIGC technology with scenic spots to enhance the interactive experience of tourists and create a new model of smart scenic spots.

Fig. 5. <Sima Gang's Little Companion Ganggang> (source: china.com)

Fig. 6. <Diverse Sima Gang is here> (source: china.com)

6   Challenges and Prospects of Human-Computer Interaction Design

Human-computer interaction design is facing many challenges today. With the progress of technology, the ways of human-computer interaction become more and more diversified, including voice interaction, gesture interaction and so on. This variety, while providing more interaction possibilities, also increases the complexity of the design. Product design teams need to keep the user experience at the center, considering the needs and habits of different user groups, as well as switching and integration between different interactions. In the process of human-computer interaction, users access a large amount of data, such as personal information, behavioral data, etc. How to protect the privacy and security of this data from misuse or disclosure is an important challenge that product design teams need to face. Although the product design team can come up with a variety of innovative human-computer interaction concepts and schemes, the implementation of technology is often limited by hardware, software, network and other aspects. How to achieve a good user experience within these limitations is a problem that product designers need to solve.

With the development of artificial intelligence technology, human-computer interaction in the future will be more intelligent and personalized. The system can automatically challenge the interaction mode and interface layout according to the user's behavior and habits, and provide more intimate services. The future human-computer interaction will no longer be limited to a single interaction mode, but to the development of multi-modal interaction. Users can interact with the system through voice, gestures, eyes and other ways to get a more natural and convenient experience. The development of virtual reality and augmented reality technology provides new possibilities for human-computer interaction. Product design teams can leverage these technologies to create more immersive and interactive experiences that engage users more deeply in the interaction process. Through continuous optimization of human-computer interaction design, technology and human needs are closely combined, so that work and life become more convenient and comfortable. In the future, with the continuous progress of technology and the continuous update of design concepts, we can provide people with more efficient, convenient and humanized services to promote the sustainable development of society.

References

1. Baidu Encyclopedia: Smart Scenic Area [EB/OL]. https://baike.baidu.com
2. Liu, X.: The application of multimedia interactive devices in science museums. Technol. Commun. 9(19), 102–103 (2017)
3. Xu, R.: Research on Visual Based Remote Human Computer Interaction Technology, [d]Master's thesis in engineering, Hebei university of engineering (2023)
4. Baidu Encyclopedia: AIGC [EB/OL]. https://baike.baidu.com

Author Index

N. A. Streitz and S. Konomi (Eds.): HCII 2024, LNCS 14718, pp. 369–371, 2024.
https://doi.org/10.1007/978-3-031-59988-0